Precious Little Sleep

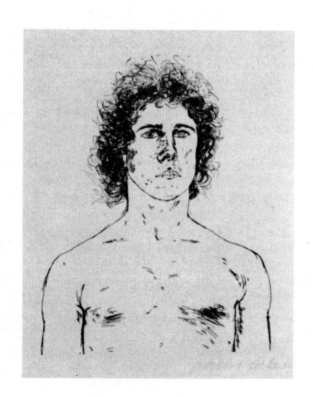

Wayne Sleep, 1969 (David Hockney)

Precious Little Sleep

The Autobiography of
Wayne Sleep

B⬚XTREE

MACMILLAN

First published in Great Britain in 1996 by Boxtree
an imprint of Macmillan Publishers Ltd
25 Eccleston Place, London, SW1W 9NF

Associated companies throughout the world

ISBN 0 7522 1135 8

Picture Acknowledgements (all other pictures are from the author's collection):
Frontispiece: David Hockney; p.1 (bottom) R.L. Palmer; p.2 (top) Hulton Getty,
(bottom) G.B.L. Wilson; p.3 (top) Leslie E. Spatt, (bottom) Royal Ballet
School/Molly Zambra; p.4 (middle) Folon Burcy; p.5 Anthony Crickmay; p.6 Jennie
Walton; p.7 (bottom) David Hockney; p.8 EMI Films; p.9 Leslie E. Spatt; p.10
(right) Anthony Crickmay; p.11 (top) Anthony Crickmay, (middle) Lia Troy,
(bottom) United Artists/Fergus Bourke; p.12 (top) Roy Round, (bottom) Catherine
Ashmore; p.13 (top) *Evening Standard*, (middle) Thames Television, (bottom) Rex
Features; p.14 (bottom) *Evening Standard*; p.15 (top) Yorkshire Television,
(bottom) Rex Features.

'For the Record' by Roy Blount Jnr first published in the USA in 1974 by
The New Yorker and subsequently in the UK in 1982 by Oxford University Press.

While every effort has been made to trace all copyright holders,
the publishers will be glad to make proper acknowledgement
in future editions of this publication in the event that any regretable omissions
have occured by the time of going to press.

The right of Wayne Sleep to be identified as Author of this Work
has been asserted by him in accordance with the
Copyright, Designs and Patents Act 1988.

1 3 5 7 9 10 8 6 4 2

A CIP catalogue entry for this book is available from the British Library.

Cover and plate sections designed by Hammond Hammond
Text typeset and designed by Keystroke
Printed and bound in the UK by The Bath Press, Bath.

CONTENTS

ACKNOWLEDGEMENTS

I am grateful to Liz Flower for helping me to get all this out of my head and into print; and for their assistance in the preparation of this book to Jeanetta Laurence of the Royal Ballet, Katy Carrington at Boxtree, Roz Hubley, and Stephen Gilchrist. And, as ever George.

The above shows an extract from a dance notation score of the ballet *Petrouchska* – one of my favourite roles – recorded in 1956 and written in Benesh Movement Notation. Benesh notation is the way in which ballets can be recorded accurately and recreated from company to company all over the world.

Choreography © Fokine 1956. Benesh Movement Notation © Rudolph Benesh 1955. (This extract was supplied by The Benesh Institute.)

ONE

Wot a Little Darling

ON 17 JULY 1948 Margot Fonteyn, Robert Helpmann and Frederick Ashton were celebrating the success of a performance of *The Sleeping Beauty*. As they sipped their first glass of champagne, I took my first gulp of air. And I was to cry solidly for six weeks, causing chaos and disruption. Even before I was born I gave my mother, Joan, a literally hair-raising experience by resting on a nerve in her womb which caused her hair to fall out. I was a late arrival and have been ever since.

I came into a female-dominated working-class family. My mother's mother, Emma, was one of six girls, and my mother had two sisters, Ruth and Vera, and just one brother, my Uncle Colin. So the house in Plymouth that I was born into was a house full of women, because I had no father of my own (and I was also to have a sister later). I was to spend the first five years of my life there.

Being a working-class girl my mother had been brought up to cope and had had responsibility placed on her at a very early age. My mother's father was flighty by nature and hardly ever at home. My grandmother became fed up with this and moved in with Harry whom she later married after her divorce and had another daughter, Sybil. As my mother's father would not allow my mother and sisters to stay with their stepfather, and in order to prevent them from being sent to a home, their grandparents, William and Maud Hortop, brought them up with their own daughters. So life for my mother (who was eight at the time) and aunts was very unsettled and rather sad.

My mother had a natural talent for singing, which became apparent when she was in the WRAF as a nurse. During the war she was stationed at Ely, where all the injured pilots came to the burns units to have the first plastic surgery. She sang to the patients and was called upon by the concert organizers for shows, and always introduced as 'Our Star'.

Her voice was such that one of the pilots, who was getting married, asked her to sing at his wedding. Because she was not Catholic, the priest would only permit her to sing 'Ave Maria' if she sang in Latin. She took lessons from Father MacSweeney, a Franciscan, who had lost his legs in combat. The doctors were not so amazed by her ability to sing Latin as they were by how she managed to heave Father MacSweeney up on to the stage. She propped him against the proscenium, then bent and hauled him, wooden legs and all, under his armpits on to the platform. From there it was three or four hefty drags to the piano stool.

After the WRAF she had various offers of a singing career. She sang in a cinema during the interval, but the biggest break came when she was offered a contract by the BBC. She turned it down, however, because she felt that with no training she would not be up to the mark. She'd had little encouragement as a child to reach any goals, and believed that as a working-class girl she knew her place. But her singing was in such demand that she was asked to do a lot of charity concerts. She had a top C that floated without effort, clear as a bell. It is one of my first memories of her, singing me to sleep and later, dancing around the room with a plate of food for me, singing to it and blowing on it to cool it down.

It was at a summer holiday camp in Selsey, working as a waitress, that she met my father. It was 1947, and he was bandleader for the season. As she usually did, she sang as she worked and he heard her. Fell in love with her, but of course he was married already. She was twenty-five, he forty-ish, in a profession she loved. There was a mutual bond. He intended to get a divorce, he kept putting it off – until finally after waiting for so long my mother lost her patience and put him off.

It didn't make any difference to me, I had my mum, and my great-grandfather to look after me while she went to work. We moved into the middle floor of a house in Percy Terrace, Plymouth, shared, as was customary, by other members of the family.

Grandad, as we called him, was something of a hero. Before the First World War he had walked from Plymouth to Manchester to find work, then at the earliest opportunity had called for his wife and daughters to join him in Cheadle, where my grandmother, at the age of thirteen, went to work in the cotton mills. She went to school for half the day and the other half was spent on the looms. There was no slacking. The foreman stood over them, watching like a hawk. He thwacked his wooden stick against the machinery if he suspected a slacker. At least he didn't hit them.

Grandad entertained me for hours on end, playing the saucepan lids with his long fingernails, or telling me stories. He showed me the slate under the skin of his arms. I can still picture it. One of the jobs he'd had was to plant dynamite in quarries. One day, up a ladder, he was placing the dynamite into the quarry face when it detonated, taking one of his eyes and almost his life. Some people thought it was no accident but was caused by one of his workmates who had a grudge against him. In hospital afterwards, a nurse was passing by his bed and saw blood spurting out of the top of Grandad's head. Her fingers stopped the flow, like the little Dutch boy and the dyke, and saved his life. He was very lucky and I thought him special.

He was full of great expressions. Once I pleaded with him to give me an apple. He asked me why I wanted it so desperately, and I told him that the kids in the lane wouldn't let me play with them unless I gave them something. He was furious. 'If they want payment, they're not worth playing with.' And then he stopped my tears with, 'Never say your mother reared a gibber.'

Another of my favourite games was to imitate Grandad shaving. I didn't have a blade in the razor, but I had the brush and the shaving soap. I stood on top of the bit bucket beside the kitchen sink and copied him. Once, when he was out, to amuse myself I thought I'd have a shave, so I climbed on the bit bucket and covered my face with soapsuds. I felt really grown up. But the difference was that this time there *was* a blade in the razor. The shaving foam turned pink and the blood started to trickle down my neck. I knew something was wrong. So I hid. When Mum got home from work I was nowhere to be seen. She made a frantic search of the house and found me cowering behind a big chair. She screamed. I was covered in blood. But to her relief, when she wiped me down with a towel she found that the cuts were not deep. And all Grandad would say was 'I told you the buggers would bite.'

Every Sunday we would gather for the communal dinner of the week. The Sunday roast was a big event. It was our weekly meat ration. I helped Grandad chop the mint while Mum prepared the roast potatoes and vegetables. I always wanted to help with the food. One Sunday we were at Auntie Florrie's (my grandmother's sister) and I opened the oven door to contribute something of my own to the roast. Very carefully I placed my plastic horse and cart on top of the meat. I shut the oven door and went out into the yard to play with my cousins, Robert, Diane and Jackie. Suddenly there were shouts of horror from the kitchen. Our one roast dinner of the week had been ruined by my contribution of melted plastic.

I was fascinated by colour and music. Every time there was music on the wireless I had this urge to get up and jig about. They couldn't stop me unless they turned the wireless off. I was never still, and as soon as I was old enough to move around I started to perform. I loved to make them laugh by crawling on the floor, blindfold, with a stick in my mouth, waggling my bottom. Uncle Gordon, my mother's cousin, used to cry, he was laughing so much.

Christmas was my favourite time of the year because of the colours. The lights and the decorations were more important to me than the presents. I got hold of the Christmas streamers, bouncing them up and down like concertinas, stripping the tree of its ornaments, causing it to crash to the ground. I just danced among the debris.

Every summer the whole family rented a field in Shawbridge on Dartmoor. It came complete with cows. We swam in the stream which ran through it, never sure which we were more frightened of, the cows which stood around regarding us with large eyes, accompanied by bemused moos, or the possible monsters which lurked under water. Each section of the family had its own tent – these were bell tents, ex-Army tents, large tents, small tents. All around a huge communal camp fire. We stayed there all through the summer, playing games, singing songs, dancing round the camp fire, being chased by wild rams, having cowpat fights, swimming, basking in the sun or being soothed to sleep by the patter of rain on canvas, which protected us from the imaginings of the night. If it sounds idyllic, that's because it was.

Back home, I was spending my days with Auntie Barbara, one of my mother's cousins, down the road because my mother was working as a waitress in Fuller's restaurant. And then came the day when cousin Jackie, Barbara's daughter went to school. She was four and I was three. I went with her to the school, but refused to leave her there. I clung to the railings, screaming that I wanted to go in too, and Auntie Barbara had to peel my fingers off the gates and drag me away. To cheer me up, she gave me my first dance lesson – tap steps on the kitchen lino.

Because I implored the teacher, I was allowed into the school a term early, and for a short time I loved everything about it. The novelty soon wore off, though, and academic achievement took second place to the dancing lessons Auntie Barbara gave me. That was to be the pattern of my life.

As I grew older I began to be fascinated by the puppet shows at the seaside. I made my own peepshow from an old cardboard box – I used cotton-wool balls for rocks and trees, cut out characters from picture books, and put coloured sweet wrappers over the peephole in the side, through which a torch could be shone. I created my own fantasy world and showed it to everybody.

And for me, any stage, any raised platform, even an orange-box, was a magnet. I would do anything, with or without an audience. At my Auntie Sybil's wedding reception in 1953 my second cousin Barry and I gave an impromptu performance of song and dance. Several of the family said that my mother should send me to dancing classes, but it took a long time to convince her. She had other things on her mind.

My mother had met Stan Sleep, a clean-looking man who worked as a clerk with Plymouth Gin. He always said the job went to his head. Actually he was more or less a teetotaller. Most eligible bachelors in those days would not have wanted to take on a woman with a child, but he did – and there was a wedding, the adoption papers came through, and there I was – Wayne Sleep. I resented him – I was four, and he had come like an intruder into what I thought was a perfect situation. I had been getting all the attention and now it had to be shared. They bought a house, so we moved to Glendower Road. Unfortunately for me there was no room for the person who had shared my life up to this time, my great-grandfather, and he went to live with one of his other grand-daughters, eventually moving in with his daughter Winnie. I missed him very much. My mother must have realized and took me to visit him frequently. Sometimes we went to his allotment, when he showed me how to plant vegetables.

When I was five, in 1953, I was enrolled in Pat Rouce's Academy of Dance. It meant a long bus ride once a week after school, but it was like entering a magic world. And I was the only boy. I didn't care. In fact I enjoyed being unique. The fact that dancing, in some people's eyes, was something only girls did didn't put me off. Nor was I put off by not being able to find tap shoes for boys – we compromised with a pair of black patent shoes with silver buckles and white ankle socks. For my first performance I found myself dressed as a toy soldier in a costume made by my mother and Auntie Ruth – the busby was made out of black cardboard and a lavatory chain. This first concert was like my peepshow, only real. I was hooked. There would be no going back.

The journey to Pat Rouce's Academy proved too long, and after a year I joined Geraldine Lamb's School of Dancing. My mother would collect me after school, take me to dancing class, wait the half hour the lesson lasted, then bring me home. Such patience. I don't think Stanley was entirely happy with the idea of his stepson attending dance classes, but I have to credit him with never making a fuss about it and he always stumped up the fees, or the necessary money for shoes and dance clothes. He was good in that way.

A couple of years later Stanley, my mother and I moved to Hartlepool in County Durham. It was a big wrench leaving Plymouth, the life there, all my cousins and my friends. Stan's sister, Winnie, had badgered him to join her in the north because she had no family nearby – except her husband Bert and son Peter. The plan was for my mother and Stan to buy a house and take in lodgers, just like Winnie did. The standard of living was cheaper in the north.

Just before we left, Stanley bought an old Austin. He had shared it with his brother in Plymouth and bought it outright when we moved. It took sixteen hours to drive from Plymouth to Hartlepool. I was sick all the way. Mum said it was because I couldn't eat dairy products, so there was a lot of acid in my stomach. I suffered from bilious attacks.

We stayed with Winnie when we first arrived. Stanley found a job as a process worker with the Steetley Magnesium Company and we found a house in Friar Terrace, opposite the bowling green and the Town Moor, a playing field with swings for children. The house was pretty dilapidated and my parents put in long hours and a lot of work before it was ready to receive its intended lodgers – who in fact never materialized, so Mum's sister, Auntie Ruth, her husband Reg and daughter Karen came to join us. They lived on the ground floor, while we were in the basement.

The house had no garden, just a small yard with a pump and an outside toilet. I grew night-scented stock, for obvious reasons, in a window-box I persuaded my stepfather to make for me. Even now I can conjure up the smell. Funnily enough I've never had a garden, still don't; I love gardens but not the toil of the soil.

I had a bath once a week, on a Saturday. The tin bath, which hung on the back of the door, was taken down and placed in front of the open gas oven. Hot water was bubbling away on top of the stove. When my hair was rinsed I loved the sound of the sizzle-splash as the saucepans of water were poured over my head into the bath.

At six o'clock, after the bath, we had home-made Cornish pasties. They are still among my favourite foods. There is nothing quite like a proper home-made pasty. They reminded me of Devon, which I missed, though most of all I missed my cousin Jackie. A year after we left Plymouth I wrote her a love letter.

A secret letter to Jackie:

Dear Jackie, I hope you are allright. I Friscy the cat. I am fine. It is Mothers day tomorrow so you can guess what day it is today give a big cis to auntie Barbra and aunti Eadi for me I all so give a cis to miss quic. I hope you pass the scholarship I had an Amon-Andress Quiz game. I recerbed your letter I love you Jackie will you marry me when I am twenty-one I will by you a lovely ring I go tap-danceing give my love to all

from silly Wayne

'I go tap-danceing.' As soon as we had arrived in Hartlepool I had been enrolled at the Muriel Carr School of Dance for weekly lessons. Her studio was hidden away above a bicycle shop; it had paint peeling off the walls and a small gas fire that leaked, but Muriel Carr was a good teacher, and taught by the book. A lot of teachers in those days could ruin a child's ability, in the case of girls in particular by forcing them too early into pointe shoes, thus crippling their feet. She didn't. I thrived under her tuition.

Every year there was the Middlesborough Tournament, a giant competition, lasting for two weeks, at which hundreds of precocious children from the age of five upwards gathered together to compete with each other in ballet, tap, modern musical (now jazz) and song and dance. Muriel entered me for the song and dance section in the youngest category. Other schools may have had more imaginative and flashy routines, but their technical proficiency was much lower. She was the best teacher in the area.

I sang and danced 'Five Foot Two, Eyes of Blue'. A song full of prophetic irony. I won. We stood on the stage, thirty of us, and Maude Wells, the adjudicator, hauled me out in front of everyone and said, 'This boy is a budding Danny Kaye.' I heard Danny Kaye on 'Uncle Mac's Children's Favourites' every Saturday morning, and I didn't think I sounded a bit like him. Funny woman. Then the adjudicator said, 'He should also learn ballet. Are his parents here?' I saw my mother sink deep into her seat. 'Ballet? *ballet*?' I could almost hear her thinking. 'My son learn *ballet*?' Boys don't do that. Song and dance – that's possible. Entertaining, that's OK too. But boys do not do ballet.

On the bus taking us home my mother asked Muriel what the adjudicator meant about 'Wayne learning ballet'. Muriel had been as intrigued by the suggestion – although in a different way – as my mother. So she talked to Maude Wells. Apparently she was impressed by my turnout. This meant nothing to me, and very little more to Mum, who thought turnout was the way one dressed. Muriel explained. My stance, my way of standing and walking, was a natural for ballet. I splayed my feet when I walked. People told me sometimes that I waddled like a duck – but a duck turns its toes in. Well, like a duck with its toes out. But it is not only that the feet should turn out, there must be a flexibility in the hip joint that allows the whole leg, thigh, knee and foot, to turn out to the side at ninety degrees. I liked the idea of being a natural. Perfect physical proportion is important too and I appeared to have that as well. But Mum and I had never seen a ballet, and in spite of Muriel Carr's explanations we still had only a dim understanding of what was meant. It was the first step in the direction my life was to take.

The only ballet my mother had ever seen was a performance of Kurt Jooss's *Green Table* during the war. She had gone with her cousin Barbara and they were hysterical with laughter the whole way through, as holes kept appearing in the darned tights of the male dancers. Not the best of first impressions.

On the last night of the tournament cups were awarded for the highest marks in the competition. I pleaded with my mother to take me to the ceremony, but we missed the bus to Middlesbrough and Mum was too tired to catch another one, so we went home again. Pity. I won the cup for the highest mark under twelve years and the overall highest mark in the song and dance section. In the end, Muriel Carr brought my lovely cups home.

Muriel already taught ballet to the girls through the syllabus from the RAD, the Royal Academy of Dancing (of which Margot Fonteyn was president), and she now applied herself to teaching me ballet. She had to send for the RAD boys' syllabus, read all the steps, and have me tested and graded by outside examiners. Between her and our first television in Friar Terrace, bought when I was eight, my learning and understanding of dance expanded no end. Or so it seemed to me.

Before we had a television the only way I could get to see musicals was by pestering Mum (not that she really needed pestering, because she enjoyed them too) to take me to the cinema or by sneaking off with cousins Peter, Robert and Karen in the hope that once we arrived, we could persuade a grown-up to take us in with them. (Children were not allowed in unaccompanied.) I saw lots of Fred Astaire's and Gene Kelly's films. In those days I preferred the flamboyance and athleticism of Gene Kelly. It wasn't until much later that I appreciated the finesse and subtleties of Fred Astaire's work. Then, I wanted to be Gene Kelly. Once I got home from the cinema, I used to fly around the house trying to imitate him – no music – our wind-up gramophone was broken so the 78s were useless. I tried to spin the turntable with my finger while pressing the needle on to the record in the vain hope of hearing Frankie Laine or Gracie Fields, neither of which I could dance to anyway.

Every Sunday afternoon there were films on the BBC. In those days there was only one channel and only one movie was shown each week. Once we had a television, I watched the old Fred Astaire and Gene Kelly films again. I knew them off by heart. But when ballet came on, as it did occasionally (the BBC still saw itself as something of an educator, all those cut-glass tones and moral values), I was not in the least interested. It was boring. No male dancers, just lots of fairies in tutus. It didn't show ballet's true qualities. But the way both Kelly and Astaire danced on film was my inspiration. It was something of their essence that I was to try to achieve twenty-five years later with my own television shows.

Dancing was one thing – there was also school, the Baltic Street Junior School. When I first arrived from Plymouth I was teased interminably for my posh accent. My broad Devonshire accent. Arrr. The kids had never heard one before. Most of them had never been out of Hartlepool. But it wasn't long before they realized that I was just like them, same background, so I joined in their taunting of others. Catholics in particular. I entered the unknown world of religious prejudice. Baltic Street was a Protestant school, and a gang of us used to lie in wait for the kids from the Catholic school down the road. When they appeared we'd chant: 'Catholic Bulldogs never get a wash, When they do they think they're posh.'

They had their own anti-Protestant chants and the whole thing would end with a chase. But it was never serious. No hard scrapping. No injuries. All we were after was a bit of fun and a bit of – very slightly scary – excitement. Unlike the serious teddy-boy gang warfare, which existed in Hartlepool like everywhere else in the fifties. That was real and often nasty. And in the dark months of winter I dreaded passing these gangs. I used to travel alone to West Hartlepool for my dancing classes. The fact that they would probably take no notice of a nine-year-old made little difference – I was not willing to put it to the test. I avoided dark corners.

When I was nine or ten Grandad died. A telegram arrived very early in the morning. My mother opened it, handed it to me, and said, 'Take this to Auntie Ruth.' She didn't tell me what was in it. I met Auntie Ruth on the stairs and gave it to her; she looked at it and burst into tears. She whispered, 'Grandad's dead.' I didn't understand the emotion my mother and Auntie Ruth felt. It had been so long since he and I had been together. We all went down to Plymouth for the funeral.

My cousin Barry and I came up with the idea that we would pay our own tribute to Grandad by picking wild flowers from Tamerton Woods. We came back with armfuls of bluebells, ferns, beech leaves and foxgloves. And bunches of beautiful daffodils which were just the other side of a stone wall and which we pretended were not from someone's private garden. Barry's father gave us some wire mesh and we created a cross filled with flowers. None of us kids went to the funeral service – we were too young.

I loved staying at Barry's house. We could really be naughty. It was a change from being held up as an example by my aunts as lovely tidy Wayne, who folded his clothes and did everything right. Barry was the ringleader in our gang of two. He jumped on the backs of lorries, and invented all sorts of scams and trouble for us to get into. I just followed, I couldn't help it. He led me into fields full of bulls to taunt them. He sneaked into stables and rode horses bare-back round fields. 'Come on up,' he'd say. Not blimming likely. I cowered and he leaped over my head. It never occurred to me to do anything like this by myself, and it beat being a member of the Life Boys, a sort of sea-cadet group, at which I was goody-goody gumdrops.

I had been brought up a Christian – I was taught to say my prayers every night and church was an important part of my life. When I was nine I had joined the choir at St Hilda's round the corner. I liked singing in the choir, which also meant I wore a red cassock and white ruff. Dressing up. I had my dance classes on Monday and choir practice every Tuesday. And what with crabbing on the rocks with cousin Peter, fishing from the end of the pier, canoeing in the sea, and school trips to Whitley Bay, life was pretty full.

After a year or two, however, my involvement with the church became even greater. One day the vicar said that two men would be coming to hold special services and classes during the following week, with what sounded to me like a really exciting way of spreading the Word. Noel Proctor (who became the chaplain at Strangeways prison) and Ken Storey were from the Church Army. Evangelists. Ken played the guitar and Noel sang hymns – not the traditional hymns, Ancient and Modern, that I was used to, but hymns that were more like pop songs. They put up a huge screen on the altar steps and projected the words so that we could sing along. They illustrated Bible stories with slides and took us through a daily chapter of *The Pilgrim's Progress*. It was mesmeric, compelling. I had never seen the church so full. I went every day after school, even playing truant from my dance classes – that's how great I thought it was. We were given tasks. My favourite was to learn as many verses from the New Testament as possible. I applied myself with gusto. On the last day of the visit we recited the verses we had memorized and those who had learned the most received a brand new Bible. I still have mine. I may not look at it much these days, but I can still conjure up the feelings.

Ken and Noel toured in a caravan and lived off a pittance from the Church Army. This was subsidized by the generosity of wellwishers, who brought food and other staples like toothpaste, boot-polish (it was the fifties) and chocolate. They invited me to join them for a week at Easter, touring round the colliery towns of County Durham. In each village we found somewhere to park the caravan, then went round gathering people to our rallies. We attracted large crowds wherever we went. My part, which brought out the performer in me, of course, was to recite twenty-three verses while Ken and Noel invited people to come up, be blessed and saved. What impressed me most was that it wasn't only young people who came but people of sixty and seventy, who discovered a new foundation for their religious beliefs.

I wrote to Noel and Ken for a long time after they left my part of the world and received much encouragement to stay on the straight and narrow in return. And I made many friends through their services at St Hilda's. I used to go with one of these friends, Angela Hall (who married someone in the Church Army and is still in Evangelism), to listen to relays of Billy Graham's rallies. He was so powerful that many people were converted simply by hearing him speak through a PA system.

This religious fervour walked hand in hand with my desire to entertain. I had also started piano lessons – at first this was tremendously exciting, but the novelty soon palled and I didn't practise. In the end the only practice I did was during my lessons. My teacher said I was wasting her time, my time and my parents' money, and ticked me off in no uncertain terms. But as well as laziness I did have two excuses for not practising. The first was that my stepfather worked nights as a process worker at the Steetly Magnesium Company and found it difficult to sleep through the din the piano was making during the day. I didn't see much of him. We tolerated each other. My sister, on the other hand, had a different relationship with him.

She was my second excuse not to practise and a much more exciting one. She was born at home, on 5 February 1958. This time I knew where she had come from. At the age of three I had asked Mum where I came from. She had told me (and I believed what I was told by grown-ups): 'Out of all the babies in the hospital I chose you.' Hmm. 'Why didn't you leave me for the Queen?' I asked her.

And there she was, one morning, my sister occupying the cot my stepfather had made for her. She was named Joanne. JO from Joan, AN from Stanley and NE from Wayne. I should also explain, at this point, that I was named Wayne after a doctor character in a book my mother was reading when pregnant and *not* after John Wayne, as is popularly thought. My mother hated John Wayne. Clark Gable was her man. My second name is Colin, after my uncle. This made my initials into WC. So Mum shoved a P in between the WC – Philip – thus giving me the ignominious title, for a man, of Woman Police Constable. For life.

I was very proud of my sister and showed her off to all my friends. She helped me occupy the very few dull moments in life. I took her for walks in her pram. My favourite game was to take her to the top of the hill, let go of the pram, chase it down the promenade and catch the handle just before it, and she, crashed into the sea. I had no conception that this might have been dangerous, or that I might have lost her. It was just fun. I did, once, knock the pram over and I thought I'd killed her. That, for a few moments, was terrible. Until she began to scream blue murder. Thank heavens. We grew up to be extremely close, in spite of the ten-year gap, and in spite of being 'Wayne's little sister' when she started dance classes – I was, by then, with the Royal Ballet. She lives in Plymouth now and is happily married to Michael and they both work in the Post Office.

Not long after Joanne was born I sat my eleven-plus examination. I had never been one of the smarter pupils in the class – I was a dreamer and there was so much more in the world, as far as I was concerned, than academic lessons. Dancing, the church, even playing on the beach or listening to *Hancock's Half Hour*, took preference to homework. So it was with some trepidation, coloured with natural nerves, that I sat this exam. I did not make it to Hartlepool Grammar, but I did do well enough to get into West Hartlepool Technical College.

I arrived, eleven years old, for my first day at the Tech. The school towered above me, a Gothic creation suitable for torture. I reeked of newness, in my first school uniform – grey socks, shorts, blazer with brand new, empty, leather satchel slung over my shoulder. The school list stipulated shorts for my age. When I got there I found out that no one else my age was wearing shorts. They all had long trousers. A really good start.

As was assembly. I waited and waited for my name to be called, to be streamed into A, B or C forms. You can guess which one I went into. We were given textbooks, more textbooks, and yet still further textbooks, rough books, copying books, fair books, rulers, compasses, pencils, the whole stationery cupboard. I crammed it into my brand new leather satchel. It was now too heavy to sling over my shoulder. Boys in the know had ex-Army backpacks. I thought I was on another planet.

The school yard was minuscule. There was no room to escape from boys who spat, boys who fought, played cards or secretly smoked. I used to stand outside the school gates until the whistle for morning lessons was blown. Then I would dive through the gates before the prefects banged them shut in my face. Sometimes they didn't let me make it. 'Tough luck, Sleepy. Late again.' Stopped by someone who probably, in later life, would collect tickets for British Rail and stop latecomers boarding their trains. Same sort of aggro.

If you were late five times your punishment was one stroke of the strap at the end of term. I was late at least fifteen times. Three strokes of the nasty two-thonged leather strap. At the end of term I joined the (long) queue outside the headmaster's office. He always complimented me on my good manners before he had me bend over. But these good manners, courtesy of Mum, never did me an iota of good in staving off a punishment. And I was a regular termly visitor to his study.

We were a very noisy and mischievous C form and some of the teachers decided that if one of us was out of order, then we were all out of order, and we would all get the strap. This had no effect on us whatsoever. It only proved that corporal punishment is a useless form of prevention. For me the real humiliation was when I, as the guilty party, had to collect the strap book from the head-master's office. It was the expression on the face of his secretary, whom I liked, when I appeared. 'Oh no, Wayne, not again.' Her sadness at my misdemeanours was worse than physical punishment. I never told my mother. Except once. The pain was too much and I winced when I sat down for tea. Mum cross-examined me, and then insisted on seeing the green and blue welts across my bum. It was all I could do to prevent her from storming up to the Tech and raising the roof. All five foot of her.

I studied all the subjects that one would suppose a dancer would need most in the world – engineering drawing, trigonometry, science, electricity, metal-work and woodwork. I was hopeless at most of them. The only thing I made that might have been good was nicked – a spanner from the metalwork class. Engineering drawing? A joke. We hid behind the tall sloping desks, out of sight of the teacher, telling jokes, flicking paper pellets – that's what our tri-squares were useful for. I made a wooden theatre in woodwork, with dovetail joints. They fitted so badly I glued it together with chewing gum. It collapsed one day soon after, when Mum leant on it while vacuuming. It ended up on the fire. I was obviously going to go far in this technical world. (I wonder, sometimes, what might have happened if I had not had a talent for dance. What a frightening thought.)

There were two good things about my time at the Tech. One was the choir. During assembly we sat on the stage behind the headmaster, facing the rest of the school. (I remember a great cheer resounding in the hall the day I made my first appearance in long trousers. Wayne and his shorts, once famous, were a thing of the past.) And my voice was not only good enough for the school choir, it was good enough for the choir of Durham Cathedral, where we sang on special occasions. Unfortunately, the clarity of my soprano did not carry through puberty. But what I learned then put me in good stead when I later appeared in musicals.

The other good thing about the Tech was Stephen Gretton. He was my best friend. We went everywhere together, sharing in the ever-secret knowledge of growing up. We spent lunches in the reference library, poring over biology text-books for gender diagrams and dictionaries for all the naughty words. That was sex education in those days. We both played rugby. I was a hooker. This meant being tumbled around in the scrum like a piece of dirty linen in a washing machine. My job was to hook the ball away from the centre of the scrum and pass it back to my team-mates. The best way I knew to do this was to kick the opposition in the shins as quickly and sharply as possible. 'Come on, Sleepy,' they yelled. I was small enough to run between the other boys' legs, almost. 'Come on, Sleepy, where's your tights, you little sissy? Where's your skirt?' Once I got seriously maddened by this baiting. I fell to the ground with the ball in my arms. Right over a brick in the ground. When another boy tackled me I rolled over to allow him to land with his full force on the brick. It was Stephen – not one of the others who really deserved to get hurt. He broke his collar-bone. The rest of them were just laughing. This little incident made me realize that it's daft to pay attention to jibes; your plans for revenge usually misfire and someone else – in this case my best friend – gets hurt. So I decided to ignore the 'dancer/sissy/tights' comments, and when I stopped rising to the bait, they stopped. In fact I became a sort of school mascot. I was good in the gym, able to do the splits and spin a bit, which gave me rarity value. And then, in my first Christmas concert at the Tech, in front of the 400 boys, and the 300 girls who always joined us from the girls' Tech for this annual get-together, I danced a sailor's hornpipe. I performed my first encore. I was accepted, by my peers, as a dancer. It was a sweet success.

Muriel Carr put me in for a Royal Academy of Dancing scholarship, while I was at the Tech, which gained me two free lessons a week. Tuesday afternoons and Saturday mornings. In Newcastle. This meant that by 3.45 P.M. on Tuesdays I would be getting twitchy in case the teacher – who didn't care for dance – wouldn't let me go in time to catch my train. I had to catch a train at 4 P.M., then take the trams in Newcastle to get to the dance studio. This meant one and a half hours of travel, each way, for an hour's lesson. I didn't get home until 8.30 at night, having done my homework on the train. But it was worth it.

At the RAD classes I met another boy who wanted to be a dancer. His name was Peter O'Brien. He teaches dance in Zurich these days. It was good to have another boy as a friend who shared the same interest as me and as someone I could compete with in class.

I sometimes stayed with him at his home in Sunderland. He had actually seen a real ballet on stage and his vivid descriptions really made me want to go. I badgered Mum to take me to the Royal Ballet when they next came to Newcastle. I bought the cheapest tickets for a performance of *Sleeping Beauty*. I climbed all those steps up to the Gods at the Theatre Royal with anticipation. And the frisson was compounded when the orchestra struck the first notes of Tchaikovsky's overture. But the moment when the curtain rose on the set and the costumes, the colour and the lights, was when I realized that this was what I wanted to be part of. I had found my world.

Mum and I turned to each other and we both said 'It's wonderful.' It wasn't so much the dancing, it was the spectacle. This was the production that the Royal Ballet had performed on its first tour of the United States in 1948, which took the country by storm. Oliver Messel was the designer, and the choreography was by Frederick Ashton, after Petipa. Magic. Unfortunately we could only stay until the end of the first act, otherwise we would miss our train home. And I hadn't seen any male dancing. There was none until the third act. I was left a little flat, wondering if the major role for men in ballet was as support for the girls. Of course, if I had been able to stay I would have seen what the men really could do.

By now I was desperate to get into show business, by any means. I saw an advertisement in the paper for boys to audition for parts in *Oliver*. I plagued my mother to let me go to London and try. Of course, at twelve, I didn't think about the practicalities of being alone in a foreign city (which London was), plus the question of board and lodging and all that stuff, but Mum did. The idea was quashed. My disappointment was like a black, heavy cloud.

My mother had been subscribing to the *Dancing Times*, where she saw an article about auditions for a scholarship to the Royal Ballet School. This struck a chord with her. If I were good enough, and lucky enough, to get the scholarship, it would mean that I would be looked after and lodgings would be taken care of. And she was determined that I should have the advantage of all possible chances that came my way. She remembered what had been denied her, for whatever reason, when she was a child. Mum asked Muriel Carr, my dancing teacher, if I would stand a chance. Miss Carr said, 'Definitely.' So my mother said, 'Really? Why didn't you tell me before that you thought he had such potential?' 'Well,' she replied, 'I didn't like to single him out in case it would upset the other students' parents.' It would be expensive to travel to London and back for these auditions, let alone spend the night there, but Mum, when she wanted to do something, always found a way. She discovered that we could travel to London by the overnight train, both ways, and not have to find accommodation.

I couldn't sleep on the train to London. It was not very comfortable, and the dark always creates apprehension. We found another hopeful RAD scholar sitting near us in the carriage, which gave us a little more confidence about being able to find Barons Court and the Royal Ballet Upper School where the auditions were to be held. We arrived at six in the morning, at King's Cross Station – not the most welcoming of places in those days. London was large, dark and rather forbidding. I was excited and not a little nervous. The competition, I knew, was going to be fierce. We found a working men's cafe and I had biscuits and orange juice, while Mum drank a cup of tea and smoked a cigarette.

When we arrived at Barons Court I joined the 400 other candidates at registration, where I was given the number thirteen – I am not of a superstitious nature – to pin on to my white singlet. We were then divided into classes of fifty and placed at the barre. Under the scrutiny of three or four adjudicators, a teacher took us through a classical ballet class. When that was over, we returned to the dressing rooms to wait for the decision. After what seemed a lifetime the door opened and the numbers of those who had passed the first round were read out. My number thirteen was one of the last to be called. I ran into the corridor to find Mum and tell her I'd got through, but I was hustled, instead, into another class with fifty other semi-finalists. The exercises, this time, were more difficult. Afterwards, the suspense was acute in the silence of the dressing-room. When the door opened, only three numbers were called. Mine was last.

Lunch break. It was one o'clock and I was reunited with Mum, who was thrilled that I'd reached the finals. This happiness was tempered by discovering that she, too, would have to be auditioned. She was to be interviewed by the Director of the School, Ursula Morton, and the Chairman, Arnold Haskell. Poor Mum – she did not look forward to this one little bit. We spent our lunch break getting increasingly nervous. The final round was coming up.

To my surprise only four girls joined the three boys in the huge studio. By contrast, the panel of judges had increased. There were many serious faces sitting behind a table the length of the studio. Quite forbidding. Some of them I recognized as being the leading dancers of the day. I had seen their pictures in the *Dancing Times*. They included Michael Somes, Ursula Morton, Errol Addison, Nadia Nerina and the greatest of all, Ninette de Valois. Other faces I did not know.

I was overawed at first. I told myself to 'keep going' and even began to enjoy the class. We were being given exercises by Harold Turner, a famous English dancer who created the Blue Boy in *Les Patineurs*. I raised a few smiles from some of the faces, although others were harder to crack. I projected as much of myself as I knew how into this final. I was determined to give them the full force of my fledgling technique.

After we made our bows we were taken downstairs to a room full of weird machines: the physiotherapy room. I lay on one of the beds while the specialist, Mr Robertson, contorted my limbs into the most peculiar positions. Finally I was placed into frogs, the position that tests your turn-out. You lie on the floor and put the soles of your feet together, close to your body. Then you let your knees drop down – the closer to the floor they get, the better the frog position is. Mine immediately hit the floor. I heard him mutter, 'Perfect turn-out.' So my duck-waddling paid dividends.

Next was the dreaded written examination. We were given a selection of titles from which to choose the subject for an essay. I settled on 'My Home Town'. This was at least something I knew about which might compensate for my bad grammar. I wrote about the division between the West Hartlepool and Hartlepool Borough Councils, how one would never ride on a West Hartlepool red bus, but stick to your own blue ones. I told the story of how the Hartlepudlians, during the Napoleonic wars, hanged a French spy – which turned out to be a monkey, washed up on the beach – and how my gran would come to Hartlepool every other summer to enjoy the carnival and the fair on the Town Moor. We would save up all year. The rifle range was my speciality, and Gran loved taking me on the the waltzers. And while I was struggling with this essay, Mum was struggling with her interview, answering questions as to the family's income, father's work and how and why I had started dancing lessons.

I was supposed, then, to go to Great Ormond Street for a projected height test, but as we had to catch the train back home to Hartlepool, this was cancelled. I have reason to be eternally grateful for this stroke of luck. When, just after I had started at the Ballet School, I was given the test, it showed I was likely to grow to between five foot two and five foot six – too short for a male ballet dancer. All hopes of a scholarship would have disappeared.

Mum and I rushed to King's Cross to catch the train home. We met the girl we had travelled down with, who unfortunately had not made it to the finals, so I stifled my own elation and sat on my desire to relive the day with Mum. Again I tried to sleep, but it was too uncomfortable, I was too excited, and I was wondering how long it would be before I heard if I'd won a place. So I was exhausted, but happy, as I dressed for school the next morning and caught the bus to the Tech. I arrived late – as usual.

A week later I came downstairs for breakfast and found an open envelope on my plate. I had been awarded one of the two Leverhulme Scholarships. I had a place at the Royal Ballet School in Richmond Park. I proudly took the letter to school that day and the headmaster read the letter out in assembly. The applause filled my head and I spent the rest of the day on cloud *ten*.

This scholarship led to my first appearance in the newspapers. 'Wayne Cuts Out Rugby in Favour of Ballet' squealed one of the headlines. It was obviously immaterial that I had given up rugby a year before because the matches clashed with my lessons in Newcastle. But who cares when it's a good story. Photographers arrived and I managed to squeeze my feet into my old rugby boots to pose for them on the beach, tackling an imaginary ball. Then it was on to the bowling green for a few *grandes jetées* on the baize lawn. If I had ever stepped on the sacred turf of the bowling green before this, let alone jumped around on it, I would have been thumped.

Because the autumn term had started at the Tech, and so that my studies (those useful dancing subjects like trigonometry and metalwork) would not be interrupted, I was to join the Royal Ballet School four months after the start of the school year in January 1962. I was in fact joining two years and a term later than most pupils, because we had not known about the school earlier. I knew that my life was going to change – I had, after all, glimpsed a world that I wanted to be a part of, and that I had no intention of leaving once in it – but I hadn't any idea just how different my life would be.

TWO

WHITE LODGE

A T THE BEGINNING of January 1962 I arrived, aged thirteen, with Mum and my stepfather, at 54 Temple Sheen Road in East Sheen. There were no spare beds at the Ballet School, so I was to be a day boy for a term. I think my parents were, well, not exactly disappointed, more let down. It didn't seem quite right to them that a scholarship boy should be farmed out, especially as I was so far from home. But they did not feel sufficiently confident to complain, and Mr and Mrs Withers, the couple I was to stay with that term, were at least welcoming. And there was the consolation of another boy from the school, Nicholas Bramble from Great Yarmouth, who was staying with them too. There wasn't really anything to be done about it, so we made the best of it. My face paled as my mother waved from the car with tears in her eyes. Over the last few years I had been her friend, her confidant as well as her son. I knew that she was going to miss me desperately. But at least she had my baby sister to help her through the more tricky times caused by my stepfather's moody nature.

The list of clothes and other stuff required for the Ballet School appeared to be endless: six pairs of underpants, vests, socks and singlets, two green school blazers and two pairs of flannel shorts. (The list said 'shorts' for those below a certain age, which included me, and I felt pretty daft because I'd been wearing long trousers for a while. And then, when I got to the school, *everyone* was wearing long trousers. Again.) We needed three pairs of day shoes, boot polish, three months' supply of toothpaste, shampoo and soap, and the most important part of the uniform – tights and ballet shoes. Plus the necessary bottle of methylated spirits to harden my feet – which was never applied. Most of this had to be bought from Barker's department store in London. My mother tried to get a grant from the local council but they would not give them out for clothes. It all cost a small fortune, which my parents could ill-afford, and I knew how difficult it was for them. Mum even gave up her treasured cigarettes and started to roll her own. But they never once complained or made me feel guilty.

Every morning Nicholas and I walked to the Sheen Gates at Richmond Park to be collected by a black minibus called the Trojan and taken to White Lodge, the school's home. White Lodge was the absolute opposite of everything I had experienced in my life to date: a nineteenth-century hunting-lodge, built for the monarch, standing in its own grounds. Even the neighbours were posh – Princess Alexandra and her husband, Angus Ogilvy. All it lacked, here and there, was a coat of paint.

The Salon, where we took class, still had its original silk wallpaper and the lobby its chandeliers and sweeping circular staircase, down which I used to slide when no one was looking. The walls of the library were curved and lined from floor to ceiling with leather-bound books on ballet and art. The garden, which we loved, was landscaped with trees (including the one Queen Victoria climbed as a child), hedges and flowerbeds, and all of this, house and garden, had – indeed still has – a tremendous view of Richmond Park, of its deer and the famous Pen Ponds; so called because the feathers of the swans were used to make Queen Victoria's quill pens.

The place itself was an absolute warren. It took ages before I stopped getting lost, and confusion was heightened by the underground passages. These had been built originally so that the servants could move from one part of the lodge to another without being seen above stairs, and the staff and pupils now used them to get around the school in the same way. There are storerooms in these underground corridors, one of which contained apples. We would take a coathanger, bend it in such a way that we could get it through the bars on the storeroom door, and spear apples. There is nothing quite like the forbidden.

Assembly was at nine o'clock, after which we started with our one and only ballet class. I thought that we would be dancing all day, which was what I wanted to do. I imagined nothing could be more perfect than to dance all day. So I was disconcerted to find that normal school timetables applied here as in other schools. At least there was no more physics, metalwork, trigonometry and engineering drawing. But because I had joined the school late I always lagged behind in academic studies, particularly in subjects I had never learned before, like Latin. Even White Lodge, in spite of its specialist application, had then to achieve a certain level of results in order to maintain its grant. In fact, the pass rate was high at O Level, with some pupils taking A Levels at sixteen.

All the pupils had one thing in common – the desire to dance. So I wasn't the only one who would rather have been leaping than conjugating Latin verbs. There were 150 girls and only thirty boys in the school, a perfect ratio I thought, with only four boys in my year to eighteen girls. The other Leverhulme scholar was Jeanetta Bumpus, who was two years younger than me. She later became a soloist with the touring company of the Royal Ballet, and eventually, as Jeanetta Laurence, Artistic Administrator of the Royal Ballet. The pupils came from all over the world and from many different back-grounds, and some people paid double fees in order to keep their children at the school and thus subsidize those who were less well-off.

Sarah Payne was my ballet teacher. Her voice was loud, and resonated round the room. She wielded a stick which she swished from side to side under our feet, encouraging us to leap higher. The girls, in those days, were much more scientifically taught than the boys. They weren't quite sure how to teach us for the best, with the result that we had a series of different teachers. We felt a bit like guinea pigs, and maybe we were. Boys do need to be taught differently. But the standard was still the highest in Britain.

At four o'clock the Trojan would return Nicholas and me to Sheen Gates. Mrs Withers was waiting for us at home with buns and tea, and after that it was homework. Mr Withers was a retired mathematician. He had suffered a stroke which left him with no feeling in one hand, and occasionally his wife pricked his fingers with a pin, to see if any sensation was returning. I don't know if it ever did. They were kind and disciplined and managed to make me feel at home, away from my large family.

Nicholas was a very odd boy. One day he asked me to take part in one of his experiments. He made me lie down on the bed, produced a large jar of Vaseline and greased my face all over. Then he slapped plaster of Paris over the Vaseline, and shoved two straws up my nostrils so that I could breathe – sort of. He left it on for half an hour. I don't remember whether I dared move or not. When the plaster was dry, he wrenched it from my face, taking with it all my eyelashes and eyebrows. Then he poured hot wax into the mould to create an effigy of my face. It cracked.

His favourite pastime, dragging me in his wake, was to visit the Victoria & Albert Museum or Westminster Abbey to peer at tombs and statues and all the death masks of saints and monarchs. This was my introduction to London, and it gave me an impression of a city populated by the macabre. But this quirky interest of Nicholas's paid off in the end. He was advised to stop dancing, because of short hamstrings, and he became one of the great wax modellers at Madame Tussaud's.

At alternate weekends pupils at White Lodge were allowed to go home. But my family was so far away and could not, in any case, afford the fare. Nicholas had a guardian while he was in London, called Joan de Robeck, who often invited me to come with Nicholas and stay for weekends at her flat in Philbeach Gardens in Earls Court. She was a very upright and correct lady, whose mores and morals came from an earlier age, and to whom manners were very important.

The first time I was offered tea at Philbeach Gardens, I nearly spluttered the lot over the carpet. It was disgusting. I thought she was trying to poison me. But this was my very first taste of Earl Grey. If you are used, as I was, to thick tea with milk, then this delicately scented, see-through tea is not only a cultural experience, it is a culture shock too. But I imbibed a lot of other sorts of culture (and manners) from her, sometimes with the full intention of learning, and sometimes without knowing it. Even after Nicholas left the school, Miss de Robeck continued to invite me for weekends, taking me to galleries, museums and on my first outings to the theatre in the West End.

But I was desperate to see my first musical, and I was finally allowed out one Saturday afternoon, in the company of a fifth-former, to see Lionel Bart's musical *Blitz*. Magic, although I don't know whether it was good or not. After this there was no stopping me. Miss de Robeck did not approve of musicals, and it took some persuading to get her to take me to *Oliver*, which she quite enjoyed – unlike the then very modern film of *West Side Story*.

I became a boarder at White Lodge for my second term. This meant I could join in all the high-spirited antics that went on after lessons were finished. As a day-boy I had been alienated to a great extent from life inside the school. The only advantage I'd had from living outside was being able to participate in the life of the church just round the corner from Temple Sheen Road, where I was a choirboy. I began to be embarrassed when my classmates came to church on Sunday and saw me singing, but I think they found it highly amusing. I had to give up the choir when I became a boarder, but religion was still important to me, and I tried to form a Scripture Union in the school, distributing badges, pamphlets and prayer sheets. I even got the boys in my dormitory to get down on their knees at bedtime and pray. It wasn't too long, however, before the sniggering became too loud to ignore and I realized they were sending me up. My evangelical fervour was distancing me from them, so I started to keep it to myself and it became, from then, an ever-dwindling light.

I shall never forget my first bath at White Lodge. This was one of those seminal rites of passage that are so often talked about. There was no privacy. The bathroom contained several basins and two upright baths, in which you sat on a ledge, with water coming up to your chin. Washing was a communal affair, quite outside my experience so far. My shyness and embarrassment led me to fill the bath with soapsuds and, with a towel draped round me, try – as quickly as possible – to submerge myself under the water. It followed that my bath night became quite an event.

All the boys assumed that there must be something wrong with my body and congregated to watch me climbing in. Paul Clarke, who was in the year above me, offered to help by holding the towel up in front of me. I accepted, in total naïvety. He peeked over the top (of course) and reported back to the others that all my vital parts were present, correct and in good order. I would not have minded, at that moment, had I been sucked down the plughole. Paul became a very good friend, however, and protected me from the few bullies that operated even here, at the school. It was the start of a lasting friendship.

Paul rose to principal dancer with the Royal Ballet. When he left, he joined the Festival Ballet, now the English National Ballet, and had tremendous success. Many years later, in the seventies, Ken Russell was filming *Valentino* with Rudolf Nureyev in the title role. There was to be a scene in which Valentino and Nijinsky improvised a mad tango together, based on an actual event, and Rudolf suggested me for Nijinsky, because he was only small, five foot two, like me. Ken was persuaded to see me as the Blue Skater in *Les Patineurs* at Sadlers Wells, and I met him in the pub next door afterwards for a drink. It was obvious that he had no intention of casting me, but was only humouring Nureyev. The role was eventually played by Anthony Dowell, although Paul Clarke was also considered for the part. Unsurprising, really, because Paul closely resembled Christopher Gable, who starred in Ken Russell's *The Boyfriend*.

Both men and women adored Paul – both for his good looks and for his personality – but, like so many handsome people, he was forever dissatisfied. He decided to change his jaw-line before starting work on the film. There was nothing wrong with it. But beautiful people are always finding imaginary flaws. He thought his jaw protruded slightly and that this might be exaggerated on film. Paul approached a few cosmetic surgeons who refused outright to alter his jaw-line. In the end he pleaded with Dick, his friend, who was a dentist, to do the operation. After much persuasion, Dick cut away half an inch either side of Paul's jaw in his own surgery. Paul's jaw was in a terrible state; he also lost feeling in the lower side of his face. Paul did not get the movie. Nine months later, his jaw had healed and he was back on top form, rehearsing a new part with the Festival Ballet.

He then went to Dick's surgery for minor work on a tooth. Paul insisted on anaesthetic, being squeemish. Dick obliged. Paul kept complaining of feeling woozy and so went to Dick's flat to sleep of the anaesthetic. Meanwhile, Dick went to clean up the surgery. When he went up, Dick was unable to wake Paul and called an ambulance. Paul was certified dead on arrival at the hospital. I was, we were, devastated by his loss and I felt so very sorry for Dick, and I always wondered if Dick blamed himself. But none of us knew that Paul had a rare heart disease (apparently known to occur sometimes in athletes), which was the real cause of his death at only twenty-nine. Dick never practised dentistry again.

In the sixth week of the second term, Dame Ninette de Valois, known to us as Madam, came to watch our class. She was looking for her future stars. Even at our tender age you could tell who was, or was not, going to make the grade. You could even pick out those who were destined for the top. We were all aware of Madam's importance – she had, after all, founded the Royal Ballet Company – and each one of us was anxious to make a good impression. Everything was going very well. Barre work was over; so was the work on the *ports de bras* (carriage of the arms and head) in the centre of the room and we lined up one by one for pirouettes from the corner. My sinuses were playing up; I realized that my nose and its desperate sniffs could not hold back the contents; a huge glob landed on Madam's shoe. I had to find a tissue to wipe it off. Some introduction. In terror, I looked up into her eyes, expecting the wrath of ages. I met her stern gaze, which melted, suddenly, and with a secret wink she gave me a warm smile and said, 'Don't worry. Get back to your exercises.' I have loved that woman ever since. And thank goodness she likes naughty boys. I have since heard many stories about how severe and ruthless she can be, but I have always found her to be a great source of inspiration, especially in guiding me through my career. She is a great humanitarian, always willing to listen to a dancer's problems, personal or otherwise.

I know she is single-minded and determined. When she was working with Lilian Bayliss, who was running the Old Vic Company, Ninette de Valois asked her if she could put on an evening of dance. Bayliss gave her usual reply: 'I will have to ask God,' and dropped to her knees. This was always her first response to requests from actors and staff for better roles, pay, conditions. Her answer would often be 'God says No.' There is not much you can say to that. In de Valois's case God's answer must have been 'Yes'. That was the beginning of the Sadlers Wells Ballet. Even if God had said 'No,' I do not imagine Madam, who is of Irish descent, would have been deterred for long. She has such vision and resolve that I am sure she would have achieved her purpose in some other way. When her company was awarded a Royal Charter and became the Royal Ballet, de Valois recognized the need to feed the company with fresh talent and created the Royal Ballet School. Thus she could nurture her fledgling dancers and keep an eye on possible unorthodox teaching methods at the same time. To this end she also formed a teachers' training course to raise the standards of ballet teaching throughout the country – and eventually the world.

Days at the school did not stop at bedtime. Every night, Miss Copeland, the Sister in charge of our dormitory, uttered the immortal phrase, 'Now boys, heads on your own pillows please!' before turning out the lights. As soon as she went, the lights came back on and the night-time activities would start.

The boys, being outnumbered by the girls, were spoilt for choice. I and the other boys would raid the larder and on rare occasions, for a dare, would creep up to the girls' dorms after midnight to share our spoils. We sat on the girls' beds – I teamed up with Primula Cotton – whispering, giggling and scoffing. The slightest noise would make us run for cover and I once hit my head on the fire extinguisher lurking over Primmy's bed. One night we put on wellington boots and, dressed in pyjamas, went for a midnight swim in Pen Ponds. The excitement of these outings was more in the daring than in the execution, because they were usually cold and uncomfortable. Except for one night.

I scaled the larder wall to find a bottle. The label said 'Highly Explosive'. Irresistible. How could I keep my hands off a bottle advertising such an evident thrill? It didn't occur to me that the contents might be what they said they were. Oh no. Something in me said it was made for me. I poured the contents down my throat – and the others found me running around the building, half-naked and screaming with laughter. They managed to whisk me into hiding just before the heavy footsteps of Sister, accompanied by the scuttle of her poodle, brought them into sight round the corner. 'Highly Explosive' was home-made wine (I now know that it was a fair epithet for the stuff) and was my first taste of – and the start of a long-lasting thirst for – booze.

Graham Powell was my chief rival when it came to dancing. He was greatly talented and I competed with him in class all the time, usually taking second place. He had been in the school much longer than I, and although we were competitive in the ballet classes, we were best friends out of it. There was nothing he could not do – painting, writing poetry, inter-school sports champion, all round good egg – and he was also very mischievous. Brilliant. We managed to get into loads of trouble.

Then one Saturday afternoon we were bored and decided to join the girls in their dorm during their rest period. This was out of bounds, and we knew it, but they were in their uniforms, and we were only sitting on their beds and gossiping. Suddenly there was a knock on the door. Graham dived under a bed and I made myself two-dimensional behind the opening door, round which appeared the head of Mr Hart, the housemaster.

'Did I just hear Sleep and Powell's voices?' And in spite of my frantic grimacing, some idiot cooed 'Yes.' We were marched off to stand outside his office door, where we waited for hours while our fate was decided. We were the only boys at that time to have ever been caned at the school. This was to make us realize the gravity of our offence. But for me the cane was nothing after the strap I'd endured at the Tech. I wonder sometimes what might have happened if they had discovered our midnight excursions. And somewhere inside I knew that caning, although a serious punishment, was the soft option.

By the time I reached my last year at the school I had given up almost all academic subjects and seemed to have far more free periods than classes. The teachers must have been pleased to see the back of me, as I still found pleasure in playing the clown in class and never achieved good marks. During prep, to relieve the boredom, I would make up poems about the girls, which were passed secretly from desk to desk, causing havoc, until the teacher would either send me out or ask me to read the poem out loud to get it over and done with.

To avoid prep I offered myself, readily, as a babysitter for the housemaster and his wife. We all had a crush on her. We were supposed to take our text books with us, to study. Ha Ha. Bang – on went the television. We watched anything, but particularly looked forward to the chance of seeing the Beatles on *Thank Your Lucky Stars*. This was our only contact with the pop world, apart from a few of the pupils playing records or tuning in a tinny transistor radio to Alan Freeman's *Top of the Pops* on Sunday afternoons.

One afternoon I heard a voice emanating from a record-player in our fifth-form sitting-room. It was French and full of passion. I fell in love with the sound of Edith Piaf. I demanded that they play 'Milord' over and over again. And then, the next week, I read that she had died. I was denied the chance, ever, to see or hear the Little French Sparrow in person.

Babysitting was taken in turns with the other four boys in my class – Graham, Peter O'Brien (who had by now joined the school), Peter Fairweather and Alan Hooper. Alan was the brain of our year, taking O Level maths in the fourth form and his A level in the fifth. He was also head prefect and the good boy in our year – making up for all the rest of us. He became, eventually, the Director of the Royal Academy of Dancing and a fine teacher before his untimely death. On a lecture tour of America for the Royal Academy he fell to his death, impaling himself on the railings ten floors below. This accident has never been satisfactorily explained.

To fill the free periods for those of us less inclined to study, Lady Agnew, our headmistress, took us around the latest exhibitions at numerous art galleries. With her we saw Goya, the first Pop Art exhibition, Modigliani – where she told me my face was like that in many of his paintings. In fact, at every exhibition she found a painting to relate to one of her students. She explained to us all the different styles of painting with such authority that several people were attracted to our group, thinking that she was a tour guide. Our numbers expanded rapidly as we moved from room to room. Although we laughed secretly with each other, we learned more from those outings than we ever could from textbooks. But that we got home in one piece from all these visits was a miracle: her driving was so erratic. She spent her time looking out for interesting sights and landmarks to point out to us. I don't think her eyes ever hit the road.

I gave up the academic subjects but not the school plays and poetry readings. And I took up the piano again. At the end of one summer term of that last year there was a concert, given in the Main Salon, for the whole school, by all the pupils who were studying a musical instrument. My tutor was away, ill, in the weeks before the concert, but I was determined to take part, and rehearsed myself in a piece by Poulenc. When my turn came to play, eager (as ever) to make a big impression, I started playing at the speed of light. I missed most of the right notes. Titters from the front row reached me which made me nervous. My hands began to shake, I lost my place and, in my desperation to finish the piece, began to make the whole thing up – my fingers flew across the keys in no particular order. I caught the general air of hysteria and with tears of laughter streaming down my face I brought the piece to an abrupt end, stood up to bow and received a standing ovation. Lady Agnew, however, was not amused, and voiced her general disapproval to the school. I was summoned to the music teacher, Miss Perrott (whom we called Parrot Face, naturally), and asked to account for my display. I tried to explain that as my piano teacher was ill, I had tried to learn the Poulenc by myself, but all she would say was that I should never have been performing in the first place. I had never answered anyone in authority back before (my mother considered rudeness a cardinal sin), but this pushed me over the edge and I told her she was a 'bloody old bag'. There were no repercussions to my surprise – but I had found my sharp tongue.

One of the great perks of being at the RBS was that we were allowed some-times, as a privilege, to watch the ballet companies at the Royal Opera House during dress rehearsals. The first ballet I saw from the amphitheatre was *Giselle*, in 1962. The two leading dancers were Margot Fonteyn and Rudolf Nureyev – Nureyev, a leading dancer with the Kirov Ballet Company, had just defected. I did not imagine, then, that one day I would dance on the same stage as him with the Royal Ballet. I remember he was so different from all the other dancers.

There was an arrogance in his walk. He warmed up on stage, holding on to a piece of scenery, long before his first appearance. The dancers who were already on stage, rehearsing, were obliged to dance around him – he had no intention of moving out of their way. And I wondered, we all did, how it was that he was allowed such latitude. But when he took flight and showed off his marvellous technique we understood why he got away with being the rebel of the ballet. I watched the partnership between him and Fonteyn with awe. His passion was a perfect foil to her radiance, her acting ability and the pure line of her body in the dance. Together they brought new and invigorating life into the staid old classics. It was a unique and near perfect partnership which made me gulp with emotion.

It was Nureyev's arrival which changed attitudes towards male dancers. No longer were they merely the prop and background for the ballerina's predominating art – up-and-coming dancers were allowed to show off their technique and encouraged to establish an equality with their partners on stage. Nureyev put male dancing firmly on the map. I was going to enter this world at exactly the right time. The future seemed exciting – more exciting than before, if that were possible.

Some of the older dancers resented Nureyev's intrusion and his foreign ways. They minded that he demanded things of them in rehearsal, instead of asking politely as is the accustomed reticent English way. Many years later I was playing Puck to his Oberon in Ashton's *The Dream* and we were working on some steps before the curtain rose. He shouted some abuse at me – I wasn't doing what was wanted, apparently – telling me to move out of the way. I asked him why he could not speak to me in civil tones.

'I learn your polite English,' he replied, 'where does it get me? Nowhere. I learn other words and THEN they move their ass.' (I learned later on in life that he was right. There are occasions, unfortunately, when only strong language achieves ends.) But I must stress that the other side of him was charming. It would get him out of sticky situations and, when he was inclined that way, you could refuse him nothing. A complex god.

As I moved up the school our outings to various theatres expanded to include visits to the Sadler's Wells Theatre, the D'Oyly Carte Opera Company and the Old Vic. Occasionally the school was also given tickets for events at the Royal Albert Hall, where I saw the Moiseyev Dance Company, the Red Army with their extraordinary acrobatic dancing and the occasional Sunday concerts. I remember that at one of these Sunday evenings there were girls going round the audience handing out free packets of cigarettes. (No good to me – I was not then, am not now, interested in smoking.) I couldn't work out why until I looked round the audience and realized that most of them were in army uniform. The school had been given free tickets for the El Alamein Reunion Concert. Vera Lynn received an ovation for her wartime repertoire, and then the stage was taken by this strange and glamorous woman who slunk on to the stage in the tightest-fitting sequinned gown. She began to sing, in that gravelly voice that was so famous, 'Tell me what the boys in the back room will have . . .' I could not take my eyes off Marlene Dietrich – I had never experienced such charisma. Field-Marshal Montgomery made a speech, and to round off my evening, the Queen Mother walked right past me.

These outside visits always resulted in impromptu concerts in the Salon. After the Red Army concert we practised cobblers. I found them easy, perhaps because I was small. Cobblers, for those that don't know, is the evocative term for jumping in the squat position while extending legs alternately out in front of you off the ground. Our visits to the dress rehearsals at the Royal Ballet resulted in my winding myself up, like a yoyo on a length of string, and hurling my body, spinning, across the room from one side to the other, where, unable to stop, I hit the wall. I was rescued, picked up, dusted down – then unabashed, I started again, believing, as do all thirteen-year-olds, 'I can do that.'

The Bolshoi Ballet came to London, and even though I was thirteen and in the third form I was small enough to be chosen by the Bolshoi teacher, along with the eleven-year-olds from the school, to be in a production called *School of Ballet*. I was to appear both with the famous Russian company *and* on stage at the Royal Opera House. When I saw those (fabulous) dancers and their athletic way of dancing which was so different to our precise English technique, I realized that this was the way I wanted to dance. It was a revelation, a *coup de foudre*. I wanted, like them, to jump higher, turn more, cover more ground, take risks and send currents of excitement through the audience. I was open-mouthed but I knew it was the way for me to go.

Some, perhaps more sophisticated, Western tastes thought the Bolshoi productions and choreography heavy and old-fashioned. This was not surprising, as they were not allowed to experiment as widely as Western dancers with their creative skills, nor were they then open to or influenced by the latest movements in Western style, music and culture. It meant that some of their dancing was preserved in aspic even if other parts were more like a liberating force.

School of Ballet started with we younger ones going through simple basic class exercises. The next scene was the *corps de ballet* going through their paces, and the ensuing scenes developed through the levels of the greater and expanding techniques of the soloists, until it was the turn of the principal dancers. One of them, Vladimir Vasiliev, became my idol. He jumped highest, turned most and took more risks than anyone I had ever seen. Who would have thought that within a year of leaving Hartlepool, I would find myself on stage at Covent Garden with the Bolshoi!

I also understudied some of the younger boys in the Bolshoi version of *Cinderella*. I found this verged on the humiliating, and I was forced to realize that I was not growing in comparison with the other boys in my form. Depression started to creep in, and I began to try all sorts of experiments to increase my height. One was hanging from the lintels of the doors in an attempt to stretch my body – but that only pulled my arms out of their sockets. In another, I lay on the bed and hung on to the bedstead while someone pulled on my feet. They called it putting me on the rack. I was open to any idea. Someone advised manure in my shoes. Now I may be green but I'm not cabbage-looking, and even I thought that a dodgy suggestion.

Our teachers, at the time, held on to the prevailing wisdom that if boys did the splits and stretched their limbs too frequently, they would lose the elasticity in the tendons and consequently their natural spring and jump. So these vital exercises were banned. The result for me, being a stocky person, was that my muscles began to overdevelop. I really needed those stretching exercises, to lengthen the muscle, and was so concerned about the growing bulk of my thighs that I wrapped plastic bags round them at night to reduce their size. I ended up with sweaty sheets and no miraculous change to my thighs by morning. My natural turn-out was starting to turn in and I was in danger of stiffening up. Just one of the theories of male dance tuition at the time. Nowadays teaching for boys is more scientific and stretching has its rightful place in the development of the body. It could be said, however, that some dancers over-extend these days, thus distorting the classical line.

One morning a week the boys from the fourth form up went to the Upper School in Barons Court to take class from a variety of teachers. Afterwards we sneaked up to the Covent Garden Studio to watch our heroes from the Royal Ballet take class: Anthony Dowell, Christopher Gable, Antoinette Sibley, Merle Parke, Nadia Nerina, Svetlana Beriosova, Annette Page, Donald Macleary, Alexander Grant and, of course, Fonteyn and Nureyev. All of them, and many other talented dancers, in one studio. They all had their own individual fan club and following. Every principal dancer was a star and fans queued for ages to see their favourites. Fierce discussions and disagreements erupted over which of these idols gave the best performance in a particular role.

In those days a dancer, in his study for a role, was required to research into the style of the period and then to interpret it as near as possible to the original performance. And he brought not only his technique but also his personality and spirit to the part. This created the theatrical experience. It strikes me that many dancers today rely on technique alone to entertain and please the public. Many ballets, therefore, appear to lack the style and artistry with which they were originally created. They have less depth than those we saw through the glass door of the studio. I can't help feeling that audiences today are sometimes being sold short – but I suspect this simply reflects these laid back times.

In my final year, the fifth form boys were summoned to the Director's office to be told – yet again – that we were to have a new teacher. We gave a collective sigh of resignation. It was unlikely, we reckoned, that this would provide much change. But we were wrong, and I think she was the making of us.

Her name was Joan Lawson. She was a ballet historian who had written several books on ballet and mime, and, even better, had travelled to Russia several times to make a specific study of their teaching methods for boys.

Miss Lawson proved to be a wonderful teacher. She took us back to the basics – to the point of teaching us how to breathe properly: not through the diaphragm, but from the back, into the rib cage. We gained knowledge and insight into our bodies and discovered that until then we had only been going through the motions. The exercises were explained to us in great detail. We were made aware of our muscles, their function in the body and how they operated for each move. We were taught how to use the muscles in our back, rather than in our shoulders, to lift our arms. This understanding relieved us of the constant haranguing to stop hunching our shoulders, or lifting our hips, or arching our backs – all of which caused enormous strain on our joints. It was a genuinely liberating feeling to discover the full extent of our bodies, to feel the power we could generate.

Joan Lawson was and is an eccentric and wonderful character with a great sense of humour. Suddenly class was inspired. She told us stories of the days when she performed in the music halls with the Anna Pavlova ballet company. She described her passion for the Russian teachers, Chebukiani and Messerer, and mimed Russian folk stories. The effect of her teaching was to provide us with the addition of theatrical skills to complement our classical technique.

We were accustomed to stand to attention at the barre when awaiting the arrival of the teacher, and to show our appreciation at the end of the class – the reverence – a deep bow. Miss Lawson would glide into the room, usually in a long flowing garment, greet us with a deep curtsey and immediately inquire how we were. We once complemented her on her long pleated skirt. 'Thank you, dear,' she replied. It was the first nylon one ever made. If I was having trouble with my pirouettes she would excuse it with, 'Don't worry, dear, you can never turn after you've washed your hair.' I had a huge head of curly hair which, when washed, expanded to obscure my vision completely.

Sometimes she came in covered with scratches and plasters and would explain that she had been up the apple tree or pruning her roses. On less jolly entrances, she would say, 'Sorry boys, I've been up all night looking after Mother.' Miss Lawson lived with and looked after her mother, who was an invalid and confined to a wheelchair.

A few years later, when I was a student at the Upper School and could not get home for Christmas, she invited me, and any other boys in the same predicament, to her house in Golders Green for the delights of her chocolate or lemon mousse. A few years ago I went back for lessons with Joan after I tore my medial ligament and had been in plaster for five weeks. I had only three weeks to recover if I was to take the lead in the West End revival of *Song and Dance*. With her help and enthusiasm, not only was I dancing on the first night but the recovery was far less painful than it might have been.

O Levels loomed. We moved into the new boys' wing, built over the sunken garden. Mr Hart and his family were beneath us on the ground floor – so our pillow fights and extra-curricular fooling around had to be kept at a minimum. Alan Hooper and I were prefects by then, and so it was up to us to keep discipline. Alan succeeded. I did not. My final term there was spent mainly sitting in the bath. Wrapped in blankets, loaded with textbooks and sitting in the deserted bathroom, I studied into the early hours, trying to catch up on lost lessons before the exams. I took five subjects and just passed in English Literature, History and Art.

But the peak of my final year at White Lodge was that a few of us were given minor parts in the Upper School graduation performance of *The Sleeping Beauty* at the Theatre Royal, Drury Lane. In the last act of the ballet, characters from fairy-tales entertain Princess Aurora and her Prince at the wedding. I was to play the Wolf opposite Jeanetta Bumpus as Red Riding Hood in the eponymous tale. During rehearsals the person in charge of the costumes said to Dame Ninette de Valois, 'Don't worry, Madam, we will have a mask to fit the boy in time for the performance.' To which she replied, 'Don't worry. There is no way you are going to put a mask over that young man's face!' A special wolf's head was made for me, leaving my face uncovered so that my expression could be seen by the audience. This decision of Madam's once again proved her ability to maximize the individual talents of her dancers. Jeanetta and I were called back many times by the audience and Madam insisted that we receive our very own curtain call at the end of the performance. It was unusual for students from White Lodge to be given such preferential treatment. We loved it.

This was the first time my mother had seen me dance on stage since I joined the school. She and my grandmother came to the performance, and when the orchestra struck up their first chords, my grandmother jumped out of her seat and screamed. She had never heard a live orchestra before, and was not prepared, sitting there in the dark of the auditorium and waiting for the curtain to rise, for the rousing start of Tchaikovsky's music. Although my part was very small it taught me the truth of an old adage: 'There are no small parts, only small players.' And although I am small in height, I learned then to give more than one hundred per cent no matter how minor the role and also to respect its importance in a production as a whole. It was a terrific end to my final year at White Lodge.

THREE

STUDENT LIFE AND FIRST ROLES

I PASSED INTO THE Upper School in September 1964 and went to live at the YMCA in Tottenham Court Road. My scholarship ran out at the end of my time at White Lodge so it was necessary for me to apply for a grant. By this time my parents had returned to Devon so it was Plymouth that granted me a Major Award. This just about covered the cost of staying at the YMCA and my travel to Barons Court, the Royal Ballet School's home in West London. It was £5 per week. I paid 30 shillings to the Y, where I shared a room with Alan Hooper; travel was ten shillings; which left me with £3 for food, dance shoes, clothes – and everything else. I was living on a diet of chocolate and chips. I began to feel dizzy in class. Then one day, after a series of pirouettes across the floor, my head and the room both continued to spin long after my body stopped. The next thing I remember was the teacher propping me up against the mirrors. I was summoned to the Bursar's office and grilled, as it were, about my condition. It soon became apparent that I couldn't afford to eat, at least not in any nutritious way and the Bursar asked me why I had not come and asked for help from the Benevolent Fund. I had never heard of the Benevolent Fund. It had never occurred to me that I could just walk in and ask. They gave me £2 extra a week – this made it up to a magnificent £7. The feeling of wealth was overwhelming, especially in comparison with the struggle I'd previously had to make ends meet. This small amount of money made a huge impact on my life and to this day I have never felt richer.

The curriculum at the Upper School was much more dance-orientated. Having gained my three O levels, I decided to quit while I was ahead and pursue only the Terpsichorean muse. A two-hour ballet class was followed by lessons in mime and character dancing or the study of different styles of dance, such as the mazurka, czardas or polonnaise, or by classes in which we learned the Royal Ballet repertoire and how to place your hands on a ballerina's body, in a *pas-de-deux* (where a boy partners a girl), without causing embarrassment to either dancer.

Most boys preferred the smaller girls, whom of course they found easier to hike aloft, and I was often left to partner the taller girls, whose waists appeared to me at eye-level. I struggled to lift them above my head, only to find that their feet had hardly left the floor. The classes would collapse into laughter as everyone watched all my determined efforts come to nothing or, even worse, saw us land in a heap on the floor. There was only one girl I partnered well. She was my size.

Her name was Jan Francis, and she is now a well-known actress. But my (often thwarted) exertions and experiences in these *pas-de-deux* classes stood me in good stead some eight years later, in Kenneth MacMillan's *Elite Syncopations*. He had the brilliant wheeze of partnering me with the tallest girl in the company – Vergie Derman. On her points she towered a foot over me.

We were assigned a series of different teachers, all with their own theories. We had learned to expect this. Now, of course, there is the teacher's training course, and the teaching is more uniform. Then the teachers were mainly ex-professional dancers from the Royal Ballet and really did include some of Britain's finest: Pamela May, Julia Farron and Barbara Fewster. They not only taught us technique but also imparted their experience as performers, and their knowledge of stagecraft and artistic interpretation. Even standing still and walking were studied, to give the correct deportment and dignity. The perfect example of this was Nureyev, who commanded attention merely by his manner of standing. The stillness created an energy which made you want to know more.

Two of the teachers stand out in my memory for different reasons. The first, Louis Ressiga, came from France. His methods of training strengthened our bodies, but we found them somewhat bizarre – dumbbells, for instance – so we were a fairly undisciplined rabble in his classes. He had a very short fuse, which we took perverse delight in lighting: in particular by linking arms and taking the mickey out of his Frenchness by high-kicking *à la* Folies Bergère. We knew that would make him lose his rag. He reported me, once, for using elastic bands round my shoes, instead of sewing elastic into them, thus making them prone to fly off during exercises. I was suspended for a week as a punishment and made to watch classes rather than participate. It might seem a harsh punishment for such an apparently little misdemeanour, but in reality it did me a favour. I learned a great deal from observing the mistakes and consequent corrections of other dancers, and it instilled in me the habit of sitting in on other classes – to absorb more knowledge and to train both mind and eye to be quick and alert.

The other teacher was Donald Britten, a principal from the Royal Ballet's touring company. He was an excellent demi-character dancer in virtuoso performances, dancing the Jester or the Neapolitan as well as the Prince. He and I were similar in physique (although he was taller), thick-set, strong, more tough than lyrical, and he taught me many of the roles I was to inherit. We all had great faith in Donald, for his abilities, his professionalism and his teaching. But he had a changeable temperament and I, by this time often depressed about my height, had days of moodiness which I could not shake off. When our low moods coincided, the relationship between us was anything but sympathetic and class would end with a distinct lack of concord between us. He cared enormously, however, and often invited us to his house, where he and his wife, Elaine Thomas, a dancer with the Company, enlarged on Joan Lawson's teachings. With the aid of a chart of the muscles of the body, he pointed out our individual weaknesses and how to strengthen them, helping us to understand the relationship of muscle, ligament and bone.

Our first classes at Barons Court were at 9 A.M., a time of day I loathed. I have always found it difficult to get up in the morning. I often took late-night trips to Old Compton Street in Soho with other boys from the YMCA; boys who were studying at universities and colleges, training to be doctors, barristers, hairdressers, chefs, prime ministers. We sat on doorsteps chatting to girls wearing outrageous beehives and long black leather boots, girls who were our age, but already working the streets. They mocked and mimicked us without mercy while we flirted with them.

It was during these evenings of dissipation that I met Gordon Henson. He lived around the corner from the Y – which he referred to as his 'club'. He always wore a suit (usually grey check), a bow tie, rather large rings on his fingers, and an obvious (except to him) black toupée. He took snuff and bicycled everywhere round the West End. His accent was very correct, and his delivery – well, nothing short of theatrical. He had appeared as a comic in shows on Clacton Pier, and had been in ENSA during the war. He must have been about seventy.

To make money Gordon went to the auctions at Debenhams and brought back loads of cheap lots in the shape of watches, record players and umbrellas – which he would then try to flog to us students. At last I had my own Dansette record player. It was the dizzy height of possession. He also handed out free tickets to shows, which he got from friends who were stage staff in various theatres. I saw a great many flops in this way – because they were the only shows prepared to give away tickets.

Gordon lived in one room with only a small gas-ring on which he boiled eggs. He told us tales of his days in music hall, snorting snuff from his little gold snuff-box. He had no telephone himself, but there was one available in the flat below if there was ever an emergency. This emergency came some years later, when I called on him to find him in bed, not looking at all well and wheezing. He put it down to 'only a cold' contracted while cleaning his bicycle. It didn't look like 'only a cold' to me: for one thing, he had not glued on his toupée, and he *never* received visitors without it. I insisted on calling a doctor, who, although it was late in the evening, came immediately on hearing the symptoms. The diagnosis was a heart attack. His left ventricle had failed.

The ambulance arrived within half an hour, during which time the old devil managed to sell me a pair of shoes for a fiver and I managed to glue his hairpiece on reasonably straight. Dignity and self-respect were all-important. He even made the ambulance men wait when they arrived so that I could gather together his wallet, his best pyjamas and some barley water, and he made me grab the fiver. As we sped down Shaftesbury Avenue towards St George's Hospital at Hyde Park Corner (where it was then), I pointed out all the theatres we were passing, and he, lovely old man that he was, kept telling the nurse, between gasps of oxygen, that one day I would appear in them all.

The ambulance men got to St George's in record time, but when we arrived the lift was not working. Gordon was wheeled round the back to the goods lift, accompanied by the inelegant odour of cabbage and other rotting matter. He was taken into a ward and the door was shut on me. I, frustrated, could do no more. He died at five o'clock that morning.

Being students, as well as watching dress rehearsals we were given a rotation of free passes to watch the Royal Ballet perform at the Opera House. Sometimes we were allowed to watch from the wings, which was far more exciting as we could see behind the scenes and watch the dancers prepare for their entrances. Nureyev once threw his ballet shoes at me to soften and mould so that they would fit like a glove. We were already aware of his mercurial temperament, and, even then, were never sure how he would treat us when he came off stage. He might be friendly – or he might be fierce. One ballet I saw from the wings was *Marguerite and Armand*, based on *La Dame aux Camélias*. Sir Frederick Ashton created the roles for Fonteyn and Nureyev, and has allowed no one else to play them since. Their interpretations were – still are – unsurpassable. Nureyev was so absorbed in his role that after a series of jumps in which he held a riding whip, when he left the stage and ran into the wings he would lash out at anyone in his way. It only took one slash for us to learn to duck during his exit. And once, when watching *Giselle*, my enjoyment of Rudolf's poetic Albrecht was somewhat marred by feeling, not a slap, but a pinch on my bottom as he came off stage. It was his cheeky way of being friendly, but it left me, the awkward student, red-faced and a tad confused in front of the *corps de ballet* all lined up to go on stage.

The students' performance at the end of my first year was *Les Deux Pigeons* and the Bournonville ballet *Napoli*, which I particularly enjoyed because of its bouncing Danish leaps. Graham Powell was the principal in *The Two Pigeons*, partnered by Lesley Collier, with Marguerite Barbieri as the Gypsy Girl and Nicholas Johnson as the Gypsy Leader. I played the Gypsy Boy, the first of many child roles. Graham and Lesley's rendition was received with enormous acclaim and they graduated together into the company at the end of the year. Graham was a very close friend, and I felt his acceptance into the company, and the consequent loss to me, quite deeply on a number of levels. We were in the same year, so it was quite hard to see him move on before me, and I began to think my height seriously militated against me; that because I was small I might never find a place in any ballet company, let alone the Royal Ballet. This was an infinitely depressing thought. And so, at the beginning of the second year, I decided to look again at ways of making myself grow.

I had heard of pills that could make you taller and asked my local doctor about them. Dame Ninette learned of my inquiries and called me to the office. She told me of one boy who had taken them and grew to six foot four. He started too small – and ended too tall.

Madam did not want that to happen to me and told me not to 'be so silly. Go away and forget about it, Sleep. You'll just have to spin twice as fast and jump twice as high.' A few years later a pill did arrive, one with which you could regulate height. It was too late for me because I was past the age where it would have been effective. And I noticed that some who took this pill did not build up their muscle power in ratio to their height, and worse, sometimes exhibited personality disorders. So there I was, seventeen, stuck at five foot two and never likely to grow another hair's breadth.

I earned some extra money during this year by performing small walk-on parts with the Royal Ballet, and by taking a job as a dresser at the New Theatre (now the Albery), on the original production of *Oliver*. This was my first insight into West End theatre and removed all the illusions I had ever harboured about the roar of the greasepaint and the smell of the crowd. Many of the actors had been in the production for years and the atmosphere backstage was about as charismatic as a factory conveyor belt. I dressed two actors, one of whom weighed at least twenty stone. I had the charming experience of having to reach down into his heavy, wet, sweaty coat sleeves to turn them inside out to dry during the interval. Another of my chores was to nip over the road to the pub opposite and bring back six pints of beer for my thesps to down during the performance. Soon afterwards I heard that one of them had fallen to his death from a bridge on stage during a performance. I did wonder if ale had anything to do with it. Drinking during a performance is usually a bad idea.

The Bolshoi came to the Festival Hall during my second year in the Upper School. The only way I could afford the cheapest ticket was to queue all night outside the hall. The trouble was that the box office did not open until 10 A.M. Class was at nine. Not only that, by the time I obtained my tickets and scooted back to the Upper School it was well into mid-afternoon. Yet again I found myself being hauled over the coals. Alan Hooper, by then a pillar of good behaviour, was with me, and I think this softened the blow. However, we had missed three classes that day; but the suspension only lasted a couple of days this time. On seeing the company perform I realized it would have been stupid to have any regrets. Ah, the brilliance of Vasiliev and his wife Maximova.

In my first term of the second year I was summoned to a rehearsal room where Sir Frederick Ashton and Robert Helpmann were rehearsing the Ugly Sisters for a new production of *Cinderella*. They were looking for the smallest person they could find to play the part of Napoleon. I fitted the bill. Obviously. But the moment Helpmann saw me he said 'Far too tall!'. The only time I have been accused of that . . . But I got the part. Helpmann was famous for his quick wit. He was once dressed in a fur coat in New York when a cop came up to him and said, 'Move along, fairy!' To which Helpmann responded by raising his hand, as if it was a wand, and said, 'Disappear!' I was so pleased to be in rehearsal with the Royal Ballet and then to be going on stage with these two brilliant artists, who had been leading dancers in their day and were also choreographers.

The scene consisted of Helpmann and Ashton fighting to dance with the tall and handsome Duke of Wellington (played by Derek Rencher), instead of the squat and ugly Napoleon. (Such wonderful stereotyping of nations.) Sir Fred, playing the more humble sister, was left with me and at the end of his solo took a flying leap into my arms. It brought the house down. At the start of rehearsals I put a lot of business into the interpretation of the role, but gradually I honed it down. It was a valuable lesson – that less is more. Further cameo parts followed Napoleon and during my final two terms at the Upper School I began to feel more confident. Although I was told that my dancing was good enough, I was still worried that my size might mitigate against me.

The part of Napoleon required little actual dancing and, although I was too small for the *corps de ballet*, my acting ability could be used to great effect in character roles. It resulted in an invitation to join the Royal Ballet Company when I finished at the Upper School. Ironic, in the end, that it was my lack of inches that helped me to a coveted place in the company.

Alan Hooper joined the touring company, and Peter O'Brien and Peter Fairweather came with me into the resident company, as did four friends made during my time at the Upper School: Marguerite Porter, Christine Aitken, Marilyn Trounson and Caroldene Horn. But of all the girls in my form at White Lodge only Bridget Skemp gained a place.

Our graduation performance was at the Royal Opera House at a matinée in July 1966. One of my parts was the Blue Skater in *Les Patineurs*, choreographed by Sir Fred. Even though I slipped and fell over, landing on my back during the performance, the audience clapped well into the interval.

In *Dance and Dancers*, September 1966, John Percival wrote that one looks for promise, talent and potential in a young dancer, and that when 'a 17-year-old boy, making his debut in one of our most famous leading roles, not only equals but in some respects surpasses all his predecessors . . .', one is both surprised and thrilled. Percival had not seen Harold Turner who created the part, but he did not believe that any other dancer 'ever whirled so fast in the final *sautés* as Wayne Sleep did . . . how many jumped higher than Sleep, or acted with his impudent wit? . . .' He ended his review of the whole matinée by praising my Dr Coppelius (my other part in the graduation performance), and saying that my 'quart-sized gifts are packed into a half-pint frame' and that obviously it would affect the parts I would be able to play. He ended by saying 'someone is going to need to apply a fairly tight rein to Mr Sleep. What a pleasant change, though, to find a young man so mettlesome and so unstereotyped. I would guess that we are in for some fun.'

I also entered for and won, the Adeline Genée Scholarship, run by the Royal Academy of Dancing, which offered tuition to the value of £150 with a teacher of my choice. It took me so long to choose a teacher that by the time I approached the Royal Academy for the money, they had (more or less) gone bust.

'Oh,' they said, 'there's only £70 left.'

'Oh,' I said, 'in that case you'd better keep it.'

I forewent the tuition.

In the summer after I graduated I was invited by Leo and Janet Kersley to perform for the Harlow Ballet Club in Essex. Leo had been with the Rambert Company and Sadler's Wells in their infancy. I found this much more exciting than going home for a holiday, and I took classes at the Max Rivers Studios in London with Eileen Ward and Kathleen Crofton. When I went down to Harlow to dance a solo from *Swan Lake* I met John Gilpin and Lucette Aldous, who were to dance the highly technical *pas-de-deux* from *Don Quixote*. I couldn't believe that I was sharing the same stage as these two great stars. I also met Sir Anton Dolin who, after seeing my work, nicknamed me 'The Mighty Atom'.

So I graduated into the company in the autumn of 1966 with flying colours – to hold a spear twice a week. A spear-carrier is the lowest of the low, in ballet as in theatre. We are there as extras, crowd fodder, to look pretty and – much of the time – are not required to move. But although I knew that I was starting in the company from the bottom, the difference between expectation and reality was even greater than I might have imagined. Success in a ballet company does not happen overnight, no matter how special or outstanding your talent. There are always dancers ahead of you, waiting their turn for the principal roles. You join the queue. You might jump it, briefly, if a choreographer creates a part for you in particular, or if the director prefers your way of dancing to another, but this may be for only one ballet in a season.

New dancers, new members of the company, join the *corps* and understudy other dancers. If they are very fortunate they might understudy one or two principal roles in a year but no one should hold their breath in anticipation of dancing that solo. First of all, each major role is shared by two or three principal dancers, each of whom, in any season, may get only one chance to perform the part. Each ballet is performed about six times in a season, and there may be three or four others being performed as well. Second, it may be through injury, retirement or sometimes pregnancy that an understudy gets a shot in the spot. And third, the odds are shortened even further because the Royal Ballet shares Covent Garden with the Opera, so there are only three performances a week. It is a shameful waste of talent and the system only serves to highlight the need for a theatre dedicated to dance, where dancers and choreographers alike have a showcase for their talents. I couldn't fathom then, as I still can't, why ballet is regarded as the poor relation to opera.

I was lucky, however. Within a year of joining the company, I was given various roles to understudy. They included the demi-character roles belonging to Alexander Grant (such as the Neapolitan Dance in *Swan Lake* and the Three Ivans in *Sleeping Beauty*), the classical roles of Brian Shaw (the Bluebird *pas-de-deux*), plus various small acting and mime roles. But I expected a long wait before any of them might be given to me. For instance, Alexander's brother, Gary, was to take over the role of Alain. He was in the touring company, and when the two companies amalgamated, he danced the part. Some years later I was offered

Widow Simone's (usually reserved for older character dancers) in *La Fille Mal Gardée* – which I accepted, on the condition that I would be allowed to play Alain. At eighteen, I had, however, already played the Notary . . . already set in character roles. At one performance as the Notary Clerk to Ronald Plaisted's Chief Notary, we over-acted so much, taking the attention off the leading players, that we were given a huge dressing down. 'Know your place, Sleep!' For a while I felt it might be my doom to be cast for ever in character parts, but really it was a measure of how Sir Fred viewed my acting capabilities.

Understudy life was frustrating. You attended rehearsals and tried to keep out of the way of the first cast who were learning their steps. As an inferior life-form you were rarely given the chance of a run through in the studio, let alone on stage, and had to practise by yourself, without music even, which required an enormous amount of self-discipline. I found it incredibly hard to motivate myself into learning, let alone practising, a role which I might never perform. Others, I know, did not have the same difficulty.

Not only did you have to learn and practise by yourself, you had also to keep yourself in the peak of condition – *just in case* you were called, which could happen at a moment's notice sometimes. And coming from the school, where classes kept us in the peak of physical condition, into the company where there was only an hour and a quarter total exercise in the morning classes, meant that the decline in stamina and physical ability was almost visible. The principal dancers rehearsed for up to three months, intensively, for one performance in a particular role. Taking outside classes was frowned upon and yet the under-study was expected to keep himself fit and able, *and* to know the role on the off-chance that he might take the stage. And there is only one chance – to prove you know the piece and that you have the stamina. Little rehearsal if any. Imagine the pressure. One shot at a role. It has to be good – no mistakes, no second chances.

If that sort of pressure was bad enough (the girls and the taller boys were always exhausted), for me the boredom and monotony of life at *corps de ballet* status was worse. To avoid terminal catalepsy in the morning classes, or while watching rehearsals for my putative roles I would indulge in pirouette practice at the back of the class. The principals would be learning their steps and I would be turning in a corner. By clever application of this particular method I failed to learn seminal portions of many roles, so it was just as well that I was hardly ever called on to replace a dancer. But there are two occasions I do remember.

I had to go on at short notice for an injured Michael Coleman in a three-scene ballet, choreographed by Kenneth MacMillan, called *Rituals* – a piece devised round the Japanese Bunraku puppets and puppeteers – to music by Bartok, which might seem a strange choice, but is well suited, in fact, to the formality and ritual of Japanese performance. The costumes and make-up followed the discipline of Kabuki.

I was called to the office one morning, told I was to learn the first scene – in a day – and so spent it locked in a rehearsal room learning the steps from a dance notator, Monica Parker, who always assisted MacMillan with his ballets. During the performance Michael stood in the wings, a badly swollen ankle meaning that he had to signal the steps to me with his arms. My eyes hardly left the wings throughout the whole performance, so that my dancing was slightly askew. A critic described my performance, quite properly, as 'sinister' (well, I was always looking to the left). If only he'd known.

The second was a ballet called *Les Noces*, to music by Stravinsky, choreographed, originally, by Nijinsky's sister, Bronislawa Nijinska. She, speaking only French, directed us. It was the most extraordinary and avant-garde piece, even in the 1960s, so how it must have been received in the 1920s when it was first produced, I find it hard to imagine. The only way to describe it, without a video, or a physical explanation, is as a compendium of leaps, jerks and energy. It was so different from anything else we had so far encountered that a few of us newcomers erupted, on first trying these movements, in bursts of nervous laughter. I think Nijinska thought some of us an undisciplined rabble. And the situation was exacerbated by her husband, who had this little black book of misdemeanours into which he would scribble our names when we misbehaved. He was kept quite busy. The net result was, of course, that when I had to go on in *Les Noces*, I did not know it perfectly. Tragic? Comic? Who knows, but it was certainly scary. It taught me that I never wanted to perform if I was under-rehearsed.

Hell though understudying was, I was glad I was not a girl. For them, it was worse. For instance, Lesley Collier, who joined the company a year before me, had to wait much longer for solos as there were so many ballerinas before her, but she eventually reached the peak and danced like a dream. The talent, the star quality, begins to be obvious by the age of fifteen, after much of the pubertal change has taken place, but the status in class is *always* clear. You have to wait your turn. I also knew that because of my height I would never play the romantic leads. But I do have one reason to be grateful for my size. I could have no long-term place in the *corps de ballet*. I stuck out, or rather, down. So I was slotted into the existing repertoire with small character roles, though it was no compensation for knowing that I would never play Romeo or Albrecht or anyone else of that stature – literally and figuratively. But my rapid rise to solo parts did cause some envy, bad feeling, mutterings, which I was not unaware of. The company could, I suppose, have not used me in solo roles, or used me very little, until I had paid the dues of time served in the *corps*.

But as the year stretched on, I began to suffer a loss in stamina. This, thanks to the daily two-hour classes at the Upper School, had been extremely high, but now, because I was dancing in hardly any of the productions, and classes were only an hour and a quarter each day, I could almost feel it dropping away. I was forced to take classes at the Dance Centre in Floral Street, just round the corner from the Opera House. Outside classes were the only way of keeping up a modicum of strength. The company did not like this, but I really don't know what they expected dancers to do. You need motivation to practise, and if there is no dancing, if there are no roles in sight, your attitude can tend towards the lacklustre. Marguerite Porter was an advocate of the mind-over-matter school of thought. She and I stood together in front of the mirrors while she repeated, over and over again, 'You are as strong as a lion. You are as strong as a lion.' There may be truth in it, but there is nothing like the right kind of exercise to keep your body in the right state.

It was as a lowly understudy that I had my first ever trip in an aeroplane, when in the autumn of 1966 the company embarked on an Eastern European tour of Poland, Czechoslovakia, Bulgaria, Romania and Yugoslavia, starting in Luxembourg. It gave me an insight into the deprivation and minimal way of living endured by those who lived behind the Iron Curtain, particularly in comparison to our way of life in the West. Prague was the most stunning part of the tour and I was lucky enough to be there before the Russian tanks (nothing at all to do with me) moved in two years later. Warsaw was a very different kettle of fish, in fact a tub full of them. One of the dancers went for a shower, only to find that the maid was keeping goldfish in the bath. Another joy there was the first taste of horsemeat – with a fried egg on top. And one by one the company members went down with food poisoning. Many of my fellow dancers did not seem to be enjoying the tour, but I was so enthralled by being in my first professional job, by flying for the first time, by being abroad for the first time, that I found the whole thing fascinating. And ever since I have had a preference for the taste of Romanian beer and the Polish vodka, Zubrowka. For me the trip was magic. For most of the others I think it was akin to a journey round the nether regions of purgatory.

Once we were back home things started to improve for me. Sir Fred, Director of the company, had worked in every aspect of theatre which enhanced his genius as a choreographer and he had a fantastic eye. When he choreographed he knew exactly what he was looking for in the way of style – especially in the use of the arms and the head – and he would keep pushing his dancers in rehearsals until he found precisely what he was looking for. He always choreographed to a dancer's particular strengths. This often made it difficult to replace the original cast in a production. I was lucky to work very closely with him during my first few years with the company and he created several roles specifically for me.

The first was Saturday's Child in *Jazz Calendar*, a ballet based on the nursery rhyme which starts: 'Monday's child is fair of face.' I was born on a Saturday and, as the poem says, Saturday's child does work hard for his living. Sir Fred set the Saturday section in a ballet class, which he then found difficult to choreograph as class consists of so many different steps. He had a hard time making up his mind which ones to use, and changed the choreography every day. The ballet gave the boys a chance to show off their technique and I was given a separate entrance, because I was the one, (un)surprisingly, chosen to arrive late. I was able to whizz around on one leg which was something I was already well known for, as I could go faster than anyone else and somehow still remain on the spot. At the end of the sequence I was able to show another strength of my technique and execute twenty entrechats-six consecutively – while the others had to drop like flies around me. (Entrechats are crossing, uncrossing and recrossing the legs in mid-air in one leap. Entrechats-six is in fact three crossings and uncrossings of the legs.) It didn't require much acting at the end to collapse on top of the teacher, who was beating his stick to the rhythm of Richard Rodney Bennett's jazz score – my legs were like jelly.

Sir Fred's open-mindedness to all kinds of influences was shown in the finale of *Jazz Calendar* – when the company mimicked going round on a revolve and waving at the audience, as seen in the TV show *Sunday Night at the London Palladium* – and in his choosing the young, unknown designer Derek Jarman to create a very basic colourful set which reflected the hippie era. This became a landmark of design for the late sixties. Jazz had never been heard at the Royal Opera House before, and this, along with Jarman's set and costumes, rather rocked the staid and established style of the ROH. It would be nice to say it brought it up to date, but it takes a long time for styles and moods to filter through the traditionalism. But if *Jazz Calendar* is performed today, it is viewed as a period piece – like so many of Ashton's works over the last fifty years, its design and music evokes the era in which it was created. It was popular with the audience but it was certainly not one of Ashton's best.

At the first-night party afterwards I was dressed like something from a novel by Dickens – lace cuffs and jabot-fronted shirt bought in the Kings Road, a high-collared double-breasted black satin jacket, flared trousers and cuban-heeled boots. This was the cutting edge of fashion. But I must have looked a bit of a joke to the two people to whom Sir Fred introduced me. I began to make polite conversation and Sir Fred kept pushing my head down, making me feel like a jack-in-the-box. I was bewildered, until I heard him say, 'I'm sorry, Ma'am. These young people do not know how to behave in front of royalty.' And Princess Margaret replied, 'Never mind, Freddy. I liked your twirls, Sleep.' Lord Snowdon giggled.

The ballet was not popular with the critics, but was very much so with the audiences, even to the point of repeating the finale on the last night of the season. An encore is something that never happens in ballet, so it was to be an interesting coincidence that, ten years later, the same thing happened with Kenneth MacMillan's *Élite Syncopations*. This was another ballet that was loved by the public and not by the critics. One review in the *Spectator* said '*Jazz Calendar* is a capriccio – light, pretty, frivolous and absolutely not what we might have expected from the Royal Ballet's Director or, for that matter, from the Royal Ballet.' Pompous, or what? Some time later we took the ballet to America, but a classical ballet with a rhythmic hip hardly stood up against the great jazz dance tradition in the States of choreographers such as Jack Cole and Bob Fosse.

My salary when I joined the company was fifteen guineas a week. With the first week's salary I bought a pair of leather casual shoes with brass bars for fourteen guineas. I left the YMCA and found an Indian landlord in the Harrow Road. There was a strong, pervasive smell of Indian cooking, day and night, which I found overpowering, and I needed, after only a very short time, to find somewhere else. It happened in one of those strange and coincidental ways that occur in life.

One of the items Gordon Henson had managed to sell me was a second hand Zeiss Icon camera, and I became very keen on photography. I took pictures of rehearsals at the Opera House. I spent hours going round markets taking shots of the stalls all lit up at dusk. One evening in Berwick Street market I started chatting to an elderly (well I thought she was) lady who had seen me dance. I told her I was looking for somewhere to live – and she invited me to share her flat in Irving Street, off Leicester Square. I leapt at this chance to live in Central London and be so close to the West End theatres again. Diana Roberts (as she was called) was a ballet fanatic and worshipped Nureyev. I frequently had to plough my way through mounds of press-cuttings and pictures of her idol spread over the floor, all of which she would catalogue in her scrapbooks. I was faced with daily interrogations as to whether the great man had smiled at me that day, whether he changed his leg warmers, what was his favourite food. More questions than I had answers for. It was pretty boring, and absolutely the last thing I wanted to talk about at home was ballet gossip.

But Diana became a great friend and thought of herself as my London mum. She allowed me to give dinner parties (at which she would produce her speciality – trifle) and have friends to stay. Graham Powell and I resumed our close friendship, and he often stayed, along with Pamela Scott, Jeanetta Laurence and Marguerite Porter from my student days. We continued to have outrageous fun together – one night Graham produced some slimming pills, which, when combined with alcohol, have a rather devastating effect. Diana returned to find us dancing, stark naked, round the flat. Unshockable, she merely asked us to pipe down so she could watch *Peyton Place* on the television.

I raided Carnaby Street to add to my wardrobe for the first of many American tours in the spring of 1967. I found a high-collared double-breasted grey suit, an orange shirt with long pointed collar, a black cravat, a check cap with a black tassel all worn with my cuban heeled boots, of course, to make me look taller. Once on board the chartered BOAC jet we stripped to dressing-gowns and tracksuits so that our clothes were immaculate on arrival in New York. We were, after all, ambassadors for the Royal Ballet Company, and by extension, for Great Britain. The company was regarded by Americans as the best in the world, along with the Kirov, and over the years had built up a fine rapport and a dedicated following there. In England I always hid my Royal Ballet label inside my bag to avoid being recognized as a ballet dancer, but in America we wore these credentials with pride. We were greeted with the warmest and friendliest respect I had ever encountered.

Our first night was at the New Metropolitan Opera House in the Lincoln Center. I rather wished I could have performed at the Old Met, which had such a history – Caruso performed there, and it was there that the Sadler's Wells Ballet (before it became the Royal Ballet) first performed in 1948 and took America by storm. By 1967 the Old Met was a heap of rubble. I paid a sort of pilgrimage to the site, and still have a brick I brought back from the ruins.

Our first season at the New Met was fraught with accidents and injuries. We opened with *Cinderella*. Svetlana Beriosova was dancing the title role and at the end of Act 1 the large coach in which she was being pulled round the stage overturned and nearly plummeted into the orchestra pit, with her in it. Like a true professional she recovered and received an ovation on her entrance in Act 2, as there were those who had thought they might never see her again. I was playing Napoleon again, and Clive Barnes of the *New York Times* singled me out for review.

> A final word for the orchestra, crisply conducted by John Lanchbery, and a diminutive young man, Wayne Sleep, making his New York debut and nearly stealing the show in the bit part of a suitor dressed up as Napoleon. Mr. Sleep, the star of last year's Royal Ballet School graduation performance, is a wonderful performer. New York will – not this season but in years to come – see much more of him, and his debut should be properly noted.

I felt an immediate rapport with the New York audience. They were so generous with their appreciation, to the point, sometimes, that we were not able to hear the orchestra. They burst into happy applause on seeing a well-executed step. This spurred us on to jump higher and to give them everything we had.

By the second week of the season the physiotherapy room was overbooked. It was discovered that the floor of the main rehearsal studio at the Met was concrete overlaid with wood, which meant that the shock to the muscles when landing was not absorbed and the jarring of the bones resulted in frequent injury. The floor should be raised a few inches above concrete to provide bounce and cushion – not as flexible as flooring for gymnasts, but soft enough to counter the impact of a body. On the first night of *The Sleeping Beauty*, Brian Shaw, famous for dancing the Bluebird solo, fell. When he could not get up, several members of the company carried him to the dressing-room, where it was found that he had snapped his Achilles tendon. He never danced virtuoso parts again. Several other dancers were sent home with injuries.

I was understudying many principal roles, including the Mandolin Dance from *Romeo and Juliet* and the Bluebird. Merle Parke was concerned about my partnering her because of my lack of inches, and tannoyed me to the stage. She needed to be certain that we would suit, and to see that I was up to it. So she Tannoyed me to the stage and put me through my paces until she was satisfied I could perform. Ironically, having proved myself, I never did dance the *pas-de-deux* with her because of a plastered ankle.

I was rehearsing as a replacement for another injured dancer when I slipped and sprained my ankle. I was miserable. My ankle swelled to mountainous proportions in front of my eyes. After the X-ray, a plaster bandage was wrapped round it to keep it immobile. This was the accepted remedy at the time, and I know now that it was entirely the wrong thing to do. A sprain should be kept moving and swelling reduced as far as possible with liberal applications of ice. This also helps to stop the fluids solidifying. The doctor in New York acted according to the received wisdom of the time and bandaged it tightly. Worse still, it was bandaged at an angle which eventually required intensive massage and other therapies to straighten it out. I was three months in America with a bandage round my ankle and could not dance any of the major roles allotted to me, only performing in the *corps de ballet*.

My injury did do me one favour. Because I couldn't dance I had time on my hands; I was invited to the famous Fire Island, just south of New York. The island is covered with individually designed wooden houses with huge glass windows fronting the ocean and New Orleans-style boardwalks. It attracted socialites and theatre people. At weekends it became a veritable *Who's Who* of New York personalities, complete with actors, transvestites and the just-plain-old-rich. I hopped from one all-night party to another and on through to the brunches and barbecues. My invitation caused some antagonism among the other dancers, many of whom had tried, for years, to wangle one, without success. It was an odd convention, but when a dancer was injured he was supposed to become a hermit, not whoop it up at first-night parties and socialize with the high and mighty, such as Sol Hurok, the impresario who was responsible for bringing over the RB. I was receiving treatment from the physiotherapist and saw no point in sitting alone, with my leg up, in a small unfriendly hotel room contemplating the loss of the roles I had worked so hard for as a student, when I could be out having fun. But by the end of the tour I had few friends left in the company.

Injuries that put a dancer out of action for any length of time are not taken lightly by the company, especially if you are a new member. They care, of course, about your health and well-being – how could they not – but a dancer in whom they have invested time and money is also a commodity. And if you're unusable, you're useless. So it behoves dancers to put themselves right as soon as possible. Over a period of time you begin to know how to treat injuries in the optimal way to get the quickest results, often, these days, with physiotherapists, specialist muscle experts, exercise trainers – and loads of ice.

It was during this period of prolonged injury that Michael Somes, the Assistant Director and former partner of Margot Fonteyn, began to be highly critical of me. I think he recognized the rebel in me and, because he was the essence of the old style of the Royal Ballet, he felt I should be knocked into line. So I was among the dancers whom he liked to dominate by bullying and sarcasm, or by the sheer power of his will. He could be quite frightening. Sometimes he made me rehearse and rehearse, repeating my steps over and over again until I felt ill with nausea. Some of the more sensitive dancers found these methods difficult to handle, to the point, sometimes, of being unable to cope with his demands. With the rest of us it produced results. And perversely, we rather revered him – particularly when we realized (as we grew with the company) that he only leaned heavily on those dancers he respected and whom he thought had talent. That he included me in that number was really borne home to me a few years later, when it was Michael Somes who interceded on my behalf with Kenneth MacMillan and Peter Wright when I wanted leave of absence.

In America the salary of even the *corps de ballet* was tripled to comply with the AGMA (Equity's American equivalent) minimum. This also stipulated overtime payments, which we did not have at home in those days. One boy carried a suitcase of baked beans with him to New York, and sat alone in his hotel room eating them, cold, out of the can. He saved enough to buy himself a house when he got back. Others liked to spend their money on goods that were cheaper and of better quality, such as towels and sheets. I spent most of my money in New York on two things.

I filled my trunk with records from Sam Goody's, the famous record store where you could buy any record in existence. I made a beeline for the musicals, which were by now a passion. It was not easy, then, to get Broadway shows on record in London, as record industry support of British theatre (or even of any theatre) was minimal. So Sam Goody's was an Aladdin's cave.

With the rest of the money I went to the theatre and to my first Broadway musical – *Mame*, starring Angela Lansbury. I have never forgotten her first entrance. Wearing a gold lamé trouser suit (very outré in those days) and short slicked-back blonde hair, Mame stood at the top of a curved staircase, blew a fanfare on a bugle and slid down the banisters. Oh, the importance of an entrance. I'd seen musicals in London, but nothing quite as impresssive as this. America led the field of the stage musical and it was very obvious that there was more precision and polish, more energy and pizazz in the States. It was not until Andrew Lloyd Webber came along in the late 1960s that Britain started to equal America in this genre.

I waited outside the stage door to get an autograph from Angela Lansbury. I could have no inkling then, as a mere member of the corps, that one day I would choreograph a short tango sequence for her and the other stars of the film *Death on the Nile*, or that, in the strange way that happens in life, she would crop up in other periods of my life.

So I arrived back in London that summer of 1967 having ended my first year in the company with a plastered and almost useless ankle. And the lingering memory of my time in the States that topped the lot was of a visit to the continental baths one evening at midnight. While we soaked in hot steam, each wrapped only in a towel, this fabulous creature entertained us with her singing, accompanied only by a pianist. Some début for Bette Midler and Barry Manilow . . .

FOUR

HOME AND AWAY

S EASONS AT THE Royal Ballet start in September. For the Autumn season
of 1968 Nureyev was invited to mount a new production of *The Nutcracker*
with the set and the costumes designed by Nikolas Georgiadis. Nureyev
gave me the part of the Nutcracker Doll. It was hell being small – one look at me
and I was typecast. Dolls, children, animals, chickens, old notary clerks: I feel as
though I have played most of the animal kingdom during my dancing life. In fact,
when Rudolph, some years later, appeared on 'The Muppet Show', he asked
me if I would partner him dressed as Miss Piggy in a scene called Swine Lake. I
said yes, then asked the producer what I would do for my own solo, appearing
as myself. The reply was sharp – who is this Wayne Sleep? I've never heard of
him.' I declined. Nureyev was so famous, so volatile. You could love him and
hate him in the same breath. You never knew whether he would tolerate the
faces staring at him through the doors of the rehearsal rooms or whether he
would rush to the doors, waving his arms and yelling 'F★★★ off!' I, as a callow
uncomprehending youth, thought he was deliberate in his antagonism, that it
was personal, but he was the same with everyone. One of the few people he
respected was Margot Fonteyn, and even to her he could be unmannerly on
occasion. But she understood. Their relationship was very special.

But this was the essence of the man. His talent and power and capability was
greater than everything else – and he knew it. He was the only person who
warmed up *on stage* (he was not supposed to, he just did it – not, of course, in
full performance but at dress rehearsals in front of an invited audience), holding
on to the scenery at the side of the stage. The rest of us, mere mortals, were
obliged to do the same as ever, find space in the wings. He questioned everything: lights, music, everything. He was unpredictability incarnate. He didn't
suffer fools. And he hated, he *hated* the hobby horses that Nikolas Georgiadis
devised for *The Nutcracker*, with their short fat, stubby, not long and elegant,
heads, the type that Morris Dancers often use.

As the Nutcracker Doll I led the cavalry into battle against the rats. We all
trooped on, dressed, or enclosed, in these hobby horses, and kept falling over
the canopies that covered our legs. I thought they were unhorselike, wide,
unmanageable, and they pleased Nureyev not one whit. He stormed on stage
after the dress rehearsal, with the invited audience still in their seats, and started
screaming 'Niko!' The designer, a good friend of Nureyev's, being a temperamental Greek, screamed back. And in the middle of this torrent of Russian and

Greek, which I doubt was suitable for translation, Rudolf grabbed the horse I was standing in and started to pull it apart. Fibreglass flew everywhere and we were all spluttering with nervous laughter, trying to make light of the whole thing. At the same time I was aware that Rudolf's blows might become more erratic and that I, the not soon-to-be-ex-horse, could be the recipient of the next whack. A voice protested somewhere – 'There's a boy in the middle of that horse' – but it made no difference to Nureyev. He did not stop until that particular animal was destroyed, and only then was it safe for me to step out. Rudolf was utterly exhausted by the dress rehearsal.

But this sense of danger always hovered around Nureyev. When it was posted on the company notice board that I was to partner Carol Hill and Lesley Collier in the Pastorale of *The Nutcracker*, I was filled with some trepidation. Being rehearsed by Nureyev could be exciting and exhilarating, or it could be nerve-racking. You never knew. He could be funny, affectionate, but never dull – you didn't know what you'd get. Part of the fun was the dread and anticipation. In the Pastorale I was given some real dancing; lots of jumps and entrechats, exactly what I like to do, without bothering with the little finicky bits. Rudolf was very annoyed at my execution of the smaller steps and shouted when I leapt into the air for a triple turn: 'You can do the tricks, but you're too lazy for the intricate stuff. Galosh, galosh.' This was his way of saying 'dreadful feet'. He was right: I just wanted to fly.

The costumes were beautifully designed by Georgiadis. I was dressed as a Dresden doll, but the costume was very heavy and this made it difficult to move around in. I did manage, at least, to lose the tricorne hat in the dress rehearsal, as it kept pulling me off balance.

Rudolf Nureyev's production of *The Nutcracker* brought that ballet into the twentieth century, compared to other productions of the time. It was the only full-length work that he did for the Royal Ballet. His use of the ballerina who classically dances the Sugar Plum Fairy to double up as the twelve-year-old Clara (more usually played by a young ballet school pupil) was innovative and gave her a better role. The Pastorale he created for Carol, Lesley and me featured some of his best choreography in the production and took my mind off the Cadbury ('I'm a Cadbury's fruit and nut case' – remember?) music, which is not my favourite. Nureyev was brilliant and exacting, but changeable and difficult. In mitigation, there is always a great deal of strain involved in putting on and choreographing a three-act ballet, particularly if you are expected not only to rehearse the whole company, but also learn the leading role yourself and perform it on the first night. But the pressure was great and so it was easy to forgive – not least because he could be great fun and, over all, was very generous to me professionally. He once allowed a few dancers, including myself, to use his private studio in his house in East Sheen to create a short ballet film. David Drew was the choreographer and Rudolph's friend, Wallace Potts, who he had met in America, the cameraman and director.

I became very friendly with Iris Law, Sir Fred's personal assistant, and later to be appointed Artistic Administrator. To kill time between rehearsals I often sat in her office, chatting, and we discovered a mutual interest in theatre. At least twice a week I would queue for returns at the National Theatre, and saw John Dexter's *Black Comedy* (my memory has Derek Jacobi as one of the leads), Peter Shaffer's *The Royal Hunt of the Sun* with Robert Stephens, Zeffirelli's production of *Much Ado About Nothing* with Albert Finney and Maggie Smith – and many more. In the summer of 1968 Iris invited me to join her and her friend Gwyneth Williams on holiday in Stratford-upon-Avon, where she introduced me to the productions of the Royal Shakespeare Company. Over those two weeks we saw every play in the repertoire, including *Twelfth Night* with Judi Dench and Donald Sinden; Judi with Barrie Ingham in *The Winter's Tale*; and Ian Holm as Romeo to Estelle Kohler's Juliet. Ian Holm is only a fraction taller than me, and it was hard to see someone of the same height playing, and brilliantly so, the ultimate romantic lead. It seems an unfair difference between being an actor and being a dancer. After the shows, Iris, Gwyneth and I would sit in the Dirty Duck, the pub down the road from the theatre, rubbing shoulders with our favourite actors. I was a real fan of the company – a groupie, even to the extent of worming my way in through the stage door using the name of the Royal Ballet to present flowers to Judi Dench.

Around this time I moved out of Diana Roberts's flat. A friend in the *corps de ballet*, David Gayle, told me of a spare room in the maisonette where he lived in Montagu Sqaure. The other flatmates were June, a harpist, who was downstairs, and Kik and his girlfriend who lived across the landing. Eileen Turner, who had been an actress, was our landlady. She had the most appalling little dog which spent its days when I was around trying to hump my leg. She used to shout things like: 'I'll have yer guts for garters' whenever it misbehaved, which was frequently. Not that it did any good.

My room had Regency striped wall paper. I hated it. One day I covered all the walls in tinfoil. Eileen was horrified. 'My lovely room, what have you done to my lovely room!' She went into deep dark mutterings every time she saw my improvement, or even thought about it. I also became a dab hand at dead flower arrangements. Not through intent – they were meant to be alive, but I never got around to throwing them away and replacing them. I just added. A real art form, which Eileen found equally distressing. I considered it to be high chic and in the forefront of fashion. I wasn't there much of the time. The shared kitchen arrangements – putting our names on jars and tins – provided me with the perfect excuse to eat out. I would usually not get in until two in the morning, and by eight the phone was ringing and plans were being made for that coming evening. It was another reason for Eileen to wag her finger and tell me, 'You'll be over soon, dear, burning the candle at both ends.' I don't think I was the best tenant she ever had, but I did have fun during my year there. I grew to know everyone in the house very well, particularly June.

I was very keen on art and drawing, and June would occasionally sit for me. Drawing from life was not one of my talents. One evening I asked her to wear something that would show off the outline of her body – to improve my skill, I said. I prepared for the event by putting out two glasses and a bottle of vodka, and turning the lights down so low that I couldn't even see my sketch pad, let alone June's outline. After several doses of vodka I plucked up the courage to pounce. We became good friends for a while, to the extent that she came with me for Christmas to Plymouth. This visit was not an entire success, for a variety of reasons. I was growing away from my roots, as so many people do; June was definitely middle-class with a 'posh' accent, which, however nice you are can sometimes seem patronizing.

My relationship with June coincided with the offer of my first acting role. Outside the rehearsal room in Barons Court there was a notice-board where 'yellow perils' were stuck, leaving messages for the dancers. These were yellow pieces of paper usually containing ominous messages like 'Please see me – Ashton'. One day the message I pulled off the board asked me to telephone John Dexter. I couldn't believe it. He had directed an opera at Covent Garden and I thought he might be considering me for a dancing role in another production. But it was far more exciting. He had seen me as Saturday's Child in Sir Fred's *Jazz Calendar* and was inviting me to audition for a part in the movie of Leslie Thomas's novel *The Virgin Soldiers*.

The audition was for the producer, Ned Sherrin. As I was waiting for my turn one boy came out in tears. One of the questions asked by John – it was his dry sense of humour – was 'And are you a virgin?' This poor boy had apparently said 'yes' and burst into tears. Dexter's idea was to cast one very small actor and one very tall actor as the gay lovers in the film. Mine was the cameo comedy part of the short soldier. In spite of the audition, I think it was a foregone conclusion in Dexter's mind and afterwards he took me to dinner at San Lorenzo's in Beauchamp Place and we discussed the part. I really felt I was breaking into new territory as an actor.

I found him easy and friendly company. With me he was not at all the frightening or intimidating person of his reputation. He took me under his wing and encouraged me in my enthusiasm for acting, giving me books such as Stanislavsky's *An Actor Prepares* (which I think I read most of), and he took me to see plays at the Old Vic: Laurence Olivier in *The Dance of Death*, Alec Guinness and Simon Ward in *Wise Child*, and in *Hedda Gabler*, Jill Bennett. She wasted no time in telling me how wrongly placed my voice was. Jill was always pretty forthright. If I was serious in my intention to become an actor, I needed, urgently, to take voice lessons. John arranged a meeting for me with Cecily Berry, who was to become the RSC's voice coach. She had already helped the dancer Christopher Gable when he left the Royal Ballet to pursue an acting career after injury problems. I went to her a couple of times, but she was too busy and didn't take me seriously because I had no intention of leaving the

Royal Ballet to become a full-time actor. She did give me this funny little bone prop, however, which was supposed to be placed between the front teeth while trying to articulate. It made me sound like nothing better than a demented duck.

Instead I went to Mary Duff, who taught at RADA. She had nurtured such actors as Dorothy Tutin and Albert Finney and was a well known eccentric character with her white powdered face and doubtful black hair. Her flat was in Queensway, a tiny three-roomed affair four flights up. She was famed for once having asked a hopeful actress after a gruelling audition, 'I've only one question for you, dear. Can you type?' She gave me many exercises to help me lower my voice. The relaxation needed to create resonance is very hard for a dancer to achieve. We learn to take shallow breaths in the chest and the upper back – if you place your hands on a dancer's upper back you can feel the ribs expand there. To have to breathe from the lower abdomen and to let your stomach out to make the voice resound like a drum is unnatural for a dancer, and it was not always easy to switch between the two. Mary took me through many roles, from *Henry V* to contemporary plays, and I longed to appear with other actors in a production. She taught me that 'anyone can read, thousands of people, but few will have the one insight that creates', and that, apart from technique, an actor must have that special ingredient, imagination. Imagination is what ignites the spark of a character – it might be anything from vocal mannerisms, or the feet and the walk, or hand gestures, to the way of holding a head, or a hairstyle. Or a line in the text that resonates. You only need one imaginative key and the rest is there.

In the winter of 1968 I invited Mary to see Ashton's *The Dream*, in which I was playing Puck. Its choreography is athletic, with spins, jumps and entrechats, *and* the character is mischievous – right up my street. And no size problem. Mary did enjoy the performance, but found it lacking in comparison to a full-throated theatrical rendering. Dance, after all, can only convey the essence of a piece, the emotions, and not every single nuance of the written text. So however brilliant Ashton's choreography, and lovely though Mary thought the production was, she felt it lacked the essential depth of the spoken play. I was, I think, slightly disappointed in her reaction, although I understood what she meant. But for me, our discussion and forays into the finer points of the text meant that I could bring more meaning into the dance.

Puck is, without doubt, one of my favourite roles, and I was later given the speaking part to perform in Benjamin Britten's opera, with Geraint Evans and James Bowman, directed by John Copley, at the Opera House. I am still waiting, however, for the opportunity to act the role in the play itself.

John Dexter also introduced me to the Royal Court Theatre, where he worked with George Devine and the designer Jocelyn Herbert. He introduced me to playwrights such as Peter Shaffer and David Storey. Some years later I created the mime movement for *Cromwell*, one of Storey's plays directed by

Anthony Page. I was insecure in the company, and wondered what they were thinking much of the time. In that illustrious company it was easy to feel insecure. It also made me reflect, yet again, on the differences between the world of the theatre and that of the dance. The theatre had so many household names. It was a puzzle to me why, apart from Rudolf Nureyev and Margot Fonteyn, the ballet had none. Under those circumstances, I could be forgiven for feeling like the poor relation.

In John Dexter's circle, Sunday lunches featured in a big way. Everyone seemed to lunch and lunch, wine and dine. Maggie Smith and Robert Stephens, who were married at that time, used to host famous brunch parties on Sundays. Once, John Dexter threw a birthday party for me at the San Lorenzo restaurant and invited various household names, such as Albert Finney, Jill Bennett and my acting hero – Derek Jacobi. This was the first time I had met him. I was still in awe of these stars; it was a world that I was trying very hard to grasp hold of, to understand, feel a part of. But I loved the excitement, the buzz of being around them.

I wore Kings Road clothes – three-tiered silver, red and blue platform shoes from Mr Freedom, T-shirt with an embroidered ice-cream sundae on the front, and bell-bottoms. The shoes stayed on until no one was looking – the day of the platform shoe was very useful. It was an extraordinary time. The sixties were boisterous, outrageous and loud. You could do anything, say anything, as noisily as you liked. Today such excesses are frowned on, both in one's personal life and on the stage. It is not done to look impressed these days. This is not a criticism, just an observation. But I did enjoy myself then, even if it was exhausting. Dancers, on the whole, have to lead tunnel-vision lives and the last thing they usually want to do after a performance is go out to dinner and socialize – especially if there is an early class the next morning. The chores are endless. You have to wash your own dance gear every day, sew elastics on shoes and, in general, eat, drink and sleep ballet. But my hunger to experience every corner of life outweighed the prospect of waking up aching with tiredness the next morning.

I had to try to obtain permission from the Royal Ballet to work outside my contract. The company were very protective of their dancers and were loath to let us do any outside work which might harm its, or its dancers', reputation. It was, after all, the leading ballet company with a Royal Charter. Dignity was prized. But Iris was my saviour and she smoothed the way so that I was granted permission to accept my first acting job.

For my part as this gay soldier, in love with another private and holding hands on parade, in *The Virgin Soldiers*, I was sent first for a very short haircut and then to an army barracks to train. Unbelievable. A very real sergeant-major drilled us for hours on end, up and down the parade ground. It was hard to take seriously. But if you didn't, and I was a major culprit, you were made to run round the perimeter of the parade ground, holding a sten gun in the air above your head, until you were ready to drop. I might have spent more time running than drilling.

This was authentic army training. A bit of a rude shock. So I wanted to be an actor? Some life. Here I was, stiffening my muscles and compressing my ankles by stomping up and down all day, and then rushing back to the Opera House for the evening performance. Army uniform to ballet tights.

After training, a jet was chartered to take the film crew and cast on location to Kuala Lumpur. It was the first time I had met the film's stars: Hywel Bennett, Lynn Redgrave, her mother Rachel Kempson and Nigel Davenport. I was already a fan of Lynn's, having seen her in *Much Ado About Nothing*. She was really one of the boys, with no side to her at all. She was one of the few people who could handle John Dexter; she had a capacity for deflecting his anger. She would calm him down with a flippant joke, or make him smile by sending it all up. She was also a softie: when we went to see *Gone with the Wind* in Singapore, Lynn started to cry even as the beginning credits were rolling. 'They're all dead, all dead,' she lamented. You couldn't help but love her. I liked her mother too, although I did not have much occasion to meet her. I saw very little either of Hywel Bennett or of Nigel Davenport – our paths barely crossed in the scheme of things.

We boarded a bus for Port Dixon, a small resort situated between jungle and sea where we were housed in chalets overlooking the phosphorescent water. I began to experience the odd jibe and comment such as 'Why do you want to act?' and 'You're a ballet dancer,' and 'Don't you realize you're keeping actors out of work,' all muttered between pints of lager. I kept my mouth shut for once, knowing I was in for a difficult time. Even John Dexter began treating me like one of his whipping boys. The security and equality I had felt in London started to recede and I began to feel exposed and vulnerable without the protection of the Royal Ballet. Dexter was known to choose one person to persecute – luckily it wasn't me, but I did experience a coldness compared to the times in the Kings Road in London. Here I was just another actor. I felt betrayed, too, because I felt that in London Dexter had built my confidence, and here he seemed to be slicing it out from under me. But this was my vulnerability, my perception. Dexter was behaving as he usually did when directing, and I was treated no differently from anyone else. I was only slightly consoled by the fact that even Derek Jacobi, in his early years at the National, had come under the lash. I suppose when directors are successful there is no end to what a potentially out-of-work actor will put up with, but not me. I was all ready to leap straight back on a plane to London. But I was stopped by Claude Watson, the assistant director, who behaved humanely and sympathetically and was a stabilizing influence in this test of tenacity.

One of the first scenes to be filmed was a soldier being blown to pieces by a landmine while playing football on the beach. The actor turned out to be Robert Bridges whom I had dressed in *Oliver*. Our roles were not exactly reversed, but at least I was now in front of the camera and not backstage dealing with a sweaty costume.

My slight superiority did not last long. My first scene was set in a swamp. Here there were two hazards: the first was trying to stay on the ledge built under water so that more than just my tin hat was visible; the second was leeches. Glamour indeed. I managed to avoid them by wrapping plastic bags round my legs before putting on the uniform.

My partner in the film was Gregory Phillips. He had been a child actor, starring with Judy Garland in *I Could Go On Singing*. He helped me towards a natural performance. In film you are seen ten times larger than life and so understatement is a rule; whereas a dancer on the stage at Covent Garden is taught to project to the balcony, to reach out over the orchestra pit into the amphitheatre. I thought waiting for one's stage entry was a test of the nerves, but it was nothing in comparison to the endless hours spent hanging about while making a movie. Each scene takes hours to set up, particularly when filming on location. When the sun went behind a cloud, we would have to stop to re-set the lighting, or wait for a patch of blue to reappear into which we fitted our lines.

I joined in everything. There were trips to Buddhist shrines and to massage parlours, where you did in fact have a massage, but like anywhere else if you paid for a bit more, you got a bit more. One of these places was like a corridor with cubicles off, open to the sky, but covered with netting – to keep the insects out, I guess. What it did not keep out was the locals, who used to climb up and watch. Whether it was to see how Westerners behaved, or to see if we were different anatomically from them, or just to have a laugh at our expense, heaven only knows. It annoyed the girls, who would yell abuse and gesticulate. Really effective in the face of laughter.

After Port Dixon, the film unit moved to Singapore to film the parade ground shots in Selerang Barracks. This was a spooky place – famous for the incident during the Second World War when all prisoners-of-war were herded into the barracks square (normally, it could only accommodate 800 – over 15,000 men were made to stay there) until the British signed an agreement not to try to escape. The army dogs could not be persuaded, not by any means, to ascend to one floor of the barracks. Animals obviously *do* have ESP. This was where the Japanese had tortured the British during the Second World War. I felt no vibes, however.

We were not allowed on to certain parts of the grass, because so many were buried under it. It was, sometimes, like acting in a graveyard – with no tombstones. But the whole place reminded me of my Uncle George who was a prisoner-of-war in Burma. He was one of only two survivors who came back to England from HMS *Exeter*. When they were blown up in the water they were taken to a prisoner-of-war camp in Burma and tortured there. Nails were pulled out, appendixes were taken out without any anaesthetic, and they all suffered from the vitamin B deficient disease, beriberi, as a result of the unending meagre diet of bad rice. Uncle George watched most of his fellow-prisoners die in front of him; he was one of the few to survive, and was eventually taken to Australia to recuperate. I have a letter from him to the family, in which he talks about coming home. He eventually came back, with TB, about six months after the end of the war. And his wife cooked him his favourite dessert as a special treat for his homecoming. It was rice pudding. He threw it at the wall. He just lost control. I don't believe he could help it. He always wanted to go back and kill this one Japanese guard, this one terrible guard who used to club them around the head if they didn't worship the sun. We all said, 'But you didn't worship the sun, did you?' He said, 'You would.' He died in about 1957. That's what the Serralang Barracks meant to me.

Our evenings were spent in Boogie Street – a long narrow road with a night market and hundreds of bars where you sat outside and watched incredibly exotic and beautiful women parading up and down. Many a member of the crew got more than he bargained for when he paid for an evening out with one of these stunning girls. Most of them were transvestites, selling their bodies to earn enough for a sex-change operation. I used to think Soho the ultimate in vice – but in Singapore every taxi-driver demanded that he take you to a massage parlour, a blue movie or a sex show. Soho? An academy of politeness and gentility in comparison.

We returned to England and finished filming in a derelict army camp in Kent, where one of the extras turned out to be the out-of-work David Bowie. I remember he played the guitar quite a lot around the camp. We discovered that we shared a mentor in Lindsay Kemp, the mime artist *par excellence*, who was a major influence on Bowie as a performer.

The filming was done but the work was not yet over. Ned Sherrin sent me to Clive Arrowsmith for publicity shots. Clive made an immediate impact on me – he was so rooted in the present, so in tune with the age. He kept me in touch with everything that was going on and we became pals. He had trendy good looks and a nonconformist attitude to life. I would crash out on his sofa after listening to the latest albums from Jethro Tull, Led Zeppelin, and Frank Zappa & the Mothers of Invention. And he managed to make me look good in photographs. I posed for a series of fashion shots for *Queen* magazine, to which he was a regular contributor, and he actually made me look tall – but this was by dint of not photographing me below the knees and standing me on a box to make me appear taller than the model . . .

The première of *The Virgin Soldiers* in Leicester Square was an exciting occasion – *and* I was going to see myself acting on screen, which was a fairly frightening prospect. To aid my morale and my image and to give me courage (how do you explain to your mother that you are acting a gay soldier in a film?), I invited the beautiful and elegant dancer Marguerite Porter to accompany me. It was strange (but marvellous) to hear people laughing at my words rather than my actions.

Although *The Virgin Soldiers* was not a huge success, I did learn an enormous amount about acting and filming, and I met some great people to boot. I continued to see many of the friends I had made, except for John Dexter. That friendship just petered out. But I was grateful and always will be, for the growth of knowledge and experience and for the opportunities John provided, in spite of the difficulties I encountered on the set. Funnily enough, I didn't see him for years, and then in spring 1976 he came backstage at the New York Met, where he was Opera Director, to congratulate me after a performance of *A Month in the Country* – as if nothing had happened. For him nothing had, there was no drama, it was simply the way he worked, and he would have been surprised to find that I had harboured reservations. After that we would meet quite amicably.

With the filming interlude over, it was back to the Royal Ballet and the start of rehearsals for another three-month tour to the USA in the spring of 1969. My roles since the last tour had improved considerably: Saturday's Child in Ashton's *Jazz Calendar*, Puck in *The Dream*, the Neapolitan Dance in *Swan Lake*, the Peasant *pas-de-deux* with Lesley Collier in *Giselle*, the *pas-de-trois* from *The Nutcracker*.

Sir Fred created another solo role for me in Elgar's *Enigma Variations*, which had its first performance on 25 October 1968. If the piece had been written by a Russian, Edward Elgar informed his friend Troyte Griffith, his *Variations* would have been performed as a ballet long ago. He would have been delighted to have seen Ashton's interpretation of this music, based on Elgar's friends and acquaintances. Sir Fred, as one critic put it, created a keyhole through which the audience were allowed to peer at the evocation of an autumnal Edwardian era; the mood was almost Chekhovian.

A series of tableaux portrayed the characters of Elgar's friends more by mood than by dance – which almost seemed incidental. Derek Rencher and Svetlana Beriosova were Elgar and his wife, Anthony Dowell was Troyte Griffith and Desmond Doyle played the publisher A.J.Jaeger. The Edwardian costumes, designed by Julia Trevelyan Oman, were authentic – she steeps herself in the history of her projects and is a stickler for correctness – even to the point of having to wear stiff high wing collars that cut into your neck when spinning. The stage was divided in half by an arch: one side was the interior of the house and the other was the garden. At certain moments in the music even the leaves of the trees would glide down towards the restful figure of Vivyan Lorrayne, as Isabel Fitton, lying in a hammock. Sir Fred explained to me that my sequence in the piece was not just about George Robertson Sinclair alone, but about him and his dog splashing about together on the banks of a river.

So I was to be half man, half dog. Animals again. Julia was given the task of designing a cap which, when pulled over the face, would turn into the features of a dog. One of my movements was, as the man, to hold the walking cane and spin in the air. I had to land with my head between my legs, throw the cane and come up with the cap pulled over my face and then chase the cane. Phew. But during the first technical rehearsals on stage the cap did not work properly and it was discarded. I felt we could have experimented further, so, for me, the solo was less effective than it might have been.

No matter how much I warmed up in the wings before my entrance, the piece was so fast it was always a shock to the system, rather like running a hundred metres in ten seconds. No – worse. I could not look as if I was out of breath at the end. This was the beginning of a succession of solos in which I had about a minute to prove myself and a long wait before I was due to appear. Unlike other performers (actors can nip off to the pub after they've signed in, musicians likewise) dancers must keep warming up right up to their entrance and it is impossible to take your mind off the role by reading a book or making a shopping list. All the negative thoughts of not balancing – or even falling – whizz round your head trying to undermine your confidence. Fortunately these worries would vanish once I hit the stage.

But an agonizing fear that I might miss my entrance in *Enigma Variations* after the tedious waiting developed into a recurring nightmare for me. My dream started with the preparations in the dressing-room: sticking on my moustache, slicking back my hair and parting it in the middle, Edwardian style, and wrestling with those lethal starched collars and cuffs. Leaving the dressing-room at the beginners' call I set off for the stage to find myself on the Piccadilly Line heading for the rehearsal room at Barons Court. Realizing I am doing the wrong thing I rush to the eastbound platform and urge the train to go faster, knowing I will never make it back on time, yet desperately hoping. Running into the wings I hear the music for my solo and find someone else dancing my role. I quiver in fear of the wrath of Michael Somes and wake up shaking and sweating and relieved to find it only a dream.

During one of our ballet seasons *Enigma Variations* was to be conducted by Sir Adrian Boult. He had known Elgar personally, so it was with great respect that we listened at the dress rehearsal to any tempi changes he might want to implement. He was well into his eighties, and even though he was a big man he was rather frail-looking. I thought if anything the tempi would be slower than we were used to. I need not have worried. The second he raised his baton he became like a young man again. I certainly know my solo was the fastest I have ever had to dance it. Boult must have abided by the Tommy Beecham method of maximum effort for the dancer. Sir Tommy was bored in a ballet rehearsal one day and increased the tempo so much that he, and the orchestra, finished well before the dancers. As they collapsed in heaps on the stage he laid down his baton, turned to his players and, before leaving the pit, said, 'Well – that made the buggers hop.' At the end of the performance we acknowledged Boult – sitting on his conductor's chair in the pit he was just able to turn round and take the cheers of appreciation. I was struck by his generosity. He's the first conductor I've seen to put down his baton in the pit and actually applaud the dancers.

The *Enigma Variations* was a great favourite with audience and critics alike, and has remained in the repertoire ever since.

The best things that happen to you in life, those events that often change its course, always appear unheralded by trumpets, bells or clanging of cymbals. They just appear, tap you on the shoulder and say, 'Well, here I am.' And you say something like, 'Oh, that's nice, then,' and get on with it.

One day in early 1969 while we were sweating through another barre exercise, in walked a man in a green checked suit, with bleached blond hair, thick circular-rimmed glasses, socks that were odd, correspondent shoes, and a sketch pad. Obviously someone who did not want to go unnoticed. He was accompanied by a well-dressed woman and a young man wearing a handsome snakeskin jacket. David Hockney had come to draw the company, along with Lindy Dufferin and Peter Schlesinger, also artists. I had no idea who they were – I had never heard of any of them and they were more of a hindrance than an excitement.

As only two of them were allowed in the rehearsal room at one time, Peter, rather to his annoyance, had to stand in the doorway. During my breaks I chatted to him there, and he asked if I would be willing to be drawn. This led to an invitation to join them that day, with Sir Fred, at Lindy's house in Holland Park for lunch. Sir Fred and I posed together for the artists, he in a chair with me (naked) sitting at his feet.

David invited me to have dinner with him that evening. He took me to his favourite restaurant in Devonshire Street. It was not a very large restaurant but it was quaint, with umbrellas hanging upside down from the ceiling forming a canopy. Peter Langan, the owner, seemed like a really rough-cut chef on first meeting. He didn't mince his words and was not bothered if people took offence. Visits to the restaurant became a regularity, and as I got to know Peter better I found a heart of gold and a wallet of generosity. On my first nights he would send me a crate of champagne, of which the top layer, with Peter's inimitable style, would be chilled. The first ballet he saw was *Cinderella*, in which I was the Jester. I was in the dressing-room with Sir Fred and Sir Robert Helpmann, who were playing the Ugly Sisters. After the show Peter came backstage, looking for me, and his booming voice arrived in the dressing-room with, 'I liked the one in the grey wig but who *was* the old bag in the red one?' I said, 'Have you met Sir Robert Helpmann?' Peter was always so unembarrassed by his own pronouncements that Sir Robert could not take umbrage – and in any case, there was lots of free champagne.

My mother, her sisters and many more of my relations had come that night to see *Cinderella*. I had intended to take them to a pizza house round the corner because there were so many of us, but Peter insisted we go to his restaurant. When he found it was fully booked, he got us into Provan's in the Fulham Road. What he didn't know, or didn't remember, was that there was a football match at Chelsea, and traffic was at a standstill locally. It took us for ever to get there. Peter joined us later, in a fury because he had paid a surprise visit to his restaurant on the way – only to find empty tables. His staff had hoped to avoid him by telling him they were booked up. He then let rip a stream of invective down the telephone. My seventy-year-old grandmother said she had never heard anything like it and that she had a lifetime's education in one evening. But she did enjoy herself. My mother demonstrated the foxtrot (I was about to choreograph a sequence for the film *Death on the Nile*) up and down the aisle of the restaurant, earning Peter's undying admiration. After dinner, all fourteen of us piled into taxis to go home – where Mum invited all the taxi-drivers in for a drink. Peter went back to his restaurant. I have no idea if the staff were still in work the next day.

David Hockney and Peter Schlesinger also became regular visitors to the ballet and we often went out to dinner or on to parties afterwards. David always treated us and usually paid with a drawing. They introduced me to a new world, one of designers, artists and writers. I met Ossie Clark and his wife Celia Birtwell – both of them at the peak of fashion design, she with fabrics and Ossie with couture. David doted on Celia, who features in nearly all his portraits of women, and a picture of her and Ossie was one of David's first to be hung in the Tate Gallery. There was super-tall Patrick Proctor, another artist, who had a domineering character which was belied by his sensitive watercolours. We looked ridiculous standing next to each other. I met Christopher Isherwood, who brought resonances of an earlier era with his straightforwardness and strong, old-fashioned delivery, and the poet Stephen Spender, a man of supreme gentleness. And there was Mo McDermott, David's assistant, who sculpted two-dimensional trees and animals from wood. I have a leopard of his that still stalks my sitting-room.

Everybody I met seemed to be connected to each other in some way. Lindy's husband Sheridan, Marquis of Dufferin and Ava, financed John Kasmin, who was David's art dealer. It was through the Kasmins, John and Jane, that I met one of the most important people in my life. At a party, I was introduced to a shy little old man who was sitting hunched in a corner. He was slightly merry, but then he was not alone in that – we all were. I found out he was only twenty-six (I was still only twenty and anyone over the age of twenty-two was still pretty ancient) and his name was George Lawson. He was with Bertram Rota, a bookshop specializing in twentieth-century first editions and one of Kas's closest friends. This meeting led to a close friendship that has lasted for more than twenty-five years. John Kasmin, who was separated from his wife by then, didn't like George's friendship with me. He was dismissive and apparently said to George, 'You'll soon get over this phase with this little ballet dancer.' But he was wrong, so wrong.

FIVE

TOURING AND SQUIRREL DAYS

'New York, New York, it's a wonderful town. The Bronx is up and the Battery's down. New York, New Yooork, it's a wonderful toooown.' Back again. Great. It was 1969.

My roles were expanded: I was dancing Puck in *The Dream*, the Mandolin Dance in *Romeo and Juliet*, the Peasant *pas-de-deux* in *Giselle*, *Enigma Variations* and *Jazz Calendar*. I was also given the Bluebird *pas-de-deux* in *The Sleeping Beauty*. This was a new production, first produced in London for this season, by Peter Wright and Sir Fred (who added a new *pas-de-deux* and more chore-ography for men), with set designs by Henry Bardon and costumes by Lila di Nobili. Nobbly Lil (as we called her) had designed *Ondine* for Sir Fred, and she and Bardon collaborated together to create an interesting production.

The dancers had to contend with an elaborate set, a ramp down which they entered on to the stage, and costumes which were the same colour as the back-drop, much of which was in the then fashionable orange. These costumes were ornate and very beautiful, as befits a fairytale, but were padded in such a way as to hinder the dancer's natural line. Di Nobili's idea was to recreate the look of the dancers in the old days who were, physically, more thickset and muscular. She achieved this by padding out the chests of the men and the hips of the girls. It made the costumes hot and heavy. The whole lot was topped with curly wigs. And at one point there was a seemingly random boat which wound a spiral route about the stage, steered by remote control. There was much criticism, in fact almost an uprising, when the Company did away with the world-famous Oliver Messel set and costumes. This was the production I saw when I first went to the ballet in Newcastle.

My partner in the Bluebird *pas-de-deux* was Lesley Collier. It was always good to dance with Lesley. We were well attuned because of our time together at White Lodge. The Bluebird is a part which needs tremendous stamina, which is only built up after dancing the part regularly for some time. Although dancers are incredibly fit, each part demands something different both in the use of the muscles and in the level of stamina required, so you might feel at your peak in one part, but less so in another. The Bluebird has leaps and beats which are hard enough in practice clothes but with the heavily padded (and bejewelled, I might add – the tail was heavily encrusted, the idea was to make me look like a bird) costumes it was very difficult to defy gravity.

The British version of the Bluebird is a *tour de force*. Not one diagonal, as in

Russia, but two, before the final eight entrechat-six. In my first performance I achieved the first four, and wondered how on earth I was going to get off the ground for the end of the solo. My last two jumps were so low that I hardly left the ground. You should end with a double turn in the air on to the knee, and all I could do was spin to face front, on two feet, with a flourish of the arms. If I had knelt I might have stayed there. I still had the Coda to come, which Lesley began while I threw up in the wings.

I was too small to play Romeo, Benvolio and Mercutio. Although I understood that for symmetry and form it were best that the three dancers should be of an equal height, I did resent this in a small way. I wonder, sometimes, whether convention could have been played with – particularly in the case of Mercutio, who is the joker in the pack and thus a part which I could have performed. Still, it was never likely to happen and the Mandolin Dance was a consolation and a challenge in which I could really make my mark. I was never sure whether Kenneth MacMillan, the choreographer was pleased or not. The applause held up the action.

Audience appreciation is something of which a dancer never tires. In fact it is vital and the only reward. Let's face it, the money's not good, especially compared with our counterparts in the Royal Opera. As far as your tutors are concerned, apart from the occasional 'Good, Sleep', there is always the necessary criticism. So soak up the applause while you may. It was turning into a great tour for me, which was made even better by rekindling a friendship.

Graham Powell – my chief collaborator and partner in crime at White Lodge – joined the resident company from the touring company. We went everywhere and did everything together. However, the tables had turned a little. Graham had been used to principal roles with the touring company, but on his arrival with us he had to start at the bottom again as there were no vacant roles and he had to wait for an opportunity to arise. It cannot have been easy for him to see me in the solo roles, while he remained in the *corps*. But he never said anything, nor indicated in any way that he harboured resentment. He found it frustrating, yes, because he had been touring in big roles, and it must have been very hard to have to wait his turn again. But that was how it was.

This reversal of roles did not stop us having a very good time together. Some things didn't change. We stayed out late going to parties and were often late for class. We were having fun. We often got hauled over the coals for what we would see as little misdemeanours or for partying, but in those days our 'rulers' were of the old school. So anything any member of the company did which was slightly off beam was regarded as a reflection on the status of the company.

These American tours were really quite glamorous. Sol Hurok, the impresario who had been bringing the Royal Ballet to America since 1948, set the tone with receptions at the St Regis Hotel in New York and the Beverly Hills Hotel in Los Angeles. Margot Fonteyn and the Sadlers Wells were accepted readily into New York and West Coast society and set the fashion wherever they went. Margot would be immaculate in Balenciaga or Chanel, and later Nureyev was to join her; Rudolf in thigh-high boots and full-length fur coats. They created something of a sensation wherever they went.

All the major American celebrities of the day came to the ballet, including Jackie Onassis, Rock Hudson, Elizabeth Taylor and Burt Lancaster. This was something I had not expected. Although the Royal Ballet was accorded respect in the UK, the adulation it received in the US surprised me. I imagined that Fonteyn and Nureyev were surrounded by all this glamour, all of the time. I wished I could just drop in on them, to be in the same room as all these people, but I never did. I didn't dare.

But they were kind to the rest of us, in spite of the lionizing they received. They gave parties for the company in their adjoining suites, and occasionally would take a select few off somewhere else. For this there was an elect hierarchy in operation, and you would get asked with certain people and not others. Rudolf took me to the Russian Tea Room with its red leather booths, chandeliers, and Czarist paintings on the walls. Seated in this outpost of old Russian splendour you would drink Stolichnaya with your tea. He had lemon with his.

One incident, in which Graham and I were not involved, took place in San Francisco. In the middle of a private party given in honour of Margot and Rudolf, the police arrived and instigated a search of the guests. People fled from all the exits to avoid the feel of a heavy hand. Margot and Rudolf hid on the roof in the hope of avoiding detection and capture. Their intention was to avoid not only a night in jail, but some nasty publicity. To no avail – they were discovered and taken away with all the others. Someone had informed the police that pot was being smoked at the party and so the place was raided. The newspapers the following morning were nothing less than sensational. Any ordinary mortal might have kept a low profile and stayed away from class that morning. But both Margot and Rudolf arrived, straight from spending the night in custody, for class at 10.30 sharp. Class came first, no matter what. I saw them come up the stairs. They walked in together, eyes ahead, and passed straight through us. They knew we knew, but as far as they were concerned it was nothing to do with us. And nothing was ever said.

All this took place at the time of the Haight Ashbury era, when hippies sang songs and smoked pot on the corners of the streets and everywhere you could see signs of love and peace, man. Every city had its own hippy quarter, always a bit out of town. The incipient hippies would camp out in unused warehouses and the streets around would reinvent themselves, with painted psychedelic pictures on shop doors, and osmose into hippiedom. In various towns, particularly in the Mid-West where hippies were very 'un-American', local reactionaries would burn these quarters down. Graham and I would somehow always end up in these places. It suited our sense of freedom. Patchouli oil became my favourite fragrance and we paraded around in long kaftans and red crushed velvet trousers. Peace and love, man. We were in there with them.

We toured all over America, travelling everywhere by plane. Gone were the days when the company would travel in their own train, Royal Ballet emblem prominent, accompanied by the orchestra, the stage crew, the sets and costumes. These journeys would take several days to get from East to West coast, with the result that people got to know each other rather well in the close and intimate confines of the carriages. Air travel was quicker and a hundred times more convenient but, I think, not nearly as romantic.

As we travelled our entourage got bigger. Groupies were added to the list of people who toured with us from city to city. We were followed around by fanatical fans like pop stars. Each dancer had a specific following who would sneak in to read the noticeboard to find out the latest cast changes. If they found you had a first performance in a new role three weeks away in another state, they'd book their air tickets to be there for the big moment. They took endless photographs of us all, especially one girl — Leslie Spatt's photographs were so good that the company used some of them and she has since become one of the best dance photographers in the world. They threw flowers from the balcony to the stage, weighted with stones inside the tinfoil to make sure the bouquets flew over the orchestra pit — sometimes they would hit their mark, which didn't half hurt.

There was always a huge crowd at the stage door, especially when Margot and Rudolf were performing. They always left the theatre as if it were another performance, dressed in such style that the fans never went away disappointed. We had to fight our way through the throng, trying not to answer the hundreds of questions about where they would be dining after the show. Somehow the fans would always find out, so that when we arrived at restaurants or clubs the same faces would appear at the doorway — just to get another look at their heroes. These same fans would never let Margot and Rudolf leave the stage without at least fifteen or twenty curtain calls, such was their devotion.

New Orleans and St Louis were so hot that you would have to run from the hotel lobby, which was freezing with air-conditioning, through to the outside which was 100 degrees and counting, and into the back of a taxi, also ice cold from air-conditioning. Because of the extremes of temperature, many of us suffered from colds and earaches. We woke up with stiff necks because of the draughts from the air-conditioning. We performed in huge outdoor arenas where the air was stifling. It was not unusual for some dancers to pass out, the ambient heat exacerbated by heavy costumes made of velvet.

I particularly remember performing at the Hollywood Bowl in Los Angeles. Our warm-ups before the performance would be viewed by many of the audience, who brought picnic hampers and ate their dinner while watching us limber up. The 10,000 capacity open air auditorium was a thrill to perform in. The stage comes out towards the audience. And the place was so large that for those in the cheaper seats, which were right at the back after a long climb up endless steps, it looked as if the dancers were not keeping time with the music:

there was a delay of one second before the music reached them. But in the open air, and without the orchestra pit separating us, many ballets took on new life – especially *Romeo and Juliet*, because you really felt you were in the market place in Verona (or Padua). But one night's performance sticks in my mind. We were dancing Stravinsky's *The Rite of Spring*. Just before the Dance of the Chosen Virgin, danced with dramatic brio by Monica Mason, there is a dramatic musical tremor. Up to this point the sky had been dark and overcast, but coinciding with the thrilling crescendo in the music, the heavy clouds parted to reveal a full moon. Pure magic.

In LA I fell in love with my first car. I can't drive, but the Mustang was so beautiful that I couldn't help it. Through Georgina Parkinson, a principal, I met Herbert Ross (director of, among others, *California Suite* and *Steel Magnolias*) and his wife Nora Kaye, a leading ballerina of the American Ballet Theater. After dinner we all returned to the Ross mansion in the hills to watch Neil Armstrong take the first steps on the moon. This extraordinary event was heightened by sitting under a clear sky by the pool. We could see the moon so clearly, we could have touched it, and there were men walking on it.

I went to Santa Monica to pose for Christopher Isherwood's friend, the artist Don Bachardy, and later they came to watch my performance as Puck in *The Dream*. Afterwards we had dinner with Sir Fred, who, surprisingly, had never met them. We ate at the Hollywood Roosevelt Hotel, where a lot of us were staying for 6 dollars per night and which was quite run down. It is now rather grand. The one thing in its favour was a large and magnificent swimming-pool (subsequently painted by David Hockney), in which Roberto Arias, Margot's husband, was given therapy. He had been shot and paralysed in an attempted coup in Panama, and Margot commuted to London from Stoke Mandeville hospital, where he was in a critical condition, nursing him through it, but she didn't miss one class or rehearsal. Another example of her tenacious dedication.

Some years later George Lawson and I were staying with David Hockney in the Hollywood hills and were invited to Christopher's house for dinner. When we first arrived, our hosts kept taking it in turns to disappear into the kitchen, leaving the other to entertain us. They acted as if nothing was wrong, but when we moved to the table all became clear. They were given away by the stiletto-heeled foot which prevented the door into the kitchen from closing, and finally admitted that their Spanish-speaking maid had passed out while cooking the meal, drunk, and had to be taken to hospital.

On our one day off in New York I took Graham on a trip to Fire Island. We were joined by Judy Colleypriest, a very generous woman and a number one fan who had become a friend, first by collecting our autographs, then by asking us out. We took the overnight ferry to arrive at 8.30 in the morning. I was in charge. 'We'll have a wonderful time,' I said. I had telephoned my friends there some days earlier to say we were intending to visit, but did not follow it up closer to the time, so when I called them to say we had arrived there was no answer.

They were either out for the count or had stayed out all night. This was a normal occurrence for those who lived there at the time: much informal sleeping over at other friends' houses. Non-stop party time. There was nothing for us to do except retire to the beach, where, exhausted after travelling overnight, we fell asleep. Five hours later I was the first to wake under a scorching sun. I moved, only to find that even the smallest motion was agonizing. I was burnt to a frazzle. Putting on tights for the next day's performance would be like buffing oneself with sandpaper. Graham was a human lobster. At around two in the afternoon we managed to catch up with our intended host, who apologized and fed us with gin and vodka. We were despondent, sore and angry. Getting sloshed numbed the pain. In the end it was too much bother to contact any other friends, so we accepted a ride back to Manhattan with an elderly (as she seemed to me then, though she was probably only fortyish) lady and her companion. Judy and Graham elected to go home to change. They took a taxi which, when they stopped off at a drugstore for some unguent to soothe their raging flesh, did a runner with all their bags, keys, money and clothes. Graham had to climb into Judy's building from the outside in order to let them in. It was a good thing it was a smallish house in the Village and not a Manhattan skyscraper.

I, on the other hand, had found a new acquaintance in the shape of the companion, and I went back with my new friend to her very large apartment on East 48th Street. It was beautifully decked out, just as she was. She played back the messages on her answering machine, which I could not help overhearing. Messages like 'Why aren't you in? You know who this is.' All from different men who didn't leave their names. It dawned on me that I had met my first high-class madam. I couldn't get rid of her – until she got interested in other members of the company. I think she was attracted to the aura of glamour that surrounds the Company in general in the US as much as anything else. But it was hard avoiding her.

My twenty-first birthday fell during this tour. I was woken up on my birthday morning, at about 6 A.M., to find I was covered in Michaelmas daisies – peace and love, man – courtesy Graham and Judy. They must have spent hours in the preparation. But I was furious and extremely unappreciative. It was too early, I had class and rehearsal. I still feel guilty about the way I reacted.

Some of the fans threw a surprise party for me in the evening which kept us out all night. This was one of the occasions that Graham was upbraided for missing rehearsals the following morning. I didn't, but I was late. We were both called in to see John Hart, the assistant director, who decided that, among our many sins, 'spending all your money' was as much a sin as any of the others. It emphasized our lack of personal responsibility. It came down to the reputation of the company. Graham threatened to leave.

Because of conflicting opinions, he did leave the company at the end of this tour. He joined the Australian Ballet Company, but his stay was short-lived. Over there he met Stephan and decided to give up dancing and teach instead. They went to live in Athens, where he became a teacher and Stephan worked for the KGB as a translator of news programmes into Russian from Greek. Eventually they returned to London to live, and rented a basement flat under Jane Kasmin's house in Ifield Road, Fulham. Graham rejoined the Royal Ballet Touring Company but lasted for only one season before giving up again – this time deciding to paint. He possessed a superior ability in more than one field which meant that he had a low tolerance level. He found it difficult to settle anywhere and to anything, and became subject to headaches and depression. When, after a short holiday in Greece, Stephan was refused re-entry into the UK (possibly because of his KGB connections), Graham was alone and started sliding deeper into depression.

The American tour ended and the summer holidays began. I went to Cornwall with David Gayle and various other friends, leaving June behind in Montagu Square. On return I longed for independence and a flat of my own, so I accepted (who wouldn't?) an invitation from David Hockney and Peter Schlesinger to stay with them in Powis Terrace, Notting Hill, while I looked for a place to stay. I slept in David's studio on a put-you-up bed. It was not very comfortable but I loved waking up to the smell of oil paint, and having a private view of David's paintings every morning more than compensated for discomfort. I had Hockneys staring at me from all directions. And it was a major step up from the silver-foiled walls of Montagu Square.

Every night there was a different event, and David included me in his entourage of Ossie, Celia, Mo, Peter Schlesinger, Patrick Proctor, the Dufferins, Peter Langan, Henrietta Guinness – plus a few undesirable hangers-on whom David, with his sweet nature, could not turn away. He has a generous and sensitive outlook that allows him to champion the underdogs of the world, letting them get away with a lot.

David was our meal ticket. Usually we finished the evenings at Langan's, where David would generously foot the bill. On Saturday afternoons he would give tea parties. Peter S., who was then studying painting at the Slade, would go out and buy game pies for lunch and cakes from Fortnum & Mason, which would be consumed with Earl Grey tea. For me every day was a new experience, meeting a new mix of friends far removed from the ballet world. I was fascinated, and was enjoying myself far too much to make any attempt to find somewhere to live.

But it began to be slightly uncomfortable when, after a couple of weeks, Peter started hinting about my search for a place of my own. With understandable reluctance I telephoned Diana Roberts and asked if she knew of anywhere I might stay while I made a greater effort to find a place. A friend of hers, a protégé of the well-known radio and television personality Gilbert Harding, had a spare room in his house just off Brook Green, Hammersmith. His name was Brian Masters, now famous for his book on the serial killer, Dennis Nielsen, and his latest, *The Things That Men Do*. He agreed to house me, but was apprehensive because apparently I had a flighty reputation. I was something of a Royal

Ballet rebel, because I did the unforgiveable, I played hard, but God! did I work hard. It didn't take long for Brian to realize how serious I was about my life and work, and confessed to having been taken in by rumours.

Brian's house was so different from David's. Powis Terrace had high ceilings and big rooms, Art Deco furniture and Lalique glass, large paintings and bargains from the Portobello Road. Brook Green was a small Victorian house enveloped in Liberty-type patterned wallpaper, chintz curtains and chair covers – quite traditional and at the opposite end of the decorative scale from David's Deco-ness. At that time Brian had an enviable job as a tour guide, showing people round the historical sites and monuments of Europe. He was a very literary person and read everything – an occupation which I envied, as I found it difficult to concentrate while reading. Brian tried to encourage me by suggesting some easy books. One of these was William Golding's *Lord of the Flies*. I still have not finished it . . .

I remember a special dinner when Brian invited Quentin Crisp and Penelope Keith, and I was allowed to ask David and Peter. Penelope was just on the verge of her very successful career with *The Good Life*. Quentin Crisp, with his purple dyed hair and flaky mannerisms, impressed so many people with his stories and eccentricities, but for me that kind of attitude was an everyday event around the Opera House. I enjoyed his company, though, and his always-on-show one man show.

A few months later I found my own flat at last. It was at 13 Masons Yard, behind Fortnum & Mason, above a picture framer's and up three flights of stairs. It was a two-room attic pied-à-terre, and mine. The rent was £16 – my salary at that time was £32. Brian advised me against taking on the lease, recommending that I should spend only a third of my salary on rent. But I didn't care – I was truly and happily independent. With the kitchenette, and a coffee table made from a piece of glass supported by two breeze-blocks (which I still use), I was able to try out the role of host. I shopped in Berwick Street market for food and wine, made huge casseroles and entertained, hoping to repay my friends' generosity to me.

That summer, I spent two of my four weeks of holiday in the South of France with Peter Schlesinger. A friend of his, Melissa North, invited us to stay with her in a holiday house belonging to a friend of hers, the film director Tony Richardson, in Le Nid de Duc, a small village some miles inland up a steep and winding road above Le Garde Frenet. Tony Richardson, who was directing at the Royal Court, in the West End and on Broadway, was then known mostly for his direction of *Tom Jones*. The money ran out during the shooting of the film, so in order to finish the actors agreed to forego their salaries and accept a percentage of the take instead. The film was a huge hit and they earned substantially more than their original salaries.

Tony had bought the entire village of Le Nid de Duc and converted the houses into homes for guests. All he had added was a house for himself and a large swimming pool, which had a view of the mountains behind a small valley. As he was not there at the time we visited, Melissa held court over the constant flow of friends from all over the world. Every day Melissa, her boyfriend Tchaik Chassay, Peter and I drove to a private beach, the Aqua Club, to swim, sunbathe and eat lunches of fresh fish, lobster and crab on the beach. In the evenings we would either zoom into St Tropez to dance the night away or congregate over a communal dinner in Le Nid – each time meeting new guests with whom we would drink and chat way into the early hours.

At the end of the summer Melissa invited me to the house she was staying in with Tony Richardson in Pelham Crescent, where she had a gathering of friends who had stayed at Le Nid de Duc. It was a beautiful house, with grand cages for exotic birds on the landing and some very expensive modern art. I met Tony and thanked him for his generous hospitality. His reply, short and to the point, was that he had heard I was very amusing on holiday, creating naked choreographic happenings in the evenings with the other guests around the illuminated swimming-pool. He said, 'If you were that amusing then, get up and entertain me now.' I wished the earth would open up and swallow me. The demand for instant entertainment was not something I was used to. It was a different thing altogether to do something for fun after a few drinks for a few friends on holiday. I couldn't. So I was discarded as being of no further use.

Something good did come out of this party, however – I met Karl Bowen. Karl was studying art and architecture at the Slade. He had his own private income, as he was part of the Kellogg family from Buffalo, New York. He was considered the most beautiful man of his generation – admired by men and women alike. He looked like a Botticelli painting.

He lived in a room in Islington, sharing a kitchen with Derek Jarman, then a painter, and Peter Logan, a sculptor. Karl persuaded me to leave Masons Yard and share a fifth-floor flat with him just by the Shaftesbury Theatre in Shaftesbury Avenue. My bedroom was a circular turret. I went to a foam factory (owned by friends of Diana Roberts) in the East End and had a piece cut to fit the circular room exactly. It complemented the dome above my head like a mini version of St Pauls. We painted the entire floor of the flat white – and then never washed it. I was much influenced and excited by Karl's Bohemian way of life.

Derek Jarman moved too, renting a whole floor of a warehouse just south of Tower Bridge. He lived in a glass conservatory constructed in a corner – to save on heating. In the rest of it he would give enormous parties. He started the Alternative Miss World pageants here, along with Andrew Logan, inviting two to three hundred people at a time. You could consider them the first raves. He made each party an individual theatrical event. Guests were eclectic, from Francis Bacon to Divine, the drag queen. He was a catalyst bringing together all the corners of the arts – musicians, actors, dancers, painters, designers.

Only a few months after moving in with Karl, I returned from spending Christmas with my family in Plymouth to find the front door unlocked. I knew

Karl was still away, so I entered the living-room with some trepidation. There were two strangers in the middle of the floor dismantling my stereo. They told me they were the police. I was not that stupid and started to make a run for the door, but I was not quite fast enough, because they grabbed me and threw me into the bathroom, where they tried to tie me up with some rope. Thanks to my ballet training and my lethal kick I managed to get away. I flew down the stairs shouting and screaming 'Help!', with the burglars in hot pursuit. I ran into the doorway of the first office, and as they pushed by me, I nearly fell through a fourth-floor window. Someone popped out of a door and said, 'Anything wrong?' Anything wrong? Didn't they hear me? My feelings of relief and anger were poured on to the head of this hapless person, and all I could say was, 'It took you long enough. Where were you?' Which is rude but not surprising in the circumstances. Anyway this kind person came up to the flat with me to make sure no accomplices were lurking in cupboards – not a soul, thank God. But I discovered that by the time I disturbed them they had been up and down the stairs for hours taking all my personal belongings: unopened Christmas presents, all the fashionable velvet suits that had been made me in the Kings Road, Anthony Price jackets, Ossie Clark and Celia Birtwell shirts and coats bought at a discount from their shop, Quorum. The burglars would have looked pretty stupid in my clothes, suitable as they were for a midget in a circus – but somebody must have used them for dusters. Not only did this whole episode put me off buying trendy clothes ever again, but I was also in immediate fear that the burglars would return for the stereo. Or me. So I telephoned George Lawson and asked if I could spend that night with him.

George lived in a mews house in Wigmore Place, behind Harley Street. I moved in that night and never moved back to my turret in Shaftesbury Avenue. It was the start of our close friendship. As he worked in books and I was still, in spite of Brian Masters's best efforts, unable to concentrate for more than a page, it is perhaps surprising that I fitted into his lifestyle. But we share an off-beat humour which we slot into and which to other people is like a foreign language. We leave them for dead. As he had no kitchen (not even to make a cup of tea), we dined out every night. He introduced me to some of the best restaurants in the West End. We would go to the Moulin d'Or in Romilly Street for Sunday lunch. The chef there had been Monty's batman during the war. The owner used to have a certificate on the wall testifying to the fact that he defeated the panel on *What's My Line*. Some people have strange claims to fame. If you asked him what he would recommend, he'd say, 'The restaurant next door. Haw haw.' And he made a fantastic treacle tart. For my birthday we went off to Au Savarin, where I crushed wild strawberries on a plate with Cointreau and added them to my champagne. Spoilt brat. And almost daily we enjoyed the hospitality of the legendary Elena (and her husband Aldo) at Bianchi's in Frith Street. Elena now has the L'Etoile in Charlotte Street and is even more of a star!

Karl, however, did not fare so well. He wanted to be a painter rather than train as an architect at the Slade. He was not, as the French say, happy in his skin, and there were occasions when life for him was even darker. He spent time in a mental hospital in Wimbledon, doped up to the eyeballs. He complained to us when we visited that time was going backwards. In the end he went back to New York. He was a lovely man but I think he was aware that he didn't have quite enough talent to make it to the top.

Meanwhile the Royal Ballet season continued at the Opera House. I was performing solo roles and sometimes dancing in the *corps* when there was a role suited to my size. Dancers take huge risks with their bodies. Every muscle and bone is stretched and pulled to the very limit. The physiotherapy room is always full of people with torn cartilages, snapped Achilles tendons, sprained ankles and groins and hairline fractures. One does not just rely on one's own caution, but of course when dancing or partnering fellow colleagues one must rely on their care for you. Many backs are seriously injured without this care.

The choreography for Puck in *The Dream* required me to do a handspring into the waiting arms of the two male lovers, Demetrius and Lysander. After they caught me, they flicked my body over into a sitting position and threw me ten or twelve feet into the air, from where I could land neatly and continue dancing. One evening during the spring of 1970 the second cast were performing with me. We always tried this lift before curtain up as we knew how dangerous the move was. All was fine. But during the actual performance, it went horrendously wrong and instead of flipping my back up, they hurtled me into the air with my pelvis parallel to the ground. I had no choice but to land flat on my back from a great height. In a situation like this, Dr Theatre comes into play. One's brain is totally intent on continuing the performance, aided by adrenalin and the presence of the audience. In this case I think I was also numbed by the pain and so managed to scrape through to the end. The next day I could not walk, let alone dance. The physiotherapist told me I had bruised my spine and all the muscles around it in the lower back, a condition known as a haematoma.

The final performance that season of *Enigma Variations* was a few days later. Ashton pleaded with me to perform my solo. As the ballet was relatively new, he was loath for any one but the first cast to perform it, because he always choreographed to the specialities of each dancer. I was resolved to rise above the pain, and acquiesced. I danced in a corset which didn't relieve the pain.

An understudy took my other roles for the following month and I flew to Paris to convalesce. I stayed with Jean Leger, who was a friend of David Hockney and Peter Schlesinger and worked for Helena Rubenstein. Jean's first sight of me must have been a shock. I arrived in Paris, already barely able to walk because of the injury, stammering and staggering from the combined effect of liberal doses of airline alcohol on top of being doped up on painkillers. The idea, obviously, was to become as numb as possible. And to make my own misery worse I had also thrown up on the plane. I don't care to think about the impression I made.

I felt better the next morning. No reference was made to my arrival – Jean was the soul of Parisian aloofness. David and Peter came over to Paris to join us and we spent a few days wandering – or hobbling in my case – round the Louvre, the Rodin Museum and other cerebral joys, leaving plenty of time for internal refreshment at La Coupole and Maxim's. This sybaritic exercise lifted spirits which helped recovery, although the effects of the accident have never really left me. If I have to lift a partner when I am tired, I experience, still, a dull ache in my lower back. Dancers, in particular, experience terrible depression when injured, because they lose performances for which they've trained for months, and which may not be repeated in their lifetime as a dancer. And there is the unknown of whether you will ever fully recover. Thank goodness I did.

When I began rehearsals back in London there was a 'yellow peril' from Sir Fred's assistant waiting to greet me on the notice board. 'Please see me – Iris.' When I went to see her, Iris told me that I was up for one of the parts in the film that was to be made of *The Tales of Beatrix Potter*.

The producers were Richard Goodwin (who went on to produce *Death on the Nile*, among other films) and his wife Christine Edzard (who designed the film's sets and costumes), with Lord Brabourne as executive producer. It had taken them three years to bring the idea to fruition. This was, in part, because of the understandable unwillingness of Beatrix Potter's publisher, Frederick Warne, to release the copyright on the stories and the drawings for anything so modern and potentially bastardizing as a film. Warne relented only when Sir Frederick Ashton agreed to be the choreographer and co-director. He brought with him John Lanchbery, Director of Music for the Royal Ballet, with whom Sir Fred had worked closely since 1959. The team was completed by a Russian living in Paris, Rostislav Douboujinsky, who was a designer and maker of masks.

John Lanchbery chose music from composers of Beatrix Potter's time that she might have listened to. He listened to hundreds of hours before making his final choice. He was the number one ballet conductor at the Garden and one of the few dance conductors who was respected by the orchestra, who played better, and by the dancers, who were able to dance better. Each dancer dances at a slightly different speed and he was able to accommodate the tempi to their varying technical styles.

Sir Fred and the producers had a difficult task because of the imperative that the film reflect, accurately, the illustrations in the books. So Sir Fred was not just looking for physical types, but also for the correct technique, posture and interpretation of each animal. There were Jeremy Fisher's long spindly legs to consider, the thumping attitude of Peter Rabbit, the ability to do point work for Pigling Bland, Jemima Puddleduck's waddle, the bounce of Squirrel Nutkin and the utter mischief of the Two Bad Mice. These attributes were to be determined in the dancers and there was much debate about who should play which animal. We were all scrutinized endlessly in class and rehearsal until a cast was produced. It was not until the producers saw me perform at the Garden that I was finally cast in two roles: Squirrel Nutkin and Tom Thumb, one of the Two Bad Mice. And it was realized that no one but Sir Fred should play Mrs Tiggywinkle.

Sir Fred brought Beatrix Potter's illustrations with him to rehearsals and we started off by studying and assuming the poses created by the characters in the pictures. Once we had the correct positions, Sir Fred used his supreme originality to link each tableau through dance. Mrs Tiggywinkle was accompanied by a banjo solo, reminiscent of his time choreographing the Cochran Revues. This was where he learnt much of his trade as dancer and choreographer; the revues lasted for a limited time and he had to provide a different genre of dance every other week, laying the foundations for his style and versatility.

My solo for Squirrel Nutkin was to some of the music from *Don Quixote* by Minkus. Maya Plisetskaya was famous for her role in that ballet, and Sir Fred gleefully adapted some of her moves, her split jumps and fast turns, for the squirrel – which he then nicknamed Nutkinskaya.

My partner as the other Bad Mouse was Lesley Collier. Because we had known each other since we were twelve years old, our affinity allowed us to enjoy the freedom we were given to ad-lib during the filming. She and I had been paired together (the Bluebirds in *Sleeping Beauty*, the Peasant *pas-de-deux* in *Giselle*, for instance) often. Lesley had been in the year above me at White Lodge and everyone knew, even from an early age, that she was destined for the highest status. She eventually became the leading ballerina at the Royal Ballet and went on to dance all the major roles in the classics – and left me. Sigh.

We learnt and rehearsed long before filming commenced. The costumes were the next stage, along with the very specific and detailed heads and faces of each animal. The nucleus of this part of the production was at the Knightsbridge house of Richard and Christine. In her search for complete authenticity, Christine was faithful to the colourings of Beatrix Potter's books and notes, and her sketches of the potential sets, scenes and costumes for the ballet reflected the light pastel shades of the watercolour illustrations.

Fittings for the costumes and heads were long and trying. We had to stand still for hours as layers of net were placed strategically over a unitard (a leotard and tights in one piece) to create the rounded shapes of mice, squirrels or pigs. I thought, in my innocence, that although my costumes were going to be bulky, the net would make them light. I was not far wrong for the mice, as their bodies were covered in clothes. But for Squirrel Nutkin . . . Thick heavy tufts of fur were layered and glued all over the net – and then there was the tail, this huge tail, made of bamboo and feathers, the whole weighing in at over twenty pounds. I envied, as did most of the others, Michael Coleman as Jeremy Fisher. His frog costume had no hair and the wet slimy look was achieved by a mask of light plastic. He also wore traditional ballet tights – to show off froggy legs – and so his only problem, if it was one, was the huge protruding tummy.

The heads were perfectly designed and meticulously made, capturing the exact expression of Potter's illustrations. The size of the heads was in natural proportion to the furry bodies. Obviously. I was still surprised, however, when having my Squirrel's head fitted, by how much larger it was than mine. The eyeholes were too high for me to see through and so I had to peer through the thousands of tiny holes into which the hair was threaded. I couldn't even make out the shape of the camera. I had a red light placed at the front of the set because I could only see haziness through the squirrel mask and had no idea, when finishing a spin, whether I was facing the front or the back. The red blob by the camera at least told me where I was. Sort of. The mouse head was easier to cope with, partly because I could see through the eyes, and partly because the hair was thinner. Vision was still obscured, though, which gave rise to a certain amount of claustrophobia. But we got used to it, after a while.

When filming started, finally, in October 1970, I saw five o'clock in the morning more often than I cared for. We would all meet at Richard and Christine's for a bacon sarnie and a lift to Elstree studios. We arrived there at about 8 A.M., which gave us enough time for a half-hour barre work-out. It was always freezing cold, as the studios were like aircraft hangars. We worried at first about tearing our muscles in the cold, but why did we worry? By the time we were in our costumes, by the time the lights were on and focused, we were already beginning to sweat. And we hadn't even started to dance. Cold? It was like dancing in a personal sauna.

Sir Fred arrived for the final dress rehearsals before the first take. He was accorded, quite rightly, great respect and adulation by the film crew. Just the way a genius should be treated. He sat in his director's chair with his name written across the back of it and was presented with breakfast – boiled egg, toast and a cup of tea – on a silver tray, before he started work. We were all taken through our paces before he arrived by Alexander Grant, who was Sir Fred's assistant during the filming. Alexander was also acting as a sort of 'gofer' between Sir Fred and the director, Reginald Mills. He had experience of dance in film, through assisting on the film, *The Red Shoes* and the recording of the ballet of *Romeo and Juliet*.

We discovered that the costumes created a problem for Sir Fred's choreography. Many of the moves were not possible in the restricting confines of the animal costumes, and so every step was emphasized and exaggerated. Sir Fred was often called on to provide some instant choreography. I was delighted when it came to the part in Squirrel Nutkin's story where he lost his tail – even if Nutkin wasn't. And because of these tails, we were unable to sit down while waiting between the takes. We had to stand up and lean against two planks of wood, with the tail wedged in a space between. Alexander Grant was playing Pigling Bland, and he not only had his costume to contend with, but was required to dance on his toes on piggy points. Jeremy Fisher, aka Michael Coleman, had to dance on wet floors and lily pads. We all had our eyeholes sprayed with matt paint so they would not reflect the bright lighting or the camera lens. Some of the girls cried from sore and bleeding feet. Jemima Puddleduck's costume, for instance, was made in such a way that Ann Howard had to do all her solos doubled up, with her chin almost resting on her knees. Physically it was a very taxing time.

Behind the scenery a grey cloth hung the whole length of the set. In front of this, among the painted cardboard hollyhocks, lily pads and bushes, were planted real trees and branches. Others hung on chains to look like branches. The dance floor was sand, real turf, leaves and bushes. The grey backcloth was a front projection screen made up of hundreds of thousands of tiny beads, on which were projected coloured slides of the Lake District.

At 10 A.M. we were ready for our first take, after rehearsing with the cameras. The final crimping of our costumes was done by the wardrobe mistress. The necks of our coat jackets were pulled up and pinned to disguise the join of the head to the body. No human feature, such as an Adam's apple, was to be seen. And we were ready for 'Action', except that 'Action', as the normal word for go in the film world, was never spoken. Because we were dancing to pre-recorded tape, the word 'Playback' was used instead. Doesn't quite have the same tone.

The soundtrack proved a major problem. The music had to be cued up a few seconds before our entrance – this was the pre-digital age – and sometimes we would finish half-way through a phrase, and finding the place to continue on the tape proved to be painstakingly slow. Some of the music contained repeats and it was sometimes easier to go back to the beginning of the piece and let it play through to the right moment, rather than start filming and then discover it was the wrong repeat.

Then 'Cut' would be called half-way through a solo. It was invariably in the middle of a leap and it would happen because the lights had fused, or I'd slipped on the artistic leaves, or jumped out of shot. The cameras were locked off because of the front projection and we had to dance within the small confines of the lens.

To arrive at the correct proportions between squirrel and tree, huge branches were constructed twenty feet above the ground. I was, possibly for the only time in my life, being made smaller, rather than (if it were ever possible) trying to look taller. One of my solos took place on one of the highest branches. I regarded it with a jaundiced eye. I was not able to see; I suffered from vertigo; I was going to dance on a four foot ledge, a branch miles in the air ; I was in a twenty-pound costume which had a tail twice my size. Not exactly my idea of fun. And no danger money either. (I will admit I did not ask for any – as I did some years later, but that is another story – I simply muttered under my breath. Nutkinskaya in a grumble.) I was to do triple pirouettes, leaping from branch to branch and gradually spiralling down the tree trunk. It took hours of take after take, trying to get the camera to follow me at the same speed that I was jumping. This meant, also, that I had to land in exactly the same position every time, which proved well nigh impossible. Somehow we managed to get to the end of the sequence. Tempers were frayed. I half thought about emulating the Rudolf Nureyev method of frustration, bashing and taking out my ragged edges on Squirrel Nutkin's tail. But I didn't. I had too much respect for Sir Fred.

The next morning I went to see the rushes. After all that work it was decided that the colour of the scenery was too lustrous and vivid to reflect Beatrix Potter's pale watercolours and so the continuity with the rest of the film would be broken. I was – annoyed. All that effort, energy, arduous repetition, all that striving for perfection, had to be re-adapted by Sir Fred to floor level. Squirrel Nutkin's flight from branch to branch ended on the cutting-room floor.

Filming the Two Bad Mice was much more fun. I was dancing with Lesley Collier and Sir Fred allowed us the freedom to improvise in the mischievous parts. I could clown around with impunity – for once. I fell down the stairs of the dolls' house, my bum bouncing on every beat, we smashed plates and crockery, we tore a huge eiderdown to pieces and allowed the feathers to cascade and drift in a blizzard – we wrecked the set. It gives me satisfaction even now. This was the only scene in the film which contained a real animal: a cat, which peered through a mouse-hole at the beginning of the sequence. I was pleased that the cat took as many takes as we did to get it right.

Our long mouse tails were pinned up out of the way with pink ribbons for the mime parts. But for the dance, Sir Fred insisted on incorporating them into the choreography. We used them to make shapes by holding them in different ways. At the beginning of the film, dancing in the hallway, the mice circle in and around, holding each other's tails to create patterns in the waltz. My solo as Tom Thumb was based on a traditional hornpipe of the time and my duet with Lesley was a polka, which was always the dance of potential riot.

Performances at Covent Garden carried on during the filming. Sometimes a day's filming would take so long that there was only just enough time to make it back for warm-up or maybe to grab a sandwich before 7.30 curtain-up. We often slept in the back of the car taking us from Elstree to the Garden. It was necessary. Our days, with filming and dancing, were long: as much as nineteen or twenty hours sometimes, and we needed to keep up our strength. But it was fun and worth every iota of exhaustion. In those days, when there was some sort of film industry in Britain, we had a great time sneaking on to other sets on the lot to watch, say, Frankie Howerd filming Up Pompeii, or maybe to catch a glimpse of Michael Caine in the canteen in our lunchbreak. Our set, too, was inundated with guests, not least because John Brabourne, the executive producer, is second cousin to the Queen. So we had visitors such as Princess Anne, Lord Mountbatten and Prince Charles – who unfortunately witnessed my bad-tempered fit over the uncomfortable costume and my struggles to get the head off. He engaged me and the other dancers in polite chit-chat: 'Is it true that dancers have to soak their feet in methylated spirits?'

The Tales of Beatrix Potter was filmed towards the end of 1970 and released on 1 April 1971, with a Royal Première attended by the Queen and Princess Anne. In the line-up before going into the auditorium we were all presented – a row of very small dancers equalling the height of Her Majesty, but not that of Princess Anne. I asked her what her favourite part in the film was. 'I haven't seen it yet,' she said with some surprise. I had really meant to ask which was her favourite Beatrix Potter character, but somehow it came out wrong. Ole bigmouth has to say something . . .

The film was a great success here and overseas. My own criticism of the film is that it was too long. To go out as a feature film it had to be longer than an hour, so fifteen minutes of dance was added to pad it out. Thank heavens for Sir Fred's amazing ability to add instant choreography.

Ossie Clark, whose real name was Raymond, told his mother to go and see the *Tales*, when it came to Manchester, because a friend of his was in it – playing a squirrel. She took a friend with her and as the opening credits rolled up, she fell asleep. She woke just in time to see Squirrel Nutkin run off at the end of the number. She stood up, pointed her finger at the screen and shouted, 'Ee, Doris, our Raymond knows that squirrel!'

Some time later, Richard Goodwin, the producer of *The Tales of Beatrix Potter*, called me in to choreograph tango sequences for the leading players in *Death on the Nile*: Angela Lansbury with David Niven, Peter Ustinov with Olivia Hussey, Simon McCorkindale with Lois Chiles. Bette Davis sat this one out. I waited in an unused studio for the occasional arrival, between takes, of my pupils. The only one who never showed was David Niven. After a few rehearsals in which I partnered Angela, she asked me whether David was ever going to come. I was sent to summon him. He said, 'Why do I have to come? I'm not supposed to be able to do it very well anyway.'

'Well, you've got to know Miss Lansbury's moves, or she might trip you up. You're not nervous are you?'

'Yes, dear boy.'

'But you've done hundreds of movies.'

'Yes,' he said, 'and each one gets worse.'

I discovered his mind was on other things – his daughter had been injured in an accident and he was commuting between London and Switzerland. He finally came to rehearsal and, needless to say, he was perfect on the day of the shoot. A gentle man and a gentleman.

Everybody arrived on the ballroom set and Bette Davis, who was not dancing in the scene, upstaged everybody by doing an impromptu can-can, then saying, 'Now follow that!'

SIX

CHANGES

I WAS SORRY TO see Sir Fred retire as Director of the Royal Ballet Company. He was a very gentle, nervous man and smoked like a chimney. On both hands he had one broken fourth finger which he refused to have rebroken and straightened – he hated hospitals. He had a supreme confidence which allowed him to admit when he was stuck for an idea while choreographing, and this made all of us bend over backwards to help him. By the time I started working with him he choreographed from a chair, from which he would rise only to demonstrate the use of arms, face or head or to do his famous impersonations of the two women who inspired him to become a dancer: Isadora Duncan and Anna Pavlova. From this chair he would suggest steps which we would try out for hours on end. Some dancers say that they actually choreographed his work for him. That is a ridiculous idea. He had such a sharp eye that he was able to eliminate the rubbish and keep only the essential and original movements. He loved expressive faces, which tallied with the great sense of humour that showed in his work. He was one of the few choreographers that could make comedy work. Being able to move between comedy and tragedy is very rare, a mark of genius.

Sir Fred was the most versatile choreographer I have ever worked with. He loved his pieces to tell a story and to get to the point. There were never any longueurs in his ballets. You would often find him in the crush bar, glass of champagne in one hand, fag in the other, sitting out half a ballet because it was so tedious. Everybody loved Sir Fred. He was never rude and never had grumpy moods. A gentleman of the old school.

He was given a tremendous send-off at the Royal Opera House on 24 July 1970. There was a gala in which the company danced pieces from over thirty ballets Sir Fred had created, including *Symphonic Variations*. The evening was compèred by Sir Robert Helpmann. Some retired dancers came back to perform, dancing various works which had been originally created for them. Dame Margot Fonteyn and Michael Somes danced the finale from *Daphnis and Chloë*, Rudolf offered his Poet in *Apparitions*, Vergie Derman and Donald MacLeary danced the Lovers' Duet from *The Wanderer* – to mention only a few. Sir Fred's final entry on to the stage to take the standing ovation from his loyal and loving public was most touching. There is nothing quite like applause that is prolonged with love. It slices open the hardest heart and there were many surreptitious, and open, tears. Oh, I was sorry to see him go. Sir Fred had been so kind and generous to me. He had given me more roles than someone of my age and experience could expect in the natural course of things. As we paid him the adulation he deserved, the inchoate realization that my career with the Royal Ballet might not be quite as easy in the future began to float through my mind. I would miss Sir Fred in more ways than one.

Kenneth MacMillan and John Field replaced Ashton as co-directors. MacMillan trained at the Royal Ballet School and very early on in his career with the company showed a distinctive originality in his choreography. He established a reputation for his dramatic insight into the darker, more traumatic experiences affecting the psychology of the human mind and was able to interpret, through movement in dance, the inner turmoil and emotional conflict in relationships. *The Invitation* was the first ballet to come close to being confined to an adult-only audience.

MacMillan's interpretation of Mahler's *Das Lied von der Erde* as a one-act ballet enhanced his reputation as a choreographer. The fluid coupling of beauty of movement with the dramatic content of the poems demonstrated his exceptional ability in this field. His ballets usually carried strong storylines, but his abstract ballets were sheer poetry, just movement to music, always containing new and original moves. These showed his lighter side, his lyrical invention, exemplified by the two ballets *Concerto* and *Solitaire*.

But his most famous work prior to his becoming director of the Royal Ballet was his *Romeo and Juliet*, in the early sixties. This he mounted on Lynn Seymour and Christopher Gable, but they were edged out on the first night when Fonteyn and Nureyev were called upon. On the first night in New York this remarkable couple made it into the *Guinness Book of Records* for the highest number of curtain calls. They received thirty-six. It has never been beaten.

Before Kenneth MacMillan left to become director for the Berlin Opera Ballet in 1966, he was resident choreographer for the Royal Ballet, in conjunction with Sir Fred, for some years. This was before I came into the company so I missed these particularly golden years. These two great choreographers complemented each other with their differing styles, and the combination – plus the one or two Balanchine ballets in the repertoire – meant that the artists of the company were given a versatility second to none. And it wasn't only the principals who were well served. The *corps* had a precision that was enviable, thanks to the drilling of Michael Somes. This showed in a stupendous Nureyev production of *La Bayadère*, when the *corps* was given some choreography which would challenge the stamina of the best of us. They were required to descend a long ramp, in single file, each girl doing an arabesque (standing on one leg, one arm extended in front, the other behind), a couple of small steps then another arabesque, holding it and descending, one after the other. The lead girl would have to do this movement more than sixty times. It was one of the few occasions when the *corps de ballet* received its own ovation. I'm not surprised. It was thrilling to watch, so simple yet so demanding. The Royal Ballet Company had an unrivalled reputation.

John Field joined Kenneth MacMillan as administrative director in September 1970 (MacMillan was artistic director). John had been associate director of the Touring Royal Ballet – unfairly known in those days as the Number Two Company – whose mission it was to go out into the cities and towns of the British Isles to bring the word of ballet to what we then called the Provinces. I was in the resident company, stationed at Covent Garden, and touring abroad. We felt we were the cream of the ballet establishment. I can't say that we looked down on the touring company, that would be unfair, but we did feel we had an edge. It was Dame Ninette de Valois who established, in her wisdom, the school which fed the Royal Ballet, and the resident company usually had the pick of the pupils. But sometimes potential stars from the school would be plucked for the touring company and given immediate solo roles. The touring company had weekly runs wherever there was a theatre large enough to take sixty dancers, plus a pit big enough to accommodate a forty-piece orchestra, and so performed more often than the resident company which alternated with the Royal Opera on a weekly basis. The frequency of performance allowed these dancers to grow as artists and learn faster than those 'condemned' to the *corps* in the resident company. They could improve their technique and strength, not only the physical but also the mental strength required to perform under the spotlight and in front of up to 2,000 people. Graham Powell and David Wall were picked for the touring ballet, thus bypassing the *corps*. So, in reality, the members of the touring company gained in places we couldn't. This was all about to change.

At the beginning of the MacMillan/Field era, the touring and resident companies became one. The idea was that a much smaller touring group would be chosen from the amalgamated company to travel and perform new works, using young choreographers. This group eventually became known as the New Group. This merger produced a behemoth of a company at Covent Garden of over one hundred dancers, at least fifty too many. So half the artists had to be sifted and sacked. This was a nerve-racking time for all of us, although the boys were marginally safer than the girls.

John Field had allegiance to his dancers from the touring company; Kenneth MacMillan an affinity with those dancers he knew before Berlin, including Lynn Seymour and Vergie Derman, who not only followed him there but also came back with him. But there were some of us who did not fit into either camp. Although we were not sacked, we did find ourselves marginalized, out on a limb, working but redundant. A direct (and unlikeable) experience of a new broom sweeping clean. This proverb in action went on throughout the first year. Some dancers decided to resign. There was no difficulty in ex-Royal Ballet trained dancers obtaining work elsewhere as dancers, teachers, choreographers or directors, such was the cachet of de Valois's creation.

During this new season, 1970–71, I started to choreograph my own ballets. Leslie Edwards, who had been with the company since the mid-thirties (and only stopped dancing two or three years ago), formed a choreographic group to allow young dancers to experiment and invent new ballets. At the end of the year they were allowed to mount their works on stage at the Collegiate Theatre of London University, when directors and ballet-masters would come to see the pieces. If you were good there was just a possibility that you might be asked to produce a work for a professional company. These days there is the Frederick Ashton Award, which allows the winner to develop fresh ideas.

My first ballet was set to music by the Steve Miller band. I wanted to bring popular music into the rigid formality of the classical dance world. I had a cast of five dancers: Alexander Grant, Lesley Collier, Marguerite Porter, Lois Strike and Jonathan Kelly. The piece started with foghorns to give atmosphere. Fog – through which the dancers were to emerge, *adagio*, during the opening – shrouded the stage. Very dramatic. Only I couldn't understand why the dancers looked so hesitant and unbalanced as they came forward even more slowly than I had requested. The smoke machine had leaked oil all over the floor and my dancers could hardly stand, never mind carry out my choreography.

And I was so eager to make a good impression on Kenneth MacMillan. We all were. I knew it was a disaster. Not even an explanatory announcement from Leslie Edwards helped. In the interval I felt pale and sick. Ninette de Valois gave me a few encouraging words – at least I think they were meant to cheer. 'Don't worry, Sleep,' she said. 'You'll be all right in variety.' I felt like Heinz's 58th at that moment. I felt awful. If a first attempt at choreography is a failure, it is very difficult for a dancer to be taken seriously afterwards. Or even to be given a second chance. It did not bode well for my next few years with the company under MacMillan's direction.

And indeed, the first season was full of disruptions and insecurities. My solo roles, apart from the ones created for me by Ashton, were shared out between John Field's favourites from the touring company. I seemed to be for ever going into the office and demanding them back – with the result that I would get one performance out of four for the season. It was a despairing time. Iris Law was a constant support for those of us from the original Resident Company, a stalwart. She spent a great deal of time mediating between the dancers and her new bosses. Every day it was necessary to make them aware of your existence; they forgot you too easily. Many dancers left for this reason. I have to say I resented the company at this point, but it was the policies, not the people, that were so upsetting. And I should admit that it had been easy for me up to that point. I had been flavour of the month for a very long time, and now my face fitted less well. I did not care for the strange loss of status. But I had been with the company for only three years, so I thought it best for my career to hang on for a while and see what would happen.

There were, during this first year of near turmoil, some high points. Thank heavens. Jerome Robbins (who choreographed with Balanchine and on Broadway) accepted an invitation to come over from the New York City Ballet to recreate one of his best ballets, *Dances at a Gathering*, which is set to Chopin's piano works. Rehearsals for this ballet were like auditions. Every morning Jerry sat and scrutinized the dancers. Afterwards we rushed down to the notice-board to see who had been struck off – or added. Those still on the list rushed back to the rehearsal room to learn extracts from the ballet. But even this was uncertain, as he never let you know what he thought acceptable in answer to his demands. His face was an expressionless mask. It disconcerted all of us. It demoralized us too, making us feel like children, not knowing whether we were doing right or not, whether we might succeed or fail. And Jerry was changing the cast right up until the dress rehearsal. He was famous for not giving any warnings as to whether you were going to be in or out. There is a tale, probably apocryphal, that during the rehearsals for *West Side Story*, which he choreographed and directed, he would call the cast on stage for notes. At one of these sessions he was talking and talking and walking backwards – until he fell into the orchestra pit and broke his arm. The cast must have noticed him getting closer and closer to the edge. No one said a thing.

With *Dances* I was lucky enough to get through to the Finals, as we called it, but on the final stretch Nureyev joined the company and I was put out to grass as his understudy. Ah well.

A couple of years later however, I did dance in two or three performances of Robbins's beautiful ballet. He came over to rehearsals for a remounting of *Dances* for the 1973 Coliseum season. Yet again I had sprained my ankle – I was still recovering and so I was not dancing flat out while Jerry was going through the pieces with me. Suddenly his mood changed, his face lost its impassivity, the veins stood out and he yelled at me, 'Do you want to be in this piece?' I was shocked by this change in temper and retorted (with my own inimitable petulance), 'Don't have to be.' This was greeted with complete and frozen silence from everyone in the room. Then Anthony Dowell, who was my partner for this piece and who hated any kind of scene, grabbed hold of me and guided me through the next steps – as if nothing had happened. I found out later that Jerry had not known about my ankle and assumed that I was just fooling around. A perfectionist but, like so many truly gifted people, difficult.

In 1975 Jerry returned to Covent Garden to remount one of his ballets, *The Concert*, a witty account of an audience listening to a piano concerto. It is hilarious and full of insight, and shows his real genius for staging and humour in choreography.

Once again I was up for one of the parts. I thought I was doing rather well, as he had already picked me out in New York to rehearse with him before he came to London. After one rehearsal I told him that I was unable to attend the next because I had promised, some months before, to give a talk about my career to the Friends of Covent Garden. His reaction was blunt: 'Well, if you can't come to this, don't come to the next.' So I didn't. And I have never performed in this ballet. He was an exacting master.

Every time there was a cast change the company office had to contact Jerry in New York and ask his permission. But sometimes getting Jerry's approval would be impossible; for instance, if a dancer was injured and had to be replaced at short notice. I can understand this from the choreographer's point of view. You have a deep concern about who is to dance your work. A role created for someone particular could be ruined, or at the very least make no sense, if it is danced by someone unsuited in a technical, physical or even mental way. But it is equally understandable from the company's point of view – it has to survive, and sometimes that does entail putting dancers into roles for which they are not entirely suited.

Apart from the excitement of Jerome Robbins during that season, I was inordinately grateful for my life outside the company in this very frustrating year. For one of my birthdays, I decided to take George out to lunch and went to the Royal Bank of Scotland, opposite Bertram Rota, the booksellers in Savile Row, to cash a $100 bill. The cashier refused the transaction. Well. I was wearing jeans, a leather waistcoat, beads and long hair. George had to come to my rescue, impeccably dressed as he always was – in a suit and hand-made, hand-tied bow tie. High on my list of resentments is the way people judge from outside appearances, particularly when jeans and a sweater might outvalue a suit. It was then, and still is, a ridiculous dress code. And George, with the exterior of perfection that he has, hides a personality of supreme devilry. To look at him you'd think butter would never melt, but he has the wickedest sense of humour, a great joy of life and the fun of the Trickster. Dry as dust? You only have to look at his eyes. Mayhem lurks.

After lunch I went with George to Cartier, where my neck was measured for a gold chain he had specially designed with a gold ball which fitted neatly into the groove under my Adam's apple. At first the salesman kept referring to me as madam. I have always assumed it was because of my long hair. George also ordered a chain for himself. I think he still has it. Mine is now lost. He once gave me a dozen watches for Christmas – by my birthday in July they were all gone.

I was now meeting all George's friends. One was Lady Henrietta Guinness, who lived in Eaton Mews West. We often went there for a good bottle of claret and a sumptuous meal, or to a restaurant which she owned and ran, the Louis d'Or. Unfortunately she was racked with instability. A car accident, years before, had left her with recurrent bouts of hypermania. I was a witness to one of her attacks. We arrived at her house to find her dousing the carpet with a watering can. She was particularly anxious that we move the fridge so she might dampen the area underneath. It was necessary, she explained, to do this to keep the electricity down. It probably worked, for her. We helped her to pack (including her green telephone) for a stay in a hospital in Muswell Hill. She was due to go into what she called the ball and chain department. We would visit her there. Once we found her standing on her head. George asked why. She replied, as if we were manifest fools, 'To get the change out of my pockets, of course.' In time her attacks became less frequent, thank heavens, and she eventually married an Italian chef and went to live in Italy, where they had a baby daughter.

Another friend was Jane Kasmin. That summer she drove us, in her Mini, to Carrenac in the Dordogne, where her ex-husband, John (David Hockney's agent), rented a château. Behind the Mini there was a convoy of cars transporting other guests. The journey took about three days.

The first night we stopped in Avranches, overlooking the monastery of St Michel. After a certain amount of local wine we started to dance around in the gardens of our small hotel. I was always being asked to perform, particularly when there was music playing. George, not to be left out, performed his own party trick: executing forward rolls along the edge of the lawn. As it was dark, he did not notice an insidious rock waiting for him in the grass, and he broke his nose. He came to me for sympathy, but as he bled all over my new Ossie Clark shirt, I wanted to punch him on his newly damaged nose. Ever sympathetic, me. When we moved on the next day George crammed himself into the back of the Mini, using alcohol to numb the pain. (And the self-pity.)

The château was just a few minutes from the Dordogne river, where we bathed every day. It had enormous bedrooms and I waged a constant nightly war with the ever-present mosquitoes – a creature for which I have never abated my dislike – to the extent that the walls looked like a blood-strewn insect field of battle. But that was the only downside of the holiday (except, maybe, George's nose).

Dinners were held every night, Cordon Bleu events prepared by another guest, Terence Conran, and John Kasmin, known to us as Kas. I always got the washing up – cooking was not my strong point and this was the only useful contribution I could make. These dinners were very precious to me and I remember that one evening, Mo McDermott (David Hockney's assistant), Peter Schlesinger, Ossie Clark and I were hard put not to laugh at Kas. He had got himself into a fearful state because the jelly had not set on his *boeuf à la mode en gelée*. He didn't blame himself. It was due to the change in pressure induced by a thunderstorm that night. The guests were an odd mix of the *boeuf à la mode* type and us, the frivolous.

David Hockney decided to take Mo, George and me on a day trip to take the waters at Vichy. We went in his open-topped red Triumph. David is always in a hurry, always impatient, waiting for people, always wants to get from A to B as fast as possible. He drove very fast along the twisting mountain roads, and never seemed to look where he was going. We were all scared to death. We tried to remain sanguine by deciding that he had a very quick eye, which is what allows him to paint such accurate reflections of ripples on water. Any excuse to calm our fearful breasts.

We stayed at the luxurious Pavillon Sévigny (Madam's old place). When you arrive at the spa itself you are given your own glass cup in a string bag. Ladies in nurses' uniforms ladle the water from the spring into your cup – and you then drink it. The sulphur content made a loo immediately necessary. It is very good for the system but the stink of rotten eggs can be hard to take. At dinner that evening I noticed that the majority of the guests looked half dead. So much for the water, I thought. But it was probably the smell.

David took many photographs of the spa and its surroundings. One of them was used as the subject for a six-foot acrylic painting called *Le Parc des Sources, Vichy*, with Ossie Clark and Peter Schlesinger sitting on chairs in the foreground. David went nowhere without his camera at this time; he was a fanatical photographer, recording moments from these tours, moments which often ended up as painting or etchings.

Events seemed to fold one into another on this holiday. It was such a peaceful, languid time, so different from the rest of the year. We went once to St Émilion for a gourmet lunch and loaded the cars with crates of wine from the vineyards. We returned to the château to witness, from the turrets, a tremendous electrical storm, which swept the Dordogne valley with eerie and illuminated landscapes.

Sammy Hodgkin, Howard Hodgkin's son, arrived at the château and I took him under my wing. He was only ten years old and was feeling a little lost because his parents were not arriving until later in the week. I have always enjoyed the company of children, being still a bit of a child myself. I had met Howard Hodgkin, the painter, and Julia (who is a wonderful cook and now has a flower stall outside Bibendum in the Fulham Road) when they invited George and me to stay at their mill near Bath. I am not really a fan of country living. There is a strange self-satisfaction about country-dwellers, an assumption that their life is better, to be devoutly wished for. I'm not saying that town people don't have their own form of manic self-satisfaction, just that it is different, and I happen to understand the city and its inhabitants. For me, the country and its ways verge on the incomprehensible. I find it odd that there they are, surrounded by food – OK it's in its raw form – but so many of them are really stingy and expect you to do with a small potato and a couple of strands of cabbage to enhance your one, possibly delicious, slice of meat. Fortunately, it was not at all like that at the Hodgkins'. Happy though I am to go and visit friends, it isn't long before I wish to up sticks and get back to the dynamism of the city. It is also something about the structure of life in the country, it is more ordered, less spontaneous, less loose than life in town.

It was at the Hodgkins' that I met Bruce Chatwin. I was utterly out of my depth listening to these two talk about paintings, books and Bruce's travels abroad. I found Bruce single-minded and ambitious, and this made him appear arrogant – at least to me. Neither was the slightest bit interested in ballet, although Howard did make the effort to come with Julia to see me dance at the Bristol Hippodrome. Ironic, really, that years later he designed for the Ballet Rambert. Maybe he enjoyed it more than he thought. Howard painted our portrait – a *triple* portrait – entitled 'Lawson, Underwood and Sleep', which sounded like a firm of solicitors. Nicholas Underwood was George's friend. Howard had seen us all sleeping in the back of a Citroën estate car after Paul Levy's wedding party near Oxford. I think this remarkable picture is now in America.

Bruce subsequently invited George and me to stay at his house in Gloucestershire. His wife kept her pet sheep tethered to the front door on a rope. She professed herself to be inordinately fond of it, and yet she seemed almost to run it over every time she arrived in her car. Country people have a different sort of eccentricity, too. The house had just been treated to get rid of the death-watch beetles, which fell noisily from the beams about our ears. I had wondered why the bed was covered in a thick transparent sheet. George secretly telephoned the Hodgkins, who appeared, angels of mercy, with baskets of food. I had been considering deep-frying the beetles. Lots of protein, apparently.

Beetles and other discomforts of country houses notwithstanding, this was a far cry from tin baths and camping holidays. My family was seeing less and less of me. I was not even aware of my neglect. I didn't write home, and because we had never had a telephone at home I was not in the habit of phoning home to mother. Some years later, when my relationship with my mother was a bit fraught, a friend pointed out that it was up to me to make contact with her at least once a week. As soon as I did so, our relationship improved. All she needed was 'Hello, Mum.'

And because we never had a phone, my family was accustomed to drop in on each other without notice. And would drop in on me in London. 'Hi, do you mind? We've come to stay for a few days.' Never mind the possible inconvenience. But I would have to bite my tongue and try not to appear selfish. I'm loyal to my family. But a bit of a warning would have been more convenient. My life was changing so much, everything was happening so fast, and the dual effect of this was that my family could not keep up with the different pace of my lifestyle and I did not realize how insensitive I was being. There were new people in my life, lunches, dinners, parties, trips abroad. Instead of summers at home with family, I was in another world, gallivanting round Europe and worrying about life at the Royal Ballet.

The Royal Ballet was going through some changes. I felt that both the style and the content for which the company was so famous was, well, in metamorphosis. I was not certain it was for the better. Kenneth MacMillan adored long-limbed lithe dancers. And the whole ethos of the company was on the move, as MacMillan and John Field tried to drag the company into modern times. Booing was heard for the first time at the Garden. The modernization came too soon.

Audiences throughout the country, particularly in places rarely touched by ballet, like to see the favourites, the full-length ballets, *Romeo and Juliet*, *Sleeping Beauty*, *Swan Lake*, that sort of thing – something old and classical, with a storyline that can be followed. A big ballet will always fill the house, three small ballets on a triple bill won't. It is simply a fact of dancing life. The New Group, the small touring company of twenty-two dancers, was going to large venues with small pieces, more suitable for intimate theatre. Not only that, the pieces were unrelentingly modern. The first tour included a new Glen Tetley ballet, *Field Figures*, set to very abstract music, in conjunction with two other short ballets, one of which was called *Apollo*. Although the dancing, the work, was good, it was not popular with audiences, who were used to a full company dancing the classics. People stayed away in droves.

John Field and Kenneth MacMillan had differences of opinion. After six months Field left and Peter Wright, who had collaborated with Sir Fred on a previous *Sleeping Beauty*, was brought in as Associate Director. He re-established a smaller version of the original touring company to present the popular ballets. They were still triple bills, but far more traditional, and therefore infinitely more acceptable to our audiences. As I was not being given many roles to dance at Covent Garden, I was included on this new tour and given plenty of opportunities to perform: the Blue Boy in *Les Patineurs*, which had been my graduation piece, and which was by now my trade mark, the Pot Boy in Cranko's *Pineapple Poll*, with music by W.S. Gilbert, and working in Dame Ninette de Valois's dramatic ballet, *The Rake's Progress*, against sets lifted straight from Hogarth's etchings. A new ballet was also created for us by Joe Layton.

Joe was a director and choreographer in America and on Broadway, with such credits to his name as *The Sound of Music*, *Annie* and *Barnum*. His idea for the ballet was to take the music of Noël Coward, use the setting of a cruise ship and call it *The Grand Tour*. The passengers on board this liner were Douglas Fairbanks (Paul Clarke), Mary Pickford (Doreen Wells), Alice B. Toklas (Jeanetta Laurence), Gertrude Stein (who was played by a man, Nicholas Johnson), Theda Bara, the mysterious goddess of silent movies (Sheila Humphreys) and, of course, Gertrude Lawrence (Deirdre O'Connor) and Noël Coward (played by Gary Sherwood). A terrific line-up.

Joe did not want pirouettes, jumps and double tours (double turns in the air). Instead of using the body as a whole, forming line and length as we were used to do, he liked to isolate parts of the body from each other, and have them work, not in unison, but separately yet together. Not unlike patting the top of your head with one hand and drawing circles on your stomach with the other. The smallest twitch of a shoulder takes on significant meaning in this way. Most of the dancers found it difficult to pick up, as they had never been to a jazz dance class. We were used to grand gestures, and this minimalist style was a new experience. It was, at that time, an entirely different attitude to dance, and had not been seen much in this country. Now, we are used to it, and it seems as normal as any other type of dance. But then? It seemed pretty odd to us. But we persevered – not least because of the characters and the story. Even if it was full of American sentiment.

The tale was based on a buffoon of an elderly tourist, danced by Vivyan

Lorraine, who was forever taking pictures of all the celebrities on board. She was shunned by these famous people and was made to feel like an outcast. Only the steward (Stephen Jefferies) befriended her. The climax of the piece was very poignant when the steward took her arm, led her to the centre of the floor and danced with her in front of all those Hollywood stars.

Brenda Last and I were two stowaways hiding in trunks on the ship. When the coast was clear we emerged to tear the heart out of a Neapolitan tarantella. This dance was sheer bravado, and Brenda and I matched each other perfectly in height, speed and gusto. Thinking about it now, though, I would like to have been a famous character, not just a stowaway. Charlie Chaplin, for instance, might have been there – who knows. But the tarantella was a cracking dance.

Although the dancing was relatively modern, the music by Coward was very accessible, and the storyline was straightforward. It was not that popular with the critics, however, even though it was received with great enthusiasm by the paying public.

Another ballet Joe Layton created for us on that tour was *Overture*, a ten-minute piece set to the overture from *Candide* by Leonard Bernstein. It was designed to introduce the ballets to be performed that evening. My costume had huge sleeves in which a fifteen-foot piece of silk was stored. This was extracted elegantly by other dancers to reveal the name of one of the ballets. This ballet had some good ideas, but was not really necessary and lasted only ten performances.

At Sadler's Wells, Noël Coward himself came to see a performance of *Grand Tour* and the cast were taken into the stalls to meet him. As I was not then a principal dancer with the company, even though performing leading roles, the PR lady did not bother to introduce me to him. I was within touching distance, but in spite of my extrovert nature both on and off the stage, I had, in fact, been brought up to be well-mannered and never to push myself forward. I certainly did not want to appear pushy. I don't know whether this reticence is due to some sort of inferiority complex or whether this holding back is simply due to having watched other grabbing go-getters forge their way through a crowd and hog the limelight for themselves. I don't want to look like them. So I never did meet the great man.

This little episode taught me that one should take opportunities wherever they are found. Even so, I failed another time too. On tour in America, a friend was going to see Judy Garland, who was staying at the Plaza with her daughter, Lorna Luft. I just could not bring myself to go too. It is a very odd tug of war that goes on inside you. Anyway, missing Judy Garland finally did it for me. I swore it would not happen again, that next time I would grasp these nettles with a brave hand. When Shirley Maclaine performed her concert at the Dominion, I was ushered into her dressing-room with loads of other people and watched her for forty minutes while she took the time to talk and meet all her guests individually. I was standing with the actor Anthony Andrews and Johnny Gold, the owner of Tramp nightclub. I was nervous and asked them if they knew her. That way they could introduce me. But they didn't. I was thinking, 'Leave, she doesn't know you, you're intruding on her privacy.' But when I did introduce myself at last, she gave me a huge hug and held me to her bosom in a long embrace and asked me what work I was embarking on. To my astonishment she knew all about me. Since then I have never failed to grasp nettles.

The tour with the Royal Ballet touring group lasted twelve weeks and was my first experience of touring around England. I had been spoilt by my experiences of touring in America and found that some of our cities and towns bore unfavourable comparison with places like Chicago, Washington, Houston or St Louis. The country seemed so run-down. We had to find our own digs. Once I ended up in a caravan at the bottom of a theatrical landlady's garden and started to take sleeping pills because of the discomfort and the tiredness. Alcohol and Mandrax can cause something of a high, I discovered, particularly on the Saturday-night milk train back to London, which always became a party venue. Paul Clarke and I, along with a fellow called Flo, always had some fun and riot on that train. Flo's real name was David Gordon. He was not only the ballet-master of this little company, he was also an exceptionally funny man. He was brilliant at keeping our spirits up. Nothing seemed too hard when he was around to make light of things. He became the Director of the Cork Ballet Company.

Touring did for me what I had seen it do for others. No, not total collapse into a state of hazed exhaustion. The opposite. Performing every night strengthened and improved my technique and stamina and I returned to the fine tuning I had experienced as a student. We ended the tour with a two-week season at Sadlers Wells in London. Peter Wright, with his understanding of what the public prefers and his more traditional approach, helped reaffirm the touring Royal Ballet's success and put it back on the map after the publicly disastrous splinter group.

After the tour George and I took a holiday. John Kasmin introduced us to a man called Xavier Corberro. He, like Tony Richardson, owned a whole village, but his was in Spain on the outskirts of Barcelona, with the improbable name of Esplugas Llobbregat. The village contained many of its original inhabitants, and was still a normal village with its church in the central square, but Xavier had turned the rest of it into a colony of artists. Xavier's father had been Mayor of Barcelona, but in Spain as a whole the family was best known for refrigerators.

Xavier had an obsession for building underground tunnels. He liked to say it was a method of getting from one house to another without bumping into the village priest, with whom he did not get on. But really he just liked tunnels. His house was extraordinary. The seventeenth-century architecture on the outside gave no clue to the sculptured and modern interior. In the hallway, in the entrance, your first surprise was a glass floor through which you could see one of his tunnels. Everything was perfect and opulent, including Xavier and his English wife, Marianne. He was the epitome of how one imagines the Spanish aristocrat, the hidalgo, with the right sort of hook to his nose, and slick black hair. She was blonde with a matching English rose complexion. They complemented each other to perfection.

We stayed across the cobbled street in the guest quarters, with our own swimming-pool and sunken bath. Every night we frequented the Ramblas – a very long street in Barcelona lined with palm-trees, where it was fashionable to parade. This evening parade, known as the *paseo*, seems to be a peculiarly Spanish thing. Everyone shows off their finery, meets friends, gossips, winds down on the day. We invariably ended up just behind the Opera House, in the Bohemia Bodega, where retired opera-singers would perform in a cabaret, singing the music of Verdi, Puccini and Wagner. It was faintly surreal, very funny but also rather sad. Some of the old singers took themselves seriously – failing to realize that they were being laughed at not laughed with. Looking back, the concept is more poignant than I, as a callow youth, thought then.

We drank coffee at the Ritz, where we used to see a man of extravagant appearance sitting at one of the tables. Eventually we found out who this was with his wax-curled moustache, eye-glass, large hat, flowing cloak and silver-topped black stick: none other than the legendary Salvador Dali, famed for his eccentricities (such as his leopard – or was it a cheetah?), his paintings of nightmare melting landscapes and his invention of the creature, Amanda Lear – from A-Man-Da-Li.

One evening I was taught to juggle oranges by Ignacio Medina Sidonia, another of Xavier and Marianne's guests. When we ran out of oranges, I juggled with coins. I examined one of the coins, out of curiosity, and found the image of a really ugly man. 'Gosh, this man's ugly,' I said, 'Who is it?'

My teacher looked at me. There was a slight glint in his eyes.

'It's my grandfather, King Alfonso XIII.' Sorry, Ignacio, but he was ugly.

While I was being taught the juggler's art, the sound of a drunken Hoffbrau House band playing Rimsky-Korsakov's *Hungarian Rhapsody* was warbling from the record player. It was a marriage of wonderful incongruity, and was to provide the inspiration for my next invention with the Choreographic Group. But before that came about there was more work to be done at the Opera House.

Kenneth MacMillan's first major work as Director was a full length version of *Anastasia*. A full-length ballet had not been done since Kenneth had created *Romeo and Juliet* ten years before, so this was quite an undertaking. Three-act ballets are few and far between, not least because of the expense. *Anastasia* had been a very successful one-act ballet in Berlin with Lynn Seymour in the title role, set to music by the Czech composer Bohuslav Martinu. It told the story of Anna Andersen's claim to be the daughter of Tsar Nicholas II, and her time in a clinic.

As a one-act ballet *Anastasia* was cleverly thought out and questioned the identity of the woman claiming to be Anastasia. Adding two preceding acts showed Anastasia in the court with her family. The supposition after seeing the first two acts was that Anna Andersen might well have been Anastasia. The first two acts were set to Tchaikovsky's first and third symphonies and contained a breathtakingly difficult *pas-de-deux*, danced to piano only, for Antoinette Sibley and Anthony Dowell. Antoinette played Mathilde Kchessinska, the prima ballerina and a favourite of the Tsar. She was famous for wearing real diamonds, sapphires and other jewels when performing. Barry Kay, who had originally designed the one-act ballet, created some glorious settings for the Russian palace and ball scenes. Kenneth interpreted the music of Tchaikovsky so well that it might almost have been specially composed for the ballet. But lengthening a successful ballet doesn't always work – on the lines of: you don't fix what ain't broke.

It was, however, a superb vehicle for one of the greatest dramatic dancers of the late twentieth century, Lynn Seymour. I remember being at a rehearsal when Kenneth asked her to bend her leg when it was held out horizontally to her body. She bent her knee, pointing her toes, obviously, to the floor. 'No, no, the other way,' he cried. It took some time to convince him that the knee joint did not allow her toes to point upwards towards the sky. Kenneth MacMillan always pushed people's bodies beyond their limits. He had such faith, such trust, in the abilities of his dancers that he believed they could make their bodies do anything. Even bend in the wrong direction.

I was given the frustratingly small part of Chief Revolutionary, leading the people to riot. There were only six dancers in this scene – the rest of the stage was taken up by out-of-work actors, as extras. Part of the scene showed the people being given food (in reality, currant buns) from a trolley. The extras were usually so starving that they would flatten me in their rush to get to the currant buns. Suddenly everything would stop as the sledges with the dying crossed the stage – and we had to cross ourselves. The Russian Orthodox Church crosses the heart from right to left. I could never remember the correct way. We were supposed to be so devout, and it was supposed to come naturally, and we invariably got it wrong. It was hard not to corpse. (Should I admit that I used to laugh my way through parts I did not care for?) But there wasn't much else to do. When the front cloth lifted, it revealed the Grand Ballroom, into which we all stormed, with Julie Wood, as Chief Revolutionary Woman, waving the Revolution's red flag. (Julie collected parrots. Her sitting-room was given over to cages. She had a particularly beastly bird, which always pecked. This was a white cockatoo, with a limp and a black moustache, called Hitler.)

Remembering the Revolutionary scene and the chaos on stage is fun now, but having to wait, then, for those few minutes of performance was unbearable for ever-active me. I began to take classes at the Dance Centre to combat my boredom.

The Dance Centre was in Floral Street, just a stone's throw away from the stage door of the Opera House. It was set up in the 1960s and was unique – the first of its kind. Before the Dance Centre opened dancers would have to travel all over London – taking a tap class in Camden, a ballet class south of the river and jazz in a pillared ballroom somewhere else. Most of our free time was spent commuting from one to the other. The Dance Centre, however, housed all the different styles under one roof, so you could spend the whole day in one space receiving tuition from teachers qualified in all realms of dance. The ballet teacher I went to there was Maria Fay, who was as frustrated as I was that my technique was not being put to serviceable use. Another teacher was Eileen Ward, who became resident teacher at the Royal Ballet School. I began to venture further afield, looking through the windows of the other studios, watching the aggressive and sexy style of jazz dancing. My first jazz teacher was Matt Mattox. He played one of the brothers in *Seven Brides for Seven Brothers* – the was the one who jumped backwards and forwards over his axe on a six-inch wood plank. He had been taught by Jack Cole, who invented the school of American jazz dance. When he was formulating his technique, Jack was influenced by the dancing he saw in India, where different parts of the body or limbs move independently, becoming known as isolation. The main thrust and strength is the torso and the ribcage. Jack Cole had worked with Marilyn Monroe on most of her films – she would not even walk down a staircase without Jack to choreograph it. Other Americans, such as Bob Fosse, Jerome Robbins and Michael Bennet, thrived in his wake.

Matt conducted his classes by beating a tabor, which is like a deep tambourine, but without the cymbally bits. He would walk round the class beating out the rhythms. He told me that I might, one day, make a good jazz dancer. There were other students with me who went on to be well-known names in their particular dance fields: Molly Molloy, who became the choreographer for Paradise Latin in Paris, and Jane Darling – perhaps the definitive jazz dancer – who eventually became my leading light in *Dash* and later in *Song and Dance*. Later I also went to the Place, which housed the London Contemporary Dance Theatre Company and School, for contemporary dance classes taken by cool Robert Cohan, a pupil and disciple of Martha Graham. The LCDT, founded by Bob Cohan, was one of the first contemporary dance companies in Britain. They set a terrifically high standard for anyone to follow.

While out shopping one day, George and I passed a window in Queensway. My eye was caught by several of what I thought were children's toy cars.

'I've gone off buying clothes, George, why don't you just buy me one of those?' So he did.

In fact, it was not a toy shop, but a car showroom. George bought this little two-seater blue car, a Fiat Gamine Vignale. It cost only £300 – and there were only 200 made. It was immediately christened Noddy and I persuaded George to drive us down (I don't drive) to Carrenac again for the summer, to join the

Left: Aged about one with my great grandfather (we all called him Grandad) and Whisky, the dog.

Below: Mum and Gran in 1953 with the Austin which later took us to Hartlepool.

Below: The 'Wayne swaps rugby for ballet' shot at Hartlepool which appeared in the *Daily Express* article when I had just won my scholarship to White Lodge, aged 13.

Above: Leaping at the Lodge. My second year at the Royal Ballet School.

Above: In my final year of the Lower School at White Lodge playing the Wolf opposite Jeanetta Laurence (née Bumpus) as Red Riding Hood in the Upper School's graduation performance of *The Sleeping Beauty* at the Theatre Royal, Drury Lane. I am wearing

Above: As Napoleon to Sir Frederick Ashton's Ugly Sister at the opening night of *Cinderella* at the Lincoln Centre in New York, spring 1967.

Left: At White Lodge (Lower School) in my final year with Pamela Scott, Ingrid Bolting, Antoinette Peloso, Eva Evdokimova, Fiona Fairrie, Alan Hooper, Graham Powell, Peter O'Brien, Peter Fairweather and others.

Left: With my mother and sister, Joanne, having a Christmas drink at home in Plymouth in 1969 (photo taken by my cousin, Diane).

Opposite: As Puck in Ashton's *The Dream* in the early 1970s.

Below: Another opening, another show. This time with David Hockney at the vernissage of his exhibition in 1971.

Below: The cast of Ashton's *Enigma Variations* in 1969 with the conductor, Sir Adrian Boult, and Michael Somes who rehearsed all Sir Fred's productions. I am in the front row with the walking stick.

Left: The *pas-de-trois* from Swan Lake, Act 1, in 1971.

Overleaf: Squirrel Nutkin from the 1971 film *The Tales of Beatrix Potter*.

Below: With George in Noddy in the Dordogne (photo taken by Jane Kasmin).

Opposite: Sir Anton Dolin and me (in four-inch platform heels) marching to protest at the Russian Embassy when the Panov dancers were not released from Russia.

Below: 'George Lawson and Wayne Sleep' – unfinished double portrait by David Hockney, 1972. George is playing his clavichord in our flat in Wigmore Place. We wanted to call the picture 'A flat', the note being played. David worked on it for over two years but was never satisfied.

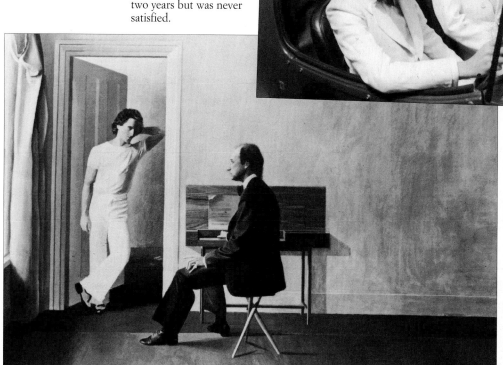

usual group of friends. I had forgotten, selfishly, that it was George's birthday the day we arrived, and I had not bought him a present. I turned to David Hockney for help.

He said, 'Ooh, don't worry, love. If you pose, I'll do a colour drawing of you and we can give that jointly to George.' It turned out to be one of the best drawings David has ever done. It was, in the end, only a head-and-shoulders portrait. This wasn't intentional, but by the time David got down to my knees we were very merry, and my legs were wandering all over the paper. So David made me legless, in more ways than one, for the gift. I presented it to George on a silver salver.

It wasn't the only unfinished portrait David did of me. In 1972 he decided to paint George and me together. He had an acrylic success with Ossie and Celia – life size – and decided to repeat it. With us. I was to stand in a doorway in white bell-bottomed trousers and white T-shirt, gazing at George playing the clavichord. Photographs were taken, Mo squared up the six-foot canvas and the project commenced. It all seemed to be going well. But around this time David and Peter started rowing. Eric Boman (a model who went on to become a photographer for *Vogue* and still lives with Peter) appeared on the scene. David went through the anguish of separation and the painting echoed his feelings. He became indecisive, repainting the background several times. He nearly had a breakdown – and the painting remains unfinished.

In Carrenac, George decided to give me driving lessons. This was a total failure. Being such good friends we can say what we like to each other. And did. George thought that my co-ordination in the dance would naturally apply to control of the car. A totally erroneous, misguided thought. I hadn't a clue, and have never felt so alien in trying to learn a physical technique. We ended up not talking to each other. Henrietta said that she would take over and took me out in Jane Kasmin's Mini.

She took me to a very narrow lane in the countryside and managed – a miracle – to teach me how to start and move forward. I was doing very well, I thought, until I saw, in the distance, some vehicle zooming towards us at speed. I panicked, turned the wheel in full lock (as I believe it's called) and ended up in the side of a hedge. Henrietta leaned over and applied the brake. It took another ten minutes for the tractor to reach us.

Henrietta decided not to give me any more lessons, so Hockney said he'd give it a try. I graduated to his BMW. At the top of a hill he got out and said, 'OK, you take over.' This car was automatic, which I assumed would make the whole thing easier. This little thought boosted my confidence as I sat behind that wheel at the top of the hill. When I set off, I found that an automatic makes no difference to the straightness of one's driving. If I veered to the left I was faced with mega-ton articulated lorries with horns to take your hair off, and if I veered to the right – well, there was a 200-foot drop. When I finally arrived at the bottom of the hill I vowed never to take driving lessons again.

Some days later I went with David and Mo on an overnight trip to Biarritz. Mo decided to read the map for the return journey, but made a terrible hash of it. David's patience was straining at the limits. Getting from A to B was of the greatest importance to him, he hated delays. I said, cocky confidence oozing from every pore, 'Give it to me, I'll take over.'

I thought that if I couldn't drive then at least I could map-read. We were getting on rather well, I thought, going at a cracking pace, when after about three hours David asked me, 'Wayne, does the sun set in the East or in the West?'

Dumb question, I thought.

'In the West, of course.' I'm nobody's fool.

'Then how come,' said David, 'the sun is setting in the East?'

What an idiot I felt. For three hours I had had the map upside down on my lap. For three hours I had taken us in quite the wrong direction. There was nothing for it but to turn round and go back to Biarritz, where we spent another night. David was unamused. Even the emollient offer of paying for the night fell on deaf ears. These days I don't map-read either.

Inspired by the Spanish juggling episode earlier in the year, I took a tape of the *Hungarian Rhapsody* on holiday with me, and a large tape-recorder. I listened to it over and over again, turning over ideas for the Choreographic Group. I must have bored the ears off the other guests with it. I decided that this new work would be based on a traditional Irish wake, so I called it *Awake*, by Wayne Sleep.

At a wake everybody gets drunk and dances around the body laid out in the coffin, to try and raise its spirit. The music of the Hoffbrau House band sounded enough out of tune and suitably quirky for this subject. In the rehearsals it was somewhat macabre to be dancing round a life-size coffin. In the piece, the coffin came on, supported by three girls and the Undertaker, played by Carl Myers, dressed in the traditional black top hat. He also carried a mug and a bottle of whisky. Carl started to flirt with the widow, Marguerite Porter (to whom he was married at the time), manoeuvring her body around the coffin and the stage, helping her to become more and more intoxicated as the band's playing also reached an advanced stage of befuddlement. To show the spirit rising from the body, thirty feet of tulle, connected by a wire, flew out of the coffin into the air.

The ballet was performed at the Collegiate Theatre. It was the first piece to show my love of humour within dance. So I was flattered that Leslie Edwards liked the humorous content enough to choose it as one of the numbers for the Friends' Christmas party later that year.

Although my roles at the Garden had diminished rather, I was given two new opportunities. One was by Peter Wright to work with Placido Domingo in the opera *Aida*. I was the Nubian slave. Somehow I misjudged my landing and ended up in bed with Amneris, played by Grace Bumbry. My size worked for me here, giving me the chance to perform another mischievous role. I painted my body dark brown with gold designs, based on the photograph of Nijinsky as the Golden Slave in *Scheherezade*.

The other opportunity came from Kenneth MacMillan. He had decided to mount a new *Sleeping Beauty* (yet another one) and, much to my surprise, choreographed a number that had not been in any other previous production, called Hop o' my Thumb, as a vehicle for me. I felt that Kenneth was beginning, perhaps, to recognize my worth. I sprained my ankle severely during rehearsals and chipped a piece of bone in my foot. That may sound like a big deal, but it happens frequently, and there is nothing to be done about it. And by this time I was quite experienced on how to treat injuries, and so I was back in time for the opening night.

Six weeks before the production was to première, Kenneth had an argument with the designer over the sets and the costumes. He thought them far too gaudy and garish. The designer was sacked. I suggested David Hockney for the sets, but the notion was rejected out of hand. It wasn't until 1990, after major successes elsewhere, that Hockney designed for the Royal Ballet. Peter Farmer was brought in for the horrendous task of creating four new acts of scenery and over 200 costumes. Somehow everything came together on the night.

This was another ballet where I had a mammoth wait of three hours before dancing a two minute solo. I arrived at the theatre at 7 P.M. and did not perform until around 10.30 P.M. You always had to check in at the half (which is thirty or thirty-five minutes before the start of a performance), regardless of when you were going on. Some nights I checked in and then sneaked out of the theatre for a sauna, where I could relax. In the last act of *Beauty* Fonteyn, playing Aurora, had to wait even longer than I did; my solo had made the act even longer. Her entrance was just after mine. We were waiting in the wings together once, and she turned to me and said, 'If it wasn't you dancing this solo, Wayne, I'd have it cut.' I don't blame her. She disliked the waiting about as much as I did, and my new solo made it even longer.

The 1973 season in New York was on the horizon. I would normally look forward to this with pleasure but I was due to dance only one role in the whole of the six weeks – Puck in *The Dream*. My previous season in New York had been a tremendous personal success, and because last time I had danced nearly every night, this time I did not wish to appear redundant in front of the knowledgeable American public. I felt underestimated and underused. Kenneth still preferred tall dancers with long legs and beautiful insteps. None of which I have.

So when the chance came to realize another ambition – I took it.

SEVEN

THEATRE DAZE

I MET THE DESIGNER Hugh Durrant at some party or other and discovered that he was designing a production by the New Shakespeare Company of Shakespeare's *The Tempest* for the Open Air Theatre in Regent's Park, to be performed in May. I asked him if there was any chance of his arranging for me to meet the director, Richard Digby Day. He was bound, I hoped, to be looking for a small athletic person to play Ariel. I had to audition at the Park for David Conville (then artistic director of the theatre) and Digby Day. They wanted to make sure I could be heard above traffic, aeroplanes, wind, birds, zoo noises, etc. And I was offered the part. My first play, my first Shakespeare. I was . . . happy.

But there was the problem of time off from the Royal Ballet. Iris arranged a strategic time for me to ask permission from Kenneth and Peter to have the spring off. I was told that my absence from the company created a place that must be filled, and I would not be invited back if someone came in to replace me. Did I really want to give up my place in the company for an acting role? They suggested I go away and think about it for a while.

I was devastated. I felt the absolute truth of being only a tiny cog in the enormous machinery of the Royal Ballet. In the ethos of the company, out of sight is out of mind. We were always being told that no one is indispensable, that there are plenty of talented dancers just waiting for an opportunity of this kind. I did not sleep. I tossed and turned, both in my bed and in my mind. A major decision – and I really did not know what was the best thing to do.

When I opened the office door I thought it was probably for the last time. I had resolved to take the part of Ariel and face whatever result that decision might bring. I would lose my place in the Royal Ballet, the place I had fought for since I was ten years old. Iris told me to go and see Michael Somes before seeing Kenneth. This sounded even worse, because I often felt that Michael was gunning for me. He was always so hard on me. Michael told me to go in and see Kenneth, but that, whatever happened, I was to keep my mouth shut. This is something I am not good at. I started to ask why (I think my mouth has a mind of its own), and was told to shut up and say nothing.

I went into the Director's office, rather meekly, and waited for them to speak. I was asked what my decision was. I explained that being offered one role, however good, on the American tour, when placed against the opportunity of acting in Shakespeare, was not enough to persuade me against the consequences of leaving the company.

'Are you sure?' I was asked.

'Positive.' Although I don't think I felt so just then. And then: 'Good luck, and we'll see you next season.'

They would have scraped me off the floor if I had not stood perfectly still.

'You mean you're inviting me back?' This was unbelievable in its own way.

'Yes.'

I was astounded. I left the office in high excitement and not a little bewildered at this apparent change of heart. Iris offered the reason. Michael Somes had heard that I was going to be dismissed and went straight to the Board of Governors. They, very well aware of my popularity with the audiences, intervened. Michael, who, I thought, did not care for me and who had alternately sat on me and pushed me in rehearsals to the limits of endurance, had stepped in and saved my career with the Royal Ballet. He has my undying gratitude for the ten happy years I had with the company after this.

I was dreading my first day of rehearsal for *The Tempest*. The read-through. This is when you meet your fellow actors, sit in a circle around the director and read the script for the first time. It took place in the most clichéd of places, a draughty church hall (in Kennington), with a tea urn and a smell of cooking cabbage. I was still very unsure, although I was taking lessons, about using my voice, particularly in front of professionals such as Michael Denison, who was playing Prospero, and Celia Bannerman who was Miranda. I mumbled my way through the morning, feeling insecure (again). All I hoped for was to make some sense of the text. There was one actor who not only knew his lines by heart, but had already defined the way the role, in his opinion, ought to be developed. This did not go down well with the director. I discovered that he preferred to have raw material, even as raw as me, to work with and to build on. The fellow who knew his lines would have to be deconstructed and brought down to earth – and then have his character reconstructed according to the director's vision. This made me feel only fractionally better, because I had no idea what to expect from rehearsals.

The first thing, thank heavens, was to map out my entrances and exits on and off the stage. But when it came to speaking . . . The moment came when the full cast were called together for a full run-through. And I had to speak. I was so overcome with nerves that my voice shook, my face flushed red and I wanted to run for cover. And I had been used to performing for at least fifteen years by then. At that moment it felt like the worst day of my life. I could feel the resentment of some of the actors, thinking of all the other good out-of-work actors who had lost a major role to a dancer. But there were others who were sympathetic and encouraging, pointing out that I was bound to be nervous, that it would get easier as matters progressed, that confidence would come. They were right – although it didn't feel like it then – but it was not easy getting there.

We opened in York for the start of a six-week tour before we came into the Open Air Theatre. The set, by Kit Surrey, was an abstract design and the floor of the stage was covered in six inches of sand to represent Prospero's island. We toured the sand in a lorry all round Britain for six weeks. We were not popular with the stage crews of the theatres we went into. It was inevitable that a dance was put in for Ariel – not easy on sand; it reminded me of filming *The Tales of Beatrix Potter*. The sand got everywhere, all over my white painted face, into my white painted nose, stuck to the follicles of my gold sprayed hair, creviced its way into the black feathers of my costume.

My speech as the Harpy was made suspended twelve feet above the ground on a wire. I ran on to the stage in a black-out and, on a given signal, was hoisted into the air. More often than not I found myself facing the back of the stage rather than the audience. I concentrated on trying to swivel round rather than on my speech. (Come to think of it, it must have been an odd sight, this feathered thing attempting to turn round while its voice was muffled against the back wall. I don't remember any giggles, though.) These minor mishaps occurred because we did not tour with a professional kirby wire flier, so every week my life was placed in the hands of the local stage crew. At one venue, instead of waiting for me to reach centre stage, the crewman winched me into the air far too soon, and I found myself soaring back and forth, careering from one side of the stage to another, banging into the scenery and grabbing anything that came towards me in an effort to stop the pendulum. After the first few lines I cut the speech, usually about two minutes long, and, clapping my hands, screamed, 'The End.' As soon as I was on firm ground I telephoned Equity (I was in a bit of a temper) to complain and they told me I did not have to fly if there was no professional there. The flying scene was cut and I gave my speech perched on a ledge. Richard Digby Day was none too happy about the change, but then he didn't see the bashing of the scenery.

I had a phobia about forgetting my lines, or 'drying'. When you are dancing, the music is a constant prompt. Learning, remembering and repeating words was a different thing. If I forgot them, I reckoned I couldn't exactly invent Shakespeare – although I have discovered since that plenty of people do. And mostly nobody notices. One story, possibly apocryphal, occurred half-way through one of the tragedies. Actor dried, pointed at his fellow actor, and said, 'And so my lord, I leave you to't.' The second actor moved to the forestage, pointed off-stage in the direction of the exiting actor, and informed the audience, 'Thus end all traitors.' Effectively scuppering the first actor's chances of getting back on stage that performance. It would make better sense if I could remember the play. I also heard that in the Scottish play, a messenger, bored with his one line of 'The Queen, my Lord, is dead', came on and said brightly, 'The Queen, my Lord, is much much better.' But that's sabotage, not forgetfulness.

There is a person in the prompt corner who is supposed to help you get back on course if you dry, but I never had any faith that it would work. There have been people who have gone completely blank – not just for a word, or a speech, even, but for the whole play. In that case it can be bad enough to induce a nervous breakdown. Or maybe the breakdown comes first. Whichever way it is, I'm told it is a devastating experience. I heard a tale of John Gielgud drying near the end of a play once. The audience was in suspense because it was at the point where he should name the murderer. He was supposed to answer the telephone and speak into it. He picked it up, and after a long silence, handed it to a fellow actor and said, 'It's for you.'

The Tempest was performed at the Open Air Theatre in repertoire during the summer season. This magical theatre is set in the centre of Regent's Park near the rose gardens, with trees and sky as a backdrop to the sets. A new set was designed by Kit Surrey for the specialized outdoor stage area of the theatre, and I asked Hugh if a new costume might be designed. The touring gear was moulting and I resembled a plucked chicken rather than a spirit. I stood in front of the rock of the new set in an all over skin-tight unitard and said, 'Now, Hugh, spray me the same colour as the rocks.' I ended up a mixture of green and grey, face and all. I was pleased with the effect, because when resting on the rocks listening to the other actors I was nearly invisible and only became conspicuous when moving to the foreground.

It was the coldest, wettest summer for years. Sometimes in the middle of a performance the clouds would roll in and burst, sending actors backstage to the portakabins posing as dressing-rooms and the audience would retire to a marquee for a glass of mulled wine. As soon as the rain stopped, we would start from where we had left off. On the odd night when it was clear and the sun shone, we contended with jets and flying feather pollen which coated our throats every time we took a breath.

Part of the set was a rock face, fifty feet high, with many hidden paths over which the actors climbed. I used to appear at the top of this rock face to recite my Harpy speech, my entrance emphasized by a loud clap of thunder and a small explosion. One evening, when I was half-way through speaking, the audience started to collect their things and leave the auditorium. I stood there, continuing with my lines, thinking, 'Well, I can't be that bad. I do it the same every night and they don't usually leave.' Then I noticed smoke billowing out somewhere in front of me, and I realized that the firework explosion accompanying my entrance had set the scenery alight and my rock was on fire. No one thought to warn me, and there I was, carrying on, good old trouper Sleep in the old-fashioned sense, cocooned in my role, oblivious to everything. Thanks, guys. As I scrambled down the scaffolding behind the rock, the stage manager was bashing an ancient fire extinguisher against the set in an effort to get it to work. He managed to douse the fire and we resumed our places for the next scene – the one in which Prospero says to Ariel: 'Well done, my proud and faithful servant.' It received a huge cheer from the audience.

David Hockney brought his father to see the play one evening. He slept all the way through it. When he woke up David asked, 'Did you enjoy the play?'

'Yes.'

'How do you know? You slept all the way through it. What was it about?'
'A tempest.'

To recover from my first venture into live acting, George and I went to Italy for a holiday. We flew first to Venice with Henrietta Guinness, and, because of her influence (a relative of hers happens to own it), we were able to swim at the Cipriani Hotel every day. Then we would zoom off to Harry's Bar for cocktails. I went to pay homage to Diaghilev, buried on the island of San Michele, and found a new grave nearby, laid with mountains of fresh flowers. It turned out to be that of Ezra Pound. I danced a few steps round Diaghilev's grave and laid a rose. I am not fanciful enough to think he saw me.

Next we all boarded a plane for Florence. There was only one person sitting in front of me. The pilot, knowing there were only a few people on board, decided on a very steep descent for the landing. I started to feel very sick and it was just at this moment that the girl in front of me turned, looked deep into my eyes and asked, in an American accent, if I wasn't Ariel in *The Tempest* in Regent's Park that summer? A fan – but not for long. I threw up all over her. No way to treat an adoring public.

Florence is a city that is not exactly short of sights. So many, in fact, that only a few things stick out after about twenty-five years: the Ponte Vecchio, the Botticellis (because they reminded me of Karl Bowen) in the Uffizi, the *David* of Michelangelo – repeated all over the city – and the skyline with the dome of the cathedral ruling over all. After Florence we went to Pisa, trying the waters at Montecatini Terme – the sulphur smell was even worse than at Vichy – where there was a band, thank heavens, whose wind instruments covered ours. In Pisa we marvelled at the leaning tower, the Campanile, and the blinding iridescent marble of the Cathedral and the Baptistry. They sit, almost like toys for giant children, in the middle of a vast expanse of green.

We were with Mary Moore and her friend, the poet Brian Patten, in Forte dei Marmi, near where Lorenzo, of San Lorenzo's restaurant in Beauchamp Place, had his family house. He had invited me and George to lunch – but we never made it. I heard later that they waited three hours for us, before they ate. George was too happy soaking up more than the atmosphere and I couldn't drive.

We went on to Siena via San Gimignano. This is a town built, it seems, of nothing but towers. Apparently if one noble built a tower, his next door noble had to build a higher one, and so on. Thirteen of these strange structures are still standing and give the place a remarkable outline as you approach. We also went through a town called Poggibonsi. I remember nothing about it – it was just the name we liked.

We arrived in Siena for the Palio, that famous bareback horse race which is conducted three times round the Campo in the city centre. Straw is laid down to minimize skidding and casualties (though I don't think there were any). I remember the nuns who had to pick up their habits to avoid the horse muck.

From Siena we travelled to Perugia, which is among the oldest university towns in Europe. In Assisi, nearby, we were prevented from entering the monastery when the guard decided that Henrietta's dress was too low cut. Undauntable Henrietta took her *Michelin Guide*, opened it, and shoved it down her offending cleavage. It did the trick. The guide allowed us in. By this time I'd had enough of the insides of monasteries and cathedrals (there are an awful lot in Italy) and slipped away on my quest to try every type of Italian cake I could. A cake stall was spotted near the monastery entrance. I usually managed to get what I wanted without language, but it did cause problems once. George and Henrietta overheard me asking for 'cacca torte'. Before the stallholder had time to get angry, they took me aside and let me know that I was, in fact, asking for 'shit cake'. I thought I was asking for chocolate . . .

Next stop was Orvieto, white wine and magpie country. We were having lunch in a restaurant, under the shadow of the cathedral when a magpie swooped in and filched the car keys off the table. We were seen frantically chasing it, up hill and down dale (well, not literally), until the wretched bird found the keys too heavy and dropped them. If I had not seen, I would not have believed.

We spent some time in the buzz of Rome and the elegant squalor of Naples, which seems to belong to another country entirely from that of Venice or Florence. From Naples we went to visit the Greek temple of Poseidon at Paestum, one of the best preserved Greek temples in the world.

Back home, my extra curricular activities continued with an appearance on the BBC's *Record Breakers*, hosted by Roy Castle. They rang Iris to ask if someone could demonstrate an entrechat-six on the programme – and she suggested me. There were the usual jokes about confusing 'entrechat' with 'entrecote'. Ha ha. An entrechat is crossing and uncrossing one's legs in a single leap, starting from a position on the ground. The opening counts as one, the crossing as two. I demonstrated, as asked, an entrechat-six which is frequently used in the repertoire. Roy told me that Nijinsky held the world record – with an entrechat-dix. Would I like to try and equal it?

I had never tried a dix before. No choreographer ever requested one. And the most I had done was an entrechat-huit when dancing Puck in *The Dream*. So, to enter into the spirit of the programme (and also because I was put on the spot in front of the audience), I agreed. Much to my own astonishment I managed not only to equal Nijinsky's record but also to beat it. I carried out six crossings of my legs, in mid-air, in one leap. An entrechat-douze. The crossing of the legs was so rapid that a qualified teacher had to look at it in slow motion playback in order to give me a place in the *Guinness Book of Records*. (A second entry came when, for charity, I was invited to do a series of grand jêtés across the wooden pier at Gateshead. I was sponsored per leap and so had to do as few as possible, as fast as possible, to get to the other end.) It is too fast for the human eye to take in so there would be little point, ever, in adding it to the repertoire.

A good entrechat-huit, with the feet opening wider, is much more effective. This is seldom used, however, because there are few dancers who are able to achieve it with any degree of certainty. Ballet dancing is not about winning records, unlike gymnastics or athletics. It *is* exciting to be able to jump high and do multiple spins but one must never forget that among all the pyrotechnics there is a character to be portrayed, and all the steps must look effortless. Dancers are taught to make everything look easy – unlike athletes, who may grimace with agony and show the effort they are making. We might be close to exhaustion but we must hide the pain behind a smiling face. You only have to watch a dancer come off stage to see the weariness drop like a cloak once out of sight of the audience.

Some years later I was invited back to *Record Breakers* for a Christmas Special. Roy Castle held the world record for the fastest taps in one minute, I for the most entrechats. As part of the routine in a comedy sketch, on air, he challenged my record, saying that he could do more entrechats than me, so I challenged his. But the joke was that it would be on his terms. I was caught. We were to start 4,800 feet in the air, with Roy doing the entrechats all the way to the ground – while I was to tap. In air. Making the noises myself. Hah.

This, of course, involved our learning to parachute and off we went to Woolwich barracks for a crash course. The most interesting part was the four-hour lecture on what to do if the whole thing went wrong – with such gems as 'If your parachute catches on the wing, someone will crawl out and cut it free for you. Then you will free fall and pull your reserve parachute.' Oh good, very reassuring. And – 'The way to let them know you are not unconscious is to tap yourself on the head.' Obvious, really. Then it was practice time.

I jumped from the aeroplane and after about six seconds of free fall, at 120 m.p.h., the parachute opened automatically. Suddenly I was at a standstill, so to speak, suspended 3,000 feet in the air. The silence was stunning after the roar of the free fall. There is no noise from traffic, tractors, trains, or anything else of life's bustle. We talked freely to each other from 100 yards apart with no difficulty or interference. My one problem was manoeuvring. A parachute has toggles which are used to steer the thing in the right direction. My instructor, following me (with another parachute), shouted directions at me: 'Wrong way. This way. Follow me. Not that way.' I could see it wasn't 'that way' – that way had a church steeple dead ahead. It did seem to be coming at me awfully fast. But I got the hang of it (quite quickly) and managed to land where I was supposed to. Landing is not unlike jumping off a twelve foot high wall. But I fell in the right way, rolled and collected up my parachute. I felt terrific. But I decided to go up again straight away in case the first time had been pure adrenalin.

The second time I noticed everything – including the sheath knife on the wall of the doorless Cessna plane. I had the knack now and enjoyed just looking at the landscape for miles around. The only trouble is that your feet cover an area of about three miles radius, so you don't see where you are supposed to land until you get nearer to the ground. Afterwards we went to the pub with the sergeant officers feeling as if we were now members of an exclusive club.

The bet? Roy won it by executing thousands of entrechats all the way down. I tapped. No one heard me. The *New Yorker* printed this poem, 'For the Record' by Roy Blount, after the *Record Breakers* programme.

> A dreamlike leap
> By England's Sleep!
> He didn't doze,
> He did a *douze*.
> His legs arose
> In curlicues
>
> He shrugged, 'OK, I'll make a run,'
> And then went heavenward (that's one),
> And five times crossed, and uncrossed five,
> And then returned to earth alive.
>
> And on TV, no less. *Voilà!*
> Sleep's the king of entrechat.
>
> Nijinsky, may he rest in peace –
> Would that he were above the ground!
> Nijinsky settled for but *dix*
> Movements in a single bound.
>
> A joy forever. He will last.
> And yet . . . his mark has been surpassed.
> Will Chaplin, too, be cast in doubt?
> Will someone edge Caruso out?
>
> But look! As consternation reigns
> Among the world's balletomanes,
> We see Nijinsky rise again.
> His spirit jumps into our ken:
>
> He climbs, descends, meanwhile with ease
> Weaving patterns with his knees,
> And stops just off the ground, and says.
> To open with some humor, '*Treize*.'
>
> And now he's serious; now he soars
> Sufficiently to cry '*Quatorze!*'
> And now, although he starts to pant,
> Up he goes – he's done a *vingt*!
>
> And now he's really going good.
> Nijinsky, folks, has just *vingt-deux'd*

We sense he could go on to *cent-deux*
But evidently doesn't want to.

For now, with one great closing spring,
He goes through untold scissoring
And disappears – a quantum leap –
And leaves the blinking world to Sleep.

Towards the end of the year, when I had returned to the Royal Ballet for the next season, I received a call from the office of Veronica Flint-Shipman, who owned the Phoenix Theatre. I was asked if I would like to audition for a part in *Winnie the Pooh*, to be produced by this very young, untried producer, one Cameron Mackintosh. The choreographer was to be Bridget Espinosa, whom I had met a few times and who was resident ballet teacher at the Elmhurst Ballet School.

At my audition at the Phoenix I was supposed to take a song with me. I knew no songs and had no music, so went unprepared. I thought, well, if they want me, they can sort something out. I showed cockiness to cover my nerves. I sang up the scale a few times, and then gave a dreadful rendition of 'Happy Birthday'. Then I was asked to study the script and read for the part of Piglet. I was brought up on Rupert Bear and Enid Blyton. A.A. Milne's books were not part of my childhood. Nobody that I knew at junior school had ever read *Winnie the Pooh*. I think it must, then, have been an essentially middle-class children's book. Today, of course, because of the cartoons and other artefacts, Winnie and his mates are everywhere. But then I had no idea of who or what Piglet was, no idea that he was a squeaky little thing, so I auditioned with a series of pig-like nasal grunts and snuffles. I didn't get the part. Then they asked me to read for the part of Tigger – which, let's face it, is much more suitable for me – which they offered to me.

I had to ask Iris Law to pave the way for another leave of absence; my second that year. This time it was easier and my request was granted without a hitch. I would not be missing any performances since they took place during the day. Piglet was played, much better than I ever could, by Maria Charles, Eeyore by Frank Thornton and Winnie by Ronald Radd. During the final run-through with the band at the Phoenix (where it was due to run mornings and afternoons over the Christmas period), I got totally lost in the songs. I thought – naturally or naïvely, I don't know – the band would be playing the tune along with me. I found I was supposed to hold the notes of the songs while they diddled around in harmonies. I found myself singing the tune of the flute or the sax on one side of the stage, but by the time I moved to the other side I would be singing the guitar or the bass line. I would probably have sung the drums, if I could. I had to learn to close my ears to the band and listen to my own voice. I just made it in time for the public.

Winnie was very low-key throughout all the rehearsals. This is a good ploy, on the whole, and can help keep your energies for a full-throated performance in front of the audience. We all expected it to be one of those performances where he'd pull out the stops on the opening night – but he never did. I believe he thought it was the way to play it. It was a lesson for me, both in the art of the director and in the business of actorly projection.

Performances of *Winnie the Pooh* were in the mornings and afternoons, so I was able to perform the Jester in *Cinderella* in the evenings. Saturdays presented the only problem. I ended up doing *Winnie* in the morning, rushing to the Opera House for the matinee of *Cinderella*, zipping back to the Phoenix for the second show at five o'clock and back to the Garden for the evening performance. It meant rapid changes of make-up from whiskers to clown, paws to ballet shoes, tail to doublet and hose – and the requisite mental attitude. I thought it might be compared to the old days of music hall, when you might open the show in one venue, whizz across town and appear in the second half somewhere else.

This was a year of great expansion, artistically, for me. Richard Digby Day, Director of the Repertory Company in York, knowing that I was dying to do a comedy role, offered me the part of Truffeldino, the servant in Goldoni's farce *The Servant of Two Masters*. It was to mean my third leave of absence from the Royal Ballet in the same season. It crossed my mind that I might be threatened, again, with the sack, but permission was granted without a murmur. I set off for York with a script the size, it seemed to me, of a telephone directory. I wondered how on earth I was going to learn all those words in the two weeks allotted to rehearsals. Actors in rep are accustomed to learning one part while playing another. For me, reading a whole script was daunting enough and as for learning it . . . I do admit to a bit of panic. And it was a leading role. Two weeks.

Rehearsals started at 9.00 A.M. and went on till six at night. Then I would go back to my digs and read, and re-read, and recite, over and over again until the early hours of the morning. Panic over (what seemed to me) lack of time, worry over not learning the part speedily enough, cleared my brain of what little receptivity it had left. I thought I would never digest the part. We rehearsed in a freezing cold hall without any semblance of a set. I imagined the staircases I would eventually be using in the fast scenes by running on the spot, counting the steps, not knowing whether the trick of throwing the plates from the top of the stairs and catching them at the bottom in those famous scenes when Truffeldino serves two masters at the same time would actually transpose to the stage or not. Our only rehearsal with the set was the day before we opened. I managed to get through the first public performance keeping my script in the wings. I'm glad to say I wasn't the only one. There were moments in the first few performances, when I had the stage to myself, where I ad-libbed, keeping to the general gist of the play. But after two weeks the piece was running both smoothly and with great pace as the farce took on its own life. I loved the laughter of the audience as I slid down poles from the upper floor, or skidded down the banisters, throwing plates, goblets and bottles of wine, chicken legs and spaghetti from level to level. Wonderful.

After the success of *The Servant of Two Masters*, Richard asked me if I would like to appear at the Bath Festival in a recital of *Sweet Mr Shakespeare*, a compilation of anecdotes and letters about the bard by famous writers and poets. By this time, the Royal Ballet was reconciled to my combining two careers, and they allowed me to continue: with the proviso that it did not conflict with any major production at Covent Garden. After *Sweet Mr Shakespeare*, Richard used the same format for a recital about Diaghilev, in which I played Nijinsky. I choreographed a solo in which I used existing photographs of his different roles, put them together in one piece, and froze in the different positions, as a flash of light, like that from a camera, captured the moment. I also told anecdotes about his relationship with Diaghilev. We performed this in the old wooden Georgian Theatre in Richmond, Yorkshire. This fine old theatre had been discovered when builders were knocking down a few walls in a warehouse. They found a hole in the floor which they realized was a theatrical trap door from the seventeenth century. They also discovered wooden boxes for the audience, pieces of hanging scenery and the candles that were the original footlights.

The restoration was made possible by the Marchioness of Zetland, who invited us to stay at Aske House. I was put in the King's Room and as I had forgotten my alarm clock, I asked if she could lend me one, but she said, 'Don't worry, we have our own ways of waking you up.' This was the butler, who woke me every morning by opening the curtains. Breakfast was served in huge silver salvers from which we helped ourselves, and then, maybe, we would walk round the gardens designed by Capability Brown, complete with peacocks. Every night after the show we stayed up late, drinking claret and port with the Marchioness's son, David Dundas. He became a composer – the jingle for the Channel 4 logo was his.

On 3 April 1973 I set off with the Royal Ballet for a tour of Brazil. We were to perform *The Sleeping Beauty* and *Swan Lake* in Porto Alegre, Bela Horizonte, São Paulo, Rio de Janeiro and Brasilia. (We were meant to perform in Buenos Aires, but students had taken over the theatre, so it was Brasilia instead.) On the way there one of the engines on the plane conked out and we were forced to land in Freetown, the capital of Sierra Leone in West Africa. We were supposed to be confined to the air base for the few hours the repair was meant to take, but when we realized that they had sent for technical back-up, the heat drove Tony Rudenko and me into the jungle. We walked through dense undergrowth until we found ourselves on a long stretch of white sand, facing the Atlantic. Lots of native children appeared – they all seemed to have old colonial names like George – and we played with them in the sea. For a laugh I taught them all a small section from *Swan Lake* (they made great, if slightly small and giggly, cygnets), and I kept on telling them to pull in their tummies. What I did not know was that the distension was caused by their diet of rice.

Eventually we left Freetown and arrived at Porto Alegre in Brazil. The heat there was intense and oppressive for performance. For relief during the daytime, I found an air-conditioned cinema which was showing the film of *Cabaret*. I had seen this already, and was rather surprised to find that many scenes were censored, in particular the homosexual ones. And yet outside the cinema, on the bookstalls in the street, were magazines devoted to the Red Baron and other famous wartime German fliers and soldiers. I found this an odd and interesting juxtaposition of moralities, and one that was almost the obverse of the culture in which I lived.

This culture shock continued. In São Paulo families begging on the street existed side by side with the lavish parties given for the company by the rich. You could travel down a road, and if you turned left you would be in slums with a hole in the ground, shared between fifty shacks, as the only sanitary facility, with electricity taken (illegally) from the street lamps; if you turned right, it would be enormous houses behind alarmed fences, with swimming-pools, servants and glossy wives. This gulf between what seemed two nations of Brazil was evident almost everywhere we went. But we were, on the whole, sheltered from these realities.

I was also rather disconcerted by the pollution of the water on Copacabana beach. But that wasn't the worst thing about it. I was swimming there one after-noon and while standing in the shallows – in only about a foot of water – the undertow pulled me off balance and took me under. As I came up for air, another wave caught me and dragged me under. They say that when you are drowning, the whole of your life passes in front of you. All I could see was dirty yellow sea water which was forcing itself into my lungs. Another wave, thank God, tossed me up on to the beach – it was the only time I have ever been grateful for rejection – with only a few sand scratches to show what I had been through. The lifeguards were rescuing another boy who must have been in more difficulties than me. This incident gave me a fear of swimming out too far, which was silly really, because it had happened in very shallow water. This fear was only conquered some years later when I learnt how to scuba dive.

We arrived in Brasilia with a police escort, to find a crowd of 25,000 already seated in the stadium. Margot and Rudolf were with us for this part of the tour. It turned out that some of the tickets had been duplicated and 5,000 of them had been sold on the black market. These unhappy people stood outside the stadium chanting 'Margot, Margot, let us in.' They considered that Margot, married to the Panamanian Roberto Arias, was one of them. And they were so noisy that the orchestra could not be heard. Some of the *corps* were in tears because they could not hear the music. Performances began falling apart. After the one-act version of *La Bayadère* (the famous one in which the *corps* descend one by one down a long ramp holding an arabesque every other step), John

Tooley, then Administrator General of the Opera House, insisted that unless something was done to stop the noise the performance would be halted. The police were called, the chanters were dispersed and the dancers continued.

Brasilia itself was like a ghost town. People came to work in this city, but no one lived there. At night it was empty, dead. Very strange. I don't pretend to understand the rationale behind it. It's a strange thing, to build a city in the middle of nowhere, and have no one live in it. Everyone who worked there lived in the surrounding satellite cities.

Our trip did not take us into the Amazon or El Salvador. Now I may never get to see it because I am not sure it will survive the vagaries of the greedy modern world. The London Contemporary Dance Company, who were in Brazil the same time as us – they got to El Salvador, and it was where Robert North, principal dancer and choreographer with the LCDT, found the music for his piece, *Troy Games*. Robert and I had been students together at the Royal Ballet school, and in Rio we found ourselves in the same hotel, the Gloria. We discussed a possible collaboration on a piece for his company and agreed to meet when we were back in London.

The audiences in Brazil were obviously starved of the quality of dance we were accustomed to, and showed their appreciation and enthusiasm both in applause and parties. Our tour evidently inspired the rich and influential in Rio to create a company for their own dancers, and many members of the Royal Ballet were called upon to perform and to help the fledgling company in its infancy.

When we came back to London we began a season at the Coliseum. This was the same Coliseum season in which I first performed in Jerome Robbins's *Dances at a Gathering*. This theatre is, in my view, the best theatre for dance in England. It has easy sight-lines for the audience and a stage as deep as that of the Opera House but wider – which means you can really let fly in circling round the stage and for diagonal leaps. I was cast by Sir Fred, who still had *carte blanche* as to who would appear in his ballets and liked to rehearse them, to dance the role of Briaxis, the Pirate Chief, in his revival of *Daphnis and Chloë*. It was the first time I was given a big role in which I was not typecast. The role required me to overcome my size and use my acting ability to its limits.

Briaxis was originally created by Alexander Grant; he had now retired from these strenuous roles. Unlike him (he is a few inches taller than I am), I had to dance roles like the Pirate Chief in such a way as to appear much bigger. Briaxis should come across as a large man, a dominant character and a leader of men, a villain who makes treacherous advances to the captured Chloë. I achieved this by characterization and the addition of fierce make-up, nose putty and a false moustache and beard. One of the best compliments I ever received was hearing, when leaving the stage door: 'I didn't think he was so small.' I'd done the trick.

I had some trouble with the one-arm lift when I raised Antoinette Sibley, as Chloë, with her back resting on my arm, above my head while running round the stage. I was not used to partnering; I was too small. Antoinette was slightly taller than me when on point and I had to manoeuvre myself to a position where the comparison would not be amusing. It meant that my body was stretched, on occasions, from toe- to finger-tip further than I thought possible. There were some who thought I should not have been cast as Briaxis, but Ashton, after auditioning me with other, taller, boys, decided that I was the one he wanted.

I gave up my summer holiday in this year, 1973, to work with Sir Fred on a new opera for the Aldeburgh Festival, Benjamin Britten's *Death in Venice*. Students from the Junior Royal Ballet school played the children and I was to understudy Tadzio, the boy pursued by Aschenbach, sung by Peter Pears. I wasn't entirely thrilled about being cast as a child (again, and a child who required angelic looks, which I knew I had not) nor about understudying, but I wanted to work with Sir Fred again and this outweighed all other considerations. Also I never questioned his casting.

I stayed in a caravan by the sea in Aldeburgh. The summer, fortunately, was a warm one. Benjamin Britten, however, was not well and could only send messages from home, where he was confined. John and Myfanwy Piper created the sets, which were mostly painted slides for back projection. Tadzio's mother was played by Deanne Bergsma, a beautiful, tall, elegant dancer famous for her Lilac Fairy in *Sleeping Beauty*, and for her immaculate *bourrée* (when a ballerina glides across the stage on point, looking as if she is gliding on ice) in *Giselle*. I have never seen the part danced better.

Death in Venice transferred to the Opera House that autumn and I had not once been obliged to perform Tadzio. I was due to go with the company to Brussels, to appear at the opening of the 'Europhalia' Festival to celebrate the beginning of the EEC, where we were due to present *Sleeping Beauty*, *Seven Deadly Sins* and *Symphonic Variations*. At Heathrow airport a call went out for me. I was asked to get back to London because the boy playing Tadzio was injured. This was the call I had been dreading. I had always felt I was totally wrong for the part. Tadzio has to have an innocence of youth as well as an angelic countenance. I could act the innocence but I knew I was no Adonis – in spite of the nickname given to me by Donald MacLeary (a principal of the Royal Ballet) of the Pocket Apollo. I had a long talk with the injured dancer, explaining that I was seriously miscast, that he was perfect, that he might never get the same kind of opportunity again. He understood, I think, the force of my arguments and did agree to perform.

I flew to Brussels, arriving just in time for curtain-up on *Sleeping Beauty*. For once I did not mind waiting for three hours to perform. The company's reception was only mild (not what we were used to) and I dubbed the 'Europhalia' Festival 'You're a Failure'. It's not surprising that our reception was less than ecstatic, because Belgium already had its own superb ballet company, created by Maurice Béjart. The Béjart Ballet, based on both contemporary and classical styles of dance, had lifted ballet into the late twentieth century. It was completely innovative, had some great dancers and often operated on the scale of a Busby Berkeley movie. I was impressed.

Back in London, a revived production (first directed by Sir John Gielgud) of Britten's opera *A Midsummer Night's Dream*, was being remounted by Covent Garden's guest opera director, John Copley. Geraint Evans, the original star, was to play Bottom again. James Bowman, the counter-tenor, was Oberon, Jill Gomez was Titania, and the lovers were Thomas Allen, Ryland Davies, Anne Howells and Josephine Barstow. I was asked to play Puck.

Puck does not sing in this opera, but speaks in metre form to the music. Bernard Haitink took me through my role. I found it difficult to interpret the dialogue in the way I wanted, because the rhythm of the music dictated the timing. I did not then have the experience to give and take, to push a beat to the limit, within those confines, and one critic said I was too clockwork. He was right. But it was quite a thrill to be dancing one night with the ballet, playing Puck in the opera the next, and then dancing (and jumping on the bed with Grace Bumbry) in *Aida*. I was on every night (that made a change) and getting three salaries . . . John Tooley asked me, 'How much are we paying you a week?' A lot, I thought, but not as much as you're getting. For once I said nothing.

During rehearsals it was fascinating to watch Geraint Evans take the part of Bottom and make it his own. Once, having been placed at the centre of the stage by John Copley, I found Geraint sidling up to me. 'Move over, boyo,' he said to me. I asked why. Maybe I was in the wrong position. He said, 'Because I haven't had centre stage in this act yet.' It was expected by performers of the old school of opera, as it were, that they would have centre stage a lot of the time. It was their due. Not that he needed to. It didn't matter where he stood, all eyes followed him anyway. Such presence.

The production opened on 2 January 1974. It proved to me that, contrary to previous thought, opera singers don't have to behave like stuffed puddings, and that there was nearly as much movement as in dance – sometimes the singers were nearly too out of breath to sing. John Copley was an excellent director. He could sing every person's part in the opera, including the soprano and had the knack of keeping us all happy, of keeping our spirits high.

Kenneth MacMillan embarked on his second full-length work in four years for the company. It was based on the story of Manon Lescaut and set to the music of Massenet, which was arranged by Leighton Lucas. *Manon* was a vehicle for Antoinette Sibley and Anthony Dowell, whose partnership was now as famous, internationally, as that of Fonteyn and Nureyev. This was special, as they were two English dancers trained totally by the Royal Ballet School.

Kenneth was in his element – creating romantic *pas-de-deux*, psychological intrigue, and a dramatic conclusion where Manon dies in the arms of her lover in the swamps of Louisiana. I was given the part of the Beggar Chief in the first act. He was a sly pickpocket with some difficult jumps and turns but with no real significance to the plot. But I was being used and it was against typecasting. *Manon* opened on 7 March 1974 and was a triumph. It is very rare, these days, for a choreographer to attempt a three-act ballet and even rarer for it to become a success. *Manon* is now danced by major companies throughout the world.

Back at home, I was on the move again. David Hockney was still living in Powis Terrace, and a flat came up for sale in the next street to him. I loved the area, we would be neighbours, and Portobello Road was only two minutes away – so George and I decided to buy it. The area had a village atmosphere. Celia and Ossie were not far up the road; Mo was in the basement flat below David; Anne Upton, another of David's friends, and her son Byron were just around the corner, where Peter Schlesinger rented a room to paint in and often used me as a model. Eugene Lambe, a friend of George's, came to live with us in the four-bedroomed maisonette on the second and third floors of a house in Powis Gardens.

George persuaded David to buy one of the first portable video-recorders by saying that if he, as a relatively rich person, didn't, how on earth would the price ever come down to our level? We used to dress up and interview each other, being amazed at seeing ourselves instantly replayed on the screen. David was invited everywhere – and we would tag along with him to all the gallery openings, fashion shows and new restaurants. Anything public. No one dared turn him away, even if he arrived with six or seven extra guests. I should say that we did not do this at private dinners.

George had a lot of mahogany and oak furniture, crystal glasses and a large collection of Moorcroft pottery from his family. I enjoyed stacking all these artefacts on top of the sideboard and transferring them to a huge glass cabinet perched on top. We hadn't been in Powis Gardens long, however, before various uninvited guests began to appear. We started to find half-eaten biscuits and grapes with chunks taken out of them. It was a mouse invasion. One night, in an effort to get rid of the beasts, we chased one poor little mouse around the dining-room. George got very over-excited, saying, 'I know where it is, I know where it is . . .' and as he jumped onto the sideboard, the precarious cabinet crashed to the floor. Goodbye Moorcroft. Hello Grace.

Grace came from a rather grand house in Islington. We were happy to rescue her because her mother's owner had a reputation for shooting cats in the back garden. George had this theory about choosing kittens: ignore those who huddle around the mother in the basket and go for the independent one hiding behind the fridge. Grace was hiding. She was half Abyssinian and half I-don't-know-what, with a brown coat and green eyes. She was bright as a button and very loving. She lived with us for fourteen years.

Among all this family furniture from Scotland was a grand dining-table over which I presided as *mâitre d'*, and we started entertaining on a grand scale. I was usually in the kitchen, while George's main job was to do what he did best – decant the wine. One day a whole roast chicken landed in the cat litter. Nobody saw, so I dusted it off (the litter was fresh and there was nothing in it) and served it up. Delicious?

I invited Sir Fred to one of our dinners. This was a grand creation, nerve-racking, and required a careful planning of the menu. The night before the dinner I rushed home on my folding bicycle (which usually ended up in the back of the car of some kind person giving me a lift) from a hard day's rehearsal in Barons Court. The preparations kept me up till 3 A.M. Roast lamb seemed fitting – I stabbed it with cloves of garlic to marinate nicely. I made chocolate mousse – that alone took three hours.

On the evening of the dinner I sent one of the guests, Henrietta Guinness, to collect Sir Fred in her Porsche. Not a bad start, I thought. David and Peter were coming – so Sir Fred could talk about sets and art. The last two guests were Karl Bowen and Jane Kasmin. On Sir Fred's arrival, eager to please, I introduced him to everyone. Karl rushed forward in awe and excitement and said, 'Oh, I love your choreography, Sir Fred Astaire.' Karl's charm was such that he could get away with things like that, and Sir Fred was flattered.

Time to eat. I produced the lamb, sizzling on a plate, surrounded by other gourmet delights. Sir Fred's face dropped as he announced that, because of a hiatus hernia, he was unable to eat anything with garlic or herbs. Oh God. Every ingredient I had bought was planned for the evening, for this one special meal. My face must have showed everything and, realizing I was in trouble, Sir Fred suggested an omelette. Well – the eggs were there – but I had never cooked an omelette. Jane was a saint and came to the rescue.

As we sat down to eat, Sir Fred turned to me and said, 'Well, dear boy, I hope you realize just who I've turned down for dinner to come here tonight.' Just before Henrietta arrived to collect him, Sir Fred had received a call from Princess Margaret asking him to dinner.

'Oh no, ma'am, I'm going to Wayne and George's.'

To his immense credit (in my eyes), Sir Fred honoured his previous engagement to me, knowing that one of his solo dancers would have been devastated, completely, in spite of culinary disasters, had he not turned up.

The following spring, 1976, we went on tour to New York and Washington. In New York I stayed at the Algonquin, one of my favourite hotels. The manager was a fan of the Royal Ballet, having followed all their successful tours for many years, so I was always given a discount. I was grateful, because I could never have afforded a room at the regular rate on my salary – even a touring salary. Henrietta and George came over on a different flight. I was due to meet them at the Algonquin, but caught them browsing through the naughty paper-backs on 42nd Street. George never could resist a bargain.

When we went on to Washington, George stayed at the Watergate Hotel with Henrietta. This wasn't long after the big Nixon scandal and impeachment.

Some of the dancers, and I, were staying at the Intrigue Hotel. It was after one of my performances here that Peter Wright informed me that I was to dance the famous Don Quixote *pas-de-deux* with Lesley Collier, in July, at the Big Top in Plymouth.

The Big Top was a blue canvas circus tent owned by the Fossett family. Because there was nowhere big enough (the Theatre Royal was not yet built) where the company might perform in Plymouth, the tent was erected in Home Park, just by the Plymouth Argyle football stadium. It seated about 3,000 people. The dancers changed in the portakabins, with outside loos. In summer the heat was incredible, to the point where many customers fainted. It was even hotter for us under the bright lights on stage. It was not for some years that air-conditioning was introduced.

I had booked fourteen seats for my family. The box office made a balls-up, and when they arrived there were no tickets left. I refused to perform unless my family were allowed in. Leslie Edwards rushed around to find them – he came back and told me he had no problem finding them because they were all as small as me. They were unperturbed by the mix-up and joked that I should do a little show outside for them, there on the concrete. I insisted that they were seated, and eventually seats were brought in for my tiny family to sit in the aisles.

This was my first performance as Alain, the idiot boy, in *La Fille Mal Gardée*. This character role had originally been choreographed by Ashton for Alexander Grant. It was a gift of a part, but it was incredibly hard to follow Alex in any role that he undertook. I last danced this role in 1990, so it was one that would remain with me for quite a long time. The repertoire in Plymouth also contained an evening of divertissements, which is a collection of extracts from different ballets, in which Lesley and I were to dance the Don Quixote *pas-de-deux*. We had performed this once before at a gala evening, but until Plymouth I had never expected to dance this virtuoso role with the Royal Ballet.

It was great to be able to go to work from home and to have my family involved in my work on a daily basis. One of my American fans, Nancy, came over. She saved her salary for the trip and stayed with us. After one of the performances, Mum gave a party for the company in Gran's house, which was large enough to accommodate everyone. Auntie Ruth prepared a huge bowl of punch, using plastic buckets to mix the potion, which consisted of vodka and plenty of my mother's home-made wine. We were all paralytic by the end of the evening. The age range at the party was from nine months to ninety years.

Sally Ashby, one of my friends in the company, stayed with Gran while we were in Plymouth. She came home one day and, thinking Gran was out, put the kettle on, checked in the fridge for food and made herself a pâté sandwich. She sat down at the table and suddenly noticed that the kitchen had been re-wallpapered since the morning. She was in the house next door. She ran for it, abandoning both tea and sandwich. The owners must have thought they had poltergeists.

EIGHT

FROM BALLET TO BOX,
VIA TURGENEV

B Y NOW MY resentment at being both underused and undervalued under Kenneth MacMillan's directorship had evaporated. My roles with the Royal Ballet were not only reinstated but expanded, and I was really enjoying the life. Kenneth started work on a new one-act ballet in which there was a good part for me. He decided to use the ragtime music of Scott Joplin. Ragtime is deceptively hard, not only to play but to dance to. It's the syncopation. The *ritenutos* and *accelerandos* are not constant and require the rhythm to be felt (even more than usual) as much as marked by time. Scott Joplin himself was adamant that one should 'hold back' with ragtime – a sort of 'slower is faster'. And Kenneth MacMillan, when rehearsing, kept saying 'Too fast, too fast.'

Some people were surprised at the choice of music, not least because the Festival Ballet had used the music in the ballet, *The Prodigal Son*, with Paul Clarke (he who did not protect my modesty with the bath-towel at White Lodge) in the title role. And also because the Oscar-winning film *The Sting* had come out the previous year and so *everybody* was playing ragtime. Scott Joplin was definitely the flavour of the moment, and Kenneth was risking being considered old hat – the music had been out of copyright for a couple of years.

But there was so much that was new about *Élite Syncopations*: the set, the orchestra, the costumes. Not to mention the choreography. The set was un-designed. The backdrop was whatever was in the theatre, anything that was stacked at the back of the stage ready for the next production. As set dressing, any old chairs were placed round the edge. This 'set' got a round of applause on the first night, which we thought quite funny, considering the amount of money that can be spent on such things.

The orchestra was a seven- or eight-piece jazz band. On stage. Usually they fiddle and scrape away in the pit with very little idea of what the dancers are doing above them on the boards. The musicians, dressed in barber-shop costumes with straw boaters, slick hair and moustaches, loved being an integral part of the per-formance, because they were being seen for a change and they could also see us.

The costumes, Lycra bodies with bright designs painted on them, were designed by Ian Spurling. Kenneth and he had collaborated before, on *The Seven Deadly Sins*. In the sixties Ian was a habitué of the Portobello Road, where he was usually spotted wearing full make-up, a cloak and a (live) white dove on his shoulder. When Kenneth asked him to design for *Élite Syncopations*, he had had a run of bad luck and was cleaning public lavatories in order to live.

Vergie Derman was the tallest girl in the company. She possessed a pair of long elegant legs and was considered one of the most glamorous of the ballerinas. On stage, sometimes, she could appear aloof; off stage she had a great sense of humour. Kenneth decided Vergie should be my partner. On her points she was more than a foot taller than me.

'Let's play around in the studio and see what comes of it,' said MacMillan. A lesser choreographer might simply have played on the difference of our heights, but Kenneth was more interested in extracting new moves and lifts to make the disparity of our heights more inventive. We experimented with various steps and lifts, lifts which seemed to fall apart under the pressure – but always ended up the right way. It was this capacity for innovation which placed Kenneth above other, more mundane, choreographers. Yet humour was a rare venture for him; he was famed for his pieces full of psychology, characterization and depth. I think the only other soufflé of a piece he did was *Valse Eccentrique*, to Ibert's *Divertissement*, with three swimmers in twenties bathing-costumes and mob caps.

Élite takes place in a Palais de Danse, complete with glitter ball. There is no real story – it is pure dance. My role gave me the chance to show off my comic abilities – not only in the *pas-de-deux* with Vergie, but also in my harassment of the rest of the cast. In the opening scene I made shy advances to Merle Parke and interrupted the other dancing couples, getting in their way. Vergie and I received a review in which our duet was compared to a love affair between a Borzoi and a Pomeranian.

The critics were not particularly kind, however. They accused MacMillan of jumping on the Scott Joplin bandwagon and it became one of those ballets which they did not like, but which was a great hit with the public. It's a strange coincidence that the two ballets that were much appreciated by the audiences, but slated by the critics, are the only two in which an encore has been demanded and given. *Élite* was one (this was at the Bristol Hippodrome, where I improvised by grabbing a broom to sweep the dancers upstage), and the other was Sir Fred's *Jazz Calendar* (where we mistimed all the music cues).

Kenneth created another ballet during the 1973–4 season, in which I was given a solo which, although tricky, was an absolute joy to dance. I shared the Autumn section of Vivaldi's *Four Seasons* with Anthony Dowell and Jennifer Penney. We had to wait through the other three seasons, and the waiting usually made us apprehensive. Kenneth's choreography was so difficult sometimes that it took a hell of a long time to get the hang of the moves. He was always that one step ahead – you'd think of something, he was already there and probably beyond you. The excitement in his work was that he was always changing gear and direction. For instance, you might be half-way through a series of turns, with your thought and momentum travelling one way – and he would ask you to reverse it, suddenly, and move off at a tangent. It required great discipline. I like to move in one direction, gathering momentum, and in *Seasons* he allowed me full rein. I could fly. I was happy.

In this work, in fact, he tailored much of the choreography to the speeds and strengths of all his leading dancers, showing off the technique of the men in particular. And this was Kenneth at the peak of his invention. He had occasionally suffered disapprobation from the critics. *The Four Seasons* was acclaimed by critics and popular with the public. There was one thing I disliked, however, and that was the set. It was designed by Peter Rice and was a rendition of a strange wooden mountainside house, looking as if it was composed entirely of matchsticks. It dominated the back of the stage. When the ballet was revived I was delighted to find that the set was struck and our costumes were reduced to unitards. These are not only comfortable (being very similar to rehearsal clothes), but are also very revealing, in the sense that there is no costume to hide behind, and one's purity (or not) of line is evident in every move.

I was really being given more to do now. I was also in *Concerto*, MacMillan's revival of his ballet set to the first movement of Shostakovich's Piano Concerto in F. This ballet, with *La Fille Mal Gardée*, *Élite Syncopations*, *The Dream*, *Sleeping Beauty* and *Swan Lake*, was included in a tour to Korea and Japan in 1975. This was exciting. Two totally alien cultures. I did not know what to expect.

One of the things that sticks with me about Korea is how much burnt countryside there was. It was difficult to believe that this was still a hangover from the Korean war two decades before. But American troops were still there and there was still some sporadic fighting. We found that Seoul remained under curfew so there was nothing to do – bar official functions – except to return to the hotel after the performance. Dennis Griffiths and I shared a room, as we had in Brazil. There are two nights in Brazil I remember. I crept into the hotel room with a friend, whispering on the phone for room service: 'Could I have dos biers and dos hamburgers?' Dennis woke up, saying 'Just make it three of everything.' Another night in Seoul, Dennis and I were kept awake by the howling of the dogs outside the window. The next day was 'Dog Day'. The rumour was that on Dog Day the relevant Korean authorities rounded up all the strays in Seoul and cooked and ate them. Now I have no idea if this is true, although I gather that dog, in some of those areas, is considered a delicacy.

One of the welcomes for the company was given by the President of Seoul – or some other important personage. The house, whoever it belonged to, was built on sticks and was the essence of simplicity. It had wood floors and no beds – at least no beds visible, apparently they were hidden behind wooden shutters. I've been fond of this pared-down style ever since. We were entertained in the garden. Just as we sat down, the band began to play. Our hosts stood, we followed. When it finished they sat, we sat. Then it was our National Anthem, so we stood again, and they stood. We sat, they sat. Then another piece of music. They stood, we stood. Something was wrong. Even I could count three national anthems for two countries. It transpired that the first piece of music had been composed for the occasion – we thought it was their anthem, they assumed it was ours.

We were in Korea for five days. The Koreans were very gentle and treated us with a great deal of warmth, friendliness and hospitality. We were quite sorry to leave, in spite of the inconvenient curfew (and the dog possibility), and head for Japan.

In Tokyo we stayed in the Otani Hotel, a huge impersonal multi-storied affair with a fabulous Japanese garden – small bridges, mini-lakes and waterfalls, rocks, maples and a sushi bar. We played at the Bunka Kaikan, which is a few stops away on the tube from the Otani. Tube travel is regimented. You stand between two white lines, the train stops, the doors open precisely opposite you, you file on. As a reflection of the country's discipline, it's fascinating.

We were rather dismayed by the audience response on the first night, it was so muted. We found the Japanese not to be the most demonstrative of people, and discovered that their polite (we thought) applause was their equivalent of a rousing, standing ovation. And we were fearing the performance had fallen flat. It required a different mind-set to perform in Japan because there is no obvious and instant feedback.

Madam Oyha, a widow who owned a big (like ICI, say) textile firm, gave a party for the company. She was one of Japan's rare independent women. She wore bright pink cheeks and lips in a pale face, and mini-skirts to show off her fine calves and ankles. She also owned a private golf course and club, the Morano. She travelled throughout the year, following and playing golf round the world, shaking hands and being photographed with celebrities, photos which she then issued in her private magazine. It was rumoured that she had endowed a new hospital near to where she lived, with the whole of the top floor, furnished with familiar trappings, reserved exclusively for her – *if* she were ever to be ill. She was a great supporter of ballet, with her own school in Osaka. All the soloists and principals received a double string of Mykimoto pearls from Madam Oyha, in token of her great appreciation. They were very fine. I gave mine to my mother.

She was a frequent visitor to Covent Garden after this tour. She sat and watched us with a powerful pair of binoculars trained at the stage – and always from the flont low. She came armed with carrier bags full of what she called her 'Pwopaganda' – a record of herself singing opera, a piece of her latest fabric posing as silk, and her magazine, full of pictures of her smiling with the famous. She kept her own driver in London throughout the year, in readiness for her yearly visit. About ten years ago she came to see me in *Cabaret* in the West End and said she would send her car to the stage door. 'How do I recognize it?' I asked. 'Same colour as this,' she said, pointing to her bright red velvet cloak. Not only red, but Rolls. She had many quirks which are the prerogative of the very rich, one of which was never touring without mountains of crates of Perrier. A quite extraordinary woman.

We went to Hiroshima. It is traditional, apparently, to take the visitor straight to the museum on arrival, before anything else. It is housed in the only building that was left standing after the atom bomb. We were given a lecture on what happened when the bomb exploded and saw photographs of the children who were sent, with pre-packed lunches, to help dig out those trapped in the ruins. Before they understood the danger they died too, from the radiation. We danced *Swan Lake* that evening. It seemed, suddenly, rather unimportant to be performing in an art form that was so ephemeral, escapist, fantasist. The experience affected each one of us. Possibly it added to the emotion. I don't know. But I have not easily forgotten.

After the performance I went to a bar where I was befriended by some Japanese. They took me to another bar. I ordered a beer, which was all I wanted, but my hosts insisted on strawberries and little bowls of savouries. I declined. They were insistent. We had been briefed about the way of Japanese customs, politeness and how one should not offend, so I gave in and ate. At the end of the evening I was faced with an astronomical bill. My weekly allowance was wiped out. I'd been set up and conned, and there was nothing I could do.

Japan is unfathomable, a land of contradictory moods. I visited Nara with a couple of friends, to see their huge wooden Buddha. After that, the company went on to Kyoto: one of the most stunning havens I have ever seen. The colours remain constant in my mind – red, white, black, against hills of green moss. It was the simplicity of the place that was most affecting, the pared-downness of the life. We were able to wander at will in and out of the houses, which were built in the twelfth century. Inside we might find neat children, dressed identically, graduated according to size. Or tables laid with due homage paid to the Japanese symmetry of life – each chopstick and tea-cup perfectly placed. It was a living meditation. It's not too fanciful to say that the mood of the place filled you with a sense of wonder, even of awe, at this creation of harmony.

We were whisked off to Kobi after this, by the bullet train. This was about as far distant in time and experience from Kyoto as you could get. It was back to the land of tube-train regimentation. When the train stops at a station you have a minute to get off and a minute to get on before the doors close. Nobody is spared, because they close automatically. The Japanese are so punctual and orderly, and the allowance for each stop is finely calculated so that the trains run to schedule. On the train, in the buffet car, I had my first experience of Kobi beef. It melts in your mouth. I found out why, later. Apparently they give the cows beer to drink, and massage their bellies. Probably the most laid-back, the most pampered cows in the world.

I went to a traditional Kabuki theatre where I sat for near on five hours in utter fascination. The stage was very plain, but 100 feet wide, with thrusts coming out into the audience. The sets were mostly simple painted cloths, which could transform the stage from sandy beach to roaring sea. One scene had a wonderful little wooden boat which bobbed across the back of the stage. The next minute the prow of it appeared on the forestage, much magnified. Brilliant. The make-up was fantastic (there were only men on stage, no women – something I only found out later). I understood not a word, and sometimes it seemed to me as though there was nothing happening, but the audience knew. All the moves are prescribed by convention, and if an actor acquitted himself well, if he executed a move, or some words, in the correct and appropriate manner, the audience shouted his name in approval. The acting was subtle, yet grand. A character sat on the stage, unmoving, for perhaps ten minutes – I started to think it was time for me to go because nothing was happening – then out of the blue he raised an eyebrow and uttered a blood-curdling screech. This produced torrents of applause and his name was shouted loud and long. I would like to have understood what was going on. But apart from it being such a different art form, it takes years to perfect the Kabuki technique. The highest accolade for a Japanese actor is to be known as a National Treasure. If only . . .

Before I returned to London I loaded myself up with cotton and silk kimonos, paper umbrellas, wooden thonged shoes, clay dolls, cotton fabrics and huge red lanterns. I went with Meryl Chappell (who had been a year ahead of me at White Lodge) to buy the lanterns. It was raining, and Meryl had an umbrella which she put in a pot in the shop among some others. We spent a long time in the shop, deliberating, and when eventually we paid the bill we turned to leave, and Meryl extracted her umbrella. This produced a stream of Japanese, and the shop owner tried to yank Meryl's umbrella away from her. I pulled it away from her, she grabbed it back. I tried to use my best mime to explain that it was Meryl's, it was raining, we had put it there when we came in. But she was having none of it. Meryl was stealing it. There was only one thing to do and we did it. We ran for it. It was, although I can think of it as funny now, quite a frightening and unpleasant experience.

Back in England it was the end of May 1975 and time for rehearsals for the Big Top in Battersea Park. I performed the Flower Festival *pas-de-deux* with Lesley Collier. This was another role usually reserved for the tall, classical principals, but it suited my technique. The Danish Bournonville style (the ballet was choreographed by August Bournonville) is full of bounce and beats, with the emphasis in the air. This style was something I had not done before, and it takes some learning. The Bournonville method consists of continual bouncing, known as ballon. I enjoyed it. I have always been able to bounce. Tigger territory.

Élite Syncopations was televized that year, live from the tent. What I found astonishing was the number of people who came, but who would never dream of crossing the river to the Opera House. I felt that we were really bringing dance to the people. We went up to Newcastle at the end of the summer, too. A tent is less formidable, less expensive, than the rarefied (sometimes) atmosphere of a theatre. I began to realize that there might be an audience for dance outside the established Opera House public.

After all this travel I wanted a quiet summer holiday. We wanted somewhere without millions of people – hard to find in August. George came up with the bright idea of Portugal. The country had just had a coup, so we thought that not too many people would venture there. We stayed in Cascais. But the locals were on holiday too, and the town was holding its annual festival to boot. I'd wanted to get away from it all and couldn't sleep; George spent time complaining about the noise of the fair outside our bedroom window. Tough. But there was fresh fish and the sun – except for George who protects himself under an umbrella. Very Scottish. One afternoon I woke from a nap to find I was the only person on the beach. There were hundreds of people on the pier and the sea wall. All laughing. I sat up and was frightened by a rat running between the rocks. I ran, clutching my lilo and unread book, as fast as I could in the opposite direction – to come face to face with a charging bull. No wonder they were all laughing. It was bull-running day, the one day in the year when the locals let bulls run through the streets and on the beach, and the brave young men of the area try and grab the the horns to crash them to the ground. There are loads of casualties and even fatalities. I saw one man run backwards in front of a bull, pulling faces, taunting it. He ran straight into a lamppost – not funny – and killed himself. A lovely quiet holiday, I don't think.

Back at the ranch, it was decided to revive a production first choreographed in 1915 by Fokine, with a score commissioned from Stravinsky by Diaghilev, and danced by Nijinsky. This was *Petrouchka*. It is taken from a traditional Russian folk-tale, about a puppet made up of the left-over pieces of wood and sawdust swept up off the magician's floor. Stravinsky found inspiration from Russian folk-tunes.

Three of us were to play Petrouchka during the season: Nureyev, Alexander Grant and me. Three totally different dancers, three totally different styles and approaches. Even our make-up would be quite different, according to how each of us perceived the part. Rudolf and Alexander had learned the role years before and had their own ideas about how it should be. It was chaos, for me, when we rehearsed together. So many conflicting opinions, conflicting moves. I was beginning to be muddled.

Essentially the problem was that although the basic steps of a ballet cannot be changed – it is rather like the text of a play – the interpretation of those steps may be quite different according to performer and choreographer. Nureyev's interpretation differed from Alexander's, which differed from Brian Shaw's – from whom I was learning, I thought. It was fortunate that John Taras, ballet master of Balanchine's New York City Ballet, came over from America to mount our revival. He had worked with Fokine himself in the thirties and forties, when Fokine had remounted the work. I insisted that I rehearse with John alone. He explained the meaning of each movement of head and body, which helped me to an understanding of how to perform the role. *Petrouchka* is a ballet where I could not rely on virtuoso solos. There are – or should be – no tricks and jumps and spins. These are used by some dancers to cover up inadequacies in interpretation. It is the mime which displays the inner depths of the unhappy character's soul.

Petrouchka is a puppet with badly made joints. His legs and his arms turn in. His head flops from side to side. All his stance is introversion, sadness, dejection.

He longs for love and escape. But he is thrown about by his master, the magician, who chucks him in a wooden box for being completely useless. He is bullied by his counterpart, his rival, the Blackamoor, whose legs and arms turn out, whose head is erect. He is full of strength, pride and extroversion.

Petrouchka and the Blackamoor compete for the love of the expressionless and emotionless Ballerina. It is a lost cause. The ballet is set in a winter fairground, with performing bears and a carousel in which the puppet show takes place. Coachmen dance Russian folk-dances and big-bosomed wet-nurses walk through the town, eating sunflower seeds to make their milk richer. The piece culminates with a chase through the town, causing the villagers to think the puppets have taken on reality. The Blackamoor kills Petrouchka. The people gather around his body, believing him human. They pick him up to find that he is only sawdust and wood. But as the orchestra play the final chords of Stravinsky's music, the soul, the ghost of Petrouchka, is seen hovering over the fairground. He thumbs his nose in revenge as his erstwhile master sees him.

Thanks to John Taras I gained a grasp of the role which otherwise might have taken years. It is one of those characters that the more you do it, the more you grow into it. I didn't have the luxury of that time scale. I needed to be immediate, to have it under my belt on the first night. I used to go to the dressing-room of the conductor, Ashley Lawrence, in the interval before the ballet. He would play a section of the music to help me into the character and to ensure we were at one in the tempi. This is not normal practice, but it was fundamental in helping me to perform this role. It was a part I *really* enjoyed dancing.

One final thing about *Petrouchka*: the ballet critic of *The Times* insisted that I was too small to play the part of Petrouchka. I mean – the creature is a doll, for heaven's sake, and what's more, was originally played by Nijinsky, who was no taller than I.

When the Kirov Ballet had come to the Festival Hall in 1971, I had heard about an amazing dancer, one of their leading principals, and forced myself to take a busman's holiday by going along to one of the classes. On that day this particular dancer did not turn up for class, but I saw him perform, eventually, and was as delighted by his performance as I had expected to be. He jumped so high, almost parallel to the floor, and could turn in almost any position. He performed steps and leaps I had never seen before, and all within the parameters of the choreography. Astonishing. He took London by storm that year. He later defected. His name was Mikhail Baryshnikov.

My first encounter with him was when he came to London to play Romeo with the Royal Ballet in the autumn of 1975. I was the solo in the Mandolin Dance. He came up to me under cover of my applause and muttered, in his heavily accented English, 'Remind me never to dance with you on stage.' It was a compliment. After the performance he invited me back to Carlos Place where he was staying, for a late supper and lots of scotch. I befriended him – partly because he knew hardly anyone in London. We sat up until two or three in the morning, conversing as best we could. After morning class I stayed behind and Micha taught me steps that he brought with him to the West. The reason he could hit the air at such an off-balanced angle, he said, was because he had trained as a gymnast before entering ballet school. He learned to jump, there-fore, with the use of a trampoline and this made him fearless when leaping. I learned that the system for training gymnasts, dancers and athletes in the Soviet Union was almost interchangeable in the earliest years of tuition. Dancers might start off as athletes or gymnasts, then as their talents showed they might be moved from one discipline to another. But a dancer, once chosen, was groomed only for one place in a company. Either for stardom, or for the character roles, or the virtuoso parts, or for the *corps*. There was no progression, no moving upwards as there is in the West. They stayed where they were put. One Russian dancer I met told me, when I inquired why he had become a dancer, that it was because the ballet school was closer to his home than the ice-rink. He also added that by becoming a dancer he would not have to join the army. I was, I admit, taken aback by the matter-of-factness in the choice of career. I don't think he loved it any the less – it's just that we regard it as a calling.

Diana Roberts asked me if I would introduce her to Baryshnikov. Her utter devotion to Nureyev was on the wane, at last. I invited Micha and his then girlfriend Jessica Lange to meet Diana at Luigi's in Covent Garden. Luigi's, at that time, was the haunt of actors, post-show, particularly of the then Aldwych-based Royal Shakespeare Company. I used to meet the likes of Mike Gwilym, Roger Rees and Nickolas Grace there. Diana paid for us all that night at Luigi's – and Baryshnikov became her new passion.

A year later I was appearing in New York and Micha was at a gala at the Met at the same time. I gatecrashed because it was my night off. He was performing with Natalia Makarova in a new piece by Jerome Robbins. Afterwards I went backstage to see him. He had discovered that the wardrobe had taken not only his costume but also his trousers. And he was expected at a reception. I went on a mission into the depths of the theatre and found a pair for him. At the party I met a girl called Nancy, who had also gatecrashed. She became a devoted fan and friend and often came to England to see me dance. She was studying psychology and took holiday jobs to raise money for these trips. One year she was working in a store when it caught fire and she fell to her death. I felt devastated.

Meanwhile I was continuing my contemporary dance classes at the Place, home of the London Contemporary Dance Theatre. Robert North and I resumed the conversation we had started in Brazil, about working together on a piece to be performed at Sadler's Wells. It certainly could not have been staged at the Opera House. It would not be until April 1980 that a major breakthrough happened at the Royal Opera House. *Troy Game*, choreographed by Robert North for London Contemporary Dance, was to be performed by the Royal Ballet. At last, a contemporary dance piece from a contemporary company in the Rep. (The review of *Troy Game* by Mary Clarke in the *Guardian* made me wonder how critics can separate their professional opinion from their personal ones: '*Troy Game* for ten men is done with slightly more vigour than originally by this company but its relentless displays of energy are wearying and Wayne Sleep – fantastic dancer though he is – turns it into a Wayne Sleep comedy number. I wanted to cheer during the comic curtain calls when the rest of the cast knocked him flat.') Lynn Seymour was also collaborating with Robert that season, and, because she was one of Kenneth MacMillan's favourite dancers, was instrumental in my getting permission to work with LCDT. It was extremely unusual for a classical dancer to go into contemporary dance, because we were not trained in it. Now it is part of the curriculum of all classical ballet schools.

Robert and I decided on the Bible story of David and Goliath, thus giving us a chance to perform together. We asked Carl Davis to write the score and worked very closely with him during rehearsals. The music echoed all the choreographic scenes perfectly in rehearsals, but once it was transposed to a full orchestra it seemed to lose much of the haunting quality it possessed on the piano. We had to make a recording from the orchestra to tour with (because of lack of funds). We were up all night, re-transposing. This was a fundamental lesson for me in the importance of arrangements and transposition. We decided, in order to thicken the plot, on a hypothetical chance meeting for David and Goliath during the night before their famous battle. This gave us a chance to show off David's cunning and Goliath's silent gullibility. The last moment in the ballet has Goliath swaying almost to the ground from a standing position, his legs held by the other members of the cast, before he finally collapses.

The production toured for about eight weeks before coming to London, and in the manner of so many productions there were changes to be made as the ballet came alive in front of audiences. I should say that, although it was a collaboration, it was far more Robert's piece than mine. My commitments with the Royal Ballet meant that I could not tour, my part was danced by Ross M'Kim, and it was Robert who engineered the changes.

I did make it to watch the first night in Aberdeen. I couldn't miss my first co-commissioned work for a professional dance company. I couldn't find any-where to stay and ended up on the floor of the digs of a couple of dancers. I had to creep out at five in the morning to avoid being caught by the landlady.

When the company came into Sadler's Wells I was able to dance my part. A few days before the first night I took to my bed with pains careering around my chest. I thought I was having a heart attack and asked George to call the doctor. He was very reluctant – it was Sunday after all – but my moans and groans convinced him, in the end, that I must be very sick. The doctor came and was far more interested in George's clavichord than in the heart-strings under my clavicle. I was insisting that I be admitted, immediately, to an emergency ward, so he gave me his diagnosis. Wind. George thought this a joke, and dismissed the whole thing as totally trivial. Laughing, he told his mother, and was taken aback when she said, 'Wind? Oh no. Poor thing. I was admitted to hospital with wind once.' George's sympathy, lacking until now, became more apparent. Apparently there is no known remedy, just rest – and probably psychological counselling. We put it down to tension and nerves – the nerves of performing in my own piece and in front of the London critics. And a fear of failure. A fledgling choreographer doesn't usually get more than one chance.

But this bout of wind helped me to lose weight, which was one consolation, because David's costume (designed by Peter Farmer) was more like a swimming-costume than anything else, and it was necessary for the body to be well-defined. The other good thing was that *David and Goliath* was chosen for the repertoire of the San Francisco Ballet after Michael Smuin had searched Britain for new pieces. My first collaboration was sold internationally.

While I was performing David at Sadler's Wells I was also rehearsing with the Royal Ballet for *A Month in the Country*, Sir Frederick Ashton's new ballet. In Turgenev's play Kolia, Vera's son, does not play a very important part, so when it was offered to me, I did not realize that I would be given some of the best dancing of my life. Kolia was only twelve years old, no easy task, even if I was small enough for the part. I started to study friends' children: the slightly ungainly way children walk and the way they look at something as if for the first time. I investigated in depth, and then discarded most of the findings, keeping only the strongest motifs. What is left out is as inportant as what is kept in. This is not unlike choreography, where the choreographer's eye has to pick out one movement from the hundreds of possibilities. The best choreographers have the keenest eyes. I also included some of the new jumps that Baryshnikov had taught me.

There was the challenge, too, of having to dance while bouncing a ball. I had to find ways of jumping and catching it, spinning and passing it under my legs, making it bounce on the music, then making it bounce high enough for me to spin before catching it. They made all sorts of balls for me, of different sizes. It had to be large enough to be seen by the audience, small enough to be held in my hand and bounce. After all the experiments I ended up going to Hamleys and buying one for 50p. It was the only one that worked. (When we took *Country* to New York, Karl Bowen came to a matinée. I was eager to impress him – and dropped the ball at the start of one of my solos. The ball is integral to the dance so I spent the rest of the solo chasing it round the stage. I felt a total idiot.

I also had to fly a kite. The props man made one out of canvas with steel supports, so heavy I could barely lift it, let alone run around the stage pretending it was in flight.

'How do you expect me to fly this thing?' I asked him.

'I've made it to last,' he said. He thought that was that. I insisted the kite be made out of balsa wood and tissue paper. This I could fly. He was hacked off because it would probably have to be repaired before every performance. But what, I said to him, if it was in the choreography that I was to jump through a paper hoop – he'd have to repair that every time. So I got my lightweight kite.

Then I discovered that though it was a doddle running around a rehearsal room, flying the thing, on stage I was confronted with obstacles, chaise-longues and other bits of furniture. So in performance I had to pick up the wind, so to speak, before I leaped over the chaise-longue or swerved round the tables, keeping it airborne.

Julia Trevelyan Oman designed the sets and costumes. She worried about my modern ball not being authentic-looking. I suggested she spray it. (It seemed obvious to me . . .) It turned up with a pattern more French than Russian, I thought, and when I expressed surprise she told me that Russia at this time was tremendously influenced by French fashion and so all the designs were an admixture of the styles of both countries. Much of the scenery was *trompe l'oeil*, and she painted a little profile portrait of Sir Fred right in the middle above the proscenium. Not many people know this. You would only see it if you knew it was there. Neat little trick.

A Month in the Country was set to music by Chopin. There were only eight dancers: Anthony Dowell, Lynn Seymour, Marguerite Porter, Alexander Grant, Derek Rencher, Denise Nunn, Anthony Conway and me. The end of the first night was very moving. All eight of us were joined on stage by Sir Fred and John Lanchbery (who arranged the score and conducted the orchestra) for a standing ovation which went on and on. Sir Fred was always nervous on a first night. He was worried that each work might be his last, that it might be a failure. In the Crush Bar, afterwards he said to George, 'Dear boy, is it just mawkish sentimentality?' George's answer was, 'It is a little masterpiece.' And so it was. The review in the *Evening Standard*, by Edward Thorpe, ran: 'A major new work by Sir Frederick Ashton is not only of great importance to the Royal Ballet but also for the whole world of dance. Last night's Covent Garden première of *A Month in the Country* added another fine work to the choreographer's unrivalled list of masterpieces.' Sir Fred need never have worried.

A Month in the Country was included in the repertoire when we went to New York, Washington and Philadelphia in the spring of 1976. My first performance as the clog-dancing Widow Simone in *La Fille Mal Gardée* was in New York. By then I had played the Notary, and the Cockerel, but was yet to play Alain. That came later. I actually found the Widow quite difficult, because the part is more usually played by an older dancer. Stanley Holden was over forty when he created the role – I was not yet thirty and did not have quite the weight and experience I should have had. But I think I managed to bluff my way through it, and my performance was not discreditable. Widow Simone's character is based on the traditional pantomime dame. She stood me in good stead and provided much inspiration when later I played Gertie, the Queen of the Circus, in *Goldilocks*.

After New York, the Company went on to Washington and Philadelphia. In Philadelphia I fell ill. For the first (and only) time I missed a performance not through injury but through illness. I lost a stone in weight and my soaking mattress had to be changed daily. A doctor was called, but could make no diagnosis. Michael Somes called from his hotel, to ask after me. (I no longer dreaded him and we had become friends.) On the last day I rallied enough to watch *Swan Lake* from the wings. But I was still delirious and can remember wondering why they were not speaking the roles.

Back in England I turned on the TV one evening to watch the news. There was an item about thirteen people who had died of Legionnaire's Disease in Philadelphia a week after we had left the city. All thirteen had stayed in the same hotel as I had. Too much of a strange coincidence, I thought. I vaguely remember, looking back, that I thought it odd that it was raining on a hot summer afternoon. It turned out to be drips from the air-conditioners sticking out of the hotel windows. We know, now, that one of the ways this dire disease is spread is through air-conditioning. I can only think I was lucky.

David Conville (who was artistic director of the Regent's Park Theatre when I played Ariel), director of the New Shakespeare Company, asked me if I would be interested in choreographing a revival of Julian Slade's musical *Salad Days*, which had been a long-running musical in London in the fifties. The cast was Elisabeth Seal, Sheila Steafel, Ian Talbot and Bill Kerr. This was my first choreography for the commercial theatre and for actors, not dancers. I was invited to all the auditions and had to set a simple routine for each person. I was amazed to find how little some of them knew about movement – most of them had been to drama school and dance, I thought (perhaps erroneously), was part of the curriculum.

And this was supposed to be a musical? But when I thought about it, I realized that all the British musicals I'd seen were very static. This was because the actors were never required to dance. Yet they could read for a part with only passable singing and no dancing ability. Dancers, on the other hand, even if they had a good voice, were not allowed even to read for a part. They were regarded merely as moving wallpaper. Something, I suspect, to do with the fact that all their performing lives are non-speaking. It follows, if you take it through to an extreme of logic, that they therefore couldn't speak at all. But if an actor couldn't dance – that was irrelevant. And the division was absolute. The British musical was dying on its feet. I insisted, because I was determined to change things, that if an actor couldn't move, he couldn't get the part.

Salad Days, among other themes, is about a piano that makes people dance and the big number is called 'Look at Me, I'm Dancing'. I found it a challenge to work within the limitations of their abilities and found it easier to let them show me what they could do, rather than enforce my will on them. Then I took what they had to offer and moulded it into the number. This experience taught me a great deal about characterization in dance, because each part in the play was so totally different. Dancing vicars and dons. How frightfully British. And it was.

Salad Days opened at the Theatre Royal, Windsor, in 1976 to full houses.

George and I had a private box, with added first night nerves, exacerbated by the presence of Joe Layton, who was staying in London. Joe had choreographed me in *The Grand Tour* some years before, and was well versed in the art of dance in the musical. One critic said my choreography was over busy. I disagreed, of course. I would have liked to put in more. I had not learned, then, that less is more. After Windsor *Salad Days* transferred to the Duke of York's in the West End.

Michael Grade came to the studio at the Dance Centre one day. He had heard that at one of the Friends' Christmas parties I had impersonated the Russian gymnast, Olga Korbut, red leotard, bunches, smile and all. It was a send-up of her floor routine for which she had won the Olympic gold. I traced the obscure music she used, and, although I can't do flips and double somersaults in the air, I portrayed her bubbly enthusiasm, her waves to the audience and her irresistible smile. She was easy to send up because her character was larger than life. She brought personality to gymnastics in the same year that John Curry brought art to ice. Michael was interested in including my Olga Korbut in John's *Ice Spectacular* for London Weekend Television. And after watching me cavort round the studio he signed me up then and there.

I decided on a beam routine, finding ways of swinging under it and back up, jumping across it and ending up prostrate below it. The damn beam kept wobbling and I thought I'd break my neck during the filming. And then, after all this death-defying effort, my Olga Korbut routine was cut from the show. Reason? John, being such a good sport and a gentle person, did not really want to send up a fellow gold medallist. It might appear bad taste. So the producer, John Schofield, asked me if I would like to do a send-up of Curry himself. The only skating I had done off the ice was *Les Patineurs*. The only skating I'd done on the ice was at Queens, in Bayswater, in rented boots that gave me athlete's foot and strained ankles. (John Curry told me that he would have had strained ankles in the boots that are generally rented out to the likes of me. The other interesting thing is that, because a skater's boots are so tightly bound round the ankle, a skater's ankles are remarkably weak. I discovered this when John appeared in a *Good Night's Sleep* without his skates and on a dance floor.) I was given lots of video tapes of his Olympic winning routine and proceeded to transfer them from ice to stage. I couldn't use his music, as his routine was included in the show. Instead I used *The Skater's Waltz*.

Before the shoot George and I were invited to Stuttgart for a few days by the Spanish Consul-General, José-Luis Castillejo. George says that Castillejo gave us each a loaded revolver, because the Spanish 'guest workers' were becoming restive and a storming of the consulate was not out of the question. I remember none of this. And I don't believe that I've ever seen, let alone handled, a loaded revolver in my life. In fact, I think I'd faint. George also says we made 'terrifying' dashes through the Black Forest to France in order to eat, because, according to the Consul, Germany was a very nice country, but the food was not to his liking. Well, yes, we did go to France to eat, quite often, but it's not that far away from Stuttgart, and as for 'terrifying' dashes . . . ? George has a fine sense of the melodramatic.

I discovered the ballroom in the Consulate, which was nigh perfect for trying out some moves for my 'ice' routine, the floor was so shiny. George was his usual helpful self, sitting in the corner, pretending to be my accompaniment, going 'Oom pah pah, oom pah pah' (this bore no actual resemblance to the music I would be using, but at least was in three-time) while I dictated the moves to him and slid over the polish of the parquet. I was able to reproduce some of John Curry's moves, but obviously some were impossible.

When it came to the show itself, it did look as though I was gliding around the ice at speed. And then the camera panned back, revealing the wind machine blowing my hair and billowing the sleeves of my shirt – with my feet rooted firmly to one spot. I also danced a tango with Millicent Martin. This was choreographed by Norman Maen, who had won an Emmy for his work on the Tom Jones specials. John filmed all his work at the Streatham ice rink, but I was very grateful to be able to film at the London Weekend television studios. The thought of possibly working my routines with the chill from the ice coursing up my trouser leg still gives me a kind of shiver. I spent some time talking to John during the filming for this show. He was a very quiet and modest person, one of those rare unassuming people who reach the top of their chosen profession. He told me that he had used the EST (Erhard Seminar Training) method to gain enough confidence to go on the ice and perform for his gold medal. A lovely man.

At around the same time I devised a number to Gilbert and Sullivan's 'A Modern Major General' for a midnight gala at the Theatre Royal, Drury Lane. I was the only dancer in the gala and was immensely flattered by the fact that Margot Fonteyn introduced me. She was my idol and I would have done anything for her, lie down in front of her à la Walter Raleigh if necessary. Ah well, I did the next best thing. After the performance I came off into the wings and placed a great deal of myself before her – I threw up. I had food poisoning. But this 'Modern Major General' routine brought me a couple of other interesting offers. One was from a producer who saw the piece and offered me my first television guest spot on the Dickie Henderson Show. The other was *very* interesting.

I was invited to America by Gilbert McKay, who had a house on the thirteenth tee of Pebble Beach, to reproduce the dance for a performance in the Bohemian Club in the Redwoods of Northern California. A private jet flew us from Pebble Beach to the Redwoods. There are very few members under fifty-five or so, as the waiting list is so long. At these annual gatherings you meet the powerful and rich, rubbing shoulders with people like Ford and Kissinger, who gave lectures while I was there. Each profession had its own camp and each camp had its own theme – the aviary where singers and comedians gathered, for instance. It was a mixture of the rough and ready and the incredibly expensive. It wasn't surprising to see a grand piano on a wooden porch. There were two communal dining-rooms in the open air, but most people brought their personal chefs. The motto of the club was 'Weaving spiders, weave not here', but was there more weaving here than at any other time of the year? The concentrated power was awe-inspiring.

After my performance on the Redwood stage, Merv Griffin invited me on to his midday chat show, televised from Las Vegas. I was to dance the Prince's solo from *Swan Lake* and partner Merv in tennis shoes and tutu. Women tried to grab my legs, not because they fancied me, but because they wanted to get into the camera lens and wave to Mum. My only way of getting there was on a jet specially sent to pick me up from the Grove. Two pilots and me in the back. One came back to pour me a drink. I said 'Cheers' – but he'd gone. Travelling alone is no fun. No one to share the joke.

Dickie Henderson was the first person to give me a guest spot on a television variety show. He was one of those traditional all-round performers who could turn his hand to everything and anything. *I'm Dickie – That's Showbusiness* was filmed at Elstree for ATV. He decided we would dance together on the show, in a set which simulated his own sitting-room. We used golf clubs, glasses and every prop in the place in a routine created by Irving Davies, who learned much of his craft from the talented but notorious Paddy Stone. Paddy choreographed many of Dickie's shows. He was notorious because he was a frightening man, sometimes sadistic in his approach – he reduced many dancers to tears. He was vastly respected in the business, and was always given three days to shoot a routine. These days you are lucky if you get a morning.

I learned how different a television rehearsal day was from one in the ballet world. When you arrive at eight in the morning there is no teacher to give a class and a warm-up. It amazed me that all the television dancers could go into their routines without even so much as a stretch. I had to creep off into a corner and do a classical ballet barre before daring to move my limbs. I might have seemed wimpish to them for all I know, but I thought they were daft not to warm up. After all the years of protection by the Royal Ballet, I now had to become responsible for myself and warming up was essential. The studio floor was concrete (memories of the Met in New York), and even though it was overlaid with a grey plasticized material I found that it jarred my limbs and deadened, somewhat, my jumps. Under the heat of the lights this covering melted gradually throughout the day and stuck to my shoes like chewing-gum. Especially after a series of pirouettes – which made holes in the surface too. The stage crew then had to patch up their pretty floor before the next take. I was not their favourite person.

This was the start of my television career. I was, at this point, as much on the box as in the ballet. I started to hear whispers in the street: 'Ooh look, it's that ballet dancer.' A novel feeling and I enjoyed it. Some well-known people resent being recognized, or resent the assumed ownership by the public, but I feel that Nureyev was right when he said, when asked if he minded about losing his privacy, 'It's part of the job.' He also added, 'The time to worry is when they don't recognize you.'

NINE

OPENING AVENUES

WITH FAME COMES responsibility. But it also opens up so many opportunities, and unless it happens to you, you have very little conception of how it can be. For me, television appearances made people consider that I might be capable of handling disciplines other than dance. Also, I must admit, it meant that my name was likely to have some kind of audience-pull. Talent is one thing, indeed is an absolute requisite for advancement in the rarefied world of classical dance, and draws its own audience out of love, but in the commercial world marketing a name is as important as talent, and helps put 'bums on seats'. And I know that audiences (mostly female) come to see me as much for 'Inn'e lovely, I'd like to put 'im in me 'andbag, and take 'im 'ome with me', as they do for my dancing, and because they have seen me on the telly.

In 1976 I had the honour to be asked to appear at the Royal Variety Performance. I talked with Louis Benjamin about what I should do, and he asked me to dance classical ballet with some of the principals of the Royal Ballet. I didn't think that would be a great idea as, quite frankly, I'd be smaller than most if not all of them. So I asked Lesley Collier if she would appear with me. She accepted, and I choreographed a tarantella for us. Eager, however, to show that I was not just a ballet dancer, I asked Bill Drysdale to choreograph a jazz finale. In between I inserted my Olga Korbut routine. Diane Langton (the singer/actress I had met when she starred in *A Chorus Line*) came along to link the scenes while I made two costume changes. Not just a little ambitious.

Diane went on the missing list for a couple of days, I don't know if she was nervous or what. Bill and I were certainly panicking. We were only two days away from the performance and she had not rehearsed the finale, where we were all to dance and sing together. Yes, I had added a song! I would have had a much easier time if I had stuck to classical ballet and there I go again – gotta try everything. I have appeared in about four other Royal Variety Performances. Once my name was not even in the programme. We were announced during the evening as two very special guests (the other being Nichola Treherne). Yes, it was my Torvill and Dean impersonation. After which the Queen said, 'What made you do that routine?' I replied, 'It was a take-off, Ma'am.' At which she smiled and whispered, 'I hope they never see it!'

So it was probably as much my being known as my talent that suggested my name to Wendy Toye when she was looking for someone to cast as Oblio in

The Point. This is a piece with an interesting history. Originally it was a cartoon, made for American television, with music and lyrics by Harry Nilssen, narrated by Dustin Hoffman, and it had won several awards. Its conversion to a stage play and its try-out in Philadelphia had not been a great success. But Harry (also famous for singing 'Without You', the theme song from the film *Midnight Cowboy*) was determined to make it work the second time around.

Wendy, who had started as a dancer with the Sadler's Wells Ballet, was now directing musicals in the West End. She rang me from the Mermaid Theatre to ask me if I would be interested in the lead part in *The Point*. She was, in fact, looking for a dancer, because she conceived the part as a mime role and thought I would fit it perfectly. I listened to the music and watched the film at the Mermaid. Then Wendy dropped out of the equation (I think she was too busy) and her place was taken by Ron Pember. Ron, an actor who occasionally directed, was a good friend of the wonderful Bernard Miles, who had founded the Mermaid Theatre. Bernard, who was to play the King, sat in as artistic director on the discussions between Ron, Harry and me about the direction *The Point* was to take. It was decided that my role, Oblio, would not be merely mime, but would also sing.

Sing? I had my doubts about this being a good career move. Harry had a wonderful voice and quite frankly I felt my ability was poor, zilch maybe. But Harry persuaded me. He said I could do it if I was prepared to *listen* enough. Listening has never been one of my best points. But he said he would take me under his wing, that he could help me. I had to give it a go. And really, I would have been a fool to pass up an opportunity such as this. It was a lesson in grasping what is offered to you – and not being afraid to ask for help.

When rehearsals started in November the choreographer backed out. I can't remember why. I was asked to choreograph the production myself. But I knew this would be more work than one person could handle, so I called in Graham Powell to collaborate with me. We only had three weeks for rehearsals, which was scarcely enough for the basic project itself, let alone all the highly technical staging it required. It was, in reality, far too ambitious a project for the Mermaid, which had old-fashioned lighting equipment and a very primitive sound system. But Harry envisaged *The Point* with video screens, back projections, sophisticated sound systems – as a production of the highest tech, way in advance of its time. Bernard Miles narrated the story from another room with a direct video link to the screen on the stage. (This might all sound very normal now, but it wasn't then.) There were slides and film inserts from the original cartoon, depictions of volcanoes and fires. And metal bars forged into a triangular set, with triangular video screens. All quite extraordinary, quite new, quite ground-breaking. Graham and I didn't have enough time in these three weeks even to choreograph a solo dance for me, and I was beginning to wonder if a simpler treatment might not be better. The technical rehearsal, where we went through the lighting, sound, video and projection, was supposed to take two days – and lasted a week. And we still weren't ready. We were all exhausted. We had rehearsed from ten in the morning to maybe twelve at night. We might arrive the following morning to find the crew asleep in the stalls – having spent all night working on problems. And then they would have to take down the metal screens, which were too big, and re-solder them on stage – while we tried to rehearse. Chaos theory had nothing on us.

I remember ad-libbing my dance solo on the first preview. I remember I danced through fifteen black-outs: the computerized lighting plot had a fit. It was not good. I was up in arms after this. Coming as I did from a subsidized theatrical background, I felt it important that the audience should be presented with a show that was at least part ready for performance. I suggested that for the second preview the audience should be invited to reclaim their money because of our technical problems. This, of course, is against the grain for commercial theatre – bums on seats. But they did concede the point, because Vivian Cox, the Mermaid's administrator, came up with the idea of rehearsing the first half in front of the audience: if it went well, the second half would be a performance; if it didn't, the audience could reclaim their money and leave. It was a hit. No one left. At the end we received a standing ovation. There is nothing an audience likes better than seeing behind the scenes or being in on the problems and tribulations of a show. It makes them feel part of it, as though they have contributed too. Matters improved by degrees. Sometimes Ron would call a halt – not because something needed going over, but because he remembered it was a rehearsal, and it might be a good idea to say 'Stop!' Just to please the audience. We ran the second act, we didn't rehearse it, and it went without hitch.

Oblio, my character, is a boy who is ostracized by his community for being different and is banned to the Pointless Forest because he has a round head instead of a pointed one, which is the norm. He goes on a long journey, meeting some strange people on the way. People such as the big operatic Balloon Ladies; the Leaf Man – who perched on a ladder with long ribbons as leaves cascading from him to the edges of the stage; the Rock Man, whose look was inspired by a piece I had seen Martha Graham perform – I hid him in a large grey-green bean bag resembling a rock until he started to sway with the music (the Rock Man sometimes had to sing an encore); and the Signpost, played by two people, one standing behind the other, with their arms going in all different directions. It is a captivating journey for Oblio, who finds out that conformity is not everything, and that victimization of the non-conformist can be overcome.

Oblio also had a puppet dog called Arrow, which went with him everywhere. Arrow was handled by a puppeteer, who controlled him by manoeuvring two sticks. I thought this would never work, because the puppeteer was going to be on stage all the time, handling the dog in full view of the audience. However, I was proved wrong. The audience accepted him, mostly due to Paul Aylett's total commitment – he became one with the dog. When the dog looked at me, so did he. They stole the show. Originally Paul wore the same black and white costume as I did. But I had him sprayed grey. My reason was that it was too confusing for the audience. Really, it was a touch of the 'move over, boyo'!

The whole experience of being in that show taught me a great deal – not only about acting, singing, and choreography, but also about the element of audience participation. This is something I now consider important when contemplating a show. In *The Point*, it was the first time I had ever walked through the auditorium on the way to the stage. The rapport was that little bit deeper.

Ron kept an eye on the dialogue, but left Graham and me to do pretty well what we wanted, which was good. And Graham, who was then living in Jane Kasmin's basement in Ifield Road, was invaluable during the fraught days of previews, rock solid, keeping morales boosted. Bernard Miles had a fund of stories he would tell in rehearsals at the drop of a hat. Something always reminded him of something else, such as when he painted backdrops for Diaghilev productions – though occasionally we were confused as to the relevance. As tempers frayed, and time was short, he became more of an irritant than a help, wasting time, we thought. But we usually felt it would be too rude and mean to stop him.

But he was good enough to help me with my diction, keeping me back after rehearsals. 'Loud and clear,' he would say. 'Don't go down at the end of your lines – up, boy, up!' His memory was not always good, and some of the cast did not like the fact that he could not remember their names. It never bothered me. He was a one man theatrical institution and worked indefatigably to keep the Mermaid alive. And he was very kind. He let Graham mount an exhibition of his paintings in the foyer during the run. I remember one evening during the performance we looked up at the screen to find Bernard, as the King, fast asleep in front of the video link camera. A hand was gently prodding him. He woke with a start and immediately went into a speech from two scenes later, cutting out a song, and forcing us to scurry to new positions.

It was great, too to work with Harry Nilssen. I am grateful that he had the nerve to let me play Oblio, that he believed in my ability to put the songs across – particularly as he used to call me 'the raw muscle', which essentially implies pure physicality. I loved both his invention and his voice. We spent many late evenings singing duets at the flat he rented from Marc Bolan in Park Lane. Marc Bolan came to the first night: it was full, in fact, of people from the music business. And it was through Harry's connections that I started to meet people from the pop world, performers such as Elton John and Freddie Mercury, managers such as John Reid, and other people who worked behind the scenes of that business: Ken and Dolly East, for instance, who became good friends.

Harry was generous and gregarious. Soon after the opening his wife gave birth and he was there for the delivery at Queen Charlotte's Hospital, which is one of those places where you can have dim lights and water births. Harry started to sing 'Happy Birthday' as the baby emerged. He reached 'Happy birthday, dear . . . ' and had to ask the nurse whether it was a boy or a girl. The nurse, being American, replied, 'It's a Beau,' hence the christening of Beau Nilssen. Some time later I received a certificate in the post to say I was now the proud godfather of Beau Harry Nilssen. I was proud, too – until I discovered later that he'd sent these certificates to several hundred other people. As I say, gregarious and generous and missed.

The Point opened in early December 1976, was an immediate sell-out, and ran until the spring when the production was to transfer to the West End. But there were technical hitches that did not seem easily surmountable. And I wasn't too happy either, because I wanted to change certain elements, but I was told there was no budget for it. So I declined the offer to perform for the West End run. While I was in *The Point* I had to dance a few times at Covent Garden and my understudy went on at the Mermaid. The notice at the box office read: 'Sleepless Nights – 4th, 9th, 12th and 15th.' *The Point* was revived the following year at the Mermaid Theatre, and in that production The Monkees performed their rock version, both on stage and on record.

The Society of West End Theatre Awards (now the Olivier Awards) nominated me for Best Performance in a Musical that year, and although I didn't win, the production itself won Best Design. The show gained a cult following. I am still stopped in the street, even today, by people who tell me, 'I saw you in *The Point*.'

Mum, Gran, cousin Robert and his girlfriend Heather came to stay with me in Powis Gardens over the Christmas while *The Point* was on. George was away in Scotland. I have to admit that sometimes while you are working it is difficult to entertain your family when you are under a certain amount of stress which can add to the pressures and problems of performing. Especially so if they are not from a performing family. (Makes them sound like seals.) One morning when we were performing twice daily, Robert drove me to the Mermaid to familiarize himself with the route. The plan was that he would bring the family to the evening show. They never turned up. After the show, I phoned home to find out what happened. They had got lost in the dark and the heavy snow, given up and returned home. Robert then kindly decided to have another go, with Heather, at reaching the Mermaid to collect me after the show. So they set off, leaving Mum and Gran in the warm. I didn't know this and I made my own way home. I found Mum in a terrible state. Robert and Heather were nowhere to be found. I spent most of the night on the telephone, ringing hospitals, police, trying to describe the car. But I still don't drive, pay scant attention to cars and didn't know the licence number. Lot of use.

In the morning I came downstairs to the sound of Robert's voice. After a pretty sleepless night, and with two shows to do, I was hardly rested and my fuse was very short. Robert and Heather had lost their way not only to the Mermaid, but also back home, and had given up and slept the night in the car. One street away. Now I can say 'poor things.' Then, I was not very sympathetic, and berated Robert for causing not only anxiety but lack of sleep. He was upset by my attitude and my impatience, which he perceived as rudeness. He saw the insensitive side of me, the side I had carefully built up over the years as a protective shell to cope with the vagaries of performance. I think I had nearly forgotten that I was brought up to be sensitive to everybody else's feelings, that I should think, always, of others before myself. But my world was so different from my family's – which is something they did not understand – and I had learned to become essentially selfish. I believe there are very few performers who are exempt from this. It is a survival tactic. I say this not in mitigation, nor as an excuse, but more as a fact of performance life. I lament it, perhaps, but I can't apologize for it. The family did make it to a show, eventually.

John Neumeier, Canadian choreographer and dancer, who had trained at the Royal Ballet and was now the Director of the Hamburg Ballet, was commissioned to create a ballet, based on Mahler's Fourth Symphony, at Covent Garden. He came to see me in *The Point* because he was thinking of casting me. He told me that he was impressed with the quiet innocence I brought to Oblio and offered me the leading character in his ballet. This was the first ballet that was created for me in the central role.

Mahler's Fourth is a difficult piece of music in that the last movement bears little or no relation to the other three. The first three movements are pure music and may be interpreted in any way you wish. The last has an incongruity that makes you think it is another composition entirely – it has sung poems about St Peter baking cakes in heaven(!). I hoped he'd leave the last scene out. Vain hope.

The rehearsals were crammed into only four weeks. This was to be a fifty minute ballet, and a twenty-minute piece is normally given eight weeks. Neumeier said to Kenneth MacMillan that it wasn't enough time. MacMillan replied that he didn't have enough time either – he was in the middle of creating a new ballet too – so John had little time to experiment.

By the time we came to the first of the two dress rehearsals, some of the choreography was still unfinished. The younger dancers were given a lot of interesting, but difficult, steps and moves. They would have been able to master it, but not in four weeks. We were all under pressure and rehearsals were tense. The *corps de ballet* tended to bash into each other, with little room to execute some of the difficult lifts and catches, which could have resulted in dangerous accidents. It didn't, as it happened, but it was more luck than judgement.

Backstage there was unhappiness, born of desperation from the difficulty and the time scale. I heard comments such as 'How's he going to finish in time?' and, 'I still can't do that step,' and because I knew they could say nothing to Neumeier, I decided to. I found him very approachable. I wanted the ballet to be a success, so it was also in my interests to promote smoothness. I asked if he would either reduce the number of people on stage or simplify the choreography. John listened quietly – he understood the concerns – but did not see why he should change his inventive choreography just because the schedule had not given him enough time. Things stayed as they were.

The ballet was about the growth of a child, his loss of innocence and ascent into adulthood. I was a child once again, but at least not dressed as one, nor remaining as one. The characterization gave me plenty of opportunity to show my technique. My choreography was difficult and energetic but not at all flashy. The other principal dancers were, Lynn Seymour and David Wall, with Jennifer Penney and Michael Coleman. The ballet started with Lynn Seymour holding me upside down by my legs as if she was giving birth to me. Then I staggered like a fawn and, as my legs gathered strength, gambolled around the stage.

At one point in the piece I had to sit perfectly still while Lynn Seymour and David Wall danced their *pas-de-deux*. I sat for fifteen minutes and at a given point got up and moved across the stage to join them in a *pas-de-trois*. It was difficult enough to walk, let alone dance, because my muscles set after being immobile for so long. I danced many sections with Stephen Beagley, who played my shadow. He had understudied Baryshnikov and was spotted by Neumeier as up-and-coming. When it came to the fourth movement, the piece was as obscure in the dance as it is in the music and there appeared to be no link with the previous three movements. I think the audience must have been fairly baffled by the whole piece.

On our opening night we were still under-rehearsed and aware of it. We had not completed a full run-through without hitches or blunders, but somehow our performance was clean. Many dancers from the Hamburg Ballet came to voice their support for John's new work and kept the applause going into the interval. But, secretly, I knew they were in a minority. I felt that this ballet, the only one created especially for me in my eleven years in the company, would have a very short life. Four performances in all.

Critically it had a mixed reception. But it was a personal success for me, even if the ballet as a whole wasn't acclaimed, because for a change the critics were relatively kind to me. Even John Percival, who seemed to dislike everything I had ever done (except my graduation piece from the school), said, 'Sleep is given a role far more rewarding than anything he has done before . . .' And others said things like 'It provides a central role for Wayne Sleep, long overdue' (David Dougall, *Sunday Times*), and 'It is not before time that Sleep has had a major work mounted on him' (*Classical Music Weekly*). And Jan Murray from the *Spectator* gave me an interesting one – I still can't decide how faint the praise is – 'Wayne Sleep must be pleased with Neumeier's efforts anyway.' Oh well.

In the end John Neumeier reworked *Fourth Symphony* for the Hamburg Ballet. It became a huge success, after more rehearsal time. But I never danced the part again.

During the rehearsals for *Fourth Symphony*, Graham Powell was taken seriously ill. He was living alone after Stephan had been refused entry into the country, and was not really happy by himself. He was trying to make a living as a painter, hiking his paintings around to galleries. He was found, more or less unconscious, at the bottom of his basement steps in Ifield Road, by Petal Miller, a soloist with the touring company, and her husband, Michael Manning, when they arrived for Sunday lunch. He had apparently been there all night.

He mumbled, 'Take me to hospital, I'm very ill,' and they took him to St Stephen's in the Fulham Road, which luckily is very near. By the time I went to see him that night he had suffered a brain haemorrhage and was in a coma. His deterioration had been rapid. I found him in intensive care, surrounded by cooling fans and packs and packs of ice. They were trying to keep his body temperature down. He looked so peaceful. I had not expected that. I held his hand and talked to him, trying to get through to him, to pierce through the unconsciousness. I asked him to press my hand if he could hear me and I was sure I felt something. But it must have been a shiver. They told me that if he did survive, he would have irreparable brain damage and be blind at the least, or even a vegetable. Graham could never have withstood that, not with the abundance of talent and energy he had.

When you sit beside someone in a hospital like this, all sorts of thoughts go through your mind, all sorts of reasons for the person being there. I wondered if the migraines and nose-bleeds he had suffered when younger had anything to do with it. He had often left classes complaining of them. I wondered if it had anything to do with the time he cracked his skull in an accident in Greece. And he hit his head again when he fell outside his front door. Maybe neither of these were factors. But the worst thing about sitting there is that there is nothing you can do, nothing. You feel so helpless.

I had to go back to the intense rehearsals of *Fourth Symphony* and was given daily reports on his condition by Petal and others who went to visit. I always picked up the phone hoping for good news – but it was always the same. When I came off stage after the first night of *Fourth Symphony* there was a telephone call waiting for me in the prop room by the side of the stage. It was George. He had waited until my first performance was over to tell me that Graham had died earlier that evening. The shock of Graham's death on top of the exhaustion of the birth of the new ballet sent me into a state of near catatonia. It was ages before I could really comprehend what had happened, ages before I cried.

In 1977, Bertram Rota, the antiquarian booksellers of which George was a director, had moved from Savile Row to a building in Long Acre, Covent Garden. The fruit and vegetable market had moved to Vauxhall and there were a number of empty warehouses ripe for conversion. John Prizeman, President of the Architectural Association, designed and converted a banana warehouse (a building which had originally been used by a carriage-maker, patronized by Samuel Pepys) into a bookshop with flats above. Prizeman did a brilliant job in restoring the building, adding a shopfront which blended perfectly with its nineteenth-century façade.

George and I moved out of Powis Gardens into the centre of London.

He bought one of the flats and I bought the one next door. I really enjoyed participating in the design of this space – an emotion quite opposite to my most recent experience of house conversion.

This was the first time I had really lived alone, and what with the strangeness of that, and the excitement of owning my very own place, I started to suffer from insomnia. There was only one cure. Videos. I bought a Betamax and watched films recorded from the television. I had no furniture and watched from (and eventually slept on) a mattress on the floor. I am now the proud owner of over 300 Betamax tapes, which are useless because my machine has died a death – and as we all know, VHS won the video battle.

I decided to base the design of my small flat on the captain's cabin of a schooner, inspired by a visit to the Maritime Museum in Portugal. Everything had to be fitted into the walls or have a dual purpose. It had Japanese wooden floors. The bathroom was specially designed with tiles that came up from the floor, continuing into the bath and then up the walls. Originally they were going to be laid on to a wooden frame, but I was concerned about possible leakage, so fibreglass was moulded over the wood, and the tiles fixed on to that. Both the bathroom and the bedroom had mirrors on the ceilings. This caused a lot of laughter and ribald comments, of course, but in reality it was to avoid any feelings of claustrophobia in such a small space. I had inch-thick glass in the windows, instead of double-glazing. The window frames had to be reinforced, the glass was so heavy. The floors were raised nine inches so that I could see out of the windows. All my books were hidden behind sliding screens, and Japanese-style paper shutters, set into wooden frames, hid the kitchen area and covered the windows. My only luxuries were a Lalique glass bowl turned into a lamp, two small Eileen Gray stainless steel and glass tables, and four Rietveld chairs. The stage door of the Opera House was only a minute's walk away and I even entertained the fantasy of extending the tannoy system to the flat so that I could stay in comfort while waiting for the half-hour call.

I had a log fire, which I left burning one evening when I went out. When I came home and unlocked the door, the fire was off, and various chairs and other items had been moved around. It was very weird. I couldn't think what might have happened. Maybe I had poltergeists. It wasn't until the next day that I found out what had happened. My neighbour, Brenda Armstrong, told me that a passer-by had seen the flickering shadows from my fire and had called the fire brigade. They had shinned up the side of the building, got in through an open window, and put the fire out. They departed without leaving a message. But they did crack a glass sculpture, a large Liberty egg. Just like poltergeists.

Brenda Armstrong had been living in Covent Garden long before the market moved. We discovered we were neighbours when we met on Lena Zavaroni's television series. I was performing some of the songs from *The Point*. Brenda had been in the theatrical profession for some time. She had been in ENSA during the war, and, among other things, was a male impersonator in top hat, white tie and tails, singing such music-hall stalwarts as 'Burlington Bertie'. I introduced her to my grandmother by saying, 'Meet Bertie.' Gran said, 'Ooh, Burlington Bertie. I've always wanted to meet him.' Confused? We were. Brenda became a family friend and was a great support to me when I was putting on my shows. She also introduced me to the Concert Artistes Association, where actors and variety artists from the old days gathered together to reminisce. I met Leslie Soroni here. He was famous for a tap dance called 'Peg Leg Pete', in which he pretended to have one wooden leg. Difficult. I saw him perform it once, and asked if he would teach it to me. 'What? Give away my act? Never!' he said. And he didn't. Even though he was over eighty.

George and I had connecting balconies six floors up so that Grace could commute. One day she was missing. I looked everywhere, even down in the street. I shouted her name, and heard a weak mewing. I looked under a parked car and saw her sitting in a puddle of dark liquid. Blood, I thought, Oh God, but it was only oil leaking from a sump. The only way she could have got there was by falling eighty feet, and the only injury she sustained was a cut jaw and irregular breathing, caused by shock.

My television appearances were becoming more frequent. I appeared with Derek Griffiths in a one-off special for Central Television. Our guests were infinitely better known than us – Peter Cook and Dudley Moore. Derek and I introduced the acts with comic sketches and danced and sang. This was in the 'good old days' (about twenty years ago), when variety shows were put together by the networks with an army of different talents – jugglers, singers, comedians, actors, dancers, etc. All doing three minute spots, all teamed up with each other. Fast, furious and fun. But the days of variety are over, the place taken by sit-coms, quiz shows, stuff from Oz etc.

Dizzy Feet was another show. This was a dance spectacular choreographed by Nigel Lythgoe and Norman Maen. I danced a Charleston, and played an American footballer in a dance sketch to music from the Beach Boys. *Dizzy Feet* won a Golden Rose at Montreux, proving that dance *was* both popular and important in its own right, not just an adjunct to variety.

In another ATV show, I was asked to dance a medley of Fred Astaire numbers for *Show Time*. This obviously called for tap, and I had done hardly any since I was five years old – I gave it up when I started ballet lessons. In those days they thought it weakened your ankles and created bulky calf muscles. Bill Drysdale was the choreographer. He was very patient because I virtually had to start from scratch. Learning the routine became my tap class – there was no time otherwise. I felt I was starting to become an all-round entertainer.

I was a regular guest on the *Lena Zavaroni Show*. Lena had knocked them for six on *Opportunity Knocks*, which she won when she was six years old with 'Ma, He's Making Eyes At Me'. She had this utterly incredible, amazing voice for one so young, but I still think it a bit odd to put a child into a talent contest that was essentially for adults. I know I won a talent contest when I was eight, but that was against others my own age. And Lena came down to London to live with a guardian and perform and become professional. She had no childhood, it seems to me, and I think that's rather sad. I was at White Lodge, yes, and being trained in a gruelling profession, but we were allowed to be children too. She was only fourteen when I guested on her shows. Grown up before her time.

One of Lena's shows travelled to Knokke, a seaside town in Holland, for three days, to take part in the Sea Swallow Award. Paul Nicholas was the guest singer and the rest of the cast consisted of twelve dancers. Dougie Squires was the choreographer, and I did a solo spot. The Sea Swallow was a competition covering shows from the majority of the European television networks. We were to perform live in front of an audience, not in a studio. We had rehearsed the numbers with breaks in the performance, to re-position the cameras, to allow for costume changes, and to get our breath back before the next routine. When we arrived, we were told this was against the rules, that we must do all the routines straight through without a break, because this was a live show. There was *chaos* in the wings and near pandemonium on stage – I ended up, totally out of breath, trying to sing 'Anything You Can Do, I Can Do Better' with Lena. In spite of all this, we won the Silver Sea Swallow Award. I thought we'd won, and was going around grinning and saying, 'Isn't it great,' when they said to me: 'What are you so happy about? It's only the Silver, so-and-so won the Gold.' I didn't know there was a Gold one too. But the BBC had won the Gold Award several years running before this, so I guess they thought it was a diplomatic time for a change. Well, I would think that, wouldn't I?

I was also a guest on the *Morecambe and Wise Show*, where I recreated Gene Kelly's dance with Jerry (from the cartoon *Tom and Jerry*). Ernie played the mouse, and I remember having to repeat my solo over and over while a special effect was made with my picking Ernie up in my hand. The three of us also danced round their living-room set to 'Good Morning' – dancing over the chairs and sofas. On my entrance in front of their famous curtain, Eric made a joke of my size looking around saying, 'Where is he?' then looked down to find I was already standing there. When I was on the *Nana Mouskouri Show* I worked with the choreographer Gillian Lynne for the first time. Gillian and I have worked together many times since.

I even danced on the wireless. On Radio 4's *Start the Week*, hosted by Richard Baker and Mavis Nicholson, I had to dance round the studio with Mavis, commenting on our movements as we careered around the studio, dodging cables and microphones. Mad.

And then I was asked if I would play Tony Lumpkin in a radio production of *She Stoops to Conquer*. The cast was awe-inspiring: Judi Dench, Michael Williams and Elizabeth Spriggs. Out of my depth? Probably. But I had decided to try everything, to grasp every opportunity that came my way. It's the only way to find out if you can do something. Taking risks is vital for a performer.

I was incredibly nervous at the first read-through of the play. My script was shaking in my hands. We were sitting in the usual circle and I looked across at Judi, whose face expressed bland mischief. I looked at her feet. She was wearing ballet point shoes and her feet were crossed in an immaculate fifth position. This little joke relieved the tension somewhat for me, until it was my turn to speak. Tony Lumpkin appeared on page ten. I'd lost the page. Michael leaned over to me, handed me a sheet and said, 'Borrow mine.' They were very good to such a radio virgin.

I was now doing more work outside the ballet than within it. The company couldn't always accommodate my technique, and they were quite pleased that I wasn't moaning about my lack of use. It was ironic that now I could be released because I was small – the tables were turning. My lack of height was allowing me to enter other arenas. If I had been taller, I would have had to remain at the Garden – on standby.

And I really could not go on asking Iris Law to negotiate everything for me. It was time to find an agent. I heard that London Management were one of the best agents for variety – in fact they were the only agents I had heard of. They, however, had not heard of me. They sent me upstairs, to the third floor, where they send all the poor relations, the unknowns, to meet Jonathan Altaras, who had just joined the firm. He was said to be young, keen and excellent at making deals. All I could see of him was that he was young. But we took each other on.

One day he received a phone call from a casting director who had been passed up the floors in the agency. This casting director, Mary Selway, was desperate for a small, agile, acrobatic actor for a part in a film, *The First Great Train Robbery*. Jonathan put me up for it. Michael Crichton was both the script-writer and the director. (He is six foot nine tall so we looked pretty odd side by side.) The film was based on the true story of the first robbery ever from a moving train, which happened in the last century. There were four main episodes, showing how the four Chubb keys were obtained to open the safe containing the gold bullion. The cast included Sean Connery, Donald Sutherland, Michael Elphick and Lesley-Anne Down.

Part of the contract involved my running across a ledge twenty feet above the ground. A doddle, I thought to myself, after Squirrel Nutkin. I was sent to Dublin (where most of the filming was to be) to learn from Dick Zyker, the stuntman. I wondered why a stuntman was necessary for a ledge twenty feet above the ground, and I soon found out. I was actually going to perform some quite daring moves and Dick was to teach me all the precautions. He fitted me with a harness and a wire. 'Just a precaution,' he said. Yes. Just a precaution. I should think so. The first stunt was to climb the wall. The second was to launch myself into the air and grab a bar, interwoven with spikes. No wonder there was a wire. And I found I still suffered from vertigo.

A couple of days later, during a night shoot, I found out that I had to dangle my legs over a building, involving some rather complicated moves and considerably higher (I thought) than the ledge twenty feet from the ground. I asked Dick how much he was getting for this sort of danger. I went to the producer and said that these stunts weren't in my contract. I was employed as an actor. For this I should get more money. His reply was to take a huge wad of £50 notes out of his pocket say 'How much?' and, without waiting for an answer, shove a bundle into my hand with a 'Will that do?' Nicely, thank you. My reservations (and my vertigo) went – just like that. I shimmied up that wall – my pockets loaded.

In the summer of 1977, we spent four weeks shooting on location at Slain Castle near Dublin, in the old Huston railway station. A gaol was built in a field. I was supposed to somersault over the spikes (for which I had practised with Dick Zyker earlier) after I had climbed over the wall. I wore a piece of rubber round my waist as protection, but it wasn't thick enough. One spike got through. They forged a tin corset for me which did the trick in the end. Being on a set with Sean Connery was fun. He had a fund of stories, which really kept us going on the night shoots.

My friend Tony Rudenko (with whom I had taught boys bits of *Swan Lake* on the beach in Sierra Leone on the way to Brazil) was living in Dublin. We got together again and were invited to lunch at Farmleigh, Miranda Iveagh's house, where we swam and played with her children. Henrietta had introduced me to Miranda some years before – they were all part of the Guinness family. So was Gareth Browne, another friend of George's, who lent his horse-drawn carriages for one of the scenes in the park. To keep fit, I went to work out in Pat Henry's gym. I was sorry to leave Dublin – the atmosphere and wit of that city are something special. It takes you to its heart and invites you to do the same. I did.

After four weeks in Jury's Hotel in Dublin we returned to London and to Pinewood Studios to finish the filming. They had built a replica of the original Crystal Palace and of the rooftops of 1860s London, and we were all in period costume, but sometimes Sean, knowing he was only to appear from the waist up in a shot, would wear his own comfortable trendy shoes. I enjoyed working on this film, and sometimes I was tempted with the notion of leaving the ballet to go into films and acting full-time. But I felt that it would be a waste of the lengthy training I had undergone, and the time it had taken to reach my current position, were I to give up dance now, and that was enough to keep me in the company. A dancer has a short enough time before the body stops him – an actor can go on pretty much for ever. I could return to acting in the future.

In April 1978 the company went to the Empire in Liverpool to perform *Swan Lake*. I danced the Neapolitan Dance in Act 3, one of the cameos choreographed by Sir Fred for Alex Grant which I enjoyed inheriting. When I came on stage there was a burst of applause from the audience – something only reserved for the Prince. My television appearances had begun to make me instantly recognizable, and a household name.

After another season in the Big Top in Plymouth, we went on tour to Athens for a week in August. We performed *Sleeping Beauty* and *Romeo and Juliet* in the ancient Greek theatre Herodeus Atticus – an open-air amphitheatre seating 6,000 people. It was a particularly fit setting for *Romeo*, with its tall columns and arches as a backdrop. The difference with this tour was the extraordinary unity created by our mixing both with the touring orchestra and the technicians. Usually when we are abroad we use local musicians, particularly in America, and at home, there is a natural division between the pit and the stage. But the touring orchestra (conducted by Barry Wordsworth, a newcomer, who became resident conductor of the touring company and of the BBC Symphony Orchestra) is much more used to mingling with the dancers and we discovered, in Athens, that both the musicians and the technicians could be great fun. It was so hot during the day that we just lay about by the pool on top of the hotel and got to know each other. It created a very happy atmosphere with no pecking order.

On the last night in Athens we said goodbye to Anthony Dowell, who was to leave the company to join the American Ballet Theater as one of its leading guest artists. He was the first of the few English dancers to achieve international stardom. His powerful leaps and jumps, and his perfect physical proportions, line and grace, singled him out among his equally athletic and brilliant contemporaries. I was sorry to see him go – I had enjoyed working with him. I'd been his Jester, and his Puck. We'd shared some nervous moments in the wings and some good ones on stage. I felt a bit like the Fool losing his King, except that Anthony wasn't old enough for Lear; but I was happy for him too.

While the company had their summer holiday during the rest of August, I was invited to Cape Town by the Capab Ballet Company, directed by David Poole. I was in two minds about whether to go, because many of my friends said I should boycott South Africa. But I was told I would be performing to non-segregated audiences. It was hard actually to know what to think. And I wondered why artists were expected to make a political stand when politicians weren't. In the end I felt that artists, at that time, should act as a link and a bridge between all races. So I went.

In Cape Town I started rehearsals as the Blue Boy in *Les Patineurs*. I was glad to see that there were several coloured and black dancers in the school. But there weren't many in the company and when I asked why, they said it was easier to get work in Europe, where there was no curfew. And there were few non-white faces in the audiences either – although there was no segregation, it was almost impossible to come to the theatre and get back to the black part of town before the curfew. It was not as I expected. Nor was arriving for rehearsal some mornings and coming face to face with dancers in army uniforms, changing into their ballet tights. Dancers were not exempt from National Service, and had to fit their curriculum around the needs of the army.

I was staying with David Poole at his house in Camps Bay. On our way home one night we found a black lady distraught by the beach. David decided to bring her home, otherwise she would end up in the local police station, something he would not wish on anyone. He insisted that she did not smoke – someone's smoking had caused a fire before – and gave her a mattress and blankets for her to sleep on. The next morning he went down to see how she was. She had disappeared with the blankets, leaving cigarette burns all over the mattress.

David had a white passport. Some of his family had 'coloured' ones and were segregated, but because he had been a leading dancer with the Sadler's Wells Ballet, and because he returned to South Africa as Director of the Cape Town Ballet, his status demanded a passport to match. I thought it a strange situation.

I enjoyed staying with David. His house overlooked the sea and I could see Table Mountain rise above the bay. Some mornings it had a mist which descended over its surface – it was known as the tablecloth. I don't know why, but the mixture of this beauty and the success of *Les Patineurs* was a strangely heady one.

In the end it was difficult to assess what was right and wrong when I was staying there. Nothing was as cut and dried as people assumed then. Would an artistic boycott have helped? Perhaps it would have prevented, rather than aided, talented black writers, dancers and performers from progressing and the plays of Athol Fugard from being seen so soon in the West End. It seems academic now. One thing I did find out was that there were a lot of talented black dancers, and I was glad to be able to suggest some of them to companies in Europe. And I would not have missed the beauty of Camps Bay for anything.

In the autumn of 1978, Anya Sainsbury (married to John Sainsbury and formerly Anya Linden, a leading dancer with the company) was putting together one of her famous charity galas for the Friends of Fatherless Families. The charity changed its title, fairly soon after, to the better-known (now) Friends of One Parent Families – when it became as common for women to leave their men as vice versa.

Her chosen venue was the Adelphi Theatre. Anya had asked me on board to help and decided to base the gala round me. It was entitled, thanks to George, *A Good Night's Sleep*. Her intention was that it should bring together all facets of theatre, and not be simply a ballet gala. At one of the Committee meetings at which the programme was being devised, someone suggested that I learn Balanchine's *Tarantella* from Edward Villella. Eddie had been a virtuoso dancer with the New York City Ballet, and the *Tarantella* was one of his most famous pieces. It was an excellent idea. I took my holiday that year in New York to it.

Anya and I were determined that it would be a particularly splendid gala. Months before the night, I asked David Hockney to design a frontcloth. I went to see him the night before he was going abroad, to get the design from him, only to discover that he had not been visited with any ideas. I sat him down, thrust a sheet of paper in front of him and coloured crayons in his hand, and said, 'I've never asked you to do anything for me before. Paint me a drop cloth, David.'

'Give me a break, Wayne, love,' he said.

I pleaded with him, and then he said, 'Ooh, love, I *do* have a little idea.' And he sketched a design. So instead of a curtain facing the audience when they entered the auditorium, there was a sixty foot lit-up Hockney. His 'little idea' eventually triggered off a whole new series of paintings.

We asked everybody to be in this gala. Dame Ninette de Valois remounted *Pride* on Maina Gielgud, ex-principal with the Béjart Ballet and now Director of the Australian Ballet. *Pride* was a solo interpreting the movements of a peacock, and was devised by Madam for herself in the twenties, so that she could perform and earn a living in the music-halls. Rather as I do now. Sir Fred created two premières for the evening: a new *pas-de-deux* for Wayne Eagling and Merle Park called *Papillon*; and *Tweedle Dum and Tweedle Dee*, to the music of Percy Grainger, with Graham Fletcher and me as the twins, and Lesley Collier as Alice. Derek Jacobi read a short introduction to *Le Train Bleu* – from which I danced the solo. This was the first time this piece had been done since it was originally choreographed for Anton Dolin by Bronislava Nijinska. I was rehearsed by Dolin himself. Marguerite Barbieri danced *Dragonfly* – first danced by Pavlova in the 1920s. My friend from *The Point*, Paul Aylett, came with his dog, now called Shambles. Stephen Sondheim gave permission for music from *Company* to be used in a piece choreographed for Peter Walker and Petra Siniawski, who had been students with me at the Upper School. Jerry Robbins also gave permission for us to use a piece from *The Concert*. I turned the tables on John Curry by asking him to dance off the ice, in a piece choreographed for him by Gillian Lynne. John also partnered Anthony Dowell in a piece from Frederick Ashton's *Façade*. This was specially pleasing because it was Anthony's style and elegance in the dance that was the strongest influence on John to change the face of ice-skating. Merle Park allowed children from her own private dancing school to perform a scene from *A Chorus Line*. Bob Cohan, of the LCDT, let Robert North and Linda Gibbs dance a *pas-de-deux* from *Nympheas* to 'Claire de Lune' by Debussy.

I asked Penelope Keith if she would appear, and she agreed to be cast as the Lilac Fairy in *Sleeping Beauty* with Anthony Dowell as the Prince and Lesley Collier as Aurora. We chose the scene from Act 2 where the Lilac Fairy enters the stage on a boat and introduces the Prince to the vision of Aurora. Penelope had only one line to say in this send-up. She had a mime scene with Anthony, but confused him utterly with her gesticulations, which were upside down, or back to front, or simply nonsensical. She then, in her frustration at not remembering any of the moves, shouted, 'I've dried.' When Anthony and Lesley started their *pas-de-deux*, Penelope went back and sat in the boat, looking pointedly at her watch and yawning at the dance unfolding on stage. Eventually she called the Prince back into the boat, and as it moved off with the Prince in it, she was left standing on the rock. It brought the house down.

We had asked several well-known playwrights to script this for us, but they ran a mile at the mention of a ballet scene. The only one who didn't was Burt Shevelove, whose idea it was.

The finale was choreographed by Bill Drysdale. It was in the style of a 1920s cakewalk for the whole company. He told us to wear whatever we wanted. Maina Gielgud wore black PVC boots and fishnet stockings.

I compèred the evening, introducing and thanking each act, but it was Burt Shevelove who brought the whole thing together by directing the evening. His way of linking the acts was inspired and completely original – he had Derek Jacobi lifted on to the stage by the *corps de ballet* as they went off after their number. He kept the pace up – normally the curtain comes down between each act, but David Hockney's front cloth was only allowed to drop in once, at the interval. Burt also insisted that each artist was to take just one bow. But nobody told Sir Fred. This was a world première by Ashton. The applause would have gone on a long time, so he took his time to come to the stage. By the time he arrived for his plaudits for *Papillon* the front cloth had come in for the interval. He was very upset. Burt came rushing backstage to tell me. We had committed a massive *faux pas*. This was a major new work, and a major new work by Sir Frederick Ashton to boot. Burt thrust a speech into my hand, told me to go on and thank Sir Fred for all that he had done that evening, and then bring him on to receive his due acclaim. But Sir Fred did not want to know. He was very upset. Princess Margaret, patron of the gala, then insisted that he go on. He refused until she said, 'We command you, Freddie'. Only then did he oblige, but reluctantly. I felt awful. Talk about a work by Sir Fred going unrecognized – and he was the last person in the world I would ever wish to upset.

The pace and style of this gala set the standard for those that followed. Until then, ballet galas had tended to be ponderous and somewhat pedantic. This was altogether more enjoyable for performers and audience alike. And apart from our stupidity about Sir Fred, there was only one other matter that marred the evening. There was a terrific party after the show in the Crush Bar at the Opera House. But unfortunately the caterer had a fault with one of her suppliers, and almost everyone came down with stomach-ache the next day. Otherwise – it was a night to remember. After the gala was over Burt said to me: 'If I had your talent I'd bottle your sweat and sell it!'

TEN

TV AND PANTO TIME

I was invited onto the *Michael Parkinson Show* – a television talk show for the first time. I was told he could be pretty tough with his questioning. I also knew he was not a ballet fan, so it was with some trepidation that I stepped out in front of the audience and the viewers. I did not meet him before the show.

He had the first few laughs on me and after that I had free rein. He was friendly, though I had expected him to be quite the opposite with a male dancer. I performed an impromptu tap solo (which I had rehearsed earlier in the day with Harry Stoneham and his band) and a short twenty-second taste of my Olga Korbut routine, without the costume, but with the wig. The *Michael Parkinson Show* had a huge audience, and on it hopefully I proved that not all ballet dancers are inarticulate.

My appearance on the show put me in 'the link', so to speak. Because I was prepared not to be precious, because I was happy to improvise and occasionally look like a fool, I was liked by the TV people and invited onto many more shows. I remember the *Eamonn Andrews Show*. I stripped to reveal my Olga Korbut leotard, put on the wig, did my routine – and at the end of it jumped into Eamonn's lap. The poor man was a tinge embarrassed and didn't know quite what to say, so called for a commercial break. Or maybe there was one coming anyway.

I also did a fair amount of radio. An interviewer challenged me, once, on why I had never done the leading roles at Covent Garden.

'Is it because of your height that you don't get the parts?'

'Of course it is,' I said.

'It seems very unfair; there are heroes that are small,' she said.

'It is unfair,' I said. 'After all, Alexander the Great was small; Napoleon was small; and how tall was Douglas Bader?'

There was a shocked silence, during which I remembered he had lost his legs during the war. I was suddenly disgusted with myself, but I couldn't unsay it. And to this day I still don't know why I said it. The only thing I can think of is that it's some kind of childhood memory, like hearing my mother say, 'Never mind, dear, Douglas Bader was only small too.' But she might have meant Kenneth More (who played Bader in the film *Reach for the Sky*) for all I know. But it is strange what little childhood aphorisms creep into your mind when under pressure. And it's ironic, given the stupidity of that remark, that I am now the proud Patron of the Wheelchair Dance Association Charity.

Margot Fonteyn presented a television series called *The Magic of Dance* and asked me to reproduce the hornpipe made famous by the eighteenth-century American dancer John Durang. I had a great time researching his diaries and his notes, and found the original music and a coloured etching, of himself, by himself. He danced any type of dance, including ballet, such as it was at the time. It must have been an extraordinary life, up and down the East Coast of Europeanized America at the time – some of it in the years before Independence. I hope I recreated what he intended – he left abbreviated notes of various steps – but there was as much intuition as fact.

This led to my being asked, by a BBC2 director, to devise a jazz ballet from a jazz score called *Adam's Rib*. I was to take six of the twelve women chosen, and set them to music by Ken Moule. I decided on Helen of Troy, Lady Macbeth, Mae West, Marilyn Monroe, Lucrezia Borgia and a brothel owner in St Louis, name unknown – or at least unremembered. I asked some of the Royal Ballet's principal dancers, such as Donald MacLeary, Marguerite Porter and Monica Mason, and the jazz dancer Jane Darling, to help. We had only two weeks to rehearse these pieces for a half-hour programme, and I can admit now that it wasn't very good choreography; it was a rush job; it was my first major choreographical piece for television; and I was out of my depth and Bill Drysdale (the choreographer) came in to help me out. But I abided by the maxim that Lynn Seymour taught me. She acted as my sounding board. If I was in doubt I'd go to her, and she'd say, 'Do everything.' So I did. Good or bad. But unless you do things, try them out, you don't know how far you can go. And even if *Adam's Rib* wasn't good, I learned a lot from doing it.

Cliff Richard was to be starring in a show called *A Christmas Lantern*, and the producers asked if I would impersonate Charlie Chaplin, with choreography by Nigel Lythgoe. I started to spend time with Chaplin's movies (researching a part is such a good time), watching his movements, mannerisms and facial expressions. This was my first Chaplin – but not my last. The tramp became one of my impersonations.

Then came my first pantomime, *Aladdin* at the London Palladium. Wonderful. I jumped at the chance. Pantomime started as a fill-in between plays, some time in the middle of the last century. They were little satirical pieces, commenting either on the politics of the day or on the play itself. The audience began to take more note of these fill-ins than they did the actual play, and so the pantomime grew. It became a huge tableau of colour and elaborate costumes and eventually developed into a full-length spectacle. It is also an incredibly English theatrical phenomenon. Try explaining it to an American or to a Frenchman or to an Italian, and they think you are bonkers. I feel quite strongly that a pantomime should be as traditional as possible – the only changes should be in the political and topical jokes.

The Royal Ballet let me go on the understanding that I perform four performances of *Enigma Variations* and *The Sleeping Beauty*, which was to be televised for American network television. *Aladdin* was to play at the Palladium for fourteen weeks, with two performances a day, over Christmas 1978. Danny La Rue was the star that year. He was Widow Twankey. I was the Slave of the Ring.

My entrance was from a twelve-foot ladder, whence I jumped down on to a trampoline placed in the wings and was hurled through the air to land centre stage and say, 'You called, Master?' I was greeted by Alfred Marks playing Abaneezer, and then I had to launch into my speech telling the Abaneezer geezer how to obtain the magic lamp. During one performance, the thing that I most feared happened. I dried. When my feet hit the stage every word of the dialogue left my head. Worse – I had no thoughts at all. It was all blackness inside.

Alfred said, 'Have you nothing to ask me, boy?'

'Nothing at all, ' I said. He rattled off my lines, pausing every now and then to see whether I'd returned to the planet, and I just stood there, shell-shocked. After jumping twelve feet off a ladder, going whizz, ping, boink and straight into 'You called, Master?' for twelve shows a week for fourteen weeks, it was not surprising my mind became blank. You could say that by that time I should be on automatic pilot, but that takes away the point of pantomime. Immediacy is the essence, spontaneity is the key. And that night I was less spontaneous than a brick.

I had a very short scene with Danny La Rue. Now there is no reason for Widow Twankey to meet the Slave of the Ring – or many other of the guest parts – but scenes were always added for Danny to meet the stars on stage, and probably take the mickey out of them. Such is the lovely looseness of pantomime.

Our scene was originally about thirty seconds. As the Slave of the Ring I was bare-chested and when, in one performance, I came on, Danny La Rue said, 'Oh what lovely little nipples,' and leaned over and tweaked them. I jumped back out of reach. Well, I was a bit taken aback.

When I went off I told my dresser. He was an old hand at this game and told me what to say if DLR did it again. And having done it once, yes, he did it again.

'What lovely little nipples.' Tweak.

I said, 'Well, at least they're mine.' And that got a good laugh from the audience and a good deal of batting eyelashes.

The next performance: Danny said, 'Well I can hang mine up when I'm hot.'

The next performance: I said, 'Well it is a bit chilly out here,' and dived under his cloak. He covered me with it and walked off the stage. I would have loved to have seen his face to the audience.

The next performance: I banged the bottom of the cloak as we went off stage.

The next performance: as I banged the bottom of his cloak, DLR took his hands away and raised them, saying 'Look no hands,' as we walked off.

The whole routine extended from the original thirty seconds to about three minutes. People came back again and again, just to see what we had added or changed. But in the end, John Avery, the front of house manager, had to caution us about this being a family show, and we didn't want to lose our audience. This was the first time I'd come across that censorship, and I was surprised, but he was right, of course, pantomime *is* a family occasion.

It made me reflect on the vast differences between performing in the ballet, the commercial theatre and the pantomime. When you are on stage in the ballet it is as if you are auditioning every night. You are watched, often by the choreographer and certainly by the ballet master. Drop below the standard – and you are likely to be out, at least for some time. In the commercial theatre, once the director has done his bit, he is gone, usually to another project, and you are pretty much left to your own devices. If it is a musical, then someone – the equivalent of the ballet master – may well watch to make sure things don't slip. In pantomime, ad-libbing and freedom to experiment are actively encouraged – but the company stage manager makes sure we don't cross the line into a vulgarity that might be deemed shocking.

Danny La Rue is one of the most generous artists I have ever worked with, and he has the most extraordinary ability to remember everyone he has ever met. We only fell out once. During one of the stage rehearsals, close to the opening night, I went off to perform in *The Sleeping Beauty*, which was being televised for American TV, having promised to return to the Palladium immediately to rejoin the technical rehearsal. I had forgotten to tell the management that I was to be presented to Princess Margaret on air after the performance. I was late, much later than expected, in returning to the Palladium. Danny did not know that I was to be let off that evening. He was furious. Quite understandably. But there were many nights when Danny and his manager, Jack, would invite me to his hospitality room by his dressing-room for drinks. I took my family – they adored Danny. He was one of the few people my mother would choose to see in performance. 'Such a lovely man.'

Pantomime taught me timing, invention and relaxation. Timing is about when to pause for a line, or a laugh, and how to make the laughter continue by building on it, rather than milking one element until the last boring squeeze. Invention is the stuff of pantomime. It can be learned, if you are willing to listen, and if you don't care about making a fool of yourself. Which, on stage, I don't. It makes you think on your feet, and you begin to learn what works and how. Some people do it much better than others. As for relaxation – it is hard to learn to come on to a stage and just 'be'. Comedians seem to manage it better than other performers. Most people need to be a character and stay in it. Pantomime teaches the ability to switch in and out of character. For instance: if I am playing Buttons, I can step out of his character and relationship to the others on the stage, come forward, and comment on the action, or the characters, as myself. Then in the next moment, I can turn back and be Buttons again. It is these three elements that demonstrate the professionalism of the pantomime player.

The following year I played Pinocchio at the Birmingham Repertory Theatre. We played to 95 per cent capacity and smashed all box-office records. Although this was a story rather than a pantomime, it was not without its moments of ad-libbing. Pinocchio (for the very, very few people who might not know) is the tale about a boy who lies, and when he lies his nose gets long and longer. In this production I stood beside a curtain, and every time Pinocchio lied, I turned to the side, behind the curtain, put on a larger nose, and returned to face the audience. All the while I dressed as a donkey. (Don't ask.) In one performance, early on in the run, this big nose fell off my face. One pantomime maxim is: you are only as good as your props. And another maxim is: if something goes wrong, use it. I couldn't pretend the nose had not fallen off – it was lying on the ground for all to see. And Pinocchio needs his nose. So there was I, clad in donkey ears, with donkey hooves attached to my hands, down on my hands and knees, chasing this thing round the stage, scrabbling with my hooves to get it on my nose (it looked like a cross between blowing peas with a straw and bobbing for apples), until I captured it and stood up in triumph. It turned into a hilarious sequence and was an ad-lib that remained in the show. But without that training at the Palladium I might have ignored the nose.

A few years later I played the Ringmaster in *Goldilocks and the Three Bears* at the Theatre Royal, Norwich. Dick Condon ran the theatre. He was a real show-business man and cared deeply about his theatre and about the local community. It was not one of those theatres which is dark and unfriendly for most of the day, only evincing life for four hours at night. The Theatre Royal was alive all day. The coffee bar was open, the restaurant was open, people were booking tickets, coming to events and just generally wandering in and out. It was a meeting place. Dick kept his eye on it. He had an office from which he could see into the foyer, and he also had a tannoy system. He knew many local people, and when they came in he would say, through the speakers, 'Oh, look. It's Mrs Thompson. Lovely to see you, Mrs T. Looking well.' He made them feel welcome, part of the whole enterprise, and this contributed to the success of the theatre.

I gave an interview, before one matinée, to the local press. The guy (I guess he was a journalist) kept prodding and pushing me. He was saying, 'You must be so in love with yourself, being recognized in the streets all the time. It must be fabulous to be a star.'

'Not always,' I replied. 'Take last night, for instance. I was sitting alone in a restaurant and four guys on the next door table started to have a go at me. For no reason. But that's the sort of thing you expect – they were just being thick and stupid.'

The next day the headlines on the front page of the local newspaper yelled: 'WAYNE CALLS NORWICH PEOPLE THICK AND STUPID.' Apart from the fact that I patently had not said that, I certainly don't think they were from

Norwich. It was a classic case of words being transposed by the press – for the sake of a story. What should have been a small item on page nine was front-page scandal. I had to go on stage every day after this. But the audiences were fine. I was the one that felt bad.

In a small way, I got my own back. There was a line in the show, a reference to the stars in the local paper. I asked Goldilocks if she had seen her stars in the paper, that they said she would meet someone who looked exactly like me. After the nonsense headline broke, I said: 'Have you seen your stars in the paper today, Goldilocks? Well, don't believe everything you read in that paper.' It got a round of applause. I found out later that the paper had just turned tabloid and was desperate for a story. And I was the fall guy.

But most of my experiences in pantomime have been enjoyable. Then I played my first Dame in *Goldilocks* at His Majesty's Theatre, Aberdeen, in 1988. I thought, having just turned forty, that it was the right age to play the Dame. I think it is the best role in pantomime. But I found the audiences came to see me as myself and to see the big dance numbers, and weren't so happy to find I was doing something different.

I have played the Dame once since – in Eastbourne, as Gertie, the Queen of the Circus in 1989. I based her partly on Widow Simone in *La Fille Mal Gardée* (I did a clog dance), but mostly on Cicely Courtneidge, who had stuck in my memory from my visits to the theatre with Joan de Robeck twenty years before. In those days I had no idea how to handle this sort of thing. I thought a dignified silence was the best course, but of course this enrages some people and actually encourages them to interpret silence as guilt. But in fact, if the press has got its claws into you, whatever you do makes very little difference. Anyone who is moderately well known can suffer from this, and the more exuberant you are, the more likely you are to fall foul. Very few people have any form of redress. And if a paper admits its wrong, the apology is to be found in the bottom right-hand corner of page twelve, next to advertisements for incontinence trusses.

But after Gertie I reverted to the Slave of the Ring, or Dick Whittington or his Cat, or, as it often is these days, Buttons – where I can play comedy and dance a big number. I have found that is what, after all, the audience pays to see. I'm no Dame, not yet . . .

I've learned so much about performing from being in pantomime. It's the best place for timing and ad-libbing and I love it. I love it for the audience participation and for the close communication the performer has with the audience. A pantomime is also likely to be the first time children come to the theatre, and it is our responsibility to make sure it is a good experience. I love all that business of 'He's behind you' and 'no, he isn't', 'Yes he is' stuff. I admit it. It's like being a child again.

In 1980 Anya Sainsbury presented another of her One Parent Family galas. This one was at the London Palladium, and was built around Anthony Dowell. Anya asked Dame Ninette de Valois to choreograph a piece about Vestris, the first dancer ever to claim world recognition. (Vestris, in his middle age, married a girl of fourteen, who became the first woman theatre manager. She bailed him out of debtors' prison when he was older and she was successful. Eventually he returned to Italy, his country of birth, and died there, alone, ill – and in debt.)

Anya asked Madam if she would create the piece on me. She was happy to say yes. My only free time of the day, which fitted in with Madam's commitments, was eight in the morning at the Royal Ballet School, before the classes started. I remember that the students, when they arrived, tried to creep in and watch through the doors as this legendary woman invented her steps. She shouted at me to 'Shut the door, Sleep.' I was surprised. 'Surely you don't mind people watching you, Madam?' I asked her. She turned and said, 'This is the first piece I've choreographed in thirty years. Now, shut that door.' Even the most experienced choreographers can be inhibited by people watching them create.

Her directions were confusing at first – I found them hard to understand. I was having to interpret her arm and hand movements with my legs and feet. She kept saying, 'No, that's not it. That's not it.' Then she hit on the happy idea of having me lie on the floor, where she put my legs into the position she wanted. 'This is what I want you to do in the air,' she said. It was a very good way of working for us.

She came to all the costume fittings. She wanted an exact replica of the famous eighteenth century print of Vestris. I was to hop on to the stage in the position of the print, holding my hat in my hand. We discovered, at the dress rehearsal, that it was not only difficult to dance holding the hat, but the coat was pulling me off balance as well, making it impossible to carry out her intricate moves. Fortunately she let me discard both hat and coat. These rehearsals with Madam were being fitted around the last week of rehearsals for my own show, *DASH*, and the gala itself took place on the night before *DASH*'s technical rehearsal at Chichester.

It was that year, 1980, that I had the idea of forming my own dance group. I went to see Bette Midler in her one-woman show at the London Palladium, in which she sang, told jokes and performed outrageous cameo characters, all with this electric personality. I thought: wouldn't it be marvellous to do something like that, myself, using dance as the vocabulary? I had invented comic characters for the Friends' Christmas parties. I was enjoying my jazz and contemporary classes, as well as ballet. So: why not perform it all together? So I started to construct a formula in which I could use six dancers, all from different dance backgrounds.

My first approach was to Jane Darling. I had met her through Bill Drysdale when I was working on one of the ATV shows at Elstree. I outlined the philosophy behind the idea and explained that it would hardly be an elaborate affair because I was financing it myself. I was entirely open about having no bookings and hoping my chosen dancers would give of themselves on spec. That was also a way I could be sure they wanted to do it. Jane was sufficiently interested in the scheme to agree. Having clinched things with the best exponent of jazz dancing, I started to look round all the dance classes for talented new dancers.

I settled on Linda-Mae Brewer, who was just over from Australia. She was a great all-rounder, if a bit raw yet, and had high technical skills in tap, ballet and jazz. I chose Conchita del Campo, a small classical dancer, as a partner for my ballet send-ups. Her technique was not great, but she had the ability (and was willing to work) to become an all-rounder. Sue Roe I chose for her toe-tapping (tap dancing on points) ability – essential for a scene I had planned. I could afford only one other dancer, so I decided on another man and asked Iwan Boermeester, trained in contemporary dance. He choreographed a piece for Jane and himself.

Bill Drysdale also introduced me to Don Lawson, a well-known drummer in the West End. He was well disposed towards dancers (because his wife, Sheila O'Neil, was a dancer), and I asked him to be my musical director. I know it is more normal that the MD is the pianist, but I feel that rhythm and percussion are more essential in a dance number. Don brought in three other musicians, all well known in their circles and very versatile: Clive Chaplin on piano, Jimmy Hastings on sax, doubling on flute, and Brian on guitar. I suspected this quartet might sound thin: but it was all I could afford.

We wrote to fifteen theatres expressing my wish to appear in them. Thirteen theatres said that a dance show could not possibly make money – and who the hell is Wayne Sleep anyway????! Two theatres, to whom I shall for ever be grateful, took up the offer. They were the King's Theatre, Edinburgh, and the Chichester Festival Theatre. I decided on Chichester for the première and that we'd go to Edinburgh a couple of months later.

Deciding on a name for this little company was very difficult. I did not want a word or a phrase with 'ballet' in it because some might think I had formed an offshoot of the Royal Ballet. Nor was it right to call it 'jazz' or 'tap', because we were using more than just those styles. I was looking for a word that was up-to-date, modern, embodying the elements I was trying to achieve. The Wayne Sleep Dance Consort, pretty though it was, sounded as though we were concentrating on sixteenth-century galliards. I wanted something with movement, élan, a name closer to a pop group than anything else – I wanted to arrest the younger generation, take dance out of its classical mould. Something to describe pace, physical body movement, short pieces, quick changes, zip, zing – *DASH*. So *DASH* it eventually became.

Rehearsals were spasmodic, slotted in around my Royal Ballet commitments. I carried a tape-recorder and various props to the small ballet room at the Opera House and unofficially held my rehearsals there, sneaking my dancers in via the canteen. This small ballet room was only fifteen feet by fifteen, and this was the room the Company had to warm up in. (The *corps* had to use the carpeted Crush Bar.) Nureyev's face when he saw the size of the room must have been a picture

– not what he was used to – no wonder he preferred to warm up on stage. We also rehearsed, for free, at the newly opened Pineapple Dance Centre. The old Dance Centre in Floral Street had closed. Gary Cockrell had given all the teachers ten days' notice to quit. I don't know why. Debbie Moore took out a lease on a warehouse in Langley Street and invited all the redundant teachers to work there. She was not a dancer (though she understood the temperament), she was an ex-model with an excellent head for business. (Her husband was an accountant.) She went into her premises with a full cast of some of the best jazz, tap and ballet teachers, and so was assured, from day one, of a certain income. She was to open two more Dance Centres, in South Kensington and in Paddington Street, followed by shops all over England. She won a Business Woman of the Year Award and eventually her company went public, when I became a director of her company, for a while.

I had not met Debbie before this, but she gave me great encouragement when I started my company and, knowing that having artists like me come to her premises was good publicity, gave me free space whenever she could. But it was all very well rehearsing people individually all over town, in any space we could get for free, but there came a point when I really had to run the show and rehearse everybody together. So I forked out for a studio for a week – underneath the stage at the Drury Lane Theatre.

Costumes were another expensive item. I couldn't afford to have them designed, so we went round the different dance shops looking for suitable stuff. Again Debbie provided help – in the form of large discounts for leotards, tights and shoes from her dance gear shops. I left them with one of the dancers, who unfortunately lost them. I had to go begging again.

I thought, naïvely, that I could run all the administration by myself, but even such a small operation as this needed an office for co-ordination. I enlisted the help of Armand Gerrard, who had just formed his own touring management company, called the Touring Office. Armand had been a stage manager with the Royal Ballet. I knew him well and knew I could trust him.

I designed both the poster and the set for *DASH*. The poster had dashes (naturally) all over it, looking like footprints in the air, with an image of a dancer leaping out of it. The set was composed of four wooden boxes with a raised section above for the band, which was to be an integral part of the show. Conchita's father owned an engineering company and he provided the metal structure which reinforced the set.

The boxes were made to rotate with the dancers standing still inside and as each turned it would reveal one part only of the dancer's body. So you see the feet, then a turn, the hips, another turn, the head. This required three openings on three sides with the fourth as a full door for the exits and entrances. Each box to represent a different style. The first in ballet shoes, the second, jazz pumps, the third, bare feet and the fourth, tap shoes. When they came out of their boxes they mingled together. The audience began to register that this was a show of mixed styles. We felt we were bringing dance out of its separate closets.

Charles Augins, a leading dancer in the American cast of *Bubbling Brown Sugar*, (he went on to choreograph *Five Guys Named Mo*), invented an Apache dance for Jane Darling with Iwan and me as gangsters. This was the first piece Charles ever did in this country. It helped to get him his Equity card. Jennifer Jackson, from the Royal Ballet, choreographed a neoclassical piece for two bodies rippling in all-over gold and silver metallic. I put together a clog dance (!) in which I used ultraviolet light to isolate white gloves and clogs and invented my own *Tarantella* using the music from the Balanchine piece. Derek Hartley from the Pineapple Dance Centre choreographed a tap number to music from Scott Joplin. I devised a solo around the music-hall dancer, Lois Fuller, for Jane; I used my John Durang hornpipe; and we paid a tribute to American musicals with a toe-tapping *Yankee Doodle Dandy*.

Charles came down to Chichester the day before the first performance to rehearse our finale on stage. I remember he sat with his head in his hands in despair at the disparity of dancers. We were six different styles, shapes, interpretation. He shook his head at our lack of slickness and the seeming impossibility of getting a classically trained dancer to produce exuberant jazz. That is what we went to bed with. The problems, and the risk, seemed enormous. Then the next day I found that my carefully designed boxes did not fit on the stage . . . Courtesy of the theatre, we brought in carpenters to make the adjustments. What with the technical and lighting run-throughs we left the stage just before the audience came in. More yet – I heard that John Percival was intending to be in the auditorium. Great. The critic who least favoured me.

I was exhausted from working with Dame Ninette, from performances at the Royal Ballet, from getting *DASH* together. We were all tired. We were all nervous. We all wanted success. And the omens to that point were scarcely propitious. But we knew we had a fast-moving show with good dancing and lots of diverse interest, even if it had been done on a shoestring, even if it was an experiment. We were all prepared to give it our all. And did.

It went without a hitch. Except for my poor dresser, who, for reasons of economy, was also wardrobe master. I yelled at him when I came off-stage (rather in the same way Rudolf could scream), sometimes because I needed a rapid change – 'Where are my gloves? Where is my hat?' – but not all my yelling was directed at him. He just bore the brunt of it and eventually it reduced him to tears. I did feel bad, because it wasn't his fault. But it is better to vent tension off the stage, even by shouting at some poor innocent, than to carry it back on stage where pent-up emotions are a dangerous quality.

But the show, the rapid changes (backstage was busier than onstage), everything: it all went like clockwork that first performance. It came together in the manner that is the stuff of many a theatrical story. Just as we hoped – just as we had worked so hard for.

After the excitement we went back to the hotel. It was freezing. My room was on a corner with the wind whistling from one window through the other. I gave my duvet to one of the girls – I wasn't able to sleep. The tension, the worry, the possible reviews, the exhaustion, even, had got to me. I went downstairs to find a late-night snifter, a little nightcap. And then I found, to my horror, that we were booked into a temperance hotel. Not a drop of drink in sight. But there was no need to drown sorrows that night, the performance had gone well.

I did fall asleep, eventually, and woke to find *The Times* shoved under my door. I admit to a certain amount of trepidation as I opened the paper, because it was the only national paper that was reviewing the show. A bad review and the theatres might not book me. And *DASH* was my baby, so, yes, really, a good review or two would be welcome. And, of course, it would also be congenial for others to see me as successful.

And, blow me down, Percival gave us a very decent review. At one point he compared my six-dancer *DASH* to the Bob Fosse Broadway spectacular *Dancin*, saying: '[*DASH's*] reliance on flair rather than spectacle must be an asset, and I, at least, found it more consistently enjoyable than its transatlantic big brother.' Well – good.

More reviewers came down to Chichester too, and Debbie Moore gathered together a contingent of her dancers – more than seventy of them – who paid to see the show and support us. Over the week audiences grew. It was rumoured that Andrew Lloyd Webber and Gillian Lynne were coming to the final performance. Whether they did or not, I have no idea, but we had a great send-off on our last night at Chichester.

I felt the success of the venture vindicated my philosophy of bringing dance, and a variety of dance at that, to a wider audience. I really liked having proved that if your ideas are good you don't need all the paraphernalia and trimmings of an expensive production. Even the lighting was supplied by whatever was hanging up in Chichester at the time. I also felt that I had only glimpsed the tip of the iceberg with a show that was successful with virtually no costumes, little rehearsal, four musicians, and six dancers. What might be done with the full support of a West End team?

I did, in fact, lose money at Chichester. It is difficult enough to recoup the cost of putting a show together, let alone make a profit, if you only have one week of performances. But it was worth it, and the money was my own so I felt no guilt. And there was the week at the King's Theatre in Edinburgh to come, followed by a late booking from the Palace Theatre, in Plymouth, for the week after. About as far apart as you can get – but par for the course if you are touring.

Edinburgh, George's home town, went very well indeed. They seem to like me in Scotland. But in Plymouth, where I come from, I lost even more money. The numbers of the people in the audience did not tally with the number of tickets sold. I was told there were 300 paid tickets. It looked to me like a lot more. The next night, through a hole in the curtain, we counted the audience. Just as I thought. At least 300 more people than the box office were saying. I asked to see the box-office manager. First he said I must be mistaken. Then that it might be one of his staff, who had been seen buying lots of clothes recently in Marks & Spencers. What an excuse. I reckoned he was guilty and just blaming some other poor sucker. I gave him until midday the next day to sort it out – otherwise I would call the police. He arrived in my dressing-room with the missing £2,000-worth of ticket stubs – they had 'been misplaced at the back of the safe'. I decided not to pursue the matter. I had my money and the point had been made. This was my first experience in producing for commercial theatre and my first experience of corruption in commercial theatre. And it made me realize how cocooned we were at the Royal Ballet, what a privileged life it was away from the rigours of the outside world.

ELEVEN

CATS AND OTHER TRAUMAS

A FEW MONTHS BEFORE *DASH*, Andrew Lloyd Webber's office telephoned to arrange a meeting. George and I were invited to supper at the Lloyd Webbers' house in Eaton Place.

Had we heard of *Old Possum's Book of Practical Cats*? Me, never. George, of course, had. Not only did he sell copies of most of T.S.Eliot's first editions, but he knew Valerie, Eliot's widow. Andrew was bent on turning these poems into a musical show. He has always produced successes with out-of-the-way subjects – Jesus, Joseph, Eva Peron. But cats? At first I thought it was a dotty idea.

Andrew was talking choreographers. I mentioned several American ones, but Andrew said no, this was to be an entirely English affair. 'I want to establish that we can produce a musical with as good dancing as any Broadway show *and* with an English choreographer.' I had difficulty seeing it myself. I held very strong opinions on musicals. I'd seen good dance routines in poor musicals and good musicals with little or no dance. I was used to waiting for American musicals to come to the UK in order to see lively, stylish and energetic choreography.

After dinner Andrew slid on to his piano stool and began to play the score. 'Try these notes, Wayne.' Oh my God. The penny dropped. This was an audition. I began to clam up. I mumbled a few notes and wished I had not had that glass of wine – Andrew's scores are notoriously difficult because of the range. George was once again at his most helpful, staring at the wall. I was pomegranate red and feeling pale inside. Did Andrew care? He said, 'Try this key, Wayne.' And I warbled some more, with George finding an even more resolute fascination with something on the wall. Sarah saved me from my pool of embarrassment by saying, when she brought the coffee in, 'I didn't know you could sing.' I could have kissed her for restoring a smattering of confidence. The audition was over. Andrew had found out what he needed to know and welcomed us to coffee.

The next day my agent called to say that Andrew wanted me to meet Trevor Nunn, who was to direct the musical. Trevor Nunn – the man who directed *Nicholas Nickleby* and *The Comedy of Errors* – was an idol of mine (I say this because I was a fan of the RSC and so admired his work), someone whom I had thought I would never work with. Cameron Mackintosh was the co-producer. This was his first venture with Andrew. I guessed Gillian Lynne would be on board, because she had done a brilliant job on Trevor's *Comedy*. (I think that is one show which ought to have transferred to the West End, but never did.) *Cats* was Trevor's first West End musical and he wanted to keep a successful team together. He brought in John Napier, who had designed many of Trevor's RSC productions, and David Hersey for the lighting design.

I thought I'd passed the audition. Then I received a message from my agent. Go to the Strand Theatre and take a song with me. What? Gulp! Help! Auditions!! Again? Trevor wanted to hear me sing. I thought well, if nothing else, it'll be an experience. Not sure who for. Cameron, Gillian and Trevor were there. I sang 'Where Is Love' from *Oliver* – in falsetto. Like many people who have auditioned for my shows since, I was ill-prepared. I bluffed my way for a while, trying to sing along to the accompanist. But I told him to stop, saying that he was putting me off. He wasn't of course, that was a lame attempt at a joke. I just couldn't sing in his key. So I sang unaccompanied. And I won my place in the show (thanks to experience in *The Point*).

Rehearsals for *Cats* started while *DASH* was performing in Plymouth. Because I could not make the first week of rehearsal I was sent some songs and asked to learn them. I went through the numbers with my *DASH* pianist, Clive Chaplin, who said he had never seen such peculiar lyrics for a musical. Clive had played in the bands of all the major American shows when they came to Britain, and he thought this *Cats* idea didn't stand a chance of running in the West End. I arrived a week later to rehearse in a Catholic church hall off Chiswick High Road, and I met the other thirty-odd people in the cast, which included Paul Nicholas, Brian Blessed and Judi Dench.

In the week before I joined rehearsals, the rest of the cast had to go away and do a project on cats. Glad I missed that one. Then before going into production Trevor decided we should do a number of improvisation rehearsals to discover, enact cat movements, traits, habits, etc., including the worst thing we'd ever seen a cat do. One silly girl pretended to be a cat in a litter box. Judi was the star – she opened her mouth wide and hissed from her larynx. Frightening. Everybody started to be a cat fetishist. Grace became my study for the production. I used to watch her intently and most of my movements were thanks to her.

No one was spared Gillian's vigorous and gut-busting warm-ups, which she demonstrated herself. 'If I can do it, you can do it.' We were compelled. This was a shock to my system, as I was used to the flow of the classical ballet barre.

We also played games to get to know each other. In one, we stood in circles, eyes closed, and I had to feel, sniff, the two people either side of me, to remember their physical presence; then on a clap of Trevor's hands, every alternate person threw themselves to the corners of the room and had to find their way back to the same place. All with eyes closed. To pick up on other people's senses. I managed to find my way back, to my surprise. Trevor said, 'Well done, very well done, Wayne. Well done.' But I didn't feel well done. I knew how I had done it. By sound. The girl next to me suffered from sinus problems and her breathing guided me back to the same place. So it worked, you could say, so what? Then Trevor said, 'Let's do it again.' This time I ended up on the piano keys.

There was another game, again in a circle. To the tune of 'Hi ho, hi ho, it's off to work we go . . .' (which we sang) we had to toss a can of Coca-Cola (I think) from one to another. When the music came to a certain point we had to pass it from one hand to the other and then on again. Pretty daft, I thought, but got into the swing of it. It's only in retrospect that I understand the principle behind this game – to be willing to let go and hand over your spotlight to the next person. A necessary facet of an ensemble show. And Trevor wanted *Cats* to be very much an ensemble show.

I had no real concept of 'ensemble', at least not in the way both Trevor and Gillian understood it. The four soloists were expected also to be at times chorus back-up for other artists, while for me ensemble – by this time having achieved senior principal status in the Royal Ballet – was the *corps de ballet* in seamless dance together, with the soloists and principals in a separate layer above. It was new to me to be part of a team in this way. I was learning, and it took me a while to grasp it. I'm pretty certain that the original intention was to bring in four soloists, Judi, Brian, Paul and me, as the backbone of the show. Ultimate ensembleship may have been the aim but it only became apparent how to achieve it through the give-and-take process of rehearsal.

These games and improvisations took up two weeks of rehearsals, during which time Trevor also helped us to create our own individual characters. Mine was almost like a master of ceremonies, small and bossy, of course, organizer of the Jellicle Ball. Paul Nicholas was taken for private dance rehearsals. I was taken for private singing coaching; in particular with Ian Adam, the famous voice coach who had helped many actors to sing, including Michael Crawford. Although I did *The Point*, the fact that I can sing – in any way at all – is entirely down to him.

After the two weeks of getting-to-know-you games and the character improvisations, Trevor had to return to Stratford-upon-Avon to organize his season at the RSC and Gillian took over at the helm. She began by choreographing the big opening ensemble dance number, and we all tried to incorporate the choreography into our own characters. Hence Stephen Tate, as Gus the Theatre Cat who was fourscore and ten, moved around the stage as his age demanded, and Paul Nicholas as the very laid back Rum Tum Tugger barely moved at all. It was only I and the younger cats who were doing the whole thing full out. Gillian was utterly bemused. Why were we not all dancing with the same amount of energy? What was going on? We explained that we were trying to interpret our characters within her choreography. She said, 'But darlings, it will look as though you can't dance! The opening of the show is an ensemble number and your characters are not even established yet.' She was right, of course.

Until *Cats*, musicals separated song, dance and dialogue, with the choreographer taking the dance rehearsals and the director the dialogue. But the composition of this musical was movement, music and sung lyrics, cleverly intertwined, and all the components needed to be worked on simultaneously.

Those of us who had been in musicals found ourselves muddled. We were accustomed to separation. Here the parameters seemed undefined. It started to make sense when Trevor came back, and he and Gillian began to work together with us in the rehearsal room. Trevor had the grand overview and Gillian filled in the details. The collaboration of director and choreographer became not only clear but obvious, and the whole process less confusing. Previous to this, most directors in England used choreographers just for the dance breaks.

Cats was taking shape.

This intensive rehearsal period started at ten in the morning. Of course I was usually late out of bed and had to take a taxi to Chiswick. One morning, nearly late as ever, we were stuck in a traffic jam in the middle of Chiswick High Road. A hearse, with coffin, was stuck in the middle. I decided to get out and walk. It started to rain – damn – I had not brought an umbrella. But something made me turn round. The spattering was not rain at all, but drops of holy water from a chalice, being flicked at me by Gladstone Liddle, the local Roman Catholic priest, who was taking the funeral service. He spouted, 'Have a nice day!' at me when I turned to look at him. Gladstone came frequently to watch our rehearsals. We struck up a friendship and I renewed my interest in religion. (Gladstone eventually became secretary to the Cardinal at Westminster Cathedral and we had many a heated religious discussion over many a dinner.)

Once, having partied with some of my cousins all night, we found ourselves, on Sunday morning, somewhere near Chiswick, and I came up with the wheeze of visiting Gladstone. To surprise him, we nabbed the front pews of his church for early morning communion. Unfortunately it was not Gladstone taking the service, but his locum. I was in my gold leather suit – which made me feel very conspicuous – so during communion we sneaked out through the side door and round to the presbytery. There we were told that Gladstone was giving communion to the Venetian Order of Nuns up the road. This sounded like a wind-up to me, so we went on a mission to find out if there really was a nunnery. We found it and crept into the hall, into which floated the angelic voices of the nuns. The doors opened and the nuns teemed out, followed by Gladstone and an all-pervading warm smell of fresh coffee and croissants. Gladstone was surprised to see us (and not a little embarrassed, I guess) and started to usher us, gold suit and all, towards the door. But perhaps the desire for coffee and croissants showed on my face, or maybe it was due to the natural and spontaneous hospitality of the Order, because one of the nuns invited us to breakfast. It happened to be feast day and we ate a very hearty breakfast, in a separate room, of course, to the nuns. I still have the vision of them, happy faces peering round the door one by one, watching us eat and tittering with laughter.

The name of my cat in the first act was Quaxo. I was to do a solo in the company tap routine, for which Gillian, who had little training in tap, called in

Lindsay Dolan. Gillian had been, like me, a Royal Ballet soloist (when it was the Sadler's Wells Ballet). In fact, when I think of it, quite a few of the original cast of *Cats* were trained in the classical form. Andrew Lloyd Webber trained at the Royal College of Music, Gillian and I at the Royal Ballet, Trevor and Judi with the Royal Shakespeare Company and various of the stage crew at the Royal Oak pub. A right royal lot.

I was also to sing the first solo – about the Gumbie Cat, played by Judi. When Gillian was setting our routine, I was dancing behind Judi, who let out a sudden and piercing shriek and stopped in her tracks, frozen. She could not put her foot down. Because I was behind her she asked: had I kicked her? I said, 'No.' I knew I hadn't. We helped her to a chair. Her face was ashen, the pain was obviously excruciating. I was reminded, all of a sudden, of the time when Brian Shaw snapped his Achilles tendon while dancing on stage. I didn't want to say this, because it wasn't my place, because it might be wrong, or, if I were right, too depressing. The ambulance came – and my private diagnosis was confirmed. Judi had torn her Achilles tendon and was admitted to the Nuffield Hospital for an operation.

I went to visit her and took a soft toy cat to cheer her up. She put on a brave face and tried to appear in good spirits (she had her watercolours and was painting), but it was apparent there was a lot of pain. She said she hoped to be better in time for rehearsals in the theatre. I said nothing. One evening I turned up with a meal from Odin's restaurant just around the corner – the complete silver service treatment, courtesy of Peter Langan. I really wanted her to feel better. But it was probably the very last thing she wanted to see – me with all that stuff from Langan . . .

Judi's injury was the start of a whole spate of difficulties. Jeff Shankley, an actor/dancer, had an operation on his cartilage. Another boy so hated being ordered about that he refused correction and was given the boot. Gillian was famous for rehearsing people until they, and she, dropped. She took two days off, too, from exhaustion. The musical director found the work and the pace too demanding and was replaced. It was proving very hard to find enough backers to finance the show. A West End musical out of Eliot's cat poems? Don't be silly. Andrew and Cameron were investing a lot of money. It was a huge risk. We were getting nearer and nearer the opening night, Judi was still in hospital, we hadn't finished blocking the show, there was still so much to do – some wondered whether it was all worth while, or whether the show was jinxed.

Andrew chose the New London Theatre for *Cats*. He had decided on it when sitting on stage during the filming of his *This Is Your Life*. It was transformed. (Except for the facilities backstage which, in common with a great many theatres, were abysmal. No windows in the dressing-rooms, no ventilation in the toilets, which were in the hallway. Far from adequate, but a home from home for me. Backstage at the ROH was not much different, then, though it has since been rebuilt.) John Napier, genius, created an amazing set – just like a rubbish dump, with the boot of a car, large tin cans, broken cutlery – all to scale. The band were hidden behind broken-down wooden fences and the stage, to my consternation, was not very large, sloped, and was covered in paper posters which were glazed to protect them. This made it incredibly slippery. I stuck rubber heels and soles on my dance shoes. This gave a grip but meant that, when spinning and pirouetting, I needed to use more power to counteract it. The coercion of these opposing forces made injuries, particularly in the knee, more likely. But you discover how best to dance within those constrictions, and you learn how to protect yourself too.

Stage rehearsals began with trying out the mechanical scenery. The stage was on a revolve, with drawbridges and ramps that led up to it. A huge rubber tyre ascended from the ground, pulling up a staircase to an opening in a huge poster, which was the backdrop. ('Oh, I see, love,' said David Hockney to George on the first night. 'The set revolves and the tyre goes up there.' So much for the element of surprise.) A trapeze swung the cats across the stage. In the second act I, as Mr Mistoffelees, descended on a rope from thirty feet in the air, reached from a narrow bridge high in the flies above. Video screens were placed at the front and the sides of the stage so that we could see the conductor relayed from behind the broken fencing. Some seating was placed on stage. Sometimes that section of the audience rushed back to the box office demanding a refund, because the seats were behind a huge wall of rubbish which blocked their view of the stage. They were not aware that the set rotated during the overture so that they would be able to see.

One morning we all went to the studio where the band had been rehearsing with Harry Rabinowitz, who conducted the first weeks of performances. Barbara Thomson, the saxophonist, Rod Argent on keyboards and John Hiseman, the drummer, also added their expertise. It was very exciting, nerve-tingling almost, sitting with the rest of the cast to hear the first band run-through. But when it was finished I realized that I had heard no solo for Mr Mistoffelees. I wondered whether it had been cut. No longer required. The outcome, perhaps, of ensemble work. If that sounds paranoiac, it probably was. I felt that I hadn't given up a year with the Royal Ballet to be under-used, and I admit that being part of a team, not a soloist, was still a new concept – I was finding it difficult because it was so long since I had done any chorus work. (Now, of course, I can't imagine why I was so bothered, and I realize I learned the backbones of proper teamwork through this somewhat fraught (for me) time with *Cats* rehearsals.)

As a dancer I hated not being given enough to do – it is, after all, life's blood – and I was worried that my solo was to be cut altogether. I called Jonathan and he reassured me that my contract stated two solos, one in the first act, and one in the second. So I talked with the management and reminded them of this. Andrew arranged for me to go to the studio with Gillian to create my solo with the rhythm section of the band. Gillian said where she wanted the big jumps and Andrew wrote the music accordingly. The stabs of the brass section were added later. This exercise made me realize how good it is if choreographer and composer can work together in such a collaboration.

Gillian choreographed a very sinuous dance for me – in which I had to perform magic tricks. Now I can juggle a little, three oranges, that sort of thing, but magic? Magic, I thought to myself, is kind of specialized. It takes years to perfect. I was delighted to have a go. The song does say 'Magical Mr Mistoffelees', so it's obvious really. A magician was brought in to teach me how to pull endless string out of my mouth, how to knock spots off handkerchiefs, how to make things disappear. All to be incorporated into the choreography, like – dance a bit, looking like a hamster with cheek pouches full, turn away from the audience and turn back pulling this stuff out of my mouth. There was so much I kept tripping over it. That, for me, was a bit of a nightmare. We dropped it, thank heavens. It would have been great if some of the tricks – 'I can pull kittens out of a hat', for instance – had been built into the scenery, but such changes would have been just for Mr Mistoffelees, and I wasn't the only cat on the block. We called in Paul Daniels, who simplified the procedure. The handkerchief trick survived and so did the one where I made a cat disappear. Every so often I would point to a part of the stage and cause an explosion in time with the music.

It is interesting to compare the way different choreographers work. Sir Fred used to sit down, and direct by voice, description and gesture. Gillian, who is always at the peak of physical fitness, always demonstrated her steps; she demanded better than our best. Doing what she asked of me went well in the studio, but when we transposed to the stage, I had a problem in re-creating the steps. The stage was smaller, and I suggested one leap to her three as I simply couldn't fit in the required steps. Or that I should just go higher to fill the music. Even the smallest changes in routine can unnerve you. We spent a few (nervous) previews trying out different combinations, but we had it in the bag for the first night.

Judi joined us on crutches, with her leg in plaster, and started to go through her moves with Trevor. But she slipped on one of the ramps and, because she found the set too difficult for manoeuvring, she sadly relinquished her roles: the Gumbie Cat and Grizabella. It was decided that Judi's understudy, Myra Sands, should play the Gumbie Cat as she had been rehearsing with me, and Elaine Page came in to play Grizabella. Elaine is very different both in physique and voice to Judi (although they are both small), and so brought an entirely different dimension to the role. Judi was going to sing the main song of the show, 'Memory', in a husky broken-down voice, as a cat whose life was on the ebb. Elaine interpreted Grizabella's solitude and lameness through movement and sang the song with a haunting, dynamic bravado.

All the cat costumes were made on the basic unitard, painted and sprayed in different colours, with knitted bibs plus leg-warmers and occasional gloves. The tails were simple rope tied round the waist. The wigs, made of yak hair to stick out, and the ornate make-up were also designed by John Napier. My costume was not Lycra, like everyone else's, but black lurex. This was supposed to be even more shiny under the lights, but unfortunately, it was quite the reverse. The lights made the lurex look like thick wool, which made me look like a fat little kitten. (Cute, maybe, but not the desired effect.) The lurex was also scratchy next to the skin and I had to wear a bodystocking for protection. This made life even hotter under the lights. I decided to wear my practice clothes during rehearsals – and even up to the first performance. I asked John if my costume could possibly be remade in Lycra, but he'd run out of makers. So I offered him the Royal Opera House wardrobe. Actually I took my costume to a friend in the wardrobe and he copied it in black Lycra, attaching the white bib from the original costume – just in time for the first performance. Good to have friends up the road.

It was decided to cancel the first previews, as there was no way we would be ready in time. But at one rehearsal a coach-load of tourists from Wales arrived at the theatre. They had not heard, no one had told them, that the previews were cancelled. They were refunded and, as a special treat because they had come all that distance, they were allowed to sit and watch the rehearsals. Even though it was rough at the edges, *Cats* was received with great enthusiasm.

A few days before the first night I found a pathetic half-drowned cat huddled in a corner in the Covent Garden Piazza. As I was an honorary member of the species, I went up to it to make sure it was all right and to give it a reassuring stroke. When I walked away it followed me down the road. I brought it back to the Piazza, thinking that its owner would be looking for it, but every time I left it, it followed me. In the end I took it home. I don't think I could have done anything else, because this cat was black, with a white bib, with two white flashes on its face – which corresponded *exactly* with my make-up. I thought this very spooky, and possibly an omen for the success of the show. Grace, however, took exception, so Bustopher Jones (a name from *Old Possum*) was eventually found a home in the country with George's trusty secretary, Penny.

When the first night finally arrived, we were all high with the nervous tension, and exhausted from intensive rehearsal and the inevitable changes that occur during previews. The preview audiences had been highly appreciative, which helped, but there is no night like a first night and no audience like a first-night audience. It was still a risk, it might get critically panned, the audience might hate it.

The applause, at the end, was tumultuous . . . but cut short. Brian Blessed came on, very much in his character as Old Deuteronomy, and held up his hand. There was a certain sighing: 'Oh God, he's going to make a speech.' But he asked the audience to leave the theatre quietly and calmly. Apparently there was a bomb scare. The timing was such, thank heavens, that it did not interrupt the performance, but the standing ovation was cut short. I think most of us felt a little deflated. It's a funny thing about performing. You give your all, and your due reward is the accolade from the audience. When you don't get it, you think, 'Oh. Was that it?' The applause helps you to come down to earth gradually.

While we were all standing in the street someone asked me if I was coming to the first-night party. I decided, on the spur of the moment, that I wasn't. I was too tired, too full of first-night nerves, and just wanted to get my head down. So I wandered home, through the streets of Covent Garden, still in my black and white costume, still in my wig and make-up, trailing my tail between my legs.

Cats, as everyone knows, was a massive success. All the trials and tribulations, all my fears and misconceptions, everything that was difficult in any way up to the first night, suddenly seemed worth while. For me, personally, it was an experience which taught me so much, about theatre, about team-work. The end result paid off.

Part of our performance was to go into the audience at various times during the show and sit on the stairs, or on the laps of the public, to move around, stare into people's eyes – do the things cats do. One girl was so overwhelming to the men she liked in the audience that we joked about her giving out her calling card. Once I came face to face with a woman in a white fur coat, so I snuggled up to it. The company manager was sent the dry-cleaning bill for the make-up I left all over it. I was attracted to another fur collar . . . I started to stroke it . . . bits came away in my hand. That was horrid, for me and for the (now mangy) owner. I ran for cover. Early on in the run, one lady's dress was ruined by wet paint on the scenery – some of the seats were in the midst of rubble above the stage.

We played to packed houses night after night. The fame of *Cats* grew and grew and tickets were like gold dust, heaven for the ticket touts. On our travels through the audience we would come across some very interesting people. Once I draped my leg over a gentleman's thigh and rested my head on a lady's arm. I rubbed my cheek against her shoulder, as cats do, and looked up into her face, to find – Joanne Woodward. I moved my leg in some embarrassment, because where there is Joanne Woodward, there is likely to be Paul Newman. Yes, indeed. And his eyes are even more blue in life than on the cinema screen. After the show they came backstage and invited a few of us for a drink. I had met Joanne Woodward before, when I was with the Royal Ballet in America. She is a great ballet supporter.

On another evening, Bette Midler knocked on my dressing-room door and I met the woman who was responsible, partly, for *DASH*. She took to my wig and wondered if she 'could do something with this' in one of her shows. Angela Lansbury came with her husband one night, and I took them to Langans for dinner. I didn't meet Barbra Streisand – she left in the interval, struck down with a migraine. But for me, the climax of these guest visits was when, after my solo in the second act, a woman stood to applaud. She asked to meet me after the show and I insisted on dancing round the floor with her, just so that I could say I had danced (alas, I'm no Fred Astaire) with the legendary Ginger Rogers. I was surprised to find she had short cropped red hair, and a freckled complexion with scarcely a trace of make-up. She looked both fresh-faced and sophisticated. I had recently seen her on stage and had felt then that she would look better without the theatrical make-up and blonde wig which created her star persona. I wondered why she felt she needed it – but I guess that's Hollywood.

A couple of months into the run I received a note from Gillian Lynne. She was disappointed, she said, to hear I had been signing autographs on stage. No way would I come out of character to sign an autograph. Our instructions were to freeze during the applause. I was unhappy not only that she believed this story, but also that she did not check the truth with me before ticking me off. The real tale went thus: a little girl in the front row handed me an autograph book during the applause. I shook my head as if to say no and she went back to her place. Afterwards, Ken Wells, Festival Ballet dancer and second lead dancer in the show, asked me if I had signed the book. I said, 'Of course I did, my dear,' meaning 'Of course I didn't.' He took my sarcasm as literal and must have told the management. I know I wasn't popular with everyone in the cast and management and I admit that much of it was my fault. The ensemble business had been a hard thing for me to get to grips with, and during that process of change, and in sticking up for what I thought, at the time, were my dues (such as with the billing on the posters, when I questioned the lack of the four star names above the rest of the artists in the show), I did not exactly endear myself. Little Wayne too big for his boots, kind of thing. So there were a few people who would have been happy to take me down a peg or two. I was beginning to understand that in the commercial theatre there was no luxury of security such as I experienced with the Royal Ballet. And this insecurity, coupled with ambition (and jealousy to some extent), can lead people to all sorts of mean tricks to keep in with the management. I, on the other hand, had a fail-safe. I could go back to the Royal.

There was one person in the *Cats* company who was constantly helpful. Sarah Brightman and I shared a covered hole in the stage where we had whispered conversations before we went on. She bolstered my confidence every night before I went out to sing my solo. We went out quite a lot over the months I was in the show. The next time we worked together was during the filming of the video recording of *Song and Dance*. By which time she was married to Andrew Lloyd Webber.

Some months into the run the whole thing was beginning to feel like a tread-mill. I had never been in a show before where I performed eight shows a week, for nine months. The longest had been four months, in *The Point*. Everyone gets low points in a long run, and I was feeling particularly low on the day a meeting was called by the Company Equity representative. Apparently Thames Television were doing a documentary on the state of the arts in West End theatres and would be in to film the finale of the second act of the show during the matinée performance the next day. Usually I am the first person to speak out in these meetings, to raise a point or have one explained. Or sometimes just be bolshy. That day I was too tired to bother and left the meeting.

The next afternoon I had forgotten about this and was in such a bad mood that I didn't even want to come and take my curtain call. But of course one always does. Bonnie Langford wiped a smudge of make-up from under my eye, which I thought odd. I was standing with Elaine Page on the stage and suddenly saw the lights of the cameras. Elaine pulled away from me, so I said to her, 'Come on, darling, you'll be out of shot. We might as well make the most of it.' Then not only Elaine, but everybody else as well, spread away from me and I got this tap on the shoulder. I turned. It was Eamonn Andrews. Clutching a big red book. 'Wayne Sleep?' Those portentous tones. 'This is your life!' Shell-shocked pause. I squeaked: 'But I haven't lived it yet . . .'

I knew absolutely nothing about it. They had all managed to keep it a secret, which I don't think is always the case. I was led away, numb, to my dressing-room, to find George with my Anthony Price dark blue satin suit and a pair of clean socks. The door closed behind me. No escape. Ten minutes later, dressed (and with the clean socks), I was ushered to the Royalty Theatre for the show.

The *Cats* cast were assembled in the balcony. Eamonn said to me, 'Whatever you do as you walk down the aisle through the audience, don't stop until you reach the stage.' I realized what he meant. Lining the aisles were hundreds (it seemed) of members of my family – some of whom I had hardly ever met. The programme started with my mother and father. Then we went to a recorded message from Margot Fonteyn in Panama. This, however, was a ruse – she had in fact flown all the way over to London and appeared as the last guest on the show. My mother had to stifle her tears. And Stephen Gretton, my friend from the Hartlepool Tech, whom I had not met for twenty-two years and who was now working for Shell and had a degree – probably thanks to my leaving and not being a bad influence on him. After I left he became top of the class. Gran threw her stick aside when the doors opened for her; she decided to walk to me unaided. Angela Lansbury spoke to me from her poolside in Los Angeles and Diana Roberts told anecdotes about when I lived with her in Leicester Square. My sister and her new husband were there, as were Uncle Bert, Auntie Barbara (who had taught me my first tap steps), and my cousin Jackie. They then played a pop record I had just made called 'Man to Man'! Lesley Collier and Jane Darling represented the dance world, along with Dame Alicia Markova and Sir Anton Dolin. And to top it all Dame Ninette de Valois came on and gave me the best compliment I have ever received in public: 'What we have here is, in my opinion, the greatest virtuoso dancer the Royal Ballet has ever produced.'

When I went back to my dressing-room for the evening performance of *Cats*, I realized that my black mood had evaporated. *This Is Your Life* was a marvellous exhilaration and I returned to the show with new life. After the performance there was a party at the hotel where all my family were gathered. George was there too, and told me how hard it had been keeping it quiet, liaising with the television company, deciding and preparing the guests. I suddenly remembered George asking me a few days before whether I'd had the suit cleaned. I had thought it slightly odd at the time, because George does not usually bother himself with that sort of domestic detail, but thought nothing further of it then. And I had seen my family only a week before when they came to *Cats*. Apparently they were going to cancel, knowing they were coming up again a few days later, but George insisted they do nothing to arouse suspicion. There were people I would like to have been included in the show, but I realized what an impossible task it had been to locate everybody. And it is wonderful to have such a record, not least because of the accolades given me by such great ballet artists.

The next night, because Margot was staying a few days, I arranged a meeting between her and Cameron Mackintosh. We dined in Langan's Brasserie, Peter's new restaurant, which he part owned with Michael Caine and Richard Shepherd. When Margot was presented with the menu she reached into her bag for her lorgnette. But it was not there. She assumed it must have been stolen while coming through customs in Panama. I remember this only because I had never seen her with glasses before. I wondered, once or twice, about the reasons that kept Margot in Panama with Roberto. I think it was her intense sense of loyalty. She never complained, even though conditions on the whole were fairly primitive and apparently all her money went on his treatments and political ambitions. I was hoping Cameron might arrange a lecture tour of the States for Margot and we mulled over the idea during dinner. In the event nothing came of it, but we spent an enjoyable evening. Margot and I reminisced about her years in the Royal Ballet. She told me that she had enjoyed being on the show and said, 'You scored and your mother scored.' I looked quizzically at her. 'With your clothes.' A high compliment from one with an impeccable dress sense.

I asked her what was the one thing in her career that had contributed to her worldwide success, thinking she might say a certain teacher, or a choreographer perhaps. She narrowed her eyes, lifted her chin, looked me straight in the eye and said, 'Tenacity.'

I was one of the few who for the nine months I was there never missed a single performance of *Cats* and I was the first member of the cast to leave. On my last night I received the token bottle of champagne and a message from Gillian on my mirror in lipstick – 'Pax, pax, pax – love Gillian.' I admit my time on *Cats* was not unalleviated happiness, and it was certainly a learning experience. I had not been that easy to work with, and it had not been easy for me either. But the friction that was generated between artist and artist, and artist and management, turned into the right dynamic tension that is sometimes so necessary when giving birth to a new work. I had not thought, to start with, that it would last six months, let alone fifteen-plus years. It is, though, the most successful show I have ever appeared in, and if I mention I was in the original cast, people anywhere in the world are impressed.

TWELVE

Song and Dance

W HILE I WAS in *Cats* I rang Andrew Lloyd Webber's office to organize a meeting. I wanted to borrow *Variations on a Theme of Paganini*, which he had composed for an album featuring his brother, Julian, on the cello. I was mulling over the idea of using it for the first act on my next *DASH* tour. The second act would be my dance impersonations. Andrew was musing on the notion of extending *Tell Me on a Sunday*, an album he had written with the lyricist, Don Black, for Marti Webb, into a two-act musical. He had tried various ways of lengthening the music and of bringing the people in the songs to life, but had not cracked it after several attempts. My request made him think that both albums could be combined into a stage concert. Marti would sing 'Sunday' in the first act and I would dance *Variations* in the second. Cameron came up with the title – *Song and Dance*. *DASH* would have to be put on hold (yet again: I had done this week after week while I was still running with *Cats*), but as *Song and Dance* was projected for twelve weeks it would give me more time to think of something for *DASH*.

Before starting work on *Song and Dance*, in February 1982, I went to the Virgin Islands with George for a two-week holiday. We changed hotels about three times – something was always wrong – and eventually gave up and hired a yacht. We sailed round the islands, mooring in different harbours each night, with a two-man crew. George and I had not the faintest idea how to sail – something that will surprise nobody, and I must say that the worst experience of a hangover I have ever had is after throwing up in the middle of the night, returning to my bunk, where the insistent rocking of the boat only exacerbated the nausea. We were too far out to swim to shore for relief. I learned that the only certain cure for sea-sickness is to sit under an apple tree. Very helpful advice when surrounded by acres of undulating water. But somehow I came back refreshed and ready to begin the new project.

Andrew and Cameron, the co-producers, booked the Palace Theatre to open *Song and Dance* on 12 April 1982. I had listened to the music over and over again on the boat, thinking that I might choreograph the piece myself. But we all decided it needed someone to keep an eye on me in performance and asked Paddy Stone. He turned it down, much to my surprise. He said, later, that he had not realized the project was to be so big. Then I heard that a contemporary dancer with LCDT, who had been in *David and Goliath*, had choreographed, with enormous success, Kate Bush's video and tour. I thought the transition from contemporary dance to pop video an intriguing leap and suggested him to Andrew and Cameron. They interviewed him and agreed. John Caird, who had worked with Trevor Nunn on *Nicholas Nickleby*, was to direct the show, and David Hersey was to design both the lighting and the scenery because it was to be full of front projections and light screens.

We went into rehearsals. Marti was in one room, we were in another. 'We' were: Jane Darling; Linda-Mae Brewer; Andrea Durant, a former principal classical dancer; Claude Paul Henry, a black contemporary dancer; Linda Gibbs, a leading dancer with LCDT; Paul Tomkinson, an ex-Royal Ballet dancer, who had been British Gymnastic Champion; Andy Norman, a jazz dancer; and Sandy Strallen, a television dancer who had appeared with me on Lena Zavaroni's shows. Harry Rabinowitz was in charge of the music.

John Caird, like Trevor Nunn (is this a particular RSC thing, I wondered?), started to play games with us. Here we are again, I thought, let the games begin . . . We found it highly amusing. We kept our tongues firmly in our cheeks and approached the games with less than serious minds. In ballet, you work on the choreography in rehearsals and the character comes out of the choreography. Once this is mastered, the oomph of character is laid on the top. In acting, you are required to lose inhibitions as soon as possible, preferably in the first rehearsal. You are encouraged to go over the top, to do ludicrous things. You may have to go to the very end and come back to something recognizable. The oomph must be present to begin with. John's job was made more difficult by the fact that there were no words in the *Dance* half to help explore the characters and he had to wait patiently in rehearsals until the initial choreography had been structured before being able to contribute.

I asked Anne Emery, who had trained under the famous fifties tap coach Buddy Bradley, to teach me tap-dancing American style. Anne was a friend of my neighbour Brenda Armstrong, and half-sister of Dick, of 'Ooh you are awful, but I *like* you! Whack!' fame. I found it very difficult to pick up this technique. It is not so easy to explain the difference – to see it is to understand immediately. But basically, the strength of American tap is below the knee, which scarcely moves, and the feet are far more rooted to the ground, producing an earthiness, almost a raunchiness, to coincide with the rhythm. It goes down into the ground and seems to derive its energy from there. It is far more laid-back and stylish. English tap, by comparison, is brighter, lighter, more upright, the knee springing high. The energy seems to stem more from the cushion of air between foot and ground. It can look rather as if you are jogging or doing an Irish jig. Linda-Mae was streets ahead of me in the tap routine, but after weeks of coaching I got there.

Andrew had originally conceived *Variations* as an album. It was, of itself, a complete piece of music. Although he was happy to write a new routine for the tap duet, he was not willing to change anything else. Quite understandable. It was part of him. But I was finding that the famous descending cello cadenza at

Previous page: With
Vergie Derman in
MacMillan's *Élite
Syncopations* at
Covent Garden in
1973.

Above: With Graham
Powell at Powis
Gardens just before
he died (photo taken
by George).

Right: As Kolia in
Ashton's *A Month in
the Country* at Covent
Garden in 1976.

Above: With Robert
North in the London
Contemporary Dance
Theatre production of
our ballet, *David and
Goliath*, at Sadler's
Wells Theatre in
1975.

Left: With Sean
Connery in the film
*The First Great Train
Robbery* in 1976.
When it came to the
final take, another
actor strangled me
as it was thought
unconvincing that
Sean's character
would have actually
strangled anyone.

Above: One of many
curtain calls in the
mid-1970s for
Ashton's *The Dream*
with Rudolph
Nureyev at the
Kennedy Centre in
Washington.

Above: With the fabulous dancer Lesley Collier in Balanchine's 'Tarantella' for the gala of *A Good Night's Sleep*.

Left: The first cast of Andrew Lloyd Webber's *Song and Dance* at the Palace Theatre, London, in 1982.

Below: Being surprised by Eamonn Andrews in 1981 on the set of *Cats* for 'This is Your Life', on stage with Elaine Paige, Bonnie Langford, Sarah Brightman, Paul Nicholas and Brian Blessed.

Below: Dancing with HRH The Princess of Wales at the Royal Opera House at the Friends of Covent Garden Christmas party, 1985.

Above: With Dame Ninette de Valois, at a party for the Theatre Museum.

Above: Playing the Emcee in Gillian Lynne's production of the musical *Cabaret* at the Strand Theatre. (Pamela Scott, second-from-the-left in the front row, was in my class at White Lodge).

Left: With Natalia Makarova in the mid-1980s (her husband, Eddie, is in the background). I was appearing at a gala at the Sadler's Wells Theatre to raise money for charity. I heard the story of how Chaplin had met Pavlova in Hollywood. Here, we tried to recreate that meeting.

Above: With Joan Lawson, Peter O'Brien and Peter Fairweather. At this White Lodge reunion in the late 1980s, we were very aware of the missing two boys, Graham Powell and Alan Hooper, from our class.

Below: With Freddy Mercury and Elton John at the Live Aid concert at Wembley.

Above: The Flying Doctor: as I received an honourary Doctorate of Letters from the University of Exeter in 1989 (photo taken by George).

Right: With my mother, Brenda Armstrong, my sister Joanne and my stepfather.

the end of the music was not working in the context of dance. Perfect though it was in concert, it lacked impact in dance performance. I tried all sorts, but there's not much you can do with a downward spiral. Sink into the floor, maybe, but that's a damp squib for an ending. I wanted to change it, to be able to create a visual intensity for the finale. Andrew was reluctant. Everytime I mentioned it I received a vacant look and no reply. I tried to explain that this was now a theatrical experience, and didn't he think that this change would be more exciting?

There is a famous saying of Ethel Merman's – 'If it ain't broke, don't fix it.' In Andrew's terms it wasn't broken. Quite the opposite. It was successful. Impasse. I got to the point, in the end, when I said to Anthony van Laast, 'Sort it out, you're the choreographer.' I downed tap shoes and created a sit-in during the rehearsals with the orchestra on stage. Harry Rab asked how we wanted the piece to end, so I told him and he said no problem. We recommenced rehearsal with the changes.

The next day Andrew came up on stage and asked me to give directions to the musicians. He joked, 'You'd better ask them to do it. They don't listen to me any more.' And he accepted the suggestions, realizing that they were right as it made the ending more exciting. On the first night he gave me a present, a smile on his face. It was a second-hand copy of *The Bunty Book for Girls*, in which he had written: 'In recognition of all you have done for me – Andrew.' I still have it on my shelf. Marti and I also received a silver pendant from him and Andrew.

In the first act, the orchestra, on stage, was on two separate platforms that wheeled slowly forwards to the edge of the stage. Marti was on a central platform which came forward at the same time. A screen came in overhead to show projections which illustrated the songs. For the second act the orchestra was at the back of the stage behind black gauze, to allow us room to dance. We had two metallic platformed staircases, almost like scaffolding, on which there were different levels for the dancers to stand. During my first solo, I held on to a trapeze to be lifted up to another level to introduce another dancer, spotlit by a special. Then I went on to dance up another ladder to the next dancer, slide down a pole for the next, and so on. It was a very inventive opening. These rostra could be repositioned anywhere we wished on stage, so that we could create an intimate space for the jazz sections, or allow a large space for the acrobatic and balletic tricks.

As the half-hour was called on the first night, many members of the audience were collecting tickets, left for them by members of the cast, at the stage door. At twenty past seven, ten minutes before curtain up, I was seen leaving by some of them. It caused a bit of a furore because they did not know I was not in the first act. I was rushing out to get a hamburger and Coke. I had been rehearsing all day and needed some food.

The first performance was received very well by the audience. The critics were mainly good, but there were one or two bad reviews – as there always are.

By this time I had learned not to read them, but someone is always going to tell you about the bad ones. They say things defensively, like, 'Well, *I* liked it anyway.' Or 'Don't you worry about those reviews, Mr Sleep.' This was from Charles, the stage doorman, when I arrived at the theatre the following night. Then he said, 'Mr Sleep. I remember when George Bernard Shaw came through the stage door the day after the first night of *Pygmalion*. I said to him – Sorry about the reviews, Mr Shaw. He said to me, Don't worry, Charles, it's like this: it's a question of mind over matter. I don't mind and they don't matter.' Good old Charles. He had been at the Palace Theatre since 1910 (I reckon he must have been born there) and always wore an immaculate suit, collar and tie.

The hardest part of the show (for me, but I hope not for the audience) was not the dancing but when I sang a duet, 'Never Ending Song', with Marti Webb at the end. This had been written specially for the show. I was so out of breath from the end of the show that it was near impossible for me to squeak a note. After a few weeks my stamina improved, but it never stopped being daunting. Andrew also added a rock-and-roll finale after the song, for Marti and me to dance together. This was the only time we were together in the show, and it invariably brought the audience to its feet, clapping along with the company.

The nearest I came to being off in the West End was when the first of my four impacted wisdom teeth began playing up. I telephoned Rod McNeil, my dentist, to book an appointment. He sent me for an X-ray and said I'd have to have an operation to remove the tooth, which felt at the time as if it was boring a hole in the side of my face. I told him flatly that there was no way I would have an anaesthetic, being more scared of being knocked unconscious with the stories of what can happen to you while under anaesthetic. It was decided that I would have a local anaesthetic and have the tooth extracted in the chair at University College Hospital on a Sunday. This would prevent me having to miss a performance. After the extraction my gum was packed with cotton wool and I was stitched up. I was given some anti-inflammatories and mild pain killers (I didn't want to be only half awake for the performance). The pain was just tolerable, and the next day when I looked in the mirror one side of my face looked like Hammy Hamster. But I insisted on performing. Rod, worried about all the spinning I had to do in performance, insisted on standing in the wings in case any stitches burst, caused by the pressure whilst turning. I got ready for the performance, drew a jaw line on the swollen side of my face to match the other side, put tons of dark shading on the swollen part of my face and luckily did not lose one drop of blood. I think that as I was so fit at the time, the rest of my body took over, plus Doctor Theatre, the old saying 'the show must go on'. I didn't miss a performance of *Song and Dance* at the Palace.

One night, Princess Margaret made an unofficial visit to the show. It was the same night that Princess Diana gave birth to her first child, William, and we heard of the birth through the stage staff during the second half of the show. I knew Princess Margaret did not know yet, so I announced the birth of the future monarch at the curtain call. When I said 'And it is . . . ' (a dramatic pause, of course, milking it for all it's worth), she raised her arms as if to say, 'Yes, yes, what is it, what is it?' I shouted, 'A boy!' I was invited to Kensington Palace to take supper with her and her two companions that evening – Brian Forbes and Nanette Newman. After supper we gathered round the fireplace and sang songs, I demonstrated a few dance steps and I was asked if I could possibly lift the Princess on to my shoulder. When I succeeded she raised her arms in a *port-de-bras* and took her due applause.

There is another night that stands out in my memory. I was dancing, when the music wound down to a standstill. I saw the musicians leaving and thought they must have gone on strike or something, so I started singing the music and contined to dance with my partners. Then the curtain came down. I stood there, feeling like a right prat. It was a bomb scare. I really hadn't thought of that. We left the stage door and, in full costume, headed across the road to Kettner's wine bar, where I bought champagne. I thought the performance must be over. But no. Not a bit of it. After a search of the auditorium by the police, who found nothing, the audience were ushered back in. We resumed the performance definitely with more bubble than we had started.

My mother brought a few relatives to come and see my performance in *Song and Dance*. My flat in Long Acre was far too small for them all, so they stayed in the Fielding Hotel, just round the corner. Noddy (the Fiat) had become quite a star, and George was giving rides round the block to each member of the family. It was a hot night and Noddy, with his top down, turned into a propelled air-conditioner, cooling us all down by turn while the rest of us waited in the Zanzibar night club. George then used Big Ears, the Bentley I'd recently acquired, to take them all back to the hotel. We passed Bow Street Police Station on the way back. Big mistake. We had parked quite properly when a red police car drew up alongside and carted George off to the police station. I had to walk.

I sat and waited for George to give a urine sample, signing autographs for the policemen's children. When George finally emerged – hours later – his parting shot to the police constable was: 'And if you want a good time I'd advise you to drink it.'

His trial came up a few months later and when asked by the judge why he was driving having drunk a bit too much, he replied, 'Your Honour. Because I could not walk.' Oh George.

Once, a few years later, when I was on tour with *Song and Dance*, we went to Scotland. We played in Glasgow and then travelled to Edinburgh. Because it was my day off I had quite a few jars. At about two in the morning I left the Caledonian Hotel and decided to walk to the house where I was staying. I thought that at two in the morning sophisticated Edinburgh would be one of the safest cities in Europe. So I walked confidently into the night – to hear, 'Give us a twirl, you little dancing poof.' I turned and saw what looked like two very large off-duty bouncers. Undeterred, I shouted, 'Who do you think you're talking to?'

'Come here and say that,' was the reply.

'No.' Dutch courage got the better of me. 'You come here.'

The problem was – they did. Two huge six foot-plus men looked down on me and gave me thirty seconds to run.

'I don't run from anybody,' I said, and started to walk away. One of them grabbed me by the shoulders.

'I thought you said I had thirty seconds to run.' My voice was higher by an octave.

'Too late.' And one of them head-butted me. The other biffed my nose. I didn't feel the sideways blow of the pavement hitting me. I thought it would be a good idea to feign death. I held my breath.

A clacking of heels ran towards me and a stiletto heel jabbed my ribs. One of the girls the bouncers had been showing off to said, 'Are you all right, laddie?'

I remained quite still. It must have worked because they all ran away. I looked up as a panda car closed on me. The police picked me up and put me in the car. Taking me home, I thought. Wrong. They wanted to cruise the streets and find the men, so that I could press charges. I was tired, fed up, in pain and I didn't want to press charges and said so.

'What do you think we are,' they said, 'a taxi service?' The car came to an abrupt halt and I was ditched on to the pavement. I had blood all over my shirt and anger was beginning to defeat my fear.

I headed back to the Caledonian. They refused me entry. I looked a mess and I was in a filthy mood. But they fetched George, who was by now my manager, and he saved me and harboured me in his suite.

The next day George treated me to a grand lunch at the Caledonian to cheer me up. He invited one of his oldest friends, Bruce Findlay, and his wife to join us. Bruce owned a record shop before managing a group called Simple Minds – whom he guided to international stardom. Lunch went very smoothly . . . except for one thing. George insisted on the ice bucket (with the champagne) remaining to hand, in case no waiters were around to replenish the glasses. The *maître d'* was a little put out and said, 'But Mr Lawson. We have served royalty here.' My temper was still ragged at the edges. I snapped.

'Well, you're serving a real queen now.'

It was during the West End run of *Song and Dance*, in the summer of 1982, that I first met Liza Minnelli. She was interested in performing the show in New York. I was thrilled. Both she and her mother, Judy Garland, were idols of mine. Icons, even. Judy Garland's films, along with those of Gene Kelly and Fred Astaire, were my most favourite when I used to bunk into the cinema in Hartlepool. I don't know how many times I have seen *A Star Is Born*. We went to dinner and discussed the possibility of doing the show together on Broadway. Eventually, however, she decided against it. So did Shirley Maclaine. Both of them wanted far more involvement in the second half, which was, at this stage, difficult to envisage. It did go to Broadway, with Bernadette Peters, choreographed by Peter Martins, but it was a completely different version, with entrances for Bernadette in the second half. It was in my contract to go with the show should it transfer to Broadway, but as the production was completely different – my contract was null and void. By this time I was beginning to understand how these things worked, so although I would have liked to appear on Broadway, it was just one of those things.

It was also around this time that I met Freddie Mercury. He came backstage after a performance of *Song and Dance* with his friend Peter Straker, and we all went out to dinner afterwards. It was the beginning of a lasting friendship. Through him I met several more people in the pop world, including Queen (of course), Elton John. I'd met Elton's manager, John Reid, before, through Ken and Dolly East. That world is fairly circular – meet one, meet all. There were many evenings when I joined Freddie and his gang at the Embassy Club in Bond Street. We all hid in the VIP bar and had some good times together. We were well looked after by both the manager, Stephen Hayter, and the owner, Lady Edith Foxwell. Lady Edith became a very close friend. She died recently and I miss her. She was vibrant, with an Irish temperament, unconventional, beautiful. There are not many people in the world of her ilk.

After six months I left *Song and Dance*. The original run was only twelve weeks, but it extended, and so I extended my contract. The show itself then ran for three years. Success. I went and sat in the sun in Corsica.

When I came back I wandered into Joe Allen's for dinner. I saw Alan Bates, dining with Tennessee Williams. Alan is one of my favourite actors, and we'd met when he came backstage, once, after *Song and Dance*. I went up to say hello. He complimented me on my tan. So I, getting carried away *as usual*, undid my shirt to show off the rest. Tennessee Williams said, 'I've seen better.' I replied instantly (why?), 'And I've read better.' Unfounded. I've never read any of his work. But I always have to say something, and sometimes it's pretty stupid. Witty retorts often come too late – long after the event – and timing is every-thing, after all. But it was all very good-humoured, and Tennessee smiled and took it in the way I'd intended. There have been other times, of course, when my hasty words have not been taken so lightly.

Even after I left *Song and Dance* I came back every time they had a new star for the first half, to lend support for two weeks. I performed with Gemma Craven, Lulu and Liz Robertson. My role was taken over by Stephen Jefferies, a principal dancer with the Royal Ballet, and later by Graham Fletcher, who had taken over my role in *Cats*. In fact, Graham took over my roles when I was with the Royal Ballet – he must have been relieved when he was able to create some of his own. I began to feel that not only had we gone some way to creating employment for dancers who no longer wanted to remain entirely classical, or go into contemporary dance, but that we had also managed with

Andrew's help to put dance on the map in the West End. We had proved it was possible to put on a dance show with the talent and a standard of dance equal to that seen in the Opera House. In fact, dance was booming – to the extent that it was even influencing fashion. Dance wear and leg-warmers hit the high street.

After three years the audiences diminished and it was decided to close the show. I was invited back for the last four weeks. Cameron's office asked me if I would rather have a salary or a percentage of the box office. There was to be a big splash of publicity and advertising so I decided to take the gamble and opt for the percentage. The houses went back to 90 per cent and my share was far higher than the offered salary. The risk paid off.

I began to plot a second tour for *DASH* during my run at the Palace. I employed Armand Garrard again as tour manager. By this time many theatres acknowledged that a dance show could attract an audience. Some were even prepared to give us a fee. Others would not take the risk and we agreed on a percentage split of box office receipts. All the money I saved on *Song and Dance* was invested in this production.

Don Lawson added two more musicians to the band and I added six more dancers: Anne Cox, Kim Rosato, Nichola Treherne, Peter Salmon, Simon Shelton and Michael de Souter. I invited a dancer who was leaving the London City Ballet to be the ballet mistress – i.e. the overseer of the dancers' technique and the show. This was Anne Allan. She was to remain my right-hand woman for many years to come.

My stage staff had to include a company manager, two stage managers, a sound engineer, an electrician and a wardrobe master. The designer was Ian Hay, an architect. He used metal frames for the background, into which coloured lights were inserted on the diagonal to represent the dashes. Suddenly the little van I had toured with before turned into a sixty-foot truck, toting hundreds of lamps, the set, a specially built rostrum to support the band and a dance floor to roll out over each theatre's stage.

All these extra people, new orchestrations for the larger band, the augmented touring truck, and more costumes (plus at least four pairs of shoes for each member of the company), meant that I had a tough financial decision to make. I could not afford to pay everyone in advance for more than three weeks, so instead of the preferred six weeks of rehearsals we only had three. *DASH* was the only unsponsored and unsubsidized dance company in Britain. That is something I feel quite proud of.

Publicity was another cost – we had to ensure everyone knew we were coming. The marketing department arranged all the interviews with the local press and the distribution of posters and other publicity material. I had designed the first *DASH* poster myself – a simple effort with the dashes representing footprints in the air. This time I decided to use a small Beryl Cook painting. Beryl Cook is a remarkable artist with a highly individualistic and very funny take of the world around her. She has a fine eye for the absurd and for strange little personal quirks that give secret pleasure. What I really like about her is that her paintings are accessible, because they are (mostly) about ordinary local people being cheeky to each other. This often makes highbrow critics denounce her as lacking depth.

Rubbish, I say.

Beryl was a landlady on Plymouth Hoe until she discovered her talent. She came to see me perform at the Palace Theatre in Plymouth and gave me a painting in thanks for her having enjoyed the show so much. It is a portrait of my back view, with enormously enlarged buttocks, supporting her on points in arabesque. It made the perfect publicity poster for the tour.

We opened in Plymouth at the newly built Theatre Royal. I stayed, as always, with Mum and Dad, and the night before the first performance I couldn't sleep at all. I felt we were not ready for an audience. My stomach was churning and I had shooting pains in my chest. The more I tried to relax the worse they became. I telephoned George in London to tell him I was having a heart attack. He said, 'Wind.' I took time off to go to a doctor the next day and have a cardiogram. Nothing, of course, it was all nerves. And we made it through the first performance, creditably as it happened, and thank goodness the Plymouth audience was loyal to their local boy. So I felt better.

It did not stop me from having a check-up with my own doctor when I returned to London eventually. Dr Vance was very tall, and wore *pince-nez* and a silver phial containing a rose in his lapel. He was one of those remarkable doctors who are excellent diagnosticians and can often tell just by looking at someone what was wrong with them. He informed me, loftily, that I was not having a heart attack.

'How would you know? Have you ever had one?' I said.

'Yes.' He looked at me over his *pince-nez*.

'What was it like then?' I was a bit piqued.

'It was rather like the *Queen Mary* landing on my chest.' I went away, more than a little chastened.

While I had been in *Cats*, George had gone to an auction to bid on my behalf for a baby grand piano and he came out with Big Ears, the Bentley. He had been unable to resist the low price and the even lower mileage on the clock. Not only could I not drive but I could not take up the piano again. George had advertised for a driver, and Mac had entered my life. He had seen a lot of life, which in general suited me fine. It meant he put up with my less than ordered lifestyle. One day he arrived in a taxi. I asked him where the car was. He said he had left it in Carlos Place, nipped round the corner for a hamburger and when he came back − it was gone. Hmmm. Yes. There were no hamburger joints around Carlos Place, I thought. So I teased him and asked how much he'd got for it. He laughed it off, saying it was probably on a ferry on its way out of the country but he knew of a really good deal on a Daimler.

So I got this totally over-the-top dark blue and silver Daimler Limousine. It came from the World Transcendental Enlightenment Company (set up by George Harrison) and had been used to ferry the Maharishi Mahesh Yogi around Britain. We nicknamed it Big Ears because it looked so funny next to little Noddy in the garage. It did eight miles to the gallon, apparently, which meant I was living (so what's new?) beyond my means. Mac drove me from venue to venue on the tour. I could sleep in the back with a duvet, or even have the odd small party (eight people with a squeeze) if desired. It was wonderful. Its number plate should have read OTT.

The audience bookings for this second tour of *DASH* were a little thin at first but began to build as word of mouth spread around the country. We had to put extra seats in the aisles at both the Theatre Royal Norwich and the Birmingham Hippodrome. And in Birmingham the clamour was so great that we decided, madly, to do two shows back to back with only a twenty minutes to effect the audience change-over. It was exhausting, but worth it.

Edinburgh was another sell-out. I stayed with George's mother and his Aunt Peggy, who live in a big limestone house in Edinburgh. Every morning I was there Peggy greeted me with: 'Would you like a wee sherry, Wayne?' I had to decline, of course. But in any case, sherry first thing in the morning is not quite my idea of sybaritic contentment. During that week I was to be interviewed on television so I invited them to come to the studio. They were very excited and dressed up for the occasion. When I told them that it would only take an hour to get to Glasgow they said, 'Ooh no, we can't go to Glasgow. We haven't been there for thirty years. That would never do.' True Edinburgh girls.

After Edinburgh, where we had a marvellous dinner party for the whole company at Prestonfield House (bagpipes and all), on to Glasgow. But even before we opened there a local paper slagged us off in a review of one of our performances in Edinburgh. We were already sold out for our week in the Theatre Royal, thank heavens, and were not dependent on reviews, good or otherwise. But I was still so angry about this vindictive and non-constructive review by the last night that I decided to tell the audience. During the finale, where I introduced the rest of the cast to an accompanying disco beat, I thanked Glasgow for the greeting I had received in the local press, which read: 'Wayne Sleep's piece of rubbish posing as light entertainment should disappear off the face of the earth forever.' I then thanked Glasgow for not disappearing after reading this review and tore it into several pieces, threw it into the air and danced under the cascade of paper.

Touring in Britain is quite an experience. It isn't a case of book your venue, arrive, set up, perform, collect your money and off to the next one. That's pure romanticism. There are always pitfalls, hitches, problems. If I didn't learn much about the general state of British theatre throughout the country, I certainly learned about the buildings themselves. No theatre is the same as the next one.

So I go straight to the theatre when I arrive in a new town. Not to the hotel or digs. Checking the space where I am to perform is my priority. Some theatres are desperately ill-equipped, which often means drastic last-minute adjustments. Some theatres don't have a sign telling you which the stage door is either, so you can be left wandering round, checking all the identical double doors hoping for a clue. Imagine that it is cold and wet and you have driven a long way, and you will get the picture.

The other drawback about small theatres with skeleton staffs is that the box office is only manned for a few hours a day. This meant the telephone would ring – and ring and ring and ring. I heard all the profits dribbling away down the phone lines in those theatres where our payment was a percentage of box office takings. But there was nothing I could do, and anyway it was part of the risk of touring.

There is one other sort of theatre that I have since learned to avoid – the theatre with no regular live productions. One of these was a cinema three times a week. What it was the rest of the time I have no idea. It had no facility for booking in advance, and was only used to people queuing on the night.

Once in my theatre, I look at the stage. For dancing this is fundamental. I need to check for holes in the floor, for unusual surfaces and for the rake of the stage. The rake is the slope that most stages have in varying degrees. Some are worse than others, notably the King's Theatre, Edinburgh, and the Bristol Hippodrome although the atmosphere in these theatres is great. These stages have the ability to make you feel as if you are dancing on the side of a steep hill. After a few performances the body does adjust and not always for the better. You may get severe back pain from having to keep your head raised up and back, causing a compression of the muscles. But if you don't keep your head up you'll look down into the pit, which then pulls you like a magnet. I have visions of being impaled on a cellist's bow. This permanent backbend means visits to the physiotherapist, a species only a little more easy to find outside London these days.

Sometimes the surface is like an ice rink. (On a rake *and* glassy . . . ? Terrific.) Sometimes it is covered with a rubberized solution on which tap dancing is totally inaudible. The solution to both those problems is to lay our portable linoleum flooring – but that brings its own problems. It is like tapping on carpet, so microphones have to be added to the front of the stage to amplify the taps.

Then I check the spotlights. They can be difficult. Set too low they are both blinding and unbalancing. They may also be effective in blanking the mind and causing next-step amnesia. And then there are the exits and entrances, the size of space in the wings, and whether there is a quick way round backstage. Each theatre differs quite considerably in all these areas – and if you don't find out, and adjust your performance accordingly, you might get very stuck on the night.

At one venue, there were only two entrances at the back of the stage, with a brick wall running up either side. I sang a song about Prince William, dressed in a babygro with a gold crown on my head. (I know . . . cute.) After the number I was to exit in a blackout. It was the first performance and I didn't remember the only exits were at the back of the stage. I couldn't find my way off. A curtain had come in half-way down the stage and, as I remembered that this would cut me off from the exits, I walked straight into the wall, scraped my forehead and yelled, 'How the ✴✴✴✴ do you get off this stage?' Just then the lights came up for the two dancers on stage to begin a romantic *pas-de-deux*. I had to waddle upstage and duck under the curtain – in full view of the audience.

Backstage, there is often a plethora of information – which can be misleading. Arrows which tell you to go one way are immensely useful until you have to find your way backwards, in which case you might end up in the orchestra pit, staring wide-eyed through a door straight into the faces of the audience, while above your head a dancer is about to take a flying leap into your arms which are not there. You can hardly shout, 'Hey, wait a minute'; only panic, and rush back to the stage without passing 'Go' and collecting £200. And then you find you are on the wrong side. The best you can do is shrug your shoulders (although in those days, I was more likely to fly off the handle, just to vent my frustration) and hope that nobody in the audience notices anything amiss.

And there are the backstage quick-change areas. Vital. There is hardly ever enough time to nip back to your dressing-room, so a makeshift area must be rigged up, usually out of black swagging on costume rails. It must have enough privacy, particularly for the girls, who, even though they are dancers and used to being looked at, do not care to be stared at by strangers, such as stage staff. It must have enough light to check self, costume and make-up, yet the light must not spill through to a blacked-out stage. In small theatres with little room backstage this can be very tricky.

Dressing-rooms. Forget all those flower- and champagne-laden, chaise-longue-bedecked dressing-rooms seen in Hollywood films. Even the biggest theatres tend to be fairly spartan (though they are likely to have a shower and well-lit mirrors), and as for the smaller ones – they could be damp and cold with the luxury of one ceiling-hung, bare light-bulb, and a basin with cold water only if you are lucky.

Somewhere during a *DASH* tour – I forget where – I had a rare two minute change between costumes, so I used my dressing-room. The music on the tannoy heralded my entrance so I rushed to the door to find it – locked. Lily, my dresser, had long enough arms to reach through the vent in the bottom of the door and turn the key in the lock. I was a couple of bars late and completely out of breath. I have often wondered who did it, and why. I know I am not always that easy to work for, demanding the dancers' best, but I did not think I was unpopular enough to be locked in my dressing-room.

But I learned quite a bit about myself, my ability to cope with the unexpected (or not, as the case may be), how to make do and mend, or simply tie a knot in the campaign of battle and move on – as some general from the Napoleonic wars is supposed to have said. In the end I found it easier to assume the worst, and then be pleasantly surprised.

Touring is character-building, stamina-testing, occasionally fun, and far more exhausting than actually performing. Different hotels every week, and standards vary – even within the same hotel chain. And very, very few hotels do food after hours, except for an occasional grudging sandwich, which is hard for a dancer – I usually do not eat before a show. (Try several athletic leaps across a room on a full stomach.) So I eat afterwards, and the choice is either Chinese or Indian late at night. And then we do not surface until late in the mornings, but the chambermaids start at 7 A.M. Vacuum-cleaners, constant chatter and radios. Radios in particular. I phoned down to the desk, once, to ask if they would turn the noise down. They turned it up, of course. This really got to me and I rushed into the corridor to yell abuse at the cleaner. She screamed and ran off down the corridor. I had forgotten I was naked.

Touring teaches you to leave more time for your next journey than you would reasonably consider possible. When we were touring *The Hot Shoe Show* I arrived at Heathrow for my flight to Manchester (late, what a surprise), and no matter how much I pleaded with British Midland they wouldn't let me on – the flight was closed. Another flight would never get me there on time for the performance. My only chance was Mac and a mad dash by car to Manchester. By the greatest spot of luck he had just delivered someone to the airport when I called his car. I would never have made it without him. Sometimes, however, being late is due to factors beyond human control. Like fog. Fog at Aberdeen, which meant that the flight diverted to Edinburgh, and we had to be bussed to Aberdeen for *DASH*. The girls changed and made up, and we all warmed up in the aisle of the bus. We were an hour late for the show.

On top of all this, there must be time set aside for rehearsal. Because we were going to perform *DASH* for four weeks over Christmas at the Sadler's Wells Theatre, I rehearsed with the cast every day to improve technique, with Anne also regimenting them into shape. I also re-lit the whole show with the chief electrician and brought in a singer who had been a contemporary dancer, to accompany a few of the dance numbers in her deep bluesy voice. The performances were sold out, though I remember one matinée when I thought we were going to be only half full. We were obliged to postpone curtain-up for forty-five minutes while the queue around the block exchanged their agent vouchers for tickets. It's great to be popular, but those already in their seats didn't feel the same way. They started a slow hand-clap, not unreasonably. Delays at a pop concert are one thing (and frequent) but in theatre? We had to make an announcement.

There is nothing quite like seeing a bubble of an idea turn into reality. Knowing that it was my own particular baby, something I had nurtured from inception, was possibly worth more than anything else. Plus the fact that I had risked my own money for this tour of *DASH*. It was worth it. The enterprise covered its costs and even made some profit. It had been a success and I was very happy about it.

In the winter of 1982, to recover from the exhaustion of the tour, I decided to take a holiday in Sri Lanka with Ian Hay. In spite of all the glorious things we saw in the month we were there, nothing, for me, quite beat the drive in and out from the airport. I love market stalls, and the road was lined with stalls of all kinds: meat crawling with flies; tables of strange religious artefacts, mostly statues of St Sebastian riddled with arrows (I couldn't fathom why, in a mainly Buddhist country); various national costumes and other Eastern bits and pieces. My idea of heaven, flies and all.

We arrived in Colombo in the middle of a festival – I think it was the Procession of the Month of Asala. Music, drums, orchid-garlanded elephants, golden Buddhas on the backs of lorries, replete with light bulbs and towing generators to power them. Raucous, colourful, different.

We hired a car and travelled around for four weeks. We stayed on a tea plantation called Tree Tops, a hotel built in the days of British rule. It was an old colonial club with all the accoutrements of home – a replica Tudor village, with narrow little streets and bright red postboxes. Odd to go to such an exotic place and find that you've not left the Old Country. We filed past the Buddha's tooth in a temple at Kandy – but it was hidden in a casket.

One evening we were sitting by the pool, relaxing, drinking, minding our own business, and a couple came up to us and asked if we would join them for a drink. I told a porky and said I did not indulge after dinner, sounding as pompous as possible. But they asked again on a subsequent evening. I moaned to Ian about 'coming all this distance to get away from it all'. About being recognized and what a bore it was. (So much for Nureyev's strictures about the responsibility of fame.) About not wanting to talk about my career or dancing in general. Moan, moan. But they were persistent, they insisted, and in the end I moaned that 'we might as well, they seemed nice enough, get it over and done with. Blah, blah, blah.'

The lady heaped praise on me, particularly for my singing. Good, I thought. Gratifying. To be recognized for something that was not my best talent – even though I was featured on the album both of Cats and of Song and Dance. And of course I had sung on TV, too. So I preened, quietly. But I was perplexed by no mention of dance. In the end I said, 'But what about the dancing?' She said, 'Yes, Leo, we know you can dance, but what a voice.'

Ah. They thought I was Leo Sayer. I explained I was Wayne Sleep. It meant nothing to them. I looked at Ian. Such jubilation on his face about my moaning. Not wanting to be recognized, indeed. And then not only not recognized but mistaken.

Not for the first time either. A younger me, with the long curly hair, was often mistaken for Leo Sayer, in the days when he had loads of chart hits and appeared on Top of the Pops. And then they didn't believe me when I told them

I wasn't. After a while I signed autographs with his name, it seemed simpler. It's funny how cross people get when they've mistaken you. As if it is entirely your fault for not being who they think you are. Years later I met Leo and confessed. He told me that he had been at a reception in the Crush Bar at Covent Garden and the Lord Mayor of somewhere-or-other came up to him and professed delight at his prowess in dance. Leo was confused, but flattered. The Mayor said he had adored him in the Neapolitan Dance in *Swan Lake*. Leo then found he was supposed to be Wayne Sleep. Touché.

We spent a couple of nights at the National Botanical Gardens and Game Reserve. We woke at five in the morning, climbed on to a small bus, and toured around for eight hours looking for wild animals. But because it had rained the previous night none of the animals were interested in visiting the larger watering holes. All we saw was a chicken. This caused all the Japanese to jump up and down with glee, rushing around taking photographs of the poor creature from all angles. I don't know which was more demented.

We decided to fly to the Maldives and catch a boat to a much smaller, remoter island. There were a dozen huts for sleeping, a generator that switched off at midnight and a communal chalet for all our meals. You could walk round the island in five minutes. To counteract the boredom we went scuba-diving twice a day.

I had not done an awful lot of ocean (or indeed sea) swimming since my near-disastrous encounter with the undertow on Copacabana Beach in Brazil. It took some courage to get into the water to start with, and then, diving down, the pressure in my ears was almost excruciating for the first twelve feet. But it was worth those twelve feet of pain. It was stunning. I fed two eight-foot moray eels on the sea bed with bits of dead fish the instructor had taken with him, saw luminous fish of indescribable beauty, and stingrays flapping about like animated duvets across the ocean floor. I found that most of the coral had been cut away by knife-happy tourists, which was not only sad from the visual aspect, it was appalling from the environmental point of view. A pity that Sri Lanka had not made the taking of coral illegal, as it is in the Red Sea. I thought it akin to cutting down trees in a national forest. Vandalism.

By the end of the week my skin was totally waterlogged and my face was a mosaic of fine cracks. But it was worth all the pain just to see the glory of the ocean bed, and it conquered my fear of swimming.

After that we returned to Sri Lanka and to Jaffna, the most northerly point on the island. Two days before we arrived the Tamils had supposedly killed some Sri Lankans. It was the start of the uprising before the civil war. We left for London just before all hell broke loose.

I arrived back in London to plunge straight into rehearsals for an eight-week stint in the Apollo Theatre, Victoria. This was a very ambitious move, because we had to hire the theatre. It meant total reliance on the ability of the box-office receipts to pay the bills. I knew it was worth a try. I had proved to my own satisfaction, at least, and to enough others too, that a show of pure dance could pay for itself. In the event I need not have worried. The Apollo seated 2,600 and we played to capacity most of the time.

Ed Kresley, whom I had met in New York, came over to assist me as choreographer. Ed had worked on the American Dance Machine, which was formed to protect the choreography and show routines from famous Broadway musicals. Don augmented the band to seven, and added two female vocalists, Lee Gibson and Anna Macleod. The music ranged from Bach to Broadway. Richard Dale designed the lighting, and Liz Da Costa came in as costume supervisor. We were expanding again.

The delight of *DASH* was that there was something for everybody. No routine went over four minutes, so that the audience concentration did not have time to waver. If you were bored by a routine – don't worry – the next one will be along in a few minutes. I was always aiming at the all-round dance lover, understanding only too well that the balletomane was not the sort of person that would come to the shows.

I incorporated a few old faves – Chaplin, Olga Korbut and John Curry – and added John McEnroe. I danced him with a tennis racquet and an invisible ball. Every bounce was accompanied by a tap step, the rhythm of which gradually got more and more angry until I finished by breaking the racquet in two. This 'sports' review was enlarged by a swimming *pas-de-deux* for a boy and girl in bathing costumes, plus cross-country running, tossing the hammer, archery, basketball, discus throwing, horse-jumping and American football. All interpreted through mime, dance and very fast costume changes.

I paid tribute to Bette Midler, my original inspiration for the show, by dressing in a big blonde wig, high heels and a tight leopard-skin frock with a tassel hanging down between the legs at the back and a tassel attached to each of the false boobs, which I twirled in time to the music. I aped Martha Graham, great American inventor of contemporary dance. She was famous for her black hair scraped back and secured by two pins in a tight bun. I'd seen a film of her doing a modern dance sculpture piece, sitting on a bench, completely covered by a bag made of lycra, under which she made weird shapes to strange music. I sent this up with four dancers hidden in stretch Lycra, rather like four large tea-bags. I wore a tight Lycra frock and a black wig (borrowed from a production of *Madame Butterfly*) which was held by two knitting needles. One of the dancers filched these during the dance and went off stage, knitting. I was gobbled up finally by one of the bags and ended up inside, rolling about on the floor with the other dancer. The only members of the audience who were not mystified by this piece were the dance connoisseurs – some of whom were furious. It's not done to send up pioneers and inventors of one's craft but I find no harm in taking the mickey just for a laugh, and it certainly doesn't detract from my admiration for their work.

One of my favourite parts was dressing in drag as one of the cygnets in *Swan Lake*. With three of the girls we did the Cygnets' Dance, step for step like the original, but with tap shoes. We all wore the requisite white tutus and feathered headdresses – but my feathers pointed forward, instead of back, so that they tickled my face to make me sneeze. The Cygnets' Dance is famous for precision. The heads and the legs must all turn at exactly the same time, and so ours did. Except that I turned in the opposite direction every time. The dance ended with my shooing the others off the stage so that I, as the prima ballerina I had obviously become, could go into the Dying Swan solo – the apogee for any aspiring duckling, however ugly. In the penultimate bar I emitted a loud quack and dropped dead.

I also decided to take the mickey out of a review in *The Times* that John Percival had once written of my interpretation of the fiendishly difficult Bluebird solo from *The Sleeping Beauty*. After my first performance in this role at Covent Garden he said something to the effect that I was more like a bluebottle than a bluebird. So I produced a send-up, and during the final jumps another dancer came on from the wings and sprayed me with a huge can of flyspray.

A classical *pas-de-deux* was accompanied by a tape which relayed my thoughts aloud. We embraced lovingly. The audience heard, 'Ugh, garlic.' I lifted her. There were heaving sighs and 'I wish she wouldn't eat pasta before the show.'

Ballroom dancing had to be included. The very tall Peter Salmon and I demonstrated the waltz, the foxtrot, the cha-cha-cha and the *paso doble*. Peter was in tails, all kosher, and I was in a tall purple beehive wig, diamanté spectacles and enough netting to rid the North Sea of all the European fish quota.

I extended my Chaplin routine by creating a six-minute ballet with Nichola Treherne and Peter Salmon. The scene took place round a bench, under which I fell. When I got up I found myself between a damsel and a large drunken bully. The bully went to kiss the damsel, but kissed me instead. This resulted in a fight where the damsel and Chaplin managed to knock the bully out and dance off happily into the sunset.

Don Lawson composed a percussion piece for drums in which he included every kind of rhythm. This was for a jungle piece, with the whole company in green and browns. Another drum solo demonstrated how the same rhythm might be applied to and interpreted by different dance styles – tap, jazz, ballet and modern. I used the Joplin piece from my first *DASH* and added a tap tribute to Fred Astaire and Ginger Rogers, which I danced with Kim Rosato, and also choreographed a Boogie Woogie Rag for the whole company.

Peter Salmon and Jane Darling danced the South American mambo, which was choreographed for the original *DASH* by Iwan, and I reprised the Hornpipe created for Margot Fonteyn's televison series *The Magic of Dance*. At one performance I went on stage to do my hornpipe to find that Don had skipped me all together, and was playing the mambo. For a few bars I struggled to do the hornpipe to the mambo. I even wondered if I might make it work, and if I did, whether Peter and Jane could possibly do the mambo to the horn-pipe. A daft notion, perhaps, but worth a try. All this passed through my mind, but before too long I hopped off stage on one leg, squawking, 'Pieces of eight, pieces of eight' – it was all I could think of at the time. Don stopped the music and I came back on stage, said, 'Hornpipe please,' through gritted teeth, and off we went. Frankly, I'm surprised that that sort of thing didn't happen more often when touring a long (and tiring) show with lots of quick changes.

In just over twelve months *DASH* did two British tours and three seasons in London. After the Apollo Victoria we went to the Bristol Hippodrome for two weeks. Then in the autumn of 1983 Paul Gregg of Apollo Leisure, the production company which not only owns many theatres around the country but also mounts tours and shows, asked me to reform *DASH* for a twelve-week tour culminating in six weeks over Christmas at the Dominion Theatre in Tottenham Court Road. This we called *A DASH of Christmas* and I added some special seasonal pieces for the run. A couple of dancers had left, so I auditioned 300 girls. Out of all of them, I chose Wendy Roe. I discovered afterwards that she had trained with Muriel Carr in Hartlepool. Small world! Alex Worrel who had been with Northern Ballet also joined me for this tour. Among the men to join was Stephen Beagley from the Royal Ballet.

We started the show with some brilliant and very effective lighting. We hung a light curtain, which in this case was a row of sixteen Parcan lamps, above the front of the stage, and these shone down on to fog created by a smoke machine, creating a curtain of light. My entrance was through this curtain. As I spread my hands, the centre six lamps extinguished, and after I stepped through they lit again behind me as if opening and closing a curtain. Then I moved to one side of the stage and pushed the curtain of light to the opposite side. The dancers were revealed. It received applause every night and set the tone for the whole show.

A few of the old favourite impersonations remained, but this was mainly an all-new show. I devised a new tap routine – and created my own accompaniment – in the Micro Tap. I wore a suit of lights and tap-danced on boards that were programmed to produce electronic drum noises when I jumped on them. I could, of course, change it from night to night if I wanted to.

And for the first time adagio dancing was added to the show. Devalda and Siricco, an adagio act, had written to me, asking if they might be included in one of *DASH*'s shows. This was the only style of dance not in the show, so they came aboard.

One night there was a near disaster. Part of the set comprised two trucks (moving platforms attached to wires) that were winched forward in time to the music. This meant that we could create several different sets. One truck was a stage with a little curtain, the other a bar. Jane Darling's husband, Peter (who was a puppeteer), hid behind the bar and operated a six-foot puppet cobra which emerged as one of the dancers charmed it with a flute. Jane slid on to the bar and danced with it. On this particular night the wires snapped on the bar truck and the platform ran out of control and careered towards the front of the stage. My heart was in my mouth. It was one of those occasions where you see something happen and there is nothing, but nothing, that you can do about it. The dancers leaped to safety just before the stage crew – thank heavens for their quick reaction – grabbed the wires and hauled the truck back before it could plunge over the edge of the stage into the audience. The rake of the stage was too steep for the wires to hold the weight against gravity, and we made sure they were strengthened before the next performance. I have no idea whether the front rows of the audience knew how close they had been . . .

I really liked the effect one can get with ultraviolet light, and extended its use during this tour. Wearing unseen black, we held luminous legs on sticks and simulated a kick routine. Then suddenly the legs twisted into impossible physical positions before they returned to the normal kick line. I also had stripes painted on the sides of the dancers' costumes, so that, when positioned, their bodies spelt *DASH*. Then it would break up and reassemble – to form ACT II. I used it again some ten years later, for the reopening of the Savoy Theatre.

The finale of *A DASH of Christmas* was pure fun. We dressed, all twelve of us, in Father Christmas outfits and did a kick-line, big white wellies and all. Big ungainly Santas booting their way around the stage. Then one night Alex Worrall tripped over her big white wellies and fell, catching the next person, and down we all went, like dominoes, all over each other, beards flying, pompoms flailing. Heaped Santas. We were almost too weak with laughter either to get up and continue or to take our bows. Audiences love a disaster, so we got some raucous applause.

I retained the routine of Prince William in his babygro for this show and the Princess of Wales got to hear about it. She asked Anne Allan, who was now giving her private dance lessons, if she could come to a performance. She asked to sit back stage, a new experience. We arranged for a chair to be put in the front wing where she would be unseen and undisturbed – except for having to duck the tennis balls that flew on stage for my McEnroe routine. So on this meeting I nearly clobbered her with tennis balls. It made her laugh.

She sat in the wings, with her detectives. During the ultraviolet dance, the stage hands (dressed in black as is usual in theatre) have to come on and move some props around. So that their faces were not picked up by the ultraviolet they wore back-to-front balaclavas with eyeholes. They rushed towards the stage to do their stuff; the detectives reached for their guns, maybe thinking 'Terrorists!' (there had recently been a bomb explosion very near the theatre) and were nonplussed to find that the crews barged straight past the Princess on to the stage to waltz off with a bit of scenery. The Princess asked me about the words of the Prince William piece. She thought she had picked up on some lyrical quip about her nose. She had. I realized she was capable of taking a joke against herself – a quality which I really like. I think I became a fan from that point. I had no inkling, then, that two years later I would dance with her.

In 1985 *DASH* went overseas. Armand was contacted by a Japanese impresario, a woman from the One World Company in Tokyo, who proposed a six-city tour of Japan. She would arrange and provide all the lighting and technical equipment. All we needed were the people, sets, props and costumes. So Armand flew into action and arranged a tour around our projected time in Japan.

We started in Oslo. We thought we were a flop. It took us time to realize that Norwegians demonstrate their appreciation with slow hand-clapping. In fact we induced them to so much slow hand-clapping that they asked us to come back four weeks later – which took care of our two-week break! In between we did Denmark and Italy and after the second Oslo trip we went to Hong Kong. In Italy we played in the Sistina Theatre in Rome. We went down so well that I was invited back to Italy several times after that to appear on Italian television shows. We performed in the Civic Hall in Hong Kong first, then crossed the ferry to Kowloon where we appeared in the huge and extraordinary Ko Shan theatre. It started with an enclosed auditorium – just like any other theatre – but when all the seats were filled, a wall peeled back to reveal lots more seats outside. The weather, thank heavens, bore no resemblance to a summer season in Regent's Park.

In each country we visited I learned to speak the opening words of the show in that language. That was fine in Norwegian, Danish and Italian (well, mostly), but goodness knows if I said 'Good evening and welcome to *DASH*' in Chinese. The nuances of the language are so fine that the audience in Hong Kong may well have heard 'May the chicken sit on your head for ever' for all I know.

And then it was on to the crowning jewel of our tour, Japan. We sent all the lighting and sound equipment back to England, knowing that it was to be provided, and flew to Tokyo. The technical staff went to meet the impresario to arrange the final minutiae of the tour, and she told them that she could not afford the generator required to power the lighting board. Could we possibly do the performance without any light except the minimal amount in each theatre? Could we *what*? We had been swamped with detailed letters and telexes from the Japanese Company specifying exactly what they would supply – even down to the coloured gel for the lamps, and now we were actually here in Japan there was nothing. Unbelievable. What the hell was going on?

I was called from my hotel to an urgent meeting. When I heard what was up, I was, frankly, aghast. A major part of *DASH* was the lighting and effects. And anyway, it was a matter of principle. I rejected any idea of performing unless she provided the generator. But she refused. I had no alternative. I could not open the show in Tokyo – or anywhere else in Japan for that matter. We were stuck – dancers, musicians, technicians, with costumes and set frozen at the airport. I phoned the British Consul. He told me that there was nothing he could do, that litigation in Japan could take up to ten years. And then the impresario dis-appeared and the consul warned me, 'You'll never be able to trace her, she'll change her name and come back as somebody else.' A lot of help he was.

I realized that I was set to lose £80,000 out of my own pocket (I was financing the tour) by not opening in Japan, and I had no chance of retrieving it, not by any means. All I could do was to offer the whole company five days' holiday, paying their salaries, per diems and hotel bills. And there is nothing worse than being hyped up to perform for six weeks – and then nothing happens. My temper was very short, funnily enough, not because of losing the money, but because I was hurt by being let down. Needless to say, I did not enjoy my trip to Japan and neither did my mother, who had accompanied me. She never ever mentioned it again.

In the end *DASH* was a show that grew and grew until it finally ended up with two sixty-foot trucks, twelve dancers, eight musicians and, in all, a staff of over thirty-five people. Over the years we hefted over 800 pairs of shoes, 200 costumes and 400 lamps. We changed the posters every season – from the first simple poster of dashes, through the wonderful meatiness of Beryl Cook, to David Hockney's front cloth design for *A Good Night's Sleep* (the gala at the Adelphi Theatre in the Strand). Many choreographers were brought in to help with new ideas and routines – among them Gillian Gregory, Anthony van Laast, Derek Deane (now Director of the English National Ballet), Beyhan Fowkes, all of them invaluable in the creation of this success.

It got to the point, though, where I found it increasingly difficult to find new and interesting routines, especially impersonations. I seem to have run out of personalities, at least of the richly fertile Olga Korbut/John McEnroe type – until Torvill and Dean came on the scene. They were the last two I added to the show and I used them, too, in a surprise appearance at the Royal Variety Show. But eventually *DASH* reached the stage where it could not grow any more and I became exasperated trying to think of new ideas. Altogether *DASH* enjoyed six British tours followed by West End seasons and one world tour.

Would I revive *DASH*? I don't think so. It was a show very much of its time. We paved the way then; I proved dance was as valuable a medium for contemporary comment as any other; there are those who tell me I made it accessible to many more people. To reproduce it would be old hat, and there is so much that has superseded *DASH* in the intervening ten or twelve years. But I am proud of what I achieved and, what's more, the exhaustion was outweighed by the enjoyment.

THIRTEEN

HOT SHOES

WHEN I FIRST formed and toured *DASH*, proving that an all-dance show could be received enthusiastically, I was approached by Jill Marshall of the BBC. She was interested in the idea of a dance show for television. Was I? Of course. But the timing was not yet right: both *Cats* and *Song and Dance* were still unformed ideas and the powers that be at the BBC decided that dance on television would pull in only a very minority audience.

But in spring 1983, during my second tour of *DASH*, while it was at the Victoria Apollo, I was approached again. The idea was the same, based on the format of *DASH* – fast-moving, quick changes, different styles of dance, and my impersonations. This time I had the other shows under my belt, and the consciousness of the potential audience was raised, so it was given the go-ahead. The producer was Tom Gutteridge, who produced the *Russell Harty Show* (a talk show) on BBC2. They hoped it would be popular, but they were unprepared for how popular it was.

It took quite some time before the title of the show was settled on. 'Hot' was a word very much of the time, of the eighties, and physically your feet are on fire. 'Shoe' – well, that's fairly obvious. And 'Show'? A show is a show is a show. I had no part in the decision as to the title. All my best titles have been made up by friends, George in particular, because he has a facility for words and I don't really. I know my limitations. Anyway the title was presented to me as a *fait accompli*. I said it sounded like a Chinese take-away.

We were given twelve weeks to produce six half-hour shows. Tom decided to shoot one show every fortnight. This meant that, in all, we had only ten days to devise, choreograph and rehearse each show. Then one day was taken up with technical rehearsals, one to record the music and two days to shoot the show. Bonnie Langford was brought in, with Finola Hughes, Cherry Gillespie and Wendy Roe. We were the permanent nucleus and other guest artists such as Lesley Collier, and various others came in from show to show.

Choreography for television is very different from that for live theatre. It meant I had to learn swiftly. Numerous choreographers created numbers in the show which varied in style from jazz to ballet to tap to classical to contemporary.

In this first series I had a pet dog, Sugar, whom I tried to teach to dance. 'Do this,' I said, and executed an arabesque. The camera then cut away to Sugar making a face of pained exasperation. 'Then do this, if you won't do that,' and I did an entrechat. Sugar looked at me under his doggy brows and stalked off, tail firmly defiant. I have never known a more dismissive pupil. And BBC writers wrote sketches about dance. I'm not sure what they expected. All sketches had to be doctored, as verbal humour is very very difficult to produce in dance.

The choreographers created scenes such as Berlin in the thirties, the Deep South, and dances about war and decadence. I brought in various classical dancers to perform pieces that were more light-hearted than their usual fare. Bryony Brind, for instance, all dressed in gold, with some Royal Ballet boys in tuxedos, danced a piece designed for her by Wayne Eagling to the music of *Goldfinger.*

One of the more fun aspects of dancing for television is the possible use of special effects. Some of our ideas were quite mad, but I loved the special FX. One science-fiction piece had me dancing up a laser beam, landing from outer space on a planet where I fought with an alien force which spun me into orbit. Another (and I think it was one of the more humorous numbers in the show; I got the idea from a chap who actually did it on *Opportunity Knocks*, to the same music) was as a muscle man flexing his muscles to music – 'Wheels' – bom, bom-bom, bom-bom bom de-bom bom bom bom – and in the final moment of muscle-popping, the camera pulled back to reveal the special effects crew blowing up the fake muscles through pipes.

I choreographed myself as a punk bumble-bee to *The Flight of the Bumble Bee*, played by Julian Lloyd Webber on the cello. I slid down the cello strings on to the floor, flew up to his lapel where he was wearing a flower, only to be swatted by him as he finished his last chord.

As I got to grips with the use of the camera I directed my first piece, choreographing 'The First Cut' by Annie Lennox, placing it in a fashion studio. Annie came down and watched the filming. I was flattered by her presence (I had not met her before), and pleased that she had allowed me to use the track. It could not have been well simulated by the orchestra, however good they were. I also interpreted 'Pinball Wizard', a number from *Tommy*, by the Who. The set was like the inside of a pinball machine and I, dressed in a silver leather suit with mirrors all over it, played the silver ball, bouncing and jumping from pin to pin. The intention was not choreographic breakthroughs, but the show was full of visual ideas.

In those days the cameras were large and bulky like Daleks. We were forever having to slow down the movement to give the cameras time to track with us. Mostly the cameramen were not really used to following dancers, who are continually moving at such speed. Most of them had worked on drama, or on magazine programmes, or the news, in all of which the action is fairly static. I would have preferred an outside broadcast camera team – the sort that films sport, for instance – but I think union rules prevented encroachment on each other's patches. It is usually best to have a hand-held camera as the cameraman can move easily in between the action like a dancer.

But I have to give the cameramen (especially Ron Green, a wonder on Camera 1) their due. They worked really hard to overcome the limitations of the unwieldy old cameras and very quickly learned how best to film dance. But they were all taller than me and were always looking down on me (literally!), and the camera, shooting from above, always foreshortens the body. So I had the stage raised two feet from the ground. It meant that I was taller than the cameras, or at least on the same level, and if the camera managed to look up to me, my legs were longer. Raising the stage also meant that we were not dancing on the concrete floor of the studio.

We had to insist on angles that we knew were best for filming dance. Some camera angles are positively unflattering and we found, quite often, that arty filming (i.e., from the corners of the stage) meant either we were being viewed from behind or the essential lines of the body was indistinct. And it seems to be a natural reaction for a cameraman to pan down to the feet when filming a tap dance. A bit fruitless, really, because the movements of the beats and taps are so subtle they are near invisible. Fred Astaire always insisted that all his body should be in camera shot – dancers do not dance just with their feet but with their whole bodies. The other instinct the cameraman had was to follow a leap through the air. This utterly neutralized the excitement of movement through space. I decided that the camera should be pulled out for a long shot for the jumps. That way you could see the distance travelled during these leaps.

Two stages were built in the biggest studio at the BBC Television Centre so that while the cameras were shooting on one set the other was being dressed and rehearsed on. Then all the cameras had to do was turn and shoot the other set. We had about three hours to shoot each three-minute number, but by the time the lighting was done, by the time the cameras had rehearsed the shots, we had maybe forty minutes actually to shoot the piece. It made all of us very nervous – we were scared that we could let the rest of the cast down by slipping, perhaps even falling over. And shooting would have to start again. I learned to choreograph in short spurts. This not only proved faster than dancing the whole piece in one, it also meant that if we boobed we would not have to start from the beginning, but from that section only.

A lot of hard work went into the costumes for the show – in two ways. We needed to ensure that the line of the dancer was paramount in the design – so the costumes should reflect our capabilities and enhance, not hide, the choreography. The other side of the hard work was that the brilliant designer we were offered for the first show was a light entertainment specialist who had designed extensively for the likes of Shirley Bassey. He viewed dance as variety, so his costumes, beautiful though they were, were full of sequins and spangles and feather boas. Glitter was not the effect we wanted, but more to the point, his costumes were not the easiest to dance in. It upset him that we brought in bits and pieces from our own previous productions and wore them for the shoot.

But it came down to a basic misunderstanding of what we were about. For example, for one piece I was to wear a pair of ballet shoes. In my dressing-room was a pair of ballet shoes, of the type only ever worn by ballerinas. I went spare.

All right, so he didn't know that the principal dancers at the Royal Ballet always had their own shoe lasts at the factory because shoes were specifically designed for the needs of that dancer. But I do think that he should have done some research. The upshot was that he reported me to the directors at the BBC.

One of them came to see me on the set and he said, 'I'd like a word with you, laddie.' How patronizing. He then reeled off a list of complaints about me from the wardrobe master and asked why I was causing so many problems. I said I had a set of counter-complaints longer than his arm, if he really wanted to talk about it, and, 'Don't call me laddie,' I added.

From then on I brought in my own costumes. One night we wanted to do ten minutes' overtime. We reached agreement with cameramen, electricians and stagehands, and everyone else on the floor, but the overtime was blocked by the guy in the wardrobe. We could not complete and the set had to stay up until the next morning to shoot the final thirty seconds. The next night he tried it again. But he was told that as I was wearing my own costume, not supplied by the wardrobe staff, he couldn't veto the overtime.

It was hard work, and like the best of hard work, it was great fun. I, and everyone else, learned more than we thought possible – and not only that – this first series was so popular, netting 12 million viewers, that we were given a second series the following year.

What we had learned, we capitalized on in the next series. For this second series Lindas Martin and Woodfield were brought in to design the costumes. What a difference. Their designs were fabulous and were nominated for the best design of the year in the BAFTA awards. Bill Miller won the BAFTA for best lighting in television. The set designs were also superb. We were given an extra six weeks, which meant that we could use three days to shoot each show. This improved the standard no end. Even so it was always a fight against time. Some nights, just to finish a sequence I would have to make it up on the spot. The intended shot would have taken too long to set up, so I would ad-lib in front of a motionless camera. Instant coffee rather than the real thing, but I had to accept the conditions – otherwise the programme would never have materialized.

Unfortunately they were unable to sell, or even repeat, *The Hot Shoe Show* series, because of the swingeing contracts with the orchestra. Orchestras are paid a fee for the recording in the studio, and another for our use of the recording to dance to. Each session in the studio recorded the requisite amount of music for each show. When Tom Gutteridge, the producer, came to finalize the shows, he decided to move a number or two from one show to another, for a better fit. We found that the orchestra were paid show by show, and piece by piece: so if music was moved around, each musician was paid again – and probably again. The more he jigged, the more they were paid. (Complicated? Confused? Quite right. We were.) This meant that for each original recording, each musician could be paid twelve times over. And if the shows were to be repeated, it would mean even more payments. This made it far too expensive a proposition either to repeat or to sell abroad. The only place the show has been shown abroad is on the public subscription channels in the US, where no one gets paid anything. Don't suppose that it will ever be shown again.

After the second series Michael Grade took over the running of the BBC. He was brought in to make the BBC work, to slim it down, make it closer to the commercial networks. He axed quite a few programmes – us and *Doctor Who*, to name but two. Admittedly we were expensive to produce, even for our regular ratings of 8 or 9 million, but we could not really complain, as we had had two very good years. But his strange excuse was not that we were costly, which was understood, but that *Hot Shoe* wasn't light entertainment enough for BBC1 and was not arty enough for BBC2. 'We don't know where you fit in.' This occasioned a puzzled and exasperated scratching of heads, because the programme had been a success precisely *because* it didn't fit into either category. It bridged the gap between light entertainment and the arts. Interesting, the different perceptions. To me that attitude indicated a lack of vision.

But I was, in any case, keen to get back to live performance. It is very difficult to give your all in front of a camera. Especially when you have to repeat and repeat, and with no applause to spur you on. The press speculated for ages afterwards as to whether we would do another series. I admit I would have loved to. But the maxim of 'quit while you're ahead' is a good one to hold on to: doing no more than two series means that the programme retains a high level of affection. Which is good.

Doctor Who, of course, did return to the screen.

Cherry Gillespie was my partner the night I was dancing when my flies came undone. It was at a Royal Charity Gala for Thames TV, for the Prince's Trust, I think and a tribute to Eric Morecambe who had recently died. It was attended by Prince Philip, that I do remember. I was dancing with Cherry in a piece for which her husband had written the music. He had done rather well from writing jingles music and he had written the music with a view to making a single for Cherry. Anyway, there we were, on stage, being recorded by the cameras, leaping about, doing lots of exciting stuff, and my waistband came unbuckled and my flies started to undo. I felt nothing. Wearing a tight jockstrap means that you tend not to feel what you are wearing over it. But the audience started muttering and people in the wings were giggling. I looked down. Oh. I was in danger of having my leaps swamped by sagging trousers and I had to change my outstretched hands for crotch-covering hands. I had to make it funny – I couldn't do it up in the middle of a very fast piece. So I was leaping around, trying to prevent all my privates being shown to all and sundry, and all and sundry were watching because it was the final act before the finale, so the rest of the cast were congregating in the wings, laughing and pointing. And the audience was rocking. Blow me – we got an ovation. Once again the audience loved being in on a disaster and what I like is having the guts to cope with things like that and turn it to advantage. Panto training as much as anything. Angela Rippon was in stitches in the wings, and Sheila Hancock said 'Don't re-record it – it was so funny.' Cherry did not realize what was going on for ages and when she did was more unhappy than amused. Live it was funny, but on TV it might look as if I had planned to do it to get a cheap laugh so I insisted that it was re-shot after the audience had left.

In the line-up afterwards, Prince Philip had a go at me.

'And as for you,' he says.

'Oh, don't,' I say. I am acutely embarrassed.

He says, 'Oh, don't worry. The same thing happened to me once.'

'Oh, really?'

'I was playing polo.'

'How did you know?'

'I suddenly felt a breeze. Trouble was, we won the cup and the Queen was presenting it, and I had to go and collect it.'

'So what did you do?'

'Oh, I held my towel over my arm like a waiter.'

So there you go.

I went to Marrakesh for a short holiday and came back just before the Variety Club of Great Britain Awards. I had to be there, because I knew they were honouring me with the 1984 Showbusiness Personality of the Year Award. I was overwhelmed. It might sound a bit Hollywood-Oscarish, but I was. It was the first time I had received any award, or reward for that matter, from any one bar the public. It was for my 'outstanding contribution' to the world of entertainment, through the success of *DASH* and the *Hot Shoe Show*. After only three years away from the Royal Ballet it was an indescribable elation to be recognized by my peers. In my acceptance speech I noted that I was the only dancer, ever, to be honoured with the award. I felt that dancers and dancing were at last being given equal status with other performers.

I must admit, however, that my friends at the Royal Ballet did think I was moving down-market. Appearing on television did not help, either. Their main objection was to the quality of the work given, rather than what the work was; more that the steps, with a whizz here, a turn there, and a leap over there, was likely to be without the creative intricacies of an Ashton. They were, of course, right. What looks good in a variety show ain't necessarily good enough for the ballet. I'd not forgotten Madam, after the fiasco of my first choreographic attempt, with the fog gun spewing its oil all over the floor, saying, 'Never mind, Sleep, you'll be all right in variety.' Her prophecy had come true.

But for Ninette de Valois variety was no bad thing. It had kept her alive in those years before a national ballet company, and neither she nor Ashton looked down on the essence of variety. It was the critics, mostly, who did. They have no conception of how hard a life it must have been – and some still have no conception of how hard a life it still is for a dancer. Full stop. A lot of pontificating goes on, without comprehension. They know the lines of the body, a good arabesque etc, emotional charges, good technique, and for them that is all that there is in dance. Step out of line, appeal to the masses, and you are immediately diminished in their eyes. There is a massive snobbery about dance – some feel it should remain exclusive.

It is not often understood that if you wanted to be a ballet dancer in Madam's days you had to go into music hall, now called variety. There were ballet companies but they were few and far between. There were certainly none established in Britain at that time (there was, of course, the Camargo Society). The dancers would come on after the comic or the singer. Phyllis Bedells, who worked closely with the Royal Academy of Dancing, one of the first English ballerinas even before Dame Alicia Markova, used to be in a revue called *By the Way*. She would come on stage, and, while dancing the relevant steps, would intone, 'Entrechat and Relevée, Come and see more in *By the Way*.'

And the public flocked in. The audience loved it. It was a bit of CULTURE, in capital letters. They were aware that they were in the presence of something clever and unattainable, that it took dedication to get there, and accorded it the proper respect. 'This is the arts, the good stuff now,' and the dancers were always greeted rapturously, never raucously.

Madam, too, created the Peacock solo 'Pride' for herself. It kept her in work. Pavlova, too. But I don't think there were many men around in the same field. All those, Ashton too, who were involved in music hall didn't mind what I was doing. And understood. I do believe I have managed to change attitudes a bit, and I know that the choreography, and sometimes the execution, isn't up to par, but as far as I am concerned, any method is legitimate if dance can bring in a bigger and wider audience.

As much as anything else I was castigated for publicizing myself. Normal publicity is just about OK, if it falls within the 'right' confines and parameters. Self publicity is frowned on by the establishment – one should not prostitute oneself for one's art, is the cry. I should, in their eyes, have stayed with the Royal Ballet and remained 'respectable', and been content with what they would offer me. But I was never, ever, going to dance the romantic leads and all my energy had to go somewhere. Madam did say to me just before I left, 'Don't leave the company.' I explained that I was not getting any new opportunities and felt that I had done as much as I could within the company. She then added, endearingly, 'Please stay. You owe it to us. We trained you!'

I knew there was more to me than just being a dancer. Hence TV appearances. I doubt that Andrew Lloyd Webber would have considered me if he had not seen and heard of me. He would have gone to the Royal Ballet, perhaps, and asked for a classical dancer – any dancer. It happened that he knew my name. I had taken the plunge, so to speak, and laid my talent and career on the line.

But *DASH* was a different matter. And it is hard to know exactly where the dividing line between publicity and self-publicity is. Reasons change as life changes. *DASH* was formed through conviction, but I could not have started it without the publicity I had already received, and once it was formed, I needed the publicity to get the bookings. So more TV appearances.

I had proved to my own satisfaction that a dance show was a viable economic proposition in its own right, and my belief was vindicated when Apollo Leisure, a production company for the Apollo Theatre Group, transferred the *Hot Shoe Show* from television to the stage. We used the most successful numbers and adapted them. Stephen Beagley came from the Royal Ballet to join us on stage with some of the other regular dancers, and we toured Britain, ending with two weeks in the London Palladium.

The start of the tour was hardly auspicious. Before our first date, in Oxford, I had warmed up at a studio in London before leaving. When we arrived at the Playhouse, I got out of the car, went straight to the rehearsal rooms, jumped in the air and whap! tore my calf muscle. I had seized up on the hour's journey in the car. I had to be strapped up, and the first week was cancelled. After that I had to dance. Sort of. It was more of a hop-hop-hopping. The start of the show had everybody dancing as if in a television screen and then we would jump down from there on to the stage. I couldn't jump, of course – I had to be lifted . . . on one leg, and then changed all the moves to my good leg. We told the audience, of course – there's no point in trying to hide obvious failings. And they loved being in on the act. 'Oh you couldn't tell,' was the most usual comment. You could, but they love knowing the ins and outs of a performer's life. It's a shared experience. I checked into every hospital and every major physiotherapist on the tour in order to have treatments and have my leg strapped up before each night's performance. Marguerite Porter, who had had a similar injury, sent me off for an injection which would help stop the muscle snapping again. It has worked so far.

At the same time, a *DASH* video, a compilation of the more popular numbers, was made and shown on Channel Four. At that point in my life I really felt that everything was before me, that everything I wanted to do would fall into place.

DASH was successful as a show and as a business. I was proud of all factors. The money enabled me to buy my own studio. I had been looking all over London for some time, for various reasons. When you are trying to put a show together you need rehearsal space. There are plenty of studios in London but you can never be guaranteed that you might be able to use one place during a whole rehearsal period. Someone has always booked the one you are using six months ago, for the next day. This not only means traipsing from studio to studio, often all over the city, but also means moving props and music, getting used to a different space and orientation. And studios vary enormously. Some are decently equipped, but some don't have pianos, some don't even have power points – and then what do you do? A dancer needs music.

Worse, perhaps, are the distractions. Next door there is rock music, pop, drums, other noises. People drop in without ceremony or peer in through the doors to see what you are doing. I usually rigged up some sort of protection, closing doors and blocking windows. But all of that is a waste of one's energy and time, both of which are better employed in the creative process.

For all these reasons, plus the cost of renting, which is fairly high, I felt the need, desperately, to have my own space. Somewhere which I did not necessarily have to clear out at the end of the day. Somewhere where I could keep all my things around me, together.

But the search was proving a mammoth task. Either the space was not big enough, or it was and the sight lines were obscured by strategic pillars. There was either not enough light (although that is remediable), or not enough wall space for mirrors. It was easy rejecting all the places I saw. I am a great believer in places that feel right. None of them did.

Then Anne Allan told me about a space in South Kensington: a mews house that had been converted into the Andrew Hardie School of Dance. Originally built as the stables and servant's quarters for the main house in Queensgate, it was converted in the early 1900s into a ballroom, replete with grand staircase, marble pillars, parquet flooring, ornamental mirrors and fireplace. When I saw it the pillars had been replaced by steel joists. A big and perfect place. It sounded right even before I saw it.

Some of the major dance companies had rehearsed their works here – Mona Inglesby with her own company, Ballet International, among many others. Andrew Hardie had died some time before, and Val Swinnard, who had been running the school ever since, no longer wanted to do so. She had closed the school and wanted to sell. Perfect. I bought it from her. She was glad, I believe, that the building was going into the hands of someone who wanted to keep it as a dance studio.

I took the staircase away, gave the parquet flooring to George for his studio in Long Acre, and dug down ten feet. I put in a sprung floor, made two changing-rooms, and created another, smaller, studio upstairs. My place. This was luxury. For all of us. We rehearsed the *Hot Shoe Show* here – but that was before I had removed the staircase and enlarged the space, so for the final rehearsals of *Hot Shoe* we still had to use a larger, outside, studio.

The most important component, however, was that there were no more unsettling flits round the city from one space to another, no more rehearsing in different environments. Creation could take place in one spot, without the constant rush. The calm was a relief – and so was the saving of about a thousand pounds in rent and travel.

I gave a big party when we opened. At about the same time the mews house opposite came up for sale, and I fantasized on the possibility of living there and simply rolling out of bed thirty seconds before having to be at work. I could think of nothing more blissful, particularly for someone who is always late. I would probably still manage to be late, but who cares? After a lot of thought, a lot of deliberation, I borrowed the money to buy it.

Upstairs it was divided into rooms that had been rented out; downstairs there were still the original stables from the 1860s, which were rented out for storage. I did the first floor up as cheaply as possible with the help of Michael, who was wardrobe master on *Cabaret* and who was to run the studio for me. I had to rent out the space when I wasn't using it to help pay for the house. I tried to keep the studio as exclusive as possible – Michael made the point that people are not as respectful of others' property as they are of their own. Gillian Lynne used it for various of her own projects as well as those of Andrew Lloyd Webber. I also let it out for the filming of various fitness videos, and I made my own video, *Step Into Ballet*, there in 1991.

I had hoped to spend the Christmas of 1986 in my mews house, but it wasn't ready. I decided to treat myself and booked into a suite in the Savoy for Christmas. Years ago, George and I had invented our own tradition of lunching at Fortnum & Masons on Christmas Eve whenever I was not working, and we managed it this year. Then we descended through the store, buying our Christmas presents on the way, getting the feel of Christmas. I don't *think* it is because of us that Fortnums now closes early on Christmas Eve . . . but George and I together can be a bit noisy. Then Mac whisked us off to the Savoy. Several friends came to visit on Christmas Day – I was rather surprised to see so many, but almost invariably they said they were only too happy to get away from their own traditional family Christmases for a few hours, and feel liberated.

I know the Savoy is expensive, I know I was paying for and doing up a house, but I felt a treat was deserved (particularly as I was in the middle of the *Cabaret* run) and I had always wanted to stay at the Savoy. The American actress Elaine Stritch lived there when she moved to England and I can quite see why. The place has views of the river and thirties furniture. It conjures up visions of Noël Coward breathing his immortal aphorisms over breakfast. It has an atmosphere like no other hotel I know. That's why.

FOURTEEN

ROYAL COMMANDS

FTER LEAVING *Cats* I appeared only occasionally with the Royal Ballet. But I was still a member and my name remained in the programmes as a senior principal dancer. I was invited back for a month in 1981, to appear in *Swan Lake*, with Natalia Makarova and Anthony Dowell, who came back for a season from America. A video was also being made of this production. This time I was not partnered in the Neapolitan Dance by Lesley Collier, now a prima ballerina, but by Rosemary Taylor – another of my White Lodge contemporaries.

It was during one of these performances this season that I first met the Princess of Wales. In the Crush Bar afterwards I said to Prince Charles: 'I haven't met your wife yet.'

He said, 'Haven't you?' and introduced me. She told me then that she had seen me dance many times at Covent Garden when she was young. She was tall and looked down on me with those pretty blue eyes, and blushed. I was hooked.

The next time I met her was when she came to the Dominion theatre to watch *DASH* from the wings. And again when I performed at a fund-raising gala for the London City Ballet, of which she was patron. Then, in the autumn of 1985, after the world tour of *DASH*, Anne Allan – now giving private dance tuition to Princess Diana – asked me if I would come along to one of their workouts. The Princess wanted to talk to me about an inchoate idea she had.

I went along to the studio in Hammersmith and was met at the door by the Princess of Wales's detective. He ushered me in to the studio where the Princess, in leotard and tights, was being taken through various steps by Anne. The workout paused and we sat down together to talk about her idea. She had always wanted to be a dancer, she said, and thought it would be great fun, if it were possible, to perform a dance routine at Covent Garden. Both she and her husband had already performed for the Friends' of the Royal Ballet Christmas party the previous year, in a spoof of the balcony scene from *Romeo and Juliet* – the Prince had climbed up a ladder to the Royal Box to sing 'Just One Cornetto'. He had performed at another Friends' party before: singing 'I Am the Pirate King' from *The Pirates of Penzance*, dressed in thigh-length boots and swashbuckling a rapier. He kept on forgetting his lines and pinned reminders on the backs of the *corps de ballet*.

When the Princess told me about her wish I did not realize at first that she meant she wanted to dance with me. I was taken aback. This I had not anticipated. 'But she's so tall,' I thought, 'we could look pretty peculiar together.' But I sat on my surprise as we went on to discuss what we might do together. She already had an idea and, what's more, the music she wanted to use. It was 'Uptown Girl', sung by Billy Joel. I was relieved that she intended the piece to be light-hearted and humorous and wanted the routine to include jazz dancing and high kicks. We started then and there to work out some steps so that I could judge how proficient she was technically. She managed a double pirouette easily and kicked over my head without any problem. I began to realize that the idea could work, in spite of the incongruity of our heights – which could not be ignored and so had to be used to our advantage and with humour. We were helped in this by the lyrics of 'Uptown Girl', which have disparity built in to them.

I rehearsed with her whenever she had enough free time. She decided, finally, that she would like to perform it at the next Friends' Christmas party, as a surprise for her husband who would be in the Royal Box. We were very careful not to let anyone know about her idea or our rehearsals. We changed venues regularly to keep the media off the scent (which we did), and when I was unable to rehearse with her later in the year because of Christmas pantomime commitments in Stoke-on-Trent, I talked on the telephone to Anne Allan, who then relayed my ideas to the Princess. On the few mornings I was able to be in London to rehearse with her I found, to my surprise, that she had perfected the steps I suggested via Anne.

I told Leslie Edwards only two days before the party. 'My dear, how marvellous,' he said. He was thrilled by the idea. Because he organized the running of the evening, he had to know, so that room would be left for a 'surprise item'.

On the day of the performance, the Princess stole away from Kensington Palace to rehearse on the stage at Covent Garden. We made sure the auditorium was empty because we didn't want to give the game away, nor did we want any gawping onlookers. The stage manager had to know, of course, and Ken Davidson, who ran the Friends' office, to ensure security, but there is such a culture of discretion at the Garden that even if more people had known, nothing would have been said. There might have been a skeleton duty stage staff there too. I asked for the lighting that we would have for the performance – if you are not used to stage lighting it can be blinding and put you off your stride.

The Princess wore both the dress and the shoes that she would be performing in that evening. 'And what are you wearing, Sleep?' she demanded. Up to that point I had not considered my outfit. I said I would find something suitable. I lifted her to check that the satin of the dress was not so shiny that she would slip through my hands. Her shoes were fairly low-heeled ('Thank heavens,' I thought), and I suggested she put elastic round them and her instep – to make absolutely certain that they wouldn't fly off, say, during a high kick. I didn't want *anything* to go wrong.

Anne Allan and Leslie Edwards were the only ones allowed into the auditorium. They sat in the stalls and guided us through our rehearsal. We had no more than an hour – it was to be a crash course in performing at Covent Garden. We went through the routine three or four times, checking our placings on the stage, making sure we hit the centre at the right time. All our practice before this had been done in a much smaller studio: we needed to be sure that the performance was big enough to reach the back of the amphitheatre – the auditorium of the Royal Opera House is very large.

We even rehearsed our bows to the Royal Box. The Princess said, 'I'm not bowing to the Royal Box.'

'Of course you are,' I teased her. 'You *must* do what I say.'

'You won't get your OBE this way.' She pretended I was being bossy.

'Excuse me,' I said, 'but I'm sticking out for a knighthood. And you must bow to the Royal Box.' So we practised. After this she was whisked away and I did not see her again until the evening.

During the afternoon, the rest of the cast assembled on stage to rehearse for the evening's show. There was a buzz of excitement – there always is before these galas. I went home to Long Acre and started to pull things out of the wardrobe to find something that would match her dress. I found a pair of white leather jeans, a pink short-sleeved shirt and a pair of white jazz shoes. Very 'Downtown Boy'.

The plan was that the Princess would enter the theatre with her husband and take her position, as usual, beside him in the Royal Box. At a certain point she was to leave the box to change into her costume. Anne Allan and I kept vigil from the wings to see when she left, so that we might meet her in the King's Smoking Room, where the royal party always retire for drinks and things. The door to the Smoking Room is across the corridor and directly opposite that of the Royal Box. Her detective let us in from the outside. He stood in the corridor, ready, among other duties, to open either door at a moment's notice.

Just inside the door of the Smoking Room was a big table. It seemed to be covered with crackers, cake, chocolates and champagne. The Princess offered me a drink. I declined. I was going to need all my faculties for our little epic. But while Anne took the Princess off to change out of her red velvet evening dress in the private bathroom in the corner of the room, I scoffed some chocolates and drank coffee. This boosted my adrenalin levels even further. Performing at Covent Garden provides its own adrenalin rush, so I was high, as one might say, already. The Princess emerged from changing, with her diamond and ruby earrings in one hand. 'Thank God for Butler and Wilson,' she said as she replaced real with costume jewellery. 'So far, so good,' I think one of us said. We were laughing about our routine, dancing around. She offered me another chocolate and took one herself. Our nerves made us giggle which, in turn, made the Princess choke on her chocolate. I banged her on her back, to help, making such a din that her detective came running in to see what on earth was going on. I don't dare think what it must have looked like to him at first glance.

We left the King's Smoking Room by the private entrance which leads directly to the backstage. We found, in our eagerness to have enough time, that we were at least half an hour too early. There were at least three items to go before us. We began to wind down because we were waiting so long. We sat on the steps, and Princess Diana kicked her shoes off. (The elastic she had attached to her shoes was a bit too tight, so concerned was she that they should stay on.) She chatted, in her easy manner, to the rest of the cast while we waited. It seemed like for ever. The act before us was never going to end – it was an opera singer performing material outside his normal sphere, stuff he would not usually be able to do. In fact many of the acts in these galas are like that – and they tend to go on too long.

But, eventually, our turn came.

As the music started for 'Uptown Girl' I ran out on to the stage. A round of applause greeted me – as I was not in the programme it was something of a surprise for the audience. Every turn, jump and pirouette I made was responded to in the same way. There is something particular about audience appreciation. I had not performed on the stage of the Opera House for some time, and was reminded how enthusiastic devotees of the ballet are. But even while I was enjoying the acclaim I was thinking, 'You wait, you lot, you ain't seen nothing yet.'

I paved the way for my partner's entrance by directing the attention of the audience into the wings. I was praying that she would not lose her bottle, get stage fright. But I need not even have let that thought cross my mind. She strode on to the stage as if she had been doing it for ever, as if she was born to it. She crossed the space, from one side to the other, taking eight steps to the middle, stopped, turning her head to the auditorium, and pausing for eight counts, then continued to the other side. As the audience realized who it was, the collective 'Aah' of surprise became almost a roar of recognition as a thousand people expelled their breaths at the same time. She repeated the sequence and paused again, looking at the audience.

We made eye contact and danced side by side, clicking our fingers, sliding into jazz movements, rolling our shoulders. Then we went into the pirouette section. I twirled, she copied, I turned again, she looked at me, 'Hah,' and upstaged me by not only repeating my moves, but turning twice to my once. I pirouetted again and she pushed me down to my knees, her hand on my head, and kicked her leg high over me. The applause was terrific. We glided to the corner of the stage, ready for the diagonal. I turned, picked her up and carried her, running across the whole width of the stage. She extended her arm to the audience, her head back, to more applause. I'm thinking, 'God, I can't drop the future Queen of England . . . ' I put her down and after more jumps across the stage together we clasped hands, ran to the back of the stage, turned to face the audience and came forward, doing step-kick, step-kick in half time to the final bars of the music. The auditorium went wild.

We bowed to the audience, and to the Royal Box. She took a long look at the box as she curtsied with a grand sweeping gesture. I mimed at Prince Charles, 'I think she and I might, you know, get together?' She ran off, I shrugged, 'Ah, well, you can't win 'em all,' in the direction of the Box, and ran after her. We came back for eight more calls. I tried to get her to take a bow by herself, but she refused. The audience was crying for an encore, and the Princess was all fired up to repeat the whole thing, but I insisted that it was best, always, to leave them wanting more. As we came off from the last curtain call, she whispered in my ear, 'Beats the wedding.' I was a bit surprised by that, but then it occurred to me that this was an occasion where the accolade was for her ability as well as for who she is. It was something she had done for herself and no one else – unlike so many other areas of her life. And the glow you feel from audience appreciation is very special. At the final curtain call for the whole company, she showed professionalism by staying in the line – the evening belonged to all the performers.

The crowds dispersed, and the Princess asked me if I would come up the stairs to the King's Smoking Room with her. The double doors opened. Prince Charles and his entourage were standing in a semi-circle facing us. He was smiling, even if rather quizzically. He said 'Well done. Have a drink.' I asked if it had been a surprise. 'Completely,' he said. For security reasons, it had been necessary to tell him on the day of the performance. The Princess was, after all, intending to be out of the Royal Box for some time. She disappeared to change, and her lady-in-waiting, Ann Beckwith-Smith, who had liaised all our meetings, breathed a visible sigh of relief. 'Only you could have done that,' she said to me, 'Well done.' I suspect there must have been some apprehension about the content of the routine.

I mingled and chatted to various people in the room. When the Princess returned, clad in her red velvet, we pulled a cracker together. I asked her if I could bring my mother to meet her. (I had invited my mother because I really did not want her to miss this performance. She had come with my cousin Robert.) I had to be quick because the royal party was preparing to leave.

I zoomed to the Crush Bar. Everyone fell silent as I entered. They all supposed the Princess to be on my heels. Such a disappointment. My voice, all squeaky, floated into this expectant silence. 'Mum,' I said, 'Mum – where are you?' I grabbed her hand and we sped back to the Smoking Room. They were just leaving. I introduced my mother to both the Prince and the Princess. Princess Diana asked her if she had been surprised. My mother said, 'Yes, I thought it might be Margot Fonteyn.' The Princess smiled and pulled a cracker with my mother. This was the only thing that didn't get wet when she slipped and fell into a puddle on the way home. Mum kept the cracker, and the gold chain that was in it, for the rest of her life.

There was a horde of cameramen waiting when I left the theatre. The media had found out about the performance within half an hour of the final curtain.

Some time later the Princess told me that not only was she thrilled at having fulfilled a childhood dream of performing at the Garden, but was also delighted about having duped some of the media. We had managed to ensure that no one, but no one, found out in advance, which is something of an achievement. The only thing that did happen – and it wasn't down to the media or the paparazzi, *per se* – was that an amateur took a series of rather blurred photographs of our performance. These images were shown all over the world. Just three minutes of dancing with the Princess of Wales gave me more world-wide coverage than in all my (then) twenty years of performing. Ironic, eh?

The Princess and I have met a few times since. We joked about doing a show together and even gave it a working title: 'Come and See Wayne and Di'. She has a ready wit and a good sense of the absurd. I once sent her a silly hat for her birthday. It had two frog's legs sticking out of the top and a slogan which said, 'Kiss me, I might be a prince.' She sent me a thank-you letter in which she said, 'Where shall I wear it? Ascot??' She always asked after the health of my parents (while they were still alive) whenever we met and used to invite them to the staff Christmas parties at Kensington Palace.

FIFTEEN

IT's CABARET TIME

ONE OF MY favourite films has to be *Cabaret*, directed by Bob Fosse – one of the best film musical directors and choreographers. So when I was approached, in the autumn of 1985, by the Theatre Royal, Hanley, Stoke-on-Trent, to play the Emcee on stage I jumped at the chance. The management had a tour of number one venues in mind, starting in Stoke, followed by a season at the Strand theatre in the West End. The proviso was that I would play the Dick part of *Dick Whittington* for them over the Christmas period. It was from Stoke that I zipped down to London for rehearsals with Princess Diana in preparation for our surprise performance at the Friends' Christmas party.

Gillian Lynne was to direct and choreograph *Cabaret*. We left any past misunderstandings and grievances behind us. She did not want a show that was a copy of the film, nor did I, as Emcee, wish to mirror the performance of Joel Grey. He had played the part both on Broadway and in the film, and it was, for me, the definitive performance. I do resemble him, both in stature and in looks, so Mark Thompson devised a different look for me. He experimented first of all with a shaven head. That didn't work, and it was changed to a black and oily wig. I was dark-lipped, black-tail-suited, and Cuban-heeled, with a glimpse of degenerate fishnet round the ankle. Quite scary and sinister right from the beginning instead of being the (albeit slightly sleazy) larky, affable, 'Gerremoff', bring-on-the-dancing-girls-type of cabaret host who degrades into something more evil and dangerous. Gillian's husband, Peter Land, was to play Cliff, and Kelly Hunter would be Sally Bowles.

Gillian decided on a creation with Brechtian undertones. It started with the rest of the cast under a white cloth, eerie and strange, from which they all emerged in black, swaying, menacing, heavy; then all shed their black costumes to become the characters. It was electrifying and powerful, but the impact of this opening led the critics to say that I gave my sinister finale at the beginning of the show, leaving me with no journey of development. In retrospect, I understand what they meant.

Gillian devised some brilliant touches, such as the tap routine to Hitler's speeches and the ricochet of rapid machine-gun fire (Kander and Ebb, the composers, thought it a great innovation), and the magic trick with a handkerchief, as in *Cats* (I had not forgotten), where a white surrender flag was shaken, whoof, and turned into a swastika. They were much struck by the whole show, thought it very different and were willing for us to take it to the West End.

There had been one or two problems and hitches on the tour in the run up to the Strand. The poster, for instance, that the Hanley management designed was about as interesting as a dishcloth, a dreadful interpretation of Berlin in the thirties. It had no style. Gillian and I thought it naff in the extreme, particularly after the simple statement of the *Cats* and *Song and Dance* posters. We wanted Dewynters to design it. The team at Dewynters were approached and did an excellent job on redesigning our poster: a red background, with a curtain through which a woman's leg in fishnets and a man's arm in a black tuxedo holding a baton appeared.

The twelve-week tour was a sell out.

While we were rehearsing in London I appeared on the Michael Aspel talk show to promote *Cabaret*. On with me was Liza Minnelli, who was appearing in concert at the Palladium. Liza asked me to come to the dress rehearsal of her show. I was sitting in the auditorium, near someone I vaguely recognized. Suddenly Liza beckoned me up on to the stage.

'Wayne, Wayne, c'mon up here, c'mon up.' So I did.

'Wayne,' she whispered, putting an arm round my shoulders, 'I'm gonna make your day.'

'Oh yeah?'

'Charles Aznavour is smaller than you.'

He was the person sitting in the stalls. A film was being made about his career and they were about to appear together in Paris.

I went along to the Palladium every night before Liza's performance to watch her warm up. She had a jam session with the band, singing, and I added the occasional dance step. It was her way of getting into the rhythm of the evening. This was new to me, and much more fun than the pain of solitary barre warm-ups.

Liza likes someone to play to when she is on stage. She gathers her friends to sit near the front so she can pick them out. Once she asked me to discreetly wave a white handkerchief. I am the opposite. I hate to catch an eye in the audience. This comes from dancing with such a gap between public and stage at the ROH. I spent each evening of that week sitting in the audience waving at her. What a great performer, and what a show.

After a tour of three months *Cabaret* came into the Strand Theatre in the West End on 17 July 1986 (my birthday). I also went to a Royal Garden Party at Buckingham Palace in the afternoon, with my mother. If it had just been me, I would not have gone, because of the opening night – but Mum, who had been unable to attend two other Garden Parties to which she had been invited, really wanted to go. I went for her. She had bought a cerise suit, with blue hat, handbag, shoes and umbrella – and was very proud of the fact that all the accessories were matching and had only cost her a fiver. There were about 2,000 people congregated in the gardens behind the Palace. Ushers picked some of us out of the avenues of people, one down which the Queen and Prince Philip would walk, and the other for the Prince and Princess of Wales. Mum and I were singled out.

I remember being prodded in the back while we were waiting by a woman who said to me, 'We've been trying to work out who you are, but can't. So we've decided you're either someone famous – or a jockey.' This was not the first time I've been mistaken for a jockey. Oliver Reed once spent a whole evening introducing me as Willie Carson. He brooked no denial and blamed me heartily for losing the 3.30 at Newmarket and his money. And thinking of mistaken identity, Jack Tinker, theatre critic of the *Daily Mail*, has more than once been mistaken for me. I get mistaken for him, too. One woman came up to me after a first night somewhere, and said 'Thank God for you and the *Mail*, Jack'. Mistaken identity is one thing, but being mistaken for a critic? It has become a great joke among our theatrical friends.

And after that jollification, it was off to the Strand double quick and into my make-up for the press night of *Cabaret* and the start of the West End run.

When I arrived at the theatre there was a bottle of champagne waiting for me, with a note: 'Good luck – love Judi.' Judi Dench had played Sally Bowles in the original London production. One lady who came to the show wrote to me saying that she was with the original Sally Bowles in Berlin in the thirties and would I be interested in meeting her and hearing about it? Would I? Of course I would. We met in the Waldorf Hotel, round the corner from the Strand theatre, for tea. She had gone to Berlin to be a film extra, as had 'Sally Bowles', because it was the place to be in the thirties. All the films were being made there. She had invested in the original production of *Cabaret*, and said it used too much stage machinery, hydraulic lifts, etc. We were much closer to the original idea of the sleazy night clubs of Berlin, but she had one criticism of the production. In those days, she said, you would never see two young men dancing together, it would always be a young man and an old one. And the old one would be paunchy, balding, yellow toothed and unattractive in other similarly disgusting ways – because they were the only ones rich enough to afford the lifestyle, such as it was. 'Of course, all our boys were beautiful. And young,' she told me. She knew one boy, one pimp, she said, who was a charmer but a dreadful show-off. He had a cigarette lighter which he proudly showed her, and then unscrewed it to reveal the little jar of cream hidden in the bottom. And it was a very old-fashioned, upright, twin-set and pearls, grand old lady that was telling me this. In the Waldorf, over cream tea.

After a year attendances were falling and there were cutbacks – just to pull it through to the summer months when the management were confident that figures would pick up again. We'd been booked solid, so the money had been coming in, but various bills had not been paid, and no one could understand where the profits had gone.

And then there were the problems with the musicians. The original MD of the show was very ill when we began rehearsals. None of us knew. He died not long afterwards. I missed him. We'd worked closely together and he had boosted my confidence no end because of his belief in me: a great boon when singing is not your primary talent.

He was replaced by Gareth Valentine. Gareth is an excellent musician, but at that time had little experience as MD. We were having half as many deps (one-night replacement musicians) as regulars and of course they didn't know the score so well. There were complaints from the cast that the tempi were out during performances. I brought in a fixer, Geoff Young, who was already in charge of some major West End shows. The management had had to drop the original one, to save money. A fixer's job is to ensure consistency of quality and to make sure deps are up to scratch. Gareth had already warned three musicians for bad behaviour, and Geoff sacked them.

'What?' I said. 'The Musicians' Union won't stand for it.'

They didn't.

I was in North Africa having my mandatory two weeks' (and well-earned) rest after a year in the part. The press found me there. They asked my opinion of the potential and looming strike action by the Musicians' Union on the show. They told me that there were pickets outside the stage door demanding that the actors not perform. Toyah Wilcox (the current Sally Bowles) and the rest of the cast defied all threats and continued to perform. Rumours abounded that I had left a sinking ship, that I had no intention of returning, that I had cleared out my dressing-room (I had, to make room for the person taking my part for two weeks) – indeed that I had instigated the whole affair in order to close the show. A cartoon appeared with me on the back of a camel, captioned – 'Last seen heading towards the desert.'

The musicians also accused me of chucking fruit at them from the stage. They did have orange peel thrown at them, I admit, but as it was in the script to be dropped on the floor of the pit, it happened every night. Out-of-work musicians stood at the stage door every night defying the cast to perform. Eventually they boycotted the show. The cast played one night without any musicians whatsoever and received a standing ovation. I returned to London to find a locked stage door. A dark theatre with no show. Gillian wrote to Equity – but they were little help. In all fifty or so staff were made redundant – actors, singers, dancers, stage management, wardrobe, dressers, box office, front of house.

Our production was very different from the original Broadway show and completely different from the film. This caused problems with some of the audience, who came expecting to see the film – and didn't. *Cabaret* was originally a vehicle for the German actress Lotte Lenya, who took the role of a landlady in Berlin. The story was seen through her eyes, and not those of a young girl trying to make it as a cabaret artist, as in the film. Lenya's part does not exist in the movie, for which the story was completely reworked. This confused many people who came to see us. But it became something of a cult piece. People either loved it or dismissed it – there was no half measure.

In August Princess Diana phoned, and said she wanted to see *Cabaret* and have a pizza afterwards. I didn't take her to a pizza joint, but I booked a table at Luigi's – which I knew would be confidential. Although pizzas were not on the menu they said if I brought her they would cook them specially.

She came backstage after the performance and was taken by a mug which I was using. Its caption said 'Let's Dance – Yah!' And on the other side was a caricature of her in leg-warmers, leotards and tights, kicking a leg in the air, holding on to bowler hat and cane. I was given the task of scouring London's markets for thirty-six of them for her to give away as presents.

I invited Gillian, Peter, George and Anne to join us at Luigi's. A huge plate arrived covered by a silver salver – and when it was lifted, there were ten pizzas to choose from. She took one look and laughed. We ate from the proper menu.

So much for pizzas.

After *Cabaret* closed in 1987 I was able to use my new space – now called the Gravity Studios – to rehearse a workshop called *Sleep with Friends*. The first half of this show was based on the marathon dances of the early 1920s. These went on for what must have seemed like weeks for the participants. Certainly they lasted for 150 hours, virtually non-stop. Some people might remember the film *They Shoot Horses, Don't They?* which was about the same subject. I concentrated on the relationships on the dance floor as much as on the characterization. These endurance tests had ten-minute breaks every three hours, which gave me a good excuse to combine different songs together in those breaks to show the relationships with their partners. I was thinking of turning it into a musical and did, to that end, work with a writer, but I ended up blue-pencilling most of his work. So it never got off the ground. It is still in the back of my mind though, and if anyone is thinking of taking it on – I have the intellectual copyright locked away in a bank vault. So there.

It was a good vehicle for some of the songs of the period: 'Ten Cents a Dance', sung by an exhausted creature with her feet in a bowl of water; 'Love Me or Leave Me', from a prospective partner, but she doesn't want to know; then a whistle sounds (this was blown by my neighbour in Covent Garden, Brenda Armstrong, who also used to bring the house down by doing a quick tap across the stage, clad only in a shirt and tights), and the whole debilitating round of dancing starts again. I had the lights go dim at one point, and when they came up again it was twenty hours later, with fatigue writ large on the dancers' faces, to the accompaniment of the MD, Gareth Valentine, singing 'When You're Smiling'. Hollywood scouts used to attend these marathons on the look-out for likely talent, so a lot of the characterization was 'Look at Me', including a faded, famous, ex-silent movie star, looking to get back into films, played by Marianne St Clair, principal ballerina of the London City Ballet. We danced a passionate tango together.

The second half of the programme portrayed rehearsals in a dance studio. I had warming up exercises, 'aah aah aah aah', up the scale and down again – and then one of the cast gets bored and goes into 'It don't mean a thing, if it ain't got that swing', everyone loosens up and slides into a jazz finish. Marianne played the ballerina, very aloof. This second half of *Sleep with Friends* became the first half of *Bits and Pieces*.

Sleep With Friends played in York and in Bath. It was not a tour, although it was billed as such in Bath. It was more in the nature of a workshop, with few props and costumes, minimal scenery and lighting. I'm sure that some of the audience were disappointed at not seeing a full-blown spectacle, but we had full houses and no one complained. Except the critics who believed it to be my next big show. My family, as always, came to see this new show.

In June I heard that Diana Roberts had suffered a massive heart attack and had been found dead beside her bed. I hoped that she had known little about it, but it saddened me beyond belief. She had been a profound help in my early years at the Royal Ballet. I, in return, had introduced her to some of her ballet heroes, and she remained good friends with many of them, such as Jeanetta Laurence, Pamela Scott and Marguerite Porter. It would not be too much to say she had been a surrogate mother to us all. We missed her, and I felt that an essential link with my past had been broken.

August saw George and I in Greece, loafing in the olive groves and the vineyards, taking in the odd ancient statue and missing my mother and my Gran, who were visiting Delphi. I came back straight into rehearsals for a touring revival of *Song and Dance*. We went to Munich (where Mum and Ruth came out to see me) for six weeks first, then to Vienna and Bregenz. I loved the way Mum always supported me.

When I got back from Bregenz I appeared on the television show *Class Mates*. In this, many and various fifth form classmates are invited to present their memories of (and make ribald comments about) the subject – in this case – me. When I walked on to the set I was faced by lots of White Lodge students I had not seen since I was sixteen. Some of them had flown in from places like America and Switzerland. It was pretty strange to see them all again, and funny to see how memories differ.

It came round to Christmas again. It was beginning to arrive quicker than before. One thing was different – I had my first Christmas in South Kensington – in the mews but the other was the same. Pantomime, for the second time in Norwich, with Dilys Watling. Which panto was it? *Aladdin*. Just to be different. And for a further change I was the Slave of the Ring. I was beginning to discern a pattern of repeats.

Time for a change, I thought, time to try something new. The cabaret circuit seemed like a good idea. Not that I knew much about it. I'd seen some performances, in good classy venues, and saw no reason why I should not attempt much the same thing. *Wayne Sleep in Cabaret*. It did occur to me that it would be hard; the proximity to the audience means that you can't hide anything. It was a long way from that exceptional and rarefied atmosphere of the Covent Garden stage, via the West End and panto, to the intimacy necessary for cabaret. I had been arriving at that point, bit by bit, I thought. But I had no idea how hard it would really be.

One surprising thing did come out of this experience. I caught chicken-pox. I was about to fly to Madrid to appear on Spanish TV in a variety special. I thought I'd have to cancel my flight. In fact I thought I'd have to cancel my appearance. I couldn't go to Madrid covered in spots like a five-year-old. Much too embarrassing. And I discovered that if you get a 'childhood' illness like chicken-pox when you are adult, you get hit much worse. So I railed at fate rather a lot.

Anne, who was coming to assist me in Madrid, came to bathe my wounds. I felt like a plague victim. I was riddled with sores and they didn't just itch, they damn well *hurt*. It was like being pierced with dozens of stiletto knives all over me and all at the same time. The knives kept me awake for three days. I looked great. Haggard, zombie-eyed, raging weals covering my skin. Lovely.

I recovered enough to go to Madrid a few days later. And judicious application of loads of really thick pan-stick make-up covered the ravages of my skin. I wondered, afterwards, whether a recent holiday in Israel where I had bathed in the Dead Sea might have made my skin more susceptible to the virus and the condition worse. I've no idea. Anyway, by the time I came back from Madrid every vestige of chicken-pox had vanished.

Just as well, because it was straight back into the next stage of the tour of *Song and Dance*, which opened in Plymouth in March. I was able to stay with my mother, which was a rare joy. It was funny being transported back about thirty-five years, living at home, as if still dancing on the kitchen table. Going home sometimes, you lose all sense of the time travelled between then and growing up. It's a sort of limbo land where you are cosseted and fussed over. The downside of that is that sometimes you are still regarded as that importunate five-year-old who wants to get on the table and perform for the family. Still, I rather like the lack of responsibility.

Then it was back on the road, this time to Amsterdam. My intrepid Mum came too, bringing Auntie Ruth. After Amsterdam – Vienna, various Scandinavian cities, Edinburgh, Glasgow. All the way through to September.

In June, right in the middle of the tour, a special gala was held to honour the ninetieth birthday of Dame Ninette de Valois. This was a BIG DO. Rudolf Nureyev took time off from his tour of South America and travelled round the clock to be there; Antoinette Sibley and Anthony Dowell partnered each other again in *The Dream*; children from White Lodge danced a hornpipe; Margot Fonteyn flew in from Panama to give a speech; and many, many other principals came to pay tribute to this most remarkable of women. All the famous ballet luminaries were there: Ashton, MacMillan, Peter Wright. And the Queen and Princess Margaret.

I interrupted the tour to appear in the gala in a piece from one of Madam's own works – as the Dancing Master in *The Rake's Progress*, based on Hogarth's prints. I was fit enough from performing daily on tour, but I had private doubts about my classical technique. It was rusty round the edges because I was not having to use it in the jazz/ballet combination of *Song and Dance*. The part of the Dancing Master requires the most perfect of perfect techniques. He is, after all, the teacher, so his fifth position and his *jetés* and pirouettes must be absolutely correct. It is textbook stuff, and the audience knows exactly what it is looking for. I had a lot to live up to. It is far easier for me to do big leaps in the air and jump around the stage than to do this perfect technique – and to do it with violin and bow in hand as well. It's hard. Hard enough for a dancer who has played the part before, and I hadn't. I suspect the Royal Ballet asked me because they thought I had played it before. I was the type of dancer that would have, were I still with the company. Besides, Madam was fond of me.

In May I started to work on my technique. I would usually fly down to London from Manchester (or wherever we were) in order to take morning class with the Royal Ballet, learn and rehearse the part with Brian Shaw, and fly back to Manchester for the evening performance of *Song and Dance*. Class made me aware of how much classical techniques, especially the men's, had changed and improved in the last few years. This was seen both in the line of the body and in the strength too. But for me the most noticeable fact was that stretching – not taught to my year in the lower school – was now mandatory. Finally I made visits to Michael Brown, the wardrobe master. I had a niggling fear that the costume might not fit, but after eight shows a week on tour I was in good shape. I need not have worried.

Madam was not told that I was performing. It was kept as a surprise. She was seated between the Queen and John (Lord) Sainsbury. The front cloth went up to reveal me and Stephen Jeffries, who was playing the Rake. After we'd danced a few steps Madam turned to John Sainsbury and said, 'Who is that new boy? We must give him more to do.'

John replied, 'It's Sleep, Madam.'

At which point she nudged the Queen – I am told it was quite a hefty nudge – and said, 'Oh it's SLEEP. HE's here!'

Madam made a wonderful speech after the performance. She said she had been given the credit for the remarkable state of British ballet, but that she was not totally responsible. 'The one person who should be here today is Dame Marie Rambert.' Rambert had died a few years before. They had been rivals in the early days, but de Valois thought it important to share this moment with her friend and rival, who would have been a hundred years old. Her generosity is one of the factors that make her such a great person, and I, for one, was in tears. She took a standing ovation under a cascade of silver petals. Both the foyer and the auditorium were covered with flowers and silk banners. I always thought the degree of decoration is in accordance with the importance of the person whom the evening is honouring, and I had never seen the Opera House so decked out, with flower baskets hanging from every light bracket. I felt that it was a privilege to have been brought up in this world, surrounded by so many remarkable people. Such was the atmosphere that I felt the whole evening was raised to a higher level than usual, almost as if it was some parallel perfect dream. It was hard to believe I was there. Madam is ninety-eight. I still visit her sometimes.

My other break in this tour was when I invited the Princess of Wales to lunch at the mews. I came back from the tour especially for the day. I had also invited Anne Allan and George. Diana had been playing tennis with Steffi Graf, so I reckoned she should have worked up a bit of an appetite. She arrived, thirsty, with the healthy pink glow you get after a good work-out. It is not an unusual colour to find in her complexion, because she often blushes, which I find very attractive. She was pleased because she had been able to return some of Steffi's serves.

She arrived, with her detective, in an old jalopy. I expect a Jag and get a jalopy? I thought it was a bit naff and said so. 'It's my disguise,' she said. And I thought, how sensible.

I had prepared a separate meal for her detective, which he ate, accompanied by George, over the road in the studio. I cooked what I considered to be a healthy meal (knowing she likes healthy foods) for Princess Diana, Anne and me, although I spoilt it rather by producing a strawberry cream gâteau from the local French deli for dessert. We also ate rather a lot of the same chocolates we'd guzzled (and on which she nearly choked) before our dance together at the Friends' party.

Her detective gave us his rendition of 'Amazing Grace' complete with bagpipe imitations. This had Diana completely hysterical with laughter. She offered to do the washing up, which I guessed was something she probably rarely had the opportunity to do these days. I didn't let her, but gave her some T-shirts and mugs from *Song and Dance* for the boys and a scarf designed by Celia Birtwell for herself. Then I rushed back for my evening performance.

A few months after the meal at home Princess Diana suggested that we lunched together. She said, 'You choose.' So I decided that we might go to the Groucho Club, of which I am a member. George again did his duty and ate with her detective. The Princess and I were joined by my ballet mistress at another table. At the end of the meal Diana insisted on paying, and her detective was called over. He produced a credit card. I had always wondered if it was true that royalty never carried money. No sooner had we parted company than I saw an article in the *Evening Standard* reporting our lunch together and even disclosing the amount that she had paid for lunch. That was quick, boys! This was one time the press beat us to it.

I told the Princess about a year ago that I was going to gut the mews and rebuild it. She said, 'Well, have you got my room ready?' So I asked her what colour she wanted it to be painted.

'Pink', she said.

'You can't,' I said. 'That's my colour.'

'You would,' she said.

She called me once on the telephone. 'Hello, it's Diana here'

'Diana who?' I don't know any Dianas.

'It's me.'

'Me? Who's me?'

'Wales.'

I was forty that year. I didn't mark it in a major way – touring, I suppose, or fatigue in general. I did have lunch at the Ritz with a few friends. I chose it because the dining-room is quite one of the most stunning I know. And I had a tea party at the mews.

Funnily enough I celebrated my forty-first birthday in 1989 in greater style, by blocking off the mews with a hosepipe (nothing but the best for me) so we could party on the cobbles. The whole thing was organized by a friend from Derbyshire, Timothy. We bought several white plastic garden urns and filled them with coronation chicken, salads, raspberries, champagne. I borrowed small round marble tables from the Pineapple Centre canteen (which backed on to the mews) and laid them out over the cobbles. I opened up the studio for dancing, and used the stables for dishing out the food. Stephen, a builder friend, acted as bouncer. Most of my friends came. But I remember particularly that Freddie Mercury couldn't. I know, now, that he was already very ill, although I was not aware of it at the time. He sent me a Lalique box in his place and his roadies to act as DJs, and a completely mad friend from Dublin provided the entertainment. When asked what he did, he always replied, 'Bird impressions.' Mr. Pussy was a drag artist. It was a great day, and my guest of honour was Evelyn Laye.

The tour of *Song and Dance* ended in 1988, towards the end of November, and I went straight into panto in Aberdeen – to play the Dame. Trudi Moffat came over from Canada to choreograph it, and she has collaborated with me on several things since; Victor Spinetti (may he live for ever) headed the cast, which also included Liza Maxwell and Martin (Paul's son) Daniels; the whole run was sold out; and we had three days off over Christmas and New Year.

SIXTEEN

TOURING AND INJURY

IN 1989 I devised another tour using the second half of *Sleep With Friends*. The set was a dance studio with the musicians behind a screen. It was the same as before, with voice warm up-exercises turning into dance numbers, and a *pas-de-deux* lesson going into a song – 'Your Feet's Too Big' – because one of the ballerinas keeps treading on the man's toes and goads him beyond endurance. Marianne St Clair warmed up as the snooty ballerina on the barre which is then lifted with her on it by two boys. She dances with it, somersaulting over it, being lifted astride it, and sliding down it. Ingenious piece, I thought, choreographed by her husband, Michael Beare, who had been at the Upper School with me. I joined her for a duet, in which the interaction took place round a bowler hat with each one trying to get hold of it through variations in movement. The jokes of the first half were too 'in'. It was understood by dancers and anyone else who had studied dance. Otherwise it seemed to pass over the heads of most of the members of the audience. I was disappointed in the reaction. I thought, in my infinite wisdom, that because I had taken so much of myself and dance to the audience that they would understand the in-jokes that go on in a dance studio. But they didn't. There was a whole new generation to convince.

The second half was much more popular, a compilation of the best numbers from *Song and Dance*, *Cats*, *Cabaret* and *DASH*. A sort of *My Greatest Hits* – ha ha. Again the orchestra was an integral part of the action and was suspended above us on the set. This second act was lavishly costumed, which appealed far more to the general audience. The first was in practice clothes and rather plain. It taught me that glitz and showmanship was still wanted. We performed part of the show for the Variety Club of Great Britain that year. I called the show *Bits and Pieces* – a weak title. When we took it into the Dominion that summer I changed it to *Wayne's World of Dance*. The first night I got stuck in the lift on my way back to the dressing-room after the first act had finished. I sat there soaking wet from perspiration for most of the interval. The second night I slipped on an oil slick. Shades of my first choreographed piece – the fog gun had leaked all over the stage and as the Emcee in an excerpt from *Cabaret* I had to lose my German accent and in broad English ask for the curtain to come down. It took twenty minutes to scrub the oil off the floor before we could continue.

The advance bookings at the Dominion had not been very good, partly because it was summer and many loyal supporters had gone away on holiday. I brought in a PR, Connie Filipello (who had worked with, among others,

George Michael). With her help the audience figures were raised by quite a substantial amount, ensuring its success. There was a not very good review in the *Daily Mail*, but Sir David English (the *Mail*'s then editor) saw the show on the first night, and wanted to congratulate me for bringing dance to the public. To show his appreciation of this he expressed a desire to run a feature article on the show in his paper. He was obviously unaware of our bad review in his own paper. When he got to hear of it he was very annoyed and made up for it by demanding a full-page spread.

I had made several appearances on the Terry Wogan show years before, but when I broached the idea of coming on to talk about my new show I was turned down. Why? I do not know. Perhaps he had a little blacklist and I was on it! It would be good to know precisely where I had transgressed. It's very hard to play by the rules if you don't know what they are. However, when Ben Elton took over the slot for a season I was invited on. I had a performance in Southend that evening at 7.30, so when I finished the Elton/Wogan show at 6.45 the only way I was going to be able to get to Southend on time was by helicopter. I captured one at a brewery near the BBC TV centre, and half an hour later I was in my dressing-room in Southend. Just before I left the show, I said to the camera, 'Don't you worry, Southend – I'll be there in time!' just in case any of the potential audience saw me live at that hour and thought the show might be cancelled.

During the thirty-week tour, Paul Gregg (the tour organizer for Apollo) and I decided that the profits of one of the shows should go to one of the charities sponsored by the Princess of Wales. Diana came to the show and was happy to come backstage afterwards to chat with the cast. She was relaxed and asked one of them if I was a hard taskmaster. To which some wag replied, 'You betcher,' and I came up with some totally irrelevant, probably irreverent, and flippant comment. So flippant that I can't remember what it was. (It was one of those times when my mouth said something before my brain was in gear.) She turned to me and gave me one of those long looks under her brows and said, 'I'LL do the jokes.' Everyone laughed. She is a very witty person, good at telling jokes, and sends amusing cards.

Iris and Gwyneth dropped work for an evening at the Royal Ballet to come and see me at the Dominion. This, for me, was a daunting prospect because they were so used to seeing top dancers from the Royal Ballet performing at the top of their powers every night. I wondered how I would fare in comparison, particularly because it had been a long time since I had appeared with the company. Would they enjoy something that was aimed at a wider audience? I was much relieved by their comments in the dressing-room afterwards. They enjoyed the show.

We ended this gruelling tour with a stint in Munich. We were all exhausted. It had seemed to be an uphill struggle since day one. Summer, low bookings, some audiences small (but appreciative), and the first faint glimmerings of touring boredom within myself. But touring is part of the business – what else could I do? As yet I had no alternative.

I was disappointed to find that even after years of trying to make dance more accessible, the first half of *Bits and Pieces* was still deemed to be for the connoisseur. Things had changed since the last time I had toured with my own show. Dance had become less popular, and by the end of the eighties the boom was over, really. Dance centres were closing down all over Britain, though that was also a question of the recession starting to bite, plus VAT on tickets. The arts are the first to be hit when money begins to get tight and we had a good time in the heady spending days of the eighties. I was unwilling to go on expending energy on soothing the fractured nerves and smoothing the damaged egos of temperamental artists. I've got quite enough with myself, thanks so much – so no more agony aunt, no more problem-solver. I'd had enough, kept my distance, and thought – that's it. The only joy was performing in front of the public. Everything else began to be an irritant. Night after night having to warm up my tired body, having to hide negative thoughts, the show must go on – all this built up like a thundercloud. I was at the end of my touring tether. Even so, all those years of discipline, all those years of training with the Royal Ballet, kept me going. Professionalism rules the day, regardless of everything.

I was living alone by then, and the lack of companionship was getting to me. I could have borne that better if I had been enjoying the touring. I was spending less and less time in my own place and more and more time dossing on friends' sofas. I let the house get increasingly messy – it seemed to me a pointless act to clean it or put it in order. Who for? Me? I didn't care. I went out as much as possible and stayed out.

I was obliged to do some structural work on the house, however, and called in some builders. I became friendly with one of them, Stephen, and his family (I am, in fact, godfather to one of his children), and we went out together quite frequently. One night we were out late at a party and when we arrived back at his place, in the early hours, he found he had forgotten his key. He couldn't wake his wife so we went round the corner to a naff caff for some breakfast. There were some very loud people in this place, so we sat as far away from them as possible. The breakfast was inedible. We sent it back. The café owner disputed our claims of inedibility, but we were backed up by mutterings of agreement from the louder end of the caff. This scared the owner. He picked up the phone and called the police. I thought, 'Oh, ha ha. He isn't calling the police. Or if he is they won't do anything.'

The next thing I knew was that Stephen and I were being asked to accompany them to the police station. What?

'What for?' I asked. 'I haven't finished my tea yet.' One of the cops put it into a plastic cup.

'Why?' I asked.

'Intent not to pay.'

I produced my 50p for the bill and slapped it on the counter. I found myself off the ground with a half-nelson round my neck. Stephen told the cop to put me down. Which he did. In the police van Stephen and I found ourselves staring at these two officers. One of them nudged the other and said, ''Ere. 'E looks like Wayne Sleep.'

The van careered across the walkway on a public park and into the station. There we were asked to empty our pockets. Stephen was first and placed keys and envelopes addressed to W.P.C. Sleep on the desk. The police looked baffled. Stephen has the build of a builder, not a dancer. I rose to my full height and said, 'He's wearing my coat.'

I emptied my pockets. One of the items was the door number of Stephen's house, which had fallen off when we were trying to wake his wife. The policeman gloated at me.

'Aha! Vandalism!'

It was Stephen's turn to rise. He said, 'That is my private property and I do not wish to press charges.'

By this time all the cleaners were gathered round and it was turning into quite a show. I was lifted by the neck again and taken to a cell. Stephen looked at the number on the door.

'There's a one on the door, but no star,' he announced. We were released an hour later with no charge. A few weeks later the headlines in the paper read: 'Wayne's Night In The Nick.' I wonder who told them about that.

I went to one of Tiffany's famous breakfasts, where they invite celebrities to drink champagne and look around the shop. There was a bangle on my side plate, and I thought, well, if it's on my side plate, it must be for me. And because I'm not one to wear jewellery, I offered it to Sian Phillips, who was sitting next to me. It was so big and chunky I could not believe it was real and thought it must have come out of a cracker. I didn't know it was worth at least £10,000 or so, pure gold, stuffed with rubies and only put on my plate to view. I went off to the West End to Bentley's, where I had a lunch meeting with two of my builders. Sitting at the table behind me was Oliver Reed, who was in London to promote his latest single – a duet with Hurricane Higgins. We joined his table for coffee and liqueurs. He was not at all like the picture that had been painted of him and I liked him instantly. It was his eloquence and knowledge of Shakespeare and the theatre that engaged me. Plus he was very funny. We decided to go out on the town. He said I could be his minder. I loved the idea. We were the Great Dane and the Jack Russell looking for fun.

We arrived at the Groucho Club at six in the evening – not the hour to be merry when all around are winding down after work. I was annoyed by two ladies who doted on Oliver, but kept calling me 'little' and 'small'. I finally stood up to my full height and shouted at them,

'I'm fed up with you calling me small. Don't do it again. Come on Olly, we're leaving.'

Silence. Broken only by a lone voice calling after me, as we left, 'Night-night, Shorty!' Too good a line to top.

We went to the restaurant nearby, where Oliver stood in the doorway and was greeted by the *mâitre d'*.

'Hello, Oliver, how are you.'

I appeared from behind Oliver and said, sweetly, 'Good evening.'

A look of horror crossed the *mâitre d*'s face and he said, 'Not the two of you together.'

We went off to a much better restaurant where the staff were not influenced by preconceptions. We invented a game – I'd give him a word, and he had to remember a quote from Shakespeare which included it. He won with flying colours and we went our separate ways.

After the *Bits and Pieces* tour, I went to Athens to direct my first cabaret. I held an open audition and saw very few good dancers. Many girls are reluctant to work abroad because they are often expected to perform more than the contract states. And the impresario wanted young girls. So I had to audition college leavers with little or no experience. I worked on them with Anne Allan, night and day, to knock some sort of shape into them. Then, when we arrived in Athens, we found the night club only half finished. This, obviously, meant a delay in opening. I was only supposed to be there for two weeks, to make sure the routines were smooth. The impresario pleaded with me to stay longer and wait at least until the stage had been built, in order to see a run-through. It wasn't on, as far as I was concerned. Pleaded is the wrong word. He demanded. But I was already contracted for a pantomime, and was not going to break a contract. He did not want to hear this. But I left. Anne managed to cancel some engagements in London and stayed on out of loyalty to the dancers.

I flew back to London to start rehearsals, but not before I had seen a run-through of sorts done on the stage by these poor unfortunates, among the rubble and open brickwork and all things electrical. I felt I was abandoning them, like the rat leaving the ship, but there was nothing I could do. They opened after Christmas, and even Ann could not stay long enough to see the first performance, so I have no idea of the end result. I spoke to some of the dancers when they returned to London. They said it had been impossible to dance, because they came on after the singing star, and he was showered every night with paper plates full of gardenias. They often came a cropper, they said, trying to dance on all the slippery gardenia petals. Lovely to look at, but hell for performing. Poor things.

If 1989 sounds like a year I was happy to get rid of, there was one highlight for me. I was given an Honorary Doctorate of Letters from Exeter University. (Yes, I know, very funny, considering I find it very difficult to finish a book, but I did feel mighty honoured nevertheless, and it is one of the most congenial things that has happened to me.) My mother and Stanley came to the ceremony, to see me dressed in the blue and red robes and black velvet cap to receive this award. I was to give the speech on behalf of all the other graduates and graduands. George and I arrived the night before to have dinner with the Chancellor, his wife and staff.

I was told not to speak for more than twenty minutes – ten to fifteen would be ideal. What? Help! I'd only prepared two minutes at best. I sat up half the night with George in order to lengthen my speech.

Mr Chancellor, Mayor, Distinguished Guests, Fellow Graduates. Nothing could have surprised me more than to have been honoured in this way by an English University. I hope they won't now take my Honorary Degree of Doctor of Letters away when I confess that I rarely write and seldom read. I do however know the alphabet. I have even choreographed letters, using the dancers' bodies to form the title of my show called *DASH*. Forming the D was easy, the A a cinch, but when it came to the S you can imagine what contortions their bodies went through to form that letter. Luckily my company was called *DASH* and not the Sadlers Wells Royal Ballet. We'd have been in real trouble there forming those words. Being the only unsubsidized company in Britain we could not have afforded the extra bodies anyway.

Looking at all the graduates here I feel a bit of a fake as I realize how hard you have all had to work to achieve your degrees. I was given mine. But then again I suppose I have had to study just as intensively in a different way to achieve my goals. At the age of thirteen, having come from a working-class background, I was lucky enough to have won a Leverhulme Scholarship to the Royal Ballet School and from there eventually won a place in the Royal Ballet at the Opera House, Covent Garden. Theatre is a great source of revenue for this country and it is the one thing in the world for which we are universally acclaimed, without reservation. And yet as a nation we spend hardly any money on making performers. Dance is particularly appealing to foreign visitors because, like music, it transcends language.

The ballets I have appeared in have relied on literature, *Romeo and Juliet*, the Scottish play, Turgenev's *Month in the Country*. I have even appeared in a musical that certainly put T.S. Eliot on the West End map, not to mention the composer, what's his name – oh yes, in alphabetical order, Andrew Lloyd Webber. Of course I'm referring to *Cats*.

But new talent must be encouraged and nurtured. For instance – I hope that when I return to this University there will be a faculty for all the performing arts, not just the Drama Department. The problem with English kids, as I know to my cost, having auditioned hundreds of them, is that they specialize in one aspect of theatre, unlike their American contemporaries who learn jazz, ballet, tap, modern singing and acting to become all-rounders.

It is heartening, however, to note that a new school for dance has just opened in Dawlish. These enterprises are greatly needed at regional level. Not everyone can go to London. Not everyone can afford the Royal Ballet

School, which in my day, believe it or not, was the most expensive school in Britain.

If I may be permitted to whip my old hobby horse, I have relentlessly tried to remove the élitism from ballet and make it more egalitarian, as it is more or less everywhere else in the world. In this country there is still, in some quarters, a misunderstanding of dance as something only girls do, or it's only for the rich and pompous. Dance is essentially an entertainment and that is what we have always tried to make our shows, first and foremost, entertaining.

My publicity people would never have chosen this day for this ceremony because it is the bicentenary of Bastille Day and I fear in terms of newsworthiness we are going to be rather eclipsed by an event that took place 200 years ago. But I do hope the local media know just how much I appreciate this honour being given to a local boy. Although I spend much of my time in London, I was born in Plymouth and still feel very attached to the West Country, and to Devon, where my family still live. In fact when my mother heard that I was to receive this degree she jokingly said [in a Devon accent] – 'Oh, I always really wanted you to be a doctor.'

Being small as a dancer I have been rather type-cast into parts such as Puck in *The Dream*, and Jester in *Cinderella*. I've played most of the animal kingdom, even Squirrel Nutkin in *The Tales of Beatrix Potter*. You could say I've always had an affinity with the seven dwarfs. After all I was born Sleepy, always been Dopey, sometimes Happy, never Bashful, often Grumpy, in winter Sneezy, but I never thought until today I'd ever be Doc.

I confess to some disappointment that the public orator chose to address us in English rather than Latin. I have just come back from a couple of days in New York, where Vice-president Dan Quayle mentioned that he very much regretted not having kept up his Latin at school as he is just about to make an official visit to Latin America.

Disraeli said: 'Upon the education of this country, the fate of this country depends.' If I were to dare to offer any advice to the undergraduates now graduates it would be to spread your knowledge and hand it on to others so they too can share in your good fortune. So may I, Sir, on behalf of all the graduates who had to work for their degrees, thank you for conferring our degrees in such a pleasant and memorable ceremony. We wish all the young men and women with very new initials after their names every success in their chosen career. I am sure they will all remember with affection, Exeter, the University that nurtured them.

I was also made a Fellow of the Royal Society of Arts. Wayne Sleep, Hon.D.Litt, FRSA. Mum was thrilled. It meant that all her sacrifices, all her scrimping to pay for classes, were worth it. She was so proud. I was a 'Doctor'. It was a long, long way from the compromise of black patent shoes and white ankle socks.

And panto in Eastbourne at the Congress Theatre. This was the contract I refused to break. Some of these seaside places are quite fun in winter, sort of woolly and wild. It gives one a different take on some of our seaside resorts. Mac drove me down in the Daimler most days. We always set off in good time but there are occasions where Fate puts a foot in it. Like the time when eighty-mile-an-hour winds blew in our face. Articulated trucks were overturned and lay on their sides by the road like beached whales. There was no way to make the matinée and phoned the theatre to tell them to get my understudy ready. In fact I did get there, just before my entrance, but he was all dolled up in my costume, shaking like a leaf, script in hand, waiting to go on. As I arrived I saw his face drop, and didn't have the heart to deny him his chance. I let him do the first scene. The audience noticed nothing – we were the same height, in thick make-up, plaited wig and hooped frock. Gertie, the Queen of the Circus had arrived.

I was invited back to the Royal Ballet, much to my pleasure, to perform the part of Alain in *La Fille Mal Gardée* at the Royal Opera House. I went with my mother to Kensington Palace for Christmas drinks, where the Princess told me she had booked tickets for my performance. Going back to the cocoon of the Royal Ballet was a welcome treat. A sixty-piece orchestra, rehearsals and classes all scheduled (none of that arranging and rushing and making do), and to perform, again, in the theatre where it had all started and which I loved so much – it was, well, just like coming home. I felt the surge of approval from a full house as I came on stage. The Princess was sitting in her box and I was so happy, and proud, to be appearing on that stage again with Lesley Collier. By then Anthony Dowell was Director of the company. But it was the last time I was to see and to work with Iris. She died shortly afterwards of a brain tumour. The redoubtable Leslie Edwards was also performing in this production, playing my father. Yes, I was glad to be back.

I was, however, surprised at how the company was performing as a whole. Although technique had improved so much since I started there, *Fille* relies a lot on the spirit of the *corps*. The style of performance had become more laid back, but during rehearsals I was determined to instill the sense of fun which is essential to the production into the dancers of the *corps*. It took time, but I was pleased with the result. As Lesley Collier said, after the performance, if *Fille* can't bring a smile to a dancer's face, what can? Indeed. But it seems that certain dancers set styles. When I was young there was Lynn Seymour and Christopher Gable and Rudolf Nureyev – all expansive and outgoing – and we copied them. These days the leading dancers are more laid-back and cool about their presentation, and so many of the company follow suit. Me? I do prefer a little oomph, a little show, a little demonstration. You are having to reach out a long way in the Royal Opera House. It could be the influence of the television, in part, which brings things so close, and extrovert acting is deemed a sin of the highest order.

I had been dancing solidly for a year and was glad to be going on holiday to Australia. The plan was to stay with David Hockney in Los Angeles on the way over. Mike Walsh, the king of Australian chat shows, who had left television to become a theatre producer, offered to give me some introductions to people in the Australian TV world. The idea was to make some TV appearances in order to test the climate for taking one of my shows over there. I went round to Mike's flat in Floral Street with George, to celebrate the start of my holiday and to pick up Mike's contact addresses. I was sitting on the floor, with one leg tucked under me and the other bent behind me. We raised our glasses to toast the fact that I had managed to complete forty weeks of dancing without injury. Mike was being very animated about his production of *Anything Goes* in Sydney, and in the course of explanation and gesture accidentally tripped over and fell on my bent left leg. I felt a tear near my kneecap. I realized immediately this was serious. I tried to get up, but couldn't, without help, and then found I could not put any weight on my leg. Oddly enough I felt no pain, except with the first tearing. After dancing for a year with no injuries, always being aware of the possibilities, always warming up before going on, always taking care, it was ironic that the moment I relaxed, away from the stage, some person unconnected with my dancing to date should fall on top of me and cause a major injury. But like so many things that are big in one's life, there is no warning, no trumpets, no prophets of doom. It just happens. And here I was, about to go on holiday, and (I hoped) to appear on TV to show myself, my ability and my shows off. Ha bloody ha.

The next morning I telephoned Shirley at the Remedial Dance Clinic and she told me to get down there jolly quick for an X-ray and a look. The bad news was that Mr Howse was on holiday and his locum always operates on a Friday, so no one could look at me – until Monday. Shirley gave me some crutches and packed me off home in a taxi. God, I felt low. I could stand only on one leg, which was very tiring. I telephoned Tony Rudenko and one of my friends, Kevin, asked them to come over, and gave them some dosh to get a takeaway. This they did, and I ate, propped up in bed, while they tried to make me laugh, but nothing they said seemed to be very funny. I was about rock bottom. But I hadn't got there yet. After they'd gone, I hobbled into the kitchen to find that they had not bothered to wash up. It was enough to make me cry with anger. It's usually immaterial to me, but when you are really down it seems like a betrayal if friends don't think about doing something simple like the washing-up. I got through the weekend, feeding myself by hobbling to the kitchen, getting a tin of baked beans, an opener, a bottle of water, carrying it back to the bedroom in a carrier bag slung over my arm. Then sat eating these cold baked beans out of a tin. Miserable between the sheets.

Edith Foxwell determined to get me out for a night, to cheer me up. She found this Chippendale-type person, who got me out of bed and took me down the stairs in a fireman's lift to the party. I held court – I felt like Ashton in the

old days. It was Monday before I could see the specialist who had booked me
into a hospital an hour away in Kent on the Wednesday. I had to taxi there –
none of my friends was available to take me – where were they? God knows. I
felt as if my left leg was hanging by a thread. Whether it was or not didn't matter, it felt like it. It turned out that I had torn my medial ligament. There is one
each side of the knee, a short connection between the femur and the tibia, and
you can tell if one is torn because you can push your leg sideways and it moves
beyond the perpendicular below the knee. The surgeon wanted to perform an
arthroscopy, which meant putting a little camera inside to determine the extent
of the damage. I didn't want any little thing wiggling away inside there possibly
making things worse and certainly inflaming the whole area. I had talked to a
few fellow dancers who had had arthroscopies and they all said that it took at
least a week before the swelling went down, which meant an extra week before
the plaster went on. And I didn't have the luxury of time. I was due to start
rehearsals for a six-month run of *Song and Dance* at the Shaftesbury Theatre in
the West End after I came back from Oz, and there was no chance of making
that in time if I let someone poke about. So there I was in bed in the hospital,
refusing to sign the form for the anaesthetic, while the surgeon tried to persuade
me that, 'It won't make it any worse,' which I did not believe, whatever he said.
I said I was prepared to take the risk of having it put in plaster straight away and
see if that mended it, and if it didn't then my run at the Shaftesbury would be
out of the window anyway, because I would have to have the ligament stitched
back together. If I had an operation I was unlikely to make the *Song and Dance*
run, but with the plaster, I reckoned it was a bit better than evens. So he
plastered me from my toes to the top of my thigh – and then I had to go back
the next day to be replastered because some of the original plaster had set on
my Achilles tendon. Lovely.

I was not going to cancel my trip. (Although I did have to cancel any TV
appearances in Australia – I could hardly be introduced as Britain's most well-
known dancer and then come hobbling on encased in plaster . . .) Apart from
the fact that I wanted a holiday, I decided that I could not possibly be seen
around the West End in plaster, obviously looking undanceworthy. At the least
the producers would have replaced me like a flash with some Russian: at the
worst the whole thing would be cancelled. I had to go, and both Los Angeles
and Australia were far enough away that no one would get twitchy.

Two days later I was sitting uncomfortably in a jumbo jet on my way to LA.
I was to stay with David when I arrived in Los Angeles. David took me to
dinner at the Helmut Newtons' apartment in the Chateau Marmont Hotel,
with Billy Wilder and his wife, and Vincent Price and Coral Browne.

David had painted the pool at the Hollywood Roosevelt Hotel: the place
had been totally revamped and was no longer $6 a night as it was when I was
last there, aged twenty-one. I found it difficult getting around in the plaster
and David sought to help, or at least alleviate the suffering, by painting a blue

and red bone on the outside of the plaster. I have often wondered what I might have got for a strange Hockney, painted on an article that was useless once it came off my leg.

In Sydney I stayed with Dolly and Ken East. They shared an apartment, then, with Elton John's manager John Reid, on Elizabeth Bay. A wonderful view – you could almost reach out and touch the yachts as they passed into the marina below. My hosts badgered Qantas into upgrading my seat to first class on the way back. It gave me more room. They did this because an airline steward had been pretty rude on the way out about my being in the ordinary cabin with my leg in plaster. In his view I should have paid extra for first class.

I came back to London via Los Angeles again, but the only thing on my mind was: what was the verdict going to be on my leg? I was certain of two things: that it would be all right, that it would not be all right. My mind went crazy, alternating between the two. When the plaster came off after six or seven weeks, the leg and ligament were inspected by the surgeon, who pronounced it healed. Relief. Such relief. But I had a leg which was less than half as fit as the other one. It was atrophied. Over the next four weeks I was to have the strictest regime and curriculum of my career.

I had forgotten how to walk correctly. I could hardly bend my knee. I telephoned Joan Lawson, who had taught me all those years ago, and who was now specializing in the reparation of dancers' body injuries. It was only a matter of weeks to the first preview.

My day started at 8.30 A.M. at the Remedial Dance Clinic with physio from Shirley, forcing the leg to bend to the point where I could bear it no longer. Then I would be off to Joan's house, in Golders Green, to learn all the basic ballet positions. It was – starting again.

Joan laid me on the floor, with my feet against the wall in first position, and we began the process of teaching my left leg how to dance again from the very beginning. Then at 3 P.M. I would go to Gordon Thompson to practise the Pilates Method of Body Control on his machines. This method is now used in all major dance companies and schools, and it allows you to keep your body fit while lying down. So a dancer, or any person with an injury, can tone up their body without having to put weight on the damaged part. The day would finish at 5 P.M., and I would get home exhausted. The whole process would begin again the next morning. And I was on a strict diet. It was pretty bleak; right then I felt as if I might be doing this for the rest of my life. And after three weeks nothing seemed to have improved, and the deadline for the first night was only three weeks away. I was beginning to entertain doubts about making it. At least the producers had not heard about the injury, and any pre-publicity interviews were done sitting down. If word had got out that I couldn't walk it would have affected the box office. And the producers still might replace me.

After a couple more weeks I asked Joan if she could come to the studio to put me through some barre work. I could just walk, and I had only a week before the first preview. It seemed impossible that I was going to make this, so they were told I had an injury, that I would miss the previews but be there for the opening night. Luckily Paul Gregg acquiesced. The previews lasted a week and a half so I had two and a half weeks to sort it out.

I went with Joan to a studio every day and tried to dance. I was frightened of putting weight on the leg – I had visions of tearing it again or, worse, an injury for life. I was jumping on a straight leg, not being able to release my knee enough to cushion the jump. At least my weight loss helped by then, because there was less pressure on the bad leg. I finally got to the Centre and started to rehearse. It was all very well getting back into dancing *per se*, but I still had to learn and rehearse the piece, so now I was working until ten o'clock in the evening re-learning steps, and learning bits that had been changed for this revival. By the time I was fitted for costumes I could walk properly, so there was now little danger that people might imagine I was unable to dance. I was continuing my 8.30 A.M. treatments, going to class with Joan, followed by body control with Gordon and finally to rehearsals in the evenings. At the first preview I hid in a box, so no one could see me, to watch my understudy. And I was still wondering if I would make it to the first night in just over a week's time. The answer, thanks to Joan, Gordon, Shirley, and any divinity (and my own determination) was 'Yes', and I was on for the press night.

I used this injury as a barometer, as an omen. If it didn't mend, it was time to give up. I was of an age to stop and turn to something else, though quite what I still was not sure. If it mended, I would take it as a sign that I was supposed to go on, that I had more to do. It mended.

The production ran for about six months in the West End and then went on tour. During this time I did a couple of galas, sacked George as my manager, and sold the car. I could not afford to keep Mac any more; the Daimler did only eight miles to the gallon and cost a lot to maintain. Mac already had other clients so he could continue to ply his chauffeuring trade. (And I was able to use him occasionally.) George was always being sacked, usually in the middle of the night (his time). He would receive a phone call at five o'clock in the morning from me on tour somewhere in the world blaming him for some local problem, such as bad service from the hotel, planes not on time, stages slippery, etc., etc. He once told me that I telephoned him in London from Los Angeles and without so much as 'Hello' said 'Where's my *other* sock?' George thought that I expected to be congratulated for having already solved half the problem!

One of the galas, at the London Palladium, was with the legendary and everlasting Carol Channing, who came over to do a special one-night performance of *Hello Dolly*, which she had created in New York. I was to do a guest appearance with Amanda, who was one of my partners from *Song and Dance*. We danced to one of the songs of the piece. Chita Rivera also came over from the States just for the gala. When the lights came up on her, she was standing with her back to the audience, which by this time was really getting into the spirit of the evening with whoops and calls and loads of applause. Very un-English. Even before Chita Rivera turned round they just went *loopy*. She once gave me a very descriptive compliment: 'Wayne, when you dance, you kick the ass out of the air.' One of my favourite quotes.

The other gala was the ninetieth birthday of the Queen Mother – at the Palladium again. The whole cast were asked to perform the finale of *Song and Dance* after we'd finished our performance of the evening. Then I was asked by Norman Maen, the director, if I would dance a Charleston (choreographed by Alan Harding) at the beginning of the evening. I thought: well, if Marti's singing until about 8.30, and if I went on at about 7.45, pretty much at the beginning of the show, then it might be possible.

The dancers and I did a rip-roaring Charleston in the first forty-five minutes of the evening; I was put in a car and rushed back to the Shaftesbury for my part in *Song and Dance*, and after our finale the whole cast was bundled into a coach – all of us still in costume – to be taken to the Palladium. We arrived *just in time* to dance part of our show as the finale of the Queen Mother's birthday show. This was the second time in my life that I had performed twice in one night in the same theatre, travelling to another to play a part in between. It was like being in the old music halls, where it was normal for an act to open the show in one theatre, zip across the river to another to open the second half, and finish by topping the bill in Islington. There were some who thought I was mad to try. I found the adrenalin rush very exhilarating and I loved it. I was actually quite sorry that it was only for one evening. My mother came to it with Auntie Ruth. This was one performance that they were never going to miss.

I had a short holiday, after which *Song and Dance* toured, and I found myself in Plymouth a few weeks before Christmas. The City Fathers asked me to turn on the Christmas lights. It was one of the simplest acts, but it was such a pleasure to do. I was treated as the local boy made good, but at the same time I felt that I had never gone away, that I was still the silly Wayne who used to follow his cousin Barry around and get in trouble with him. It is a really good feeling to be recognized and fêted by your home town, particularly if your family is still there, and Plymouth is a town of such genuine people.

There was an ad-lib I added to the show half-way through the tour. During the mime scene where I fight with one of my partners, I added in a plaintive cry 'I want my mummy.' In the last performance of *Song and Dance* in Plymouth, unbeknown to me, my mother came on at that point and shoved a dummy in my mouth. As it was near the end of the show I brought her on in the finale, to audience cheers.

This tour had been a relaxing one for me, because I didn't have to produce or direct or organize, I just had to perform. What bliss.

Then guess what – panto again.

SEVENTEEN

MARKING TIME

GOOD OLD PANTO. Good old *Aladdin*. Good old Guildford Civic Hall. Good old Sleep. Same thing over and over again. I was stuck in a rut. I needed a new agent. Nothing was happening for me except repeats. *Song and Dance* was OK, but I'd done it before and so it was not very inspiring. My agent and I had been drifting further and further apart until there seemed to be no communication whatever.

Brian Marshall was directing *Aladdin* at Guildford that year. I'd worked with him before, when he was the comedian in Danny la Rue's *Aladdin*. I confided my beefs and frustrations to him and found that he knew the variety circuit and suggested that I get a cabaret act together.

My only venture to date into cabaret had been naïve. Brian's suggestion was for me and four girls, talking to the audience and going into dance numbers – old favourites or new ones created for the occasion. I decided to give it a go. It seemed . . . a good move.

I joined his agency and he booked me a tour in the smaller theatres round the country. It was an eye-opener. *Wayne's World of Dance* was booked everywhere to do the second forty-five minutes of an evening's entertainment, and had no control over what happened in the first forty-five minutes. It could be anything from a juggler or a magician, to a singer or comedian. I found that people who came to see me (and they did) resented having to sit through a first half without my appearing, and I extended my act to two sets of forty-five minutes. We'd arrive in a theatre (some places were cinemas on alternate nights) to find a list of forthcoming attractions in the foyer saying something like 'TONITE – WAYNE SLEEP. TOMORROW – MR. WONG AND HIS AMAZING DOVES – SEE THEM SHIFT WEIGHTS.' That was the sort of quality act I was up against.

Cabaret is exposing. They see your spots, your warts, your sweat. You are in such close confines yet you have to win them over. I learned how to chat to the audience, how to hold their attention while changing clothes, shoes, wiping my face down with a towel. The best cabaret artists walk into a space, whatever size, whatever type, as if they are walking into their own living-room. But as a dancer it was not easy. We need certain things, such as decent lighting, a good floor (I toured my own), changes of costume even if only minimal. A comedian on the whole needs only spotlight and microphone. He can walk on to the stage and he has everything there and just be himself. It requires a lot of guts, and it is an absolute art to be oneself. I had to be myself and other people through the dance as well. Goodness, though, I discovered how different it was, not having the back-up of a big show, and being laid so bare in front of the public was the hardest thing I have ever done. It was a damn good experience.

But I did not care for the cabaret venues very much. It was all small theatres, small rooms, often very squashed – particularly for five dancers. In the past I had only toured in the major theatres and was unaware that these places existed. Some of the venues we performed in were dead seedy. I had a van and a stage manager, and between us and the girls, we did everything – lighting, costumes – everything. There is hardly ever any permanent staff in such places either. So it is very much down to you to turn on your own lights. And of course your publicity is only as good as the theatre's publicity – and if they don't plaster your name around, your name simply won't get around.

We had a minimal band (Musicians' Union rules) but used tapes as well. And I had to beware of letting my act look like a smaller version of previous performances – and it is difficult after having a large band, twelve dancers and big production numbers to scale it down to cabaret size. But that was part of the attraction, the intimacy. It was a buzz to make it work. It *is* the hardest form of entertainment – just you and the audience.

By then I'd covered pretty well everything in my career – starting with the classical: the Royal Opera House, then the West End, film, TV, tours, panto and, with cabaret, even the end of the pier. I have performed in major theatres, minor theatres, churches, the open air, tents, pavilions, leisure centres, night clubs.

I didn't think there was much left for me to try.

Although I was never out of work, my career was not expanding. Ten years before I had created my own place in the market. I expected others to follow in my tracks but the jungle closed behind me. I'd thought that after I broke new ground there would be loads of offers of one sort or another. But what happened? Nothing. I thought the telephone would ring. Did it? The beastly thing sat in silent conspiracy. I found that to get work I had to create work. And this was beginning to exhaust me. Low? My feet were sticking out the bottom.

On top of this, my life at home was in total disarray. I was living by myself and had let the place go almost to total ruin. Michael Jason, who had been wardrobe master on *Cabaret* and *Wayne's World of Dance* and was renting out the studio for me, came over to clean up once in a while – but even he gave up eventually. I had, I admit with some embarrassment, become rather slovenly. I have no idea what happened to that nice and tidy Wayne who was held up as such an example of neatness by his aunts for his cousins to follow. Vanished, poor sod. I left dishes in the sink, I hated opening letters especially if they were bills, and my life really needed organizing. That's when the wife of a colleague said that she had this friend called Miriam who would come and sort me out. So she arrived and put my house, my office and my life in order. Everything was cleaned up. It was neat enough to be seen on *Through the*

Keyhole for Yorkshire TV. The best reason for doing that programme is that it really makes you tidy the house . . .

Things started to pick up. I was slightly surprised to find that I could work much better when I wasn't in a mess – I'd convinced myself that it made no difference. Pure justification for my laziness. I made a video, *Step Into Ballet*, in 1991, to be released that autumn. This was when I began to take more interest in teaching and with the idea of giving back some of the knowledge that I had acquired throughout my career. The video started with the simplest things – how to put your shoes on, what best to wear for ballet class, and some basic starter exercises that any one could use. But Chrysalis, the company that made this video, never distributed the tapes so they have hardly ever been seen. I know they are sitting somewhere on a shelf in a warehouse. I also know that most of the libraries in the country have outstanding orders for this video. Curiously, I have just seen it advertised for sale on the Internet. First I'd heard of it.

1991 was the year I became more and more involved in charity events and galas. This seems to happen as you get older. Once you have directed one, the word gets round! And pleadings come from all sides for you to direct, take part, choreograph others. I think it is important for people who have made it to make themselves available to help those who are less fortunate. But I have one stipulation – and that is that most of the money that is raised should go to the charity for which the event is being held. I very much mind if organizers cream off most of the takings for 'administrative' details, and there are such people around who spend their lives making money out of charitable events. I think it is just not on.

Princess Diana has come to the ones I organize and I always donate part of the proceeds raised to one of her charities. Her presence will always draw people in (with the presence of royalty, as much as £250 upwards can be charged for a ticket). Some of the causes I am involved in are hardly known outside the world of dance – the Benesh notation system, for example, or the Wheelchair Dance Association, a charity with which I am most closely involved.

Although directing and performing in various galas in aid of different causes, I was still touring my cabaret act around the country and choreographed a Stravinsky piece for Marianne St Clair and myself at the Queen Elizabeth Hall. I did part of my cabaret act in a tent at Windsor for Zoo Check. The wooden boards in the tent were placed directly on grass, and every time you jumped on a board, the next one would flip up and hit you in the knee, if not the nose. Unpredictable, and quite exciting, if occasionally painful, but everyone, both performers and audience, took it in good spirit. The evening was organized by Virginia McKenna – we had a great dance together after the performance. I was delighted to meet her – I found her to be a person of great strength of character.

Because of the success of *A Good Night's Sleep*, which I had co-directed at the

Adelphi Theatre some years before, the Royal Society for the Protection of Birds asked me to mount a charity gala for them at Covent Garden. It was to be attended by the Princess of Wales, with a lush dinner at the Savoy afterwards.

The theme, of course, was birds – a Carnival of Birds. The organizers asked world-famous designers to link up with choreographers to create pieces on this theme. And the designers weren't just any old designers, they were luminaries: Lagerfeld, Versace, Anthony Price, Vivienne Westwood, Katherine Hamnett, Armani, Jasper Conran. Hair-raising on a number of levels, when you think about it. All that co-ordination, co-operation and dealing with some fairly large egos, difficult temperaments and young and nervous choreographers for whom this was a first night. I was to effect all the liaisons, find the choreographers and determine the order of the programme.

But I was called in half-way through, when most of the groundwork had been done. This meant that I could not shape the evening entirely to my liking, only build on what had already been achieved. So for a number of reasons directing this charity was a little trepidatious.

It is hard enough, even at the best of times, even when you know the pieces, to decide the flow of a programme, but when some of the pieces being choreographed are not likely to be finished until the evening – it is a supreme headache. I could only go by the music they were dancing to and so determining the order was a nightmare married to educated or inspired guesses; with flexibility built in, as well – some items did have to be moved around on the night. All choreographers, even the best, are capable of flops, but there was nothing I was going to be able to do about that. And the theme was rather limited and confining, particularly for a one night gala. Every piece was to be about birds.

Evelyn Glennie had already agreed to take part, so in order to vary the diet still further I asked not only the likes of Darcey Bussell, Viviana Durante and Eva Evdockimova. I choreographed a sequence for myself and thirty other tap dancers. I came on as the red red robin dressed in all-over Katherine Hamnett red sequins. I flew in from the wings and had to wear a leather harness, which I thought I was going to have to wear underneath the skin-tight sequins, but Katherine Hamnett decided that it looked very fetching over the top so she encrusted it with rubies and made a feature of it.

Sarah Brightman sang a song composed for the occasion by Andrew Lloyd Webber, thus fulfilling an ambition to sing at the Royal Opera House. Natalia Makarova, who was in London with a production from Chichester, came on in Anthony Price which received a great roar from the audience and recited a poem that none of us could understand, even though it was in English.

One of the coups of the evening was the appearance of the Bolshoi Ballet. It was also the cause of the greatest friction of the evening. The Bolshoi were being dressed by Versace, who had designed costumes that were incredibly beautiful but made partnering impossible. They were bejewelled, which meant that the man cut his hands on his partner's costume, and full-skirted, so the costume banged against her partner. They were very sorry but could not possibly dance in them and would wear their own costumes. It fell to me, in the interval, to tell Versace that the Bolshoi could not use his costumes. I was very nervous, but it had to be done. He had come all that way to see the performance and I thoroughly expected a scene. I offered as a compromise that the costumes would be paraded at the end of the show, but he said that if they would not dance in his designs, then his designs would not be shown and stipulated that I would have to make an announcement to this effect. He was very professional about it and not at all what I had expected. These fabulous costumes must have taken a lot of thought to design and a long time to make. Someone from *Vogue* said that if the costumes were not worn then the number must be cut. No way!

Oh, there were other hiccups – Eva Evdockimova broke her foot, and there was a pause of about forty seconds while some hasty juggling was done, with someone who should have been ready and was not – and forty seconds is a gap of deathly proportions if you are sitting in an audience and waiting. As it is, that evening was instrumental in showing me how vital it is to keep calm and in control, to ensure that the wheels of the event are well oiled. A gala is like mounting a West End show with only one day's rehearsal – on the day of performance. Events of this type take about six months to produce and have to run alongside everything else in one's life. A lot of money was raised, helped by the National Youth Orchestra giving their services for free.

The Carnival of the Birds taught me a lot. It was a successful evening but did not arouse the kind of excitement that some galas generate. And there were various things that I would never do again. Coming in half-way through is one. Having a too limited theme and working with too many unknown quantities (designers and more than enough choreographers) are two more. But my mother enjoyed the evening. The highlight for her was to sit next to the Princess of Wales for the entire performance.

This was the start of my directing charity galas. I have, to date, directed four more. There is Design for Dance at Her Majesty's Theatre, a Benesh event at St John's, Smith Square, one for the English National Ballet in the hallowed marble of the Foreign Office and *90 Years of Dance* at the Britten Theatre. This does not include various appearances with the likes of Barnardo's, National Youth Ballet and the Wheelchair Dance Association. I am currently in the process of putting together something to raise money for them. Many people won't give to a charity like this because they say that dancing is purely recreational. But for so many it is wonderful therapy.

Then *Aladdin* (yes, yet again – I was beginning to think I could live in that bottle) at Tunbridge Wells. The highlight of the year was to follow. I was asked to go on a concert tour with Lorna Luft (daughter of Judy Garland and half-sister of Liza Minnelli) in *Hollywood and Broadway*. This was billed as a Celebration of the Golden Era of Stage and Screen, and is just the sort of material that is close to my heart. It always takes me back to the days before White Lodge, when my mother and I would sit in the cinema, mesmerized by the glorious song and dance routines on the screen.

We were doing a tour of ninety dates, ranging from Inverness to Plymouth, Dublin to Jersey. For once the management had worked out a reasonable tour with not too much travelling from one end of the country to the other, coming back to London most nights to sleep in my own bed. Bliss. Even so, after two and a half months, and four tour dates from the end, we were in Hull and Lorna said to me, 'Wayne, Wayne, it doesn't work.' Her voice was very plaintive. I looked down to find she was clicking her heels, just as Dorothy does in *The Wizard of Oz*, when she wants to magic herself home.

The tour was a sell-out. Trudi Moffat came over from Canada to assist me with the choreography. She had also worked on *Bits and Pieces* and was now a regular help on various aspects of dance, particularly jazz, and she is a whizz with hip-hop, running-man and other street styles. Trudi choreographed a voguing number for my cabaret show, in which I impersonated Madonna. Lorna and I went on *Wogan* (this was when Gloria Hunniford fronted it) just before we came into the Palladium for a couple of Sunday dates in the April towards the end of the tour. Liza came over to see us there, bringing Lorna's father, Sid Luft, and the four of us went off to Tramp after the show to celebrate the three of them being together for once.

In the spring of 1992 I was invited by Trudi Moffat to New Orleans, where she was choreographing the spectacular for the pre-Olympic trials. I was to dance a solo in the middle of the arena, up twenty steps and on to a moving platform. I had so far to run that the heat took my breath away as I climbed the staircase. Luckily it didn't show, as I whizzed and jumped with laser beams ricocheting from my mirrored jacket. As you know I love an audience, but even more that night I loved the biggest chorus line I have ever danced with below me on the turf – 500 to be exact!

I was asked by the Benesh Institute Endowment Fund (of which I am a Patron) to organize a do for them in St John's, Smith Square. Benesh is a system of written dance notation, like notes on a stave, each line corresponding to a level of the body: head, shoulders, waist, knees and floor. With the addition of dots, crosses and lines, both position and movement is indicated. It is a system used throughout the world, and it means that if a company wants to know the steps from *Swan Lake*, the Benesh notation book will be used by a trained notator to teach the positions to the dancers. But – it takes a long time, about three or four years, to learn this system, because it is complicated and you must have a mathematical turn of mind. Benesh receive no money from the Arts Council and are totally reliant on charity to keep alive, let alone notate all the ballets and train people.

As this gala was only to be an hour long, creating less pressure for me, and less for the artists who were only available on the day, I decided to direct it. It gave time for a dinner afterwards and I was also to dance with Anthony Dowell again. The Princess of Wales came, and I sat with her and Richard Branson at dinner. My mother (my best and favourite fan as usual) was at another table and the Princess asked me to bring her over to say hello. I said to Mum, 'Just take it easy, you know,' but she threw her arms round the Princess and gave her a hearty hug. Mum had, by this time, been to at least three of the staff Christmas parties at Kensington Palace, and felt, I think, very motherly and fond. We raised a six-figure sum which was divided between Benesh and a charity of the Princess's choice.

Around this time I decided to stop letting out the studio. I was getting very little out of it because it was making just enough to pay Michael. The dance craze was over. Studios were closing everywhere, including Debbie Moore's Pineapple Centre in Paddington. (Her clothes outlets, however, were doing well.) Gordon, who was renting space for his body control studio in the Kensington Pineapple, which was also about to go, asked if he might rent my place instead. This seemed a good idea, so he took over the whole building. I like it too, because if I need to get in trim all I need to do is roll out of bed, toddle across to the studio and there I am.

In the summer of 1992 I appeared in a six-week summer season on the *Joe Longthorne Show* at the Bournemouth International Centre. Roy Walker and the Nolans were also on the bill. Although I enjoyed watching them perform and found Joe Longthorne one of the best male singing impersonators – convincing from Pavarotti to Presley – I found appearing for only seven minutes of a two-hour show unfulfilling.

Summer seasons were the guarantee, in earlier times, of never being out of work for some performers. They'd do panto, rehearsing in November, opening in December, and playing through until March. Then there'd be the annual spring holiday, and April would see the start of the rehearsals for the summer season – which would open in late May and carry on through until the end of September. Then October would be time off, and the process would start again.

During the run of the show at Bournemouth, Brian phoned to ask if I would appear on a Christmas Special for the BBC. I was to teach a remarkable puppet the fundamental ballet exercises. I was a bit dubious, but when Brian told me that Ashkenazy, the concert pianist, had taught it the piano; Yehudi Menuhin the violin; and Pavarotti had taught it to sing – who was I to say NO?

A car collected me from Bournemouth to take me to the Beeb. I met some old colleagues from the *Hot Shoe Show*, sorted out something to wear with the wardrobe, and went on to the set, where I met a dancer in a headless doll costume. I started to teach him the basic barre steps. He kept falling over and I began to get fidgety. I was supposed to tell the story of *Swan Lake* by reading the autocue. They had got it completely wrong (memories flooded back of My Time On TV eight/nine years before). I insisted on a meeting with the director in private.

'We'll have to rewrite the story. It's wrong,' I told him.

'Can't you just fake it?'

'I know it's a children's show,' I said, 'but I'm not here to lie to them.'

He then asked if I would demonstrate the dying swan. I had to inform the pillock that although it's a swan, that character and its music is not in *Swan Lake* and I was not about to demonstrate a girl's dance.

'And besides,' I said, 'I'm not here to make ballet look like the *Benny Hill Show*.'

By the time we came to the recording I was muttering under my breath various words that could not be used on a kids' show. All I wanted to do was to get it done in one take and go home and sack my agent for putting me in such a vulnerable and stupid position. The puppet arrived complete with head. It looked ridiculously large and kept falling over. I ad-libbed to cover this. One of the boots fell off. Again I covered – dreading that we would have to go back to the top and start again. As I continued to explain the story in ever more garbled English I felt a tap on the shoulder.

It was Noel Edmunds with a Gotcha Oscar. I'd been done, caught, fooled ... It's a very strange feeling – suddenly realizing that everyone, camera, crew, lighting, wardrobe, dancers, are all watching your every move, are all in on the joke except you. I was flabbergasted, and in the car on the way back to Bournemouth I tried to remember if I'd done anything or said anything really bad. I did not see the tape until I was shown it live on *Noel's House Party*. I've never laughed so much in my life. The puppet's name was, of course, Mr Blobby.

I had started to become involved again with my ballet roots with the advent of invitations to direct galas, and I began to think that it was time to move back into that world. I was enjoying directing more than performing eight shows a week, but still decided to take time out to think, to reassess whether I ever wanted to go back as a performer.

Sundays now, at least, were spent at home, with lunches cooked by Miriam for various friends with whom, through pressure of work, I was less in touch than I liked. I caught up with several old friends – Pamela Scott (Royal Ballet), Brenda Armstrong (Long Acre) and Anne Allan, who was now assistant to one of the biggest, if not the biggest, producers in Canada, and was in London to put on *Kiss of the Spider Woman*. I love it when people I have nurtured or worked with do well. Nichola Treherne is now assistant director on *Starlight Express*, *Joseph* and *Jeeves* for ALW (although I cannot take credit for her marrying my wonderful stage manager, Tim Robinson!) and Peter Salmon created, with Jane Darling, the jazz syllabus for all the students of the British Ballet Organization. Peter was with me at the Upper School, and in *DASH*. He is very tall, and in the ballet where he is the villain to my Chaplin, the juxtaposition of heights added to the comedy. But our comedy duos began in the classes of one of our ballet teachers, a Frenchman with eccentric views on how to teach. He made us jump with dumbbells in our hands, saying that it would improve our jump, and that we would jump much higher when we put them down. Of course we did, the fool. All it did was strain our lower abdomens and backs. Thank goodness the Royal Ballet School was on to it and he was replaced shortly after.

But Miriam left, and almost immediately afterwards the press were on my tail. I kept getting messages that a journalist was trying to get hold of me. As I was staying out of the limelight – deliberately – I wondered what the hell they'd dug up this time. One evening there was a ring at the bell, and I thought, instinctively, it must be this journalist. George answered the door and came back to me.

'Oh, it's nothing really. You're only dying of Aids.' We laughed, with relief. I thought they had found something true. The journalist wanted a story 'from my point of view', as she said the tabloids had already prepared a vicious story for the Sunday papers. I knew I had a clean bill of health and was looking forward to the money I could make if they printed. Everyone in town seemed to know about this story except me. By Saturday they were up and down the stairs, peering through the letterbox, and one of them yelled: 'Come out, we know you're dying.'

I then received a call from someone I'd worked with in PR, who told me the story again, and asked me what I was going to do about it. I said, 'Nothing. Let them go ahead. It's not true anyway.'

She said, 'You can't let this story go to press – even if it's not true – mud sticks.'

I called Edith, who found me a lawyer, Stephen Gilchrist, and he came round immediately and telephoned the paper in question. He let them know that action would be taken, in spades, if they printed it. He then went out on to the doorstep and asked if any of them would like to talk to him. They whizzed off. The editor would not give us a yes or no as to whether the story would be printed.

Stephen phoned me the next day to say, 'Do you want the good news or the bad news? Well, the bad news is you're not going to be rich and the good news is that the story hasn't gone in.'

All this was another reason to recoil from show-business for a while and return to the classical.

The English National Ballet put on a performance, staged like a cabaret, to raise money for the Company. Katie Wade, Director of the ENB School, asked me to choreograph and appear with her students. This was in the marble hall of the Foreign Office and a special stage was put in for the occasion. Of all the places I imagined myself dancing, as a child, the cushioned corridors of the Foreign Office was never among them. This was later to result in the ENB asking me to choreograph a gala the following year to celebrate the re-opening of the Savoy Theatre.

The Dance Umbrella organized a gala in October for Leslie Edwards, who had encouraged me all those years ago with my Olga Korbut routines when I performed at the Friends' Christmas parties. He was also the first person to help all those fledgling choreographers by putting on a workshop for them at the University of London's Collegiate Theatre. I feel quite strongly that choreography should be on the curriculum of every dance school, because even if a dancer has no intention of becoming a choreographer, it is essential he or she understand the creative process and the accompanying stresses and strains that a choreographer has to handle. Leslie received a standing ovation for all the work he had done – a lot of it had been extracurricular and pretty much unrecognized, but out of his workshops came some of the most influential and creative choreographers in the world today. I was very happy to be there. I was very happy to be part of the Leslie Edwards Appreciation Society.

In the autumn I toured my cabaret act (four girls and a blue silk suit) round the ex-pat communities of Dubai and Abu Dhabi. I felt like I was on another planet or in a different and parallel time dimension. I had a short-lived love affair out there. A camel kissed me. This was my deepest interaction in the desert. I was dared to approach this creature from behind – I had my doubts, camels have a good kick and rather large feet, but I used my Barbara Woodhouse technique by breathing down my nostrils. When I got to its flank it wound its long neck and muffin nose towards me. I daren't move. It plonked its rubber lips against my cheek. It raised its superior nose, turned its head and loped off into the desert.

That heat was followed by winter in Southend-on-Sea. A rolling grey North Sea, as opposed to rolling great sand dunes. It was *The Pied Piper* this time, with Peggy Mount, which made a change from the usual panto. There were loads of local children playing the Hamelin children and the Hamelin rats. I didn't get kissed by a rat.

In the early part of 1993 the Royal Opera House finally asked David Hockney to design an opera for them. It was *Die Frau Ohne Schatten* (The Woman Without a Shadow) by Richard Strauss. I had suggested David twenty years earlier for the *Sleeping Beauty*, when the ROH were seeking a designer. They didn't take him then (although I felt they should) because he had no track record. Since, however, he has done a great many very important designs all over the world, including Glyndbourne and the ROH was about the last to pick up on him. We had a great evening on the press night, like a family get-together, just like old times in the sixties, with Ossie and Celia and others.

Derek Deane had just become Director of the English National Ballet. The company was at sixes and sevens after the previous Director had left. Derek was sweeping through the organization, tightening things up, replacing dancers, and trying to create its style and a foundation for the *corps*. So it was an unsettled time for the dancers when I came in to do my piece for the re-opening of the Savoy Theatre.

The theatre was being rebuilt in the style of the twenties, so that it was just like the D'Oyly Carte original. For the opening I was to choreograph a ballet set to Sullivan's music. John Cranko had creamed off the best for *Pineapple Poll*, so I listened to over eighty hours of tapes, choosing various bits I felt I could use, and Carl Davis came in, cleverly tied all the arrangements together and added more composition. That was fun because he had composed *David and Goliath* so many years before, and we were definitely on the same wavelength.

I decided to link scenes from the life of Gilbert and Sullivan. Their lives together were pretty volatile and prone to argument and eruption. They even argued over the price of the new carpet in the foyer. Towards the end of their lives they did not speak to each other, except in the way of work, and they came on to take their bows at the end of their operettas on opposite sides of the stage. Neither acknowledged the other's presence.

I played the writer WS Gilbert, and brought out a tap mat, unrolled it, and argued out my duel with Sullivan (who was danced by Paul Lewis, on tour) in a tap dance. Part of the set was a white piano which was spotlit at the beginning of the piece, and when it turned round it was the Gilbert writing desk. I created quite a few dances round that prop. I found some little-known Sullivan ballet music and recreated its *pas-de-deux*. We all ended up in Venice for the *Gondoliers* dance. It was a light-hearted look at episodes from their lives and true gala material. We performed at the Savoy for a week. I pulled a calf muscle during the rehearsals for the *Suite*, which meant that I had to cancel some cabaret dates and also that I had to adapt some of my own moves for one-legged dancing.

The ENB took the *Savoy Suite* into their rep for a short time, but the critics were mostly dismissive. They complained about it being too light in tone. Well, of course it was, it is based on operetta, after all, and I, for one, had never intended it as a serious piece. But as the company relies very much on good critical notices it was wiser to drop it. But, as usual with many ballets that get indifferent reviews, the audiences adored it, wherever it went.

In the late autumn of 1993 I directed another charity performance for Benesh, together with the Huntington's Disease Association, of which the Princess of Wales is also Patron. This event was dedicated to the memory of Kenneth MacMillan, who had recently died.

The evening was called *Designed for Dance*. It was compèred by Stella Gonet and Louise Lombard of TV's *House of Elliot*, which was very fitting in that showbiz, cross-cultural, fictional way. Costumes from the Diaghilev era were paraded and numbers were danced from that period. Then I paraded costumes from Sir Frederick Ashton's ballets, and the dances included excerpts from *Les Deux Pigeons* and *Façade* among others. In the second half the cast of *Crazy For You*, which was on in the West End, did a number or two and showed their Ziegfeld-like costumes, and several West End musicals, alive and dead, also showed off their finery, and then we came to the point of the evening – the tribute to the life and work of Kenneth MacMillan.

I paraded several of his costumes from *Elite Syncopations*, *Romeo and Juliet*, *Mayerling*, *Manon*, and many others. I danced in *Elite Syncopations* and others, such as Viviana Durante, Darcey Bussell, Zoltan Solymosi, Irek Mukhamedov, Marion Tait, Joseph Cipolla and Kevin O'Hare danced in various of his creations. The evening ended with a waltz from *Carousel*, which was in the West End and which was MacMillan's last choreographic work. He died before it was finished. The whole evening was very nostalgic and there was the occasional moist eye.

The rest of 1993 was either taken up with touring *Hollywood and Broadway* again, but this time with Bonnie Langford and Kim Kriswell. I was no longer performing my cabaret act. I can only remember one serious hitch on the cabaret circuit. I arrived in Buxton, of pure water fame (not that water has anything to do with this) and found I had the band, but had left the tapes at home. I had to phone London for a bike to go to the mews, fetch the tapes and get back to Buxton in time for the opening. I had my doubts about his being able to do it – unlike Puck, he couldn't girdle the earth in forty minutes (I wish) – but he arrived back just in time and I started breathing again. But it just about wiped out the profit. Another thing I learned. Don't leave home in a hurry.

EIGHTEEN

TIMES OF SORROW

THE PANTOMIME OVER the Christmas period of 1993–4 was at the Birmingham Hippodrome, with Lesley Joseph from *Birds of a Feather*. A riot. I was playing Dick Whittington's cat this time. Fun though it is to be an all-talking, all-singing, all-dancing cat (yet again my destiny to be an animal – if I had any belief in the Eastern theory of the transmigration of souls, I might even begin to wonder whether I'd made it as a human being this time), it got very wearing by the end of the run to be always at knee level. You get patted on the head rather too much for my liking. But the real pleasure about being in Birmingham was that I could take ballet classes with the Birmingham Royal Ballet, and entertain Peter Wright and Anthony Dowell in my dressing room when they came to see *Dick Whittington*.

After *Dick* finished in February I continued my tour with Bonnie and Kim and followed that by joining the English National Ballet in the *Savoy Suite*. I also took the part of Dr Coppelius, which I had not danced since my graduation performance over twenty-five years earlier. I really enjoyed it. It is a part that can be both sinister and funny. And for this I was nominated for Performance of the Year in a Ballet by the *Manchester Evening News*. *Coppélia* came to the Royal Festival Hall after the tour for a short run.

Katie Wade, from the English National Ballet School, rang and asked me to choreograph another piece for the pupils. This piece, called *Promenade*, with music by Gottschalk, was to be taken to France for the seminar known as Jeunes Ballets de France. Students from all over the world come to take part in classes with teachers from all over the world. You are able to assess one school against another, see how you are measuring up in the international ballet world. I think it is a very important event to take part in, even though the Royal Ballet School has never bothered with it.

Promenade was devised for all the pupils in the school, not just the selected best students. They were very nervous, but received a rewarding reception at its première. As a result I was asked to choreograph ballets for other dance schools. But before I could, I received a blow that set me back many months – indeed it is only now that I feel I am coming out of it.

Some years before my mother had telephoned me. She said she was separating from my stepfather and would I buy her a house? 'Of course,' I said, without even thinking twice about it, even though I would have to get a 100 per cent mortgage. So she moved to a six-bedroomed house off Mutley Plain in Plymouth, near where we had lived all those years before.

Our relationship was as strong as it had been in the early days. It had suffered a hiatus – quite a long one – during the early part of my adult years. The reasons were often small, compounded by being many, but the major one was that she had become a Jehovah's Witness. One of their doctrines is that you must go out trying to convert people, even by knocking on doors. My mother knocked on mine, but I was not ready and so it disappointed her. Eventually she eased up and we were able to communicate, rekindling our friendship. But I still received copies of the *Watchtower*. None of this had affected my mother's loyalty to me and my career, however. She was faithful in her attendance at all my performances and did not miss one of them. Her support was invaluable, even if I did not necessarily show it at the time. I think some people almost have to be away from their family in order to realize how vital and valuable they are. I was leading a completely different life from that of the rest of my family. By the time I was forty we were beginning to draw closer together again.

Mum moved into her house – and Stanley moved in too. She did not have the heart to leave him. So he had a bed-sit in the house, and would collect a tray of food from the dining-room at meal times and take it back to his room. He did eat with us from time to time. He seemed quite content with this arrangement – this way of life seemed to suit them both. Stanley began to suffer from a breathing disorder and I even began to feel sorry for him.

My mother was beginning to suffer from arthritis in her hands. She would moan occasionally with that awful stabbing pain that sufferers get. It is very easy to be irritated both by the little gasping 'Ooh' and the fact that a sufferer tries to be 'brave' about it. Perhaps that sounds mean and selfish, but when someone you love does utter an 'Ouch' almost out of the blue, you jump and say, 'What, what is it? Tell me.' It frightens you. And then they say, 'Oh nothing, it's only my arthritis,' or rheumatism, or frozen shoulder, and you think, 'Only?' You just do not want the people you love most dearly to be in pain. You can bear none of it for them and almost feel guilty because you can't. And then that guilt makes you irritable, and so it goes round and round.

My poor mother. She had started to take mild painkillers in the form of paracetamol, on the advice of her doctor. On the packets – which you can buy over every chemist's counter in the land – it says that you may take up to eight tablets a day; people assume no harm. My mother took her daily dosage to keep the pain at bay. Two or three years later she became very ill and we were all desperately worried, even more so than we might have been normally, because in the last few years she was a Jehovah's Witness, which meant that if she needed a blood transfusion she might refuse to have one. There was something wrong with her liver, but even after taking samples, nothing was diagnosed. They were baffled.

She sank very low for a while and we feared the worst, but somehow she recovered. Her breathing was very bad sometimes, particularly after she came out to Munich to see *Bits and Pieces* in the autumn. There is something there called the Fuern, and it's due to the autumnal climatic conditions and the fact that Munich is in a bowl. The Fuern carries off a lot of elderly people every year. I always carried a doctor's telephone number with me whenever we were together, unbeknownst to her. She would have regarded it as a fuss and bother. But sometimes things were so bad she could hardly walk.

She sent me an article about paracetamol in which it said that it might collect in the body, particularly in the liver. It does not get flushed out. I don't know if this is a proven fact or not. My mother always felt it was a huge contribution to her ill-health – and she also thought the doctors knew and would not say. She was, however, taken off the paracetamol and given another painkiller for the arthritis. Although she recovered physically, she never recovered the bouncy personality we all loved.

On the morning of 2 June 1994 my sister telephoned me at 8.30.

'I've some bad news,' she said.

I thought, it's Gran. I had just been to the funeral of a friend of George's and was feeling the sadness of mortality. But my sister said it was Mum. She had just died. I couldn't believe it – I had been talking to her on the telephone on the Tuesday, two days before. She'd been in fairly good health, she said, and was laughing and joking. She took to her bed on the Wednesday morning and it was all over by Thursday. It was pneumonia. Her immune system had collapsed and her body was weakened, as a result of the medication she had been taking. I am sorry I was not there, which is something I have to bear, but I am grateful that it was quick.

Joanne took care of all the details. Cancelling a performance for a charity at Drury Lane for the London City Ballet in order to go down to Plymouth was as much as I could handle. Wendy Roe and George came down with me on the train to hand me over to my sister. I was in no fit state to come on my own. The only thing I did was to order a spray to cover the entire coffin. I knew I couldn't bear to look at it. I wanted all the wild flowers we had picked together when I was a child: bluebells, primroses, violets, ferns, moss, stones of the forest, beech branches, grasses and foxgloves. Some of the flowers rooted in the moss. I took a bunch of violets and planted them on Grandad's grave. He has no headstone and I thought it was fitting that he should have them.

The funeral was held at the Kingdom Hall of the Jehovah's Witnesses. It was a very small hall, brightly lit, and everything was so close. Quite different from the normal church and its service. My sister and I held each other up for strength, and the sadness was lightened only by my grandmother in her wheelchair. She is still alive, in her mid-nineties, and on occasions is as bright as a button. She was that day. She looked at the coffin and raised her stick to it. 'That's my Joanie in there,' she stated. I don't know if she remembered the five-year-old child she left with her own parents when she remarried over sixty-five years earlier, but I like to think so. And she interrupted the address by one of the Jehovah's Witnesses by saying, 'Give me back my shoe,' when it fell off her foot and rolled to a rest by my mother's coffin. Dear Gran. She managed to make things not quite so black.

All the family came. It was the first time, and probably the last time, I have ever seen them completely united. But my mother – with whom I had lived alone with complete happiness as a child, who had made my costumes and struggled to pay for my dance classes, the one who had loved and supported me through everything – was gone. It was, I felt, the end of an era.

Afterwards I cried. No tears to start with, just great racking sobs, howls of pain of loss and loneliness. And my biggest fear was that I would not be able to cry. So many close friends had died well before their time – Paul, Alan, Nancy, Henrietta, Graham – and I had not cried for them. But I wanted to mourn my mother.

I went to Spain on my own in November 1994 for a week. I was still desolate from my mother's death. I needed time to be away from everything and to focus my mind and research my projected tour for the following year. This was to be called *Dance* and was to be a history of dance and all its different styles. And in the way that things happen when you least expect it, I met someone called José Bergera, who is now my assistant, lives with me and keeps my life in order.

Back home it was straight into rehearsals for panto. I was playing Buttons in *Cinderella* for the first time. What a plum of a panto role for me. I can be myself, unrestrained and cheeky, do comedy (which I love and am still learning), dance for a reason to cheer up Cinderella, joke and have fun. There is almost nothing better than hearing an audience laugh at something you have said or done. I even did a *pas-de-deux* with Peggy Mount. She sent a picture of our dance to her doctor – who had sent her for two hip replacements. Amazing. This experience renewed my enjoyment in pantomime. I was also working for a very good and honest producer, Lee Dean.

The Birmingham Royal Ballet were in London over the Christmas season. This company dances in the way I used to when I was a student, both with their spirit and their technique, maybe because Sir Peter Wright was the director for twenty years or more. He produced *The Nutcracker*, which we went to see and which I think is probably the best version that has ever been done, including the one that Nureyev did nearly thirty years before, where he tore the stuffing out of the hobby horses.

After *Cinderella* I went into rehearsals for *Dance*.

NINETEEN

WHAT NOW?

OVER THE CHRISTMAS of 1994 I met the producer Alan Field. He was a friend of Brian Marshall, my agent. Field was, at that time, Adam Faith's manager, and had just toured *Alfie*. I thought he would be just the man to bring my latest idea to fruition.

I conceived a show based around the history of dance, explaining the origins of each dance style, with illustrations and examples and exuberance. Take the Lindy Hop. In 1926 Charles Lindbergh 'hopped' the Atlantic in his plane the Spirit of St Louis, and a dance craze was named in his honour, the Lindy Hop. I intended to include the hornpipe, the Charleston, ballet, contemporary, jazz, tap, clog – everything. I wanted to include dancers made famous by the music halls of the late nineteenth and early twentieth centuries, such as Lois Fuller with her silks. When she danced she actually disappeared into her waving silk. Coloured lights were projected on to the material to create flames. This number was called the Fire Dance. I wanted Little Titch with his Big Boot dance (he was only four foot six, wore two-foot long boots and danced on the toes of them), and Wilson Kepple and Betty's Sand Dance – one of the funniest ever devised. (The sand dance was an Arab dance performed on sand to make appropriate noises to accompany the music.) And Anna Pavlova's California Poppy too. She was one of the many ballerinas who danced in music halls before there were ballet companies in this country – or most of the Western world for that matter.

I also thought this show could stand on its own without a 'name' to front it, and I devised it so that I was not to be the central character, but just one of the cast. This meant that if I left, it would be able to continue touring without me. An ideal – a show that would exist by virtue of its own merit. And it was a show with an absolute reason for dance, and not just a series of musical numbers joined together. I thought it was one that could work, not for just a season, but for quite a time, and even have an offshoot, touring universities as part of the dance education syllabus. People are always interested in the origins of things, they like to know a story, and so often knowing the story helps them appreciate whatever they are watching in greater depth. It took years of research to bring the whole scheme together and I am extremely proud of it.

This was a very adventurous project and, like *DASH*, was made up of specialists in their own fields. Linda Mae Brewer (the understudy to one of the leads in *Les Misérables*) came to represent the birth of jazz dance. I employed the British tap champion and the Lindy Hop champion. Ursula Hagli and Richard

Slaughter joined to give their authentic impersonations of Pavlova and her partner Mordkin. Kerry Biggin represented the original movements of the Martha Graham style. Alistair Bull, Lizzie Leigh and Gary O'Hanran came to support other styles such as clog dance, and Bob Fosse hornpipe, Charleston and can-can. José became my personal dresser. I asked Wendy Roe, who had been in the *Hot Shoe Show* and *DASH*, to be my personal assistant. She had become a model and actress and the mother of twins, a boy and girl, Alex and Katy. I thought I had the best cast ever.

My dining-room was turned into an office and Wendy had to spend more time on the phone, almost running the production side, than in the studio assisting me. This was a fractious rehearsal period, with certain artists becoming more than difficult.

In fact the production opened almost a week late in York and we had to cancel the previews. The lighting designer, stage manager and company manager were brought in at the eleventh hour, and everyone was behind schedule. In the whole twenty-five-week tour there were no photographs of our production outside the theatres. Just a small poster would greet us on our arrival in each town, while overpowering displays for future attractions such as *Me and My Girl* and *Singing in the Rain* drowned our publicity.

Only one town did not give us good reviews – perhaps the curtain going up almost an hour late may have been partly responsible. Technical problems seemed to jinx the show.

Linda Mae Brewer lasted only six weeks, and many other members of the cast were dogged by injury, making the performances highly inconsistent. I didn't miss one performance, and found it difficult to understand how some of my fellow artists could cancel dance numbers every performance. I don't think there was one week when we performed dance numbers without somebody being absent. Ursula unfortunately snapped her Achilles tendon. I had to put more of my cabaret numbers into the show to help fill out the evening, hardly giving me a break.

By the end of the run I was glad it was over. The producer did not give a last-night party, and the costumes that I had lent to the production free of charge were dumped at my dressing-room door. I asked if the truck taking the scenery back to the store could take the boxes of my costumes to my house. The answer was no. They had to be left in Bromley.

When I finally came to collect them, many were missing – picked up by the truck? Who knows. The whole thing was upsetting from the start, so I was not surprised at this treatment by the end of the tour. I am still owed a lot of money.

After twenty-five weeks of solid dance I was mentally exhausted but happy with my physical well-being. George said that I hadn't danced better in years, so it was well worth the effort. The audience in some places gave us standing ovations and well after the curtain dropped, some would sit and listen to our brilliant band, led by Tom Steer, and dance in the stalls.

Some time during the November of the previous year I had been approached by Lady Farnham to direct a Royal Charity Gala in aid of the Friends of the Elderly at the Britten Theatre, Royal College of Music. It was entitled *90 Years of Dance* and was to be held in the presence of both the Queen and Princess Margaret, who are, respectively, the Patron and the President of the charity. I called on the talents of Agnes Oaks, Thomas Edur and Yat Seng Chang of the English National Ballet, Darcey Bussell and Jonathan Cope of the Royal Ballet, the Roly Polys and the Jiving Lindy Hoppers. Other members of the committee co-opted *Riverdance* and landed a coup with the British première of the two new stars of the American Ballet Theatre, Angel Corella and Paloma Herrera. The children of the Royal Ballet School, thanks to Dame Merle Park, danced the opening hornpipe and my dance company performed various pieces from the *History of Dance*. My band from the dance show provided the music, and Kit and the Widow did a wonderful job of compèring the whole event, linking each act with witty rhymes. One of the best things about this particular gala was that it was not too long – the other was that it raised well over £150,000, which is probably a record for a theatre as small as the Britten.

The critic, Nicholas Dromgoole, has always been very supportive of my work. In fact just after my graduation he took me to see the Kirov at the Opera House. I introduced him to Lesley Collier when I was staying with Diana Roberts, and a few years later they married. He wrote a very appreciative review of the *90 Years of Dance* for the *Sunday Telegraph* under the headline 'Masterly Sleep Pitches it Perfect'.

> My respect for Wayne Sleep grows every time he does something fresh in the theatre. Last Monday he arranged a very grand and very select charity gala, in the presence of the Queen and Princess Margaret, at the Britten Theatre in the Royal College of Music.
>
> Wayne Sleep as director really understands about galas. Nothing went on too long, the mixture was right, and the evening accelerated in fun and excitement as the rich programme unfolded. Events were compèred professionally by Kit and the Widow, and what events! . . . Wayne Sleep the performer is as exuberant as ever, and his charm, sense of fun and vibrant stage presence, create exactly the right atmosphere for a celebration of dance.

While I was putting together the *90 Years of Dance* gala for the Friends of the Elderly, Lady Farnham rang me to say that Princess Margaret would like to see the programme as she had some ideas of dance styles that she thought might be used. I telephoned her and she asked me if I would like to include the palais glide. I had to inform her I had no idea of how to dance this, to which she said, 'I see your dance education is not complete, you had better come and learn it.' I went to the Palace to show her the programme of events with Lady Farnham, pianist Patricia McNaughton (who was on the committee), and José, complete with Doc Martens. The Princess greeted us in her entrance hall where she had rolled the carpet up in order for me to learn the dance. I uttered, 'We usually roll it out for you, Ma'am.' Then she proceeded with great flourish and agility to teach myself, Lady Farnham and José the palais glide. We had to hold on to each other as it is a line dance. I thought it rather funny that José, on his second day in London, should be in this situation, not understanding a word of English, with his arm around Princess Margaret. When Princess Margaret found out about this, she said, 'Isn't it amusing, we've just taught the Spanish the palais glide!' I apologized to her for José's boots, to which she replied, 'Don't worry. I once danced it with an officer in boots and spurs and he ruined the parquet flooring.' We stayed on and the pianist played some of the music which we might use for the gala. I found Princess Margaret very knowledgeable, in fact she has always been a great supporter of dance and theatre in general, and keeps herself well informed of what is currently happening in the theatre.

At dinner after the gala I sat next to Princess Margaret. She, along with the rest of the cast, sang 'Happy Birthday' to me. It was my forty-seventh birthday.

The tour finished a week after the gala and I was exhausted. I rented a villa, with José, in the south of Spain for four weeks. I needed just to relax and wind down. Wendy came out to join us with her twins and it was great to do nothing except sit in the sun, eat fresh fish, sleep to the scent of jasmine outside my window, and watch Alex and Katy play in the pool and do all the daft and clever things children do.

Back in London the final plans for converting my mews house were underway. I was having the inside completely redesigned and rebuilt. Even the roof came off. At one point only the front wall was left standing, and because it is a listed building there were various restrictions against changing its aspect. The reason for all this change was that I needed more space inside, partly because José had come to stay and partly because I needed to separate my living arrangements from my office and work life. I had been living on the top floor only, because the ground floor was still the original 1860 stabling. I found a home in the country for all the wood and ironmongery and set about redeveloping the ground floor as well. I have created a house on several different levels, by both raising and dropping floors and adding intermediate storeys, which gives an extraordinary illusion of space. I have made room for a small studio on the ground floor, and have a kitchen and office on what is now a lower ground floor. All the rest of the house is for private living and it means that I can separate my work and home life – something I have been wanting to achieve for a very long time.

I moved out of the house on 1 November 1995, and went back to Plymouth to stay in the house I had bought for my mother a few years before, when she had decided to separate from my stepfather. He died in March that year, during the first (disastrous) week of mounting *Dance* in York. We were never that close but I hated to see the pain he was suffering from angina – it seemed to cause terrible breathing problems. I wonder sometimes if he simply lost the will to live after my mother went. Who knows. I felt no compulsion to go to the funeral. I felt for my sister more than anything else. The tour was in Chichester at the time. I am sorry, though, that the burden once again fell on my sister to make the necessary arrangements.

I was to play Buttons again for Christmas pantomime, in Crewe. Most of the cast were new (except for Peggy Mount) with Sonya, the pop singer, who was a real Scouser, very easy-going, an essential good laugh, and John Challis from *Only Fools and Horses*, who was playing his first Dame. José found a job with the crew and became the front part of Dobbin the Horse. He upstaged everyone in sight, which caused much hilarity and some consternation. How this horse managed to take centre stage in the curtain call is beyond me. There was never such a good command of the boards since 'Move over, boyo.'

One of my favourite parts of the show was when six children were asked on to the stage at the end of the show. I always asked them who they like best, expecting (in *Cinderella*) to hear them say, 'Prince Charming,' or 'Cinderella,' or sometimes even 'Buttons.' But once it was 'That cow,' meaning Dobbin the Horse. I said, 'That horse will have to go.' I mean – hardly a role model, is it? At one performance I was being heckled by a rugby team while I was interviewing the children, so I made one of them come up on stage and questioned him as if he was one of them. He was about six foot six and solidly built.

'And what would you like to be when you are grown up?' I asked him.

'A man,' he said.

'No chance,' I said. There was much laughter, from his friends in particular.

A close friend died in the spring of 1996. Lady Edith Foxwell, who owned the Embassy Club where I used to go for late drinks with Freddie Mercury, died in Kensington and Chelsea Hospital in Fulham. I am so glad that I spent a week with her in Spain less than a month before. She had skin cancer, which I tended in Marbella; she appeared incredibly cheerful, but almost as soon as she came back home she went into hospital. I feared she would not come out again, but didn't want to think about that. I was renting a flat (my house, supposed to be finished in six weeks, is still not ready six months on) just by World's End in Chelsea, and I could see the back of the hospital from the sitting-room window. I used to stare and think, 'I'm so close, I'm so close, I could touch her if I just extended my hand.' As if. I visited her just before she died and it gave me a funny feeling, walking back along the street behind the hospital, knowing I was passing her room, and probably for the last time. I shall miss her.

Since Crewe I have not been touring. I decided that it was time to give something back to the world that had nurtured me for the last thirty-six years so I have been developing workshops and master-classes. I go all over the country (and all over Europe too) and teach groups of children, and teachers and parents come to watch. These workshops consist of a day of teaching, beginning on early Sunday mornings with a general class for under nine-year-olds. These classes are not aimed at teaching basic technique – I concentrate in bringing out a high level of performance, often by teaching the children a small part from a musical or ballet. The general class is followed by pre-elementary ballet classes, then through elementary to advanced. After this I take both general tap and jazz classes, ending with a free-for-all for teachers, and including people who do not train but enjoy dance and movement. This is the fun class of the day, spanning ages from nine to ninety.

I did not have the slightest intention of teaching a technique class. But to my surprise I find that I absolutely love directing pupils in a role, especially the younger ones. At that age they have no inhibitions. And apart from the fact that I like working with children, I am finding it fulfilling on the emotional level too. I admit to be gratified by the enthusiasm with which they greet me and perform for me. And the enthusiasm works both ways, as well, I have a new energy for life.

There is a new ballet to be premièred at the Royal Opera House in November 1996. I have been asked to choreograph scenes from the stories in *Alice in Wonderland* for the National Youth Ballet of Great Britain. The ages in the NYB range from four to twenty-one. Dancers from all over Britain strive for a place in this company, which allows them to perform at the highest amateur level: 500–1,000 students audition every year.

There have been some remarkable changes in schooling of technique in classical ballet since I was a student. With the setting up of the Royal Ballet School's teachers' course, standards of teaching all round the country from the students who studied at the course make sure that the pupils are now receiving a well-thought-out syllabus. There aren't many teachers in Britain now who just teach for the sake of making a quick buck or because they were once students who didn't make it into ballet companies. While there will always be teachers with a natural vocation, making them stand out from the others, now all would-be teachers can enjoy the benefits of brilliant training.

The student of today contrasts radically with those of my era. When I looked around a class when I was learning at the Royal Ballet School I found the students to be all very different in their anatomy. Talent more than perfect physique usually won you a place. Students differed in height – there would be slightly podgy dancers or very very slim, feet didn't always have the greatest insteps (point) and one could get away with a slightly imperfect shape. Today, however, to obtain a place in any of the great ballet schools or companies, perfect physique is imperative, even before the ability of the dancer is taken into consideration. I went to a very well-known ballet school recently to watch a class of girls who all looked exactly the same. Long slender legs, slim physiques and almost identical in personality, which sometimes I found restricted and uniform. In fact it was very difficult to find one technique better than another, whereas in my day it would have stuck out a mile who were going to be the stars of tomorrow. With the almost cloning approach, a lot of it must depend on personal taste as to who is chosen for the companies. However, there are always one or two who will stand out against the rest. I am talking in general about the basic standard. When I received two free classes a week from the Royal Academy of Dancing, my tap dancing classes had to be stopped; it was not considered good for the ankles or the leg muscles. When I went to the Royal Ballet School it certainly was not part of the dance curriculum. Now tap is taught once a week to the final year at the Royal Ballet School (Lower School, White Lodge) by Bill Drysdale (who taught me for my TV shows). It has been realized that tap dancing can only help especially with rhythm and musicality.

There were very few ballet schools in the country where one could go to study dance when I was younger. Now the number of boarding schools has escalated, most regions being serviced by at least one. In these schools now not only ballet is taught, contemporary dance too has become part of most schools' teaching. Tap, as I have said before, and jazz dance are also included. Most of these schools realize the standard you have to achieve to make it into a ballet company, and giving this all-round training gives pupils more chance to get a job in musical theatre. Many schools now teach singing and acting along with their predominantly dance training.

I have been talking about schools which taught mainly ballet. There are of course schools that give an all-round musical training. These schools have also doubled since I was a child, but for some poor students, even though there are more schools giving opportunities for very good training, being able to afford to go to these schools even after being auditioned and accepted is another matter. The lucky student who wins a scholarship is a rare occurrence. Most parents, if they are not rich enough to pay for their children themselves, have to apply for local grants. These grants have become fewer and fewer over the years. I receive letters all the time begging for advice or even monetary help, and feel sorry that our country is not backing the talent that it is producing.

What happens now to the dancers who achieve places in ballet companies all around the world? The standard required has become incredibly competitive (as dance schools churn out brilliantly trained technical dancers). When I watch these dancers I find that the style has changed immensely since the time I trained. As I said before, we were always being told to use our personalities and dance with our spirits, I suppose you could say in an extrovert way, trying to create excitement during the performance between audience and artist. Now, with some companies I watch, I find that I have to go in to find their performance – it's almost as if it has become vulgar to show too much joy and feeling. Any form of exaggeration seems to be taken as old-fashioned and not conforming to the slightly introverted performances of many of the dancers today.

Technical virtuosity has reached Olympic proportions, and rather like the Olympics, performance records are broken every year. But it is important to remember that dance is not just about Olympic feats (although higher and bigger leaps are gasp-making), it is about portraying a role, and learning the stage-craft takes a good few years more after the training is complete. Only by actually performing roles does the dancer improve and learn the complexities of performance. There are too many dancers who seem content with gymnastic virtuosity of technique. The truly great dancer is one who aspires to both technical bravura and artistic performance. This is what singles him out from the rest.

In a way I am now hoist by my own petard in the sense that I really shouldn't still be dancing at forty-eight – but I am, and it seems silly not to go on while I can. However, I have no intention of clinging to the stage when I am physically no longer able to give 101 per cent. So I always have my most critical friends in the audience, to tell me the truth about my performance. So far so good.

Some twenty years ago George said, 'Of course, you're married.' I retorted 'Don't be ridiculous. I am not.' He continued, 'Yes, you are married to your work.' And in a way I suppose he was right; perhaps my personal relationships have suffered because of this. But things are much better now that I am more settled and I am looking forward to moving into my 'new' home.

Looking back, my favourite radio interview was when Roy Plomley once invited me to choose my *Desert Island Discs*. To select only eight is almost impossible. He advised me not to listen to anybody else, and said that right up to the moment of recording the programme I could change my list. So I went for the first ones that sprang to mind. My eight chosen records were:

Verdi's Requiem Mass. I had heard this while holidaying in the Dordogne in a church in St Cère. One of the soloists was Rita Hunter. The acoustics were amazing and her voice as clear as a bell. It reminded me of balmy days at Balme and Carennac.

Edith Piaf singing 'La belle histoire d'amour'. Unfortunately when I first discovered her voice in the fifth-form sitting-room at White Lodge, singing 'Milord' on a 45 rpm, later that day the news came on the radio that she had died. It was a strange feeling to have of elation and sadness all in one day.

'Without You' – a song made famous by Harry Nilssen, who was so helpful when he believed I was right for his musical *The Point* at the Mermaid Theatre.

I had to have a Beatles number, evocative of the sixties – 'All You Need Is Love'. In fact I last saw Paul McCartney at the opening of the Liverpool Institute for the Performing Arts. I had been one of its original supporters when it was just a sketch on a piece of paper a few years before. Paul and I had quite a long chat, and I was secretly pleased that I was able to introduce him to his greatest fan – my sister, Joanne. She had said to me previously that if she was not able to meet him that would be OK. It would still be worth taking a risk and the day off from work. If she did meet him, my instructions were not to tell him that she was a big fan. As soon as I introduced them the first words she said were, 'It's so nice to meet you – I'm a big fan of yours'!

I chose for my fifth record Beethoven's Choral Fantasia (Op. 80) because it reminded me of holidays with George in the little open Noddy car.

Maria Callas in *Tosca*. For no other reason than that she epitomized true artistry and technical bravura on stage. With some opera singers you might just as well buy the recording, as their actual performance on stage can seem superfluous.

I just had to have two of the great twentieth-century ballet composers, Stravinsky (*The Firebird*) and Prokofiev (*Romeo and Juliet*). Both of these records reminded me of Margot and Rudolf and American tours with the Royal Ballet.

As a joke, I chose a ninth theme tune of *Desert Island Discs*, 'Sleepy Lagoon'. When Roy asked me why, I said, 'Well, you have been able to put up with it for twenty-five years – that's a good enough test!' So they had to play it twice. I took as my luxury a poppy, saying that it was such a serviceable plant.

Over the years I have appeared as a guest on many TV shows, of which one of the funniest was in a sketch with the comedy group the Goodies. I was to choreograph and lead a football team of classical dancers (dressed in doublet and tights) against the Goodies' team (in tutus and football boots). The ballet was to look like a football match on stage at the Wimbledon Theatre, and the audience, instead of being the demure ballet crowd, was replaced with footballers and skinheads. The idea was to hurl the opposing team's leader into the net. This action was interspersed with the odd Dying Swan and Cygnets dance. A crazy idea, zany and fun. The spectators made a hell of a din, holding up banners with mad quotations such as '*Les Sylphides* is curable!' 'Baryshnikov Bites Your Knee Caps' and '*A Month in the Country* is Worth Two in the Bush'.

When I look back one party that stands out in my memory is when John Reid asked if I would like to be his guest at the Live Aid concert, now of historical fame. Elton John was the only star with a caravan just outside the stadium. All the other performers had to be escorted from the Wembley arena before going on stage. I spent much of the day going from the stadium to the enclosure beside the caravan, where I met Viscount Linley. He had not met Freddie Mercury. I must admit that I enjoyed introducing the Queen's nephew to the 'Queen'. And then of course Queen went out and played – for me at any rate – one of their greatest sets ever.

I miss Freddie especially for his great sense of fun. Each of his parties was a gala outdoing all others. I remember George and I going to one of his 'hat' parties. Yes, everyone had to wear a hat. I pulled down one of my curtains and wrapped it around my head. George wore a red leather 1920s motoring helmet and goggles, not to be outdone of course. This party was held on the lawn of his very large house in Earls Court by the Japanese garden he had built. It lasted from lunchtime into the early hours.

Another time Freddie chartered a jet to take many of his friends from London to Ibiza for his fortieth birthday. I accompanied Helen Montagu (who had produced *Dead Eyed Dicks*, a play starring Peter O'Toole which I had choreographed years before) on the flight. On board were crates of champagne. So the party actually began at Heathrow. Freddie had invited hundreds of people and put us all up in the hills surrounding his hotel, which he had taken over completely for his closest colleagues and friends. The party went on all night and the next day; back on the plane Helen and I exchanged stories and the party continued.

During my career I often found myself with other colleagues standing outside the Soviet Embassy petitioning for one cause or another. One was to help the Panovs, two Jewish dancers who had been confined to their small apartment and barred from performing. They were eventually allowed to leave the USSR and go to Israel, from where they were able to dance freely all over the West. Another time myself, Margot Fonteyn and members of the ballet and acting world congregated outside the Embassy to petition for Rudolf to be allowed to go back to Russia to see his aged mother, who was eventually permitted to come and see him.

On one of these crusades we were supposed to march from Marble Arch to the Embassy in Bayswater. I was with Sir Anton Dolin, who had no intention of walking all that way. He demanded I hail a cab, and we sailed off to a pub opposite the entrance to the Embassy. Pat (as we called Sir Anton) saw some television cameras lurking and grabbed my arm, dragging me across the road where the tired marchers were just arriving, led by Sir John Gielgud. As we joined the front line, Pat said, 'Smile – we're on *News at Ten!*'

One day I opened the *Guardian* to find my mother's name there. It wasn't anything to do with me for a change – there had throughout my career been several articles about me and my mother, and even about myself and my sister. (Lord Snowdon took the photo of Joanne and myself for the front cover of the *Sunday Times*. He was also generous enough after the session in his studio to take us upstairs to his living quarters for tea. There he showed my sister the stucco on the ceilings that he had hand crafted. I found out then to my surprise that he was also related to Oliver Messel, the designer of the famous production of *Sleeping Beauty* when the Sadler's Wells Ballet first went to America.)

The article in the *Guardian*, as I said, was nothing to do with me. It was to do with the fact that my mother had given a room to Len Wincott, enabling him to come to England for a holiday. Len Wincott was one of the ringleaders in the national naval strike of 1931 which was known as the Invergordon mutiny, when all ships leaving the harbours round Britain were to stop at twelve noon and the few that did leave were booed out of the harbour. This was to stop one shilling a day being deducted from the present salary of the ratings (regular seamen). He had been a friend of one of my great aunt's, and became friends with my mother and Gran. After the strike, which proved successful, was over, Len Wincott was blacklisted by employers all over the country. He walked everywhere to find a job but all doors were closed to him. After three years of unemployment, the Communist Party, of which he was a member, sent him to live in Russia, where he served in the Russian army and was awarded a medal for his part in the German siege of Leningrad. Not long after, he was falsely accused of being a British spy, interned in a Siberian camp for ten yeras, and was not released until Stalin's death.

In 1973 my mother read an article in the local Plymouth paper asking if anyone in Plymouth who had known Len years before would give him accommodation so that he could come and visit the city. My mother replied, and said she would guarantee his well-being by giving him free board and lodgings in our house. This, I found to my astonishment, was reported in the national press. I was used to seeing Mum in the paper, but it was usually with me after one of my first nights. Totally upstaged this time, good old Mum. (In 1983 Len was given a Royal Navy burial in Plymouth Sound. All had been forgiven.)

I've had some fabulous vacations in my life but one I remember most is when I decided to take my mother and grandmother to Venice for a few days. There was much excitement, as neither of them had been on an aeroplane before. My Auntie Sybil, Auntie Ruth and her friend Colleen, plus my stepfather, all came up to Gatwick to wave us off. Gran, who was just about still able to walk at this time (with a stick), was given preferential treatment by the staff at the airport and the three of us were given a buggy to get around in. We arrived at the steps to the plane and it was only then that my mother became slightly nervous. Gran, on the other hand, couldn't wait to board.

After take-off the stewards came round with drinks and my mother and Gran ordered their usual voddies and lemonade as they called them. 'No ice – it dilutes it,' Gran would say. After a few minutes my Mother said, 'Here – it tastes different up here.' Gran replied, 'Yes, it must be the altitude.' By this time we were all giggling and I asked the Italian stewardess if I could see the bottle. It was Stolychniya – 100 per cent proof. No wonder it tasted different to them.

They loved their holiday in Venice. One day we would go sightseeing and the next relax at the Grand Hotel des Bains and bathe at the Lido, and lie in the sun on beds complete with sheets and pillows! This was how they did not become exhausted. After all, Gran was in her late eighties and Mother well into her sixties. The great thing about going to Venice with these two old gals was that they were shown the greatest respect and given red carpet treatment. The Italians certainly know how to look after their families.

I will be touring, again, by the time this book is out, with Lorna Luft. We are appearing in another *Hollywood and Broadway*. It is like entering Aladdin's cave (and I've done enough of that in my life to know) and being able to take your pick. Touring *Hollywood and Broadway* is different, it is established, and there is good back-up. I always look forward to touring with Lorna. We have fun together and we are in tune on stage. And by the time autumn comes I will be wanting to perform again. It's the interaction with a live audience – something I've enjoyed ever since I waggled my bottom at Uncle Gordon's behest, and also something that I don't think, in the long term, I want to live without. I am lucky. I work in a profession I enjoy and which also keeps the bailiff from the door.

A few weeks ago I was up early (because of builders) and drinking coffee in the local deli around the corner when a man came up to me and said, 'Mr Sleep, I've just seen a photo of your studio in a catalogue in Paris.' 'What catalogue?' I replied. 'You must be mistaken!' 'The Francis Bacon Retrospective Catalogue.' He then went on to tell me that Francis had taken him to see my studio in South Kensington to point out where he had painted from 1930–1934. He had not only painted in my studio, he had lived on the premises too. I had given the parquet floor (when I had rebuilt the interior years before) to George, and it is now in his studio on the top floor in Long Acre, Covent Garden. The other day, for a joke, we went up to look for daubs of paint on the woodwork.

I remember once being interviewed on Radio 2. I was asked the question, 'When you look back on your life, would you like to change anything?' My immediate reply was, 'Yes, I wish I had kept my big mouth shut a bit more.' There was a pause, then I added 'No. I don't – I'd say it all over again!'

It's been forty-three years since I took my first dance lesson, and looking back over my last thirty years of professional dancing and performing, two significant achievements stand out in my mind. The first is overcoming all the obstacles I had to face before being taken seriously as an all-round entertainer, having come from the classical background of the Royal Ballet. Many dancers become teachers, few become choreographers, and even fewer become singers, actors or directors. Having resisted being pigeon-holed as just a dancer, I have felt driven to participate in all these aspects of theatre and enjoyed every minute of it. The other achievement, I feel, has been in helping to popularise dance by taking it out to people who would not normally set foot in a theatre to see a dance performance. If I have been instrumental in helping dance become more accessible, it's all been worthwhile. I have more than achieved my childhood dream of being on stage amongst the colours, lights and music. And there is still so much in the pipeline – still more dreams to be fulfilled and precious little sleep.

ROLE CALL

BALLET

(Only choreographers have been listed. Unless otherwise stated, all roles were danced with the Royal Ballet.)

A Month in the Country – Ashton
Anastasia – MacMillan
Capriol Suite – Ashton
Cinderella – Ashton
Concerto – MacMillan
Coppelia – Hynd (English National Ballet)
Creatures of Prometheus – Ashton
Dances at a Gathering – Robbins
Daphnis und Chloë – Ashton
David and Goliath – North/Sleep (London Contemporary Dance Theatre)
Don Quixote (pas-de-deux) – Petipa
Élite Syncopations – MacMillan
Enigma Variations – Ashton
Façade – Ashton
Flower Festival (pas-de-deux) – Bournonville
Four Seasons – MacMillan
Fourth Symphony – Neumeier
Geoffrey Cauley Ballet – Cauley (St Paul's Cathedral)
Giselle – Ashton after Coralli/Perrot
Jazz Calendar – Ashton
Job – de Valois
La Fille Mal Gardée – Ashton
'Le Train Bleu' – Dolin (solo in *A Good Night's Sleep*)
Les Noces – Nijinska
Les Patineurs – Ashton
Mamzelle Angot – Massine
Napoli – Bournonville
Nutcracker – Nureyev
Ondine – Ashton
Overture – Layton
Petrouchka – Fokine
Pineapple Poll – Cranko
Pulcinella – Beare (Queen Elizabeth Hall)

Renard – Drew (the Proms and Edinburgh International Festival)
Rite of Spring – MacMillan
Savoy Suite – Sleep (English National Ballet)
Shadow Play – Tudor
Sleeping Beauty – (four productions: Ashton, Ashton/Wright, MacMillan, de Valois)
Summer – Kersley (Harlow Ballet Club)
Swan Lake – Ashton after Ivanov
'Tarantella' (pas-de-deux) – Balanchine (*A Good Night's Sleep*)
The Dream – Ashton
The Grand Tour – Layton
The Invitation – MacMillan
The Rake's Progress – de Valois
The Soldier's Tale – Gielgud/Sleep (two productions: Queen Elizabeth Hall and Royal Festival Hall for BBC TV)
The Taming of the Shrew – Cranko
Tweedle Dum & Tweedle Dee – Ashton
Two Pigeons – Ashton
Vestris – de Valois (Sainsbury gala, London Palladium)

PLAYS

Durrant's *Diaghelev* at Richmond Theatre, Yorkshire (*actor*)
Pinocchio (ad. Terry) at Birmingham Rep (*actor*)
Digby Day's *Sweet Mr Shakespeare* at the Bath Festival (*actor*)
Goldoni's *The Servant of Two Masters* (Truffeldino) at York Rep. (*actor*)
Stravinsky's/Ramuz's *The Soldier's Tale* (The Soldier) at Queen Elizabeth Hall and Royal Festival Hall (*actor, dancer and choreographer*)
Shakespeare's *The Tempest* (Aerial) with the New Shakespeare Company (*actor*) at Regent's Park, London

MUSICALS

Cabaret – West End, London (*singer, dancer, actor*)

Cats – West End, London (*singer, dancer*)

The Point (Oblio) – Mermaid Theatre, London (*actor, singer, dancer*)

Song and Dance – West End, London (*singer, dancer*)

Winnie The Pooh (Tigger) – West End, London (*actor, singer, dancer*)

FILMS

The First Great Train Robbery (*actor*)

The Tales of Beatrix Potter (*dancer*)

Virgin Soldiers (*actor*)

CHOREOGRAPHY

Adam's Rib (jazz ballet for BBC TV)

Chaplin Ballet for DASH

David and Goliath (LCDT and San Francisco Ballet)

Dead-Eyed Dicks – play

Death on the Nile – film

'Praise God and Dance' in Duke Ellington tribute (St Paul's Cathedral)

Promenade (ENB School)

Savoy Suite (ENB)

Storey's *Cromwell* – play

Winding Road (London City Ballet)

Wonderland: Scenes from Alice (The National Youth Ballet)

The Soldier's Tale – Gielgud/Sleep

Royal Ballet Choreographic Group
(All performed at the Collegiate Theatre, London)

A Ballet – Sleep

A Wake – Sleep

Double You (W) – Eagling/Sleep

Hornpipe – Grant

Jeux d'enfant – Morse

The Wedding – Sleep

PARODIES

(All for DASH unless otherwise stated.)

Ballroom demonstration as Doris the Goddess of Dance

Bette Midler

Charlie Chaplin

Martha Graham

Marilyn Monroe (choreographed only)

John Curry (ice-skater)

John McEnroe (tennis player)

Mae West in *Adam's Rib* (jazz ballet for BBC TV)

Olga Korbutt (Russian gymnast)

The Four Cygnets (from *Swan Lake*) in tap shoes

The pop group Madness

Torville & Dean (renamed Bourville & Cream)

RADIO (all BBC Radio)

Desert Island Discs

Down Your Way

She Stoops to Conquer (Tony Lumpkin) with Judi Dench

Social Dancing in the 20th Century (Narrator)

The Life of Ginger Rogers (Narrator)

TELEVISION

A Christmas Lantern (with Cliff Richard)

Adam's Rib

Blankety Blank

Cinderella (two productions)

Dickie Henderson

Dizzy Feet

Élite Syncopations

Four *Royal Variety* shows

Give Us a Clue

Hot Shoe Show (for two years running with the BBC)

John Curry Ice Show

Lena Zavaroni

Marti Caine

Morecambe and Wise

Eric Morecambe tribute

Nana Mouskouri

Noel's House Party

Oscar Peterson

Showtime Special (with Derek Griffiths)

Showtime Two

Sleeping Beauty

Stargames

The Goodies

The Magic of the Dance

The Nutcracker

The Soldier's Tale

Theme Dreams

This is Your Life

VIDEO
Duke Ellington tribute
Noel's House Party
Song and Dance
Step into Ballet with Wayne Sleep
The Goodies
The Royal Ballet's *Swan Lake*
The Tales of Beatrix Potter

PANTOMIMES
Aladdin – Norwich, Bury St. Edmunds,
   Guildford, London Palladium
Cinderella – Redhill, Crewe
Dick Whittington – Hanley, Birmingham
Goldilocks – Norwich, Aberdeen, Eastbourne
Jack and the Beanstalk – Poole

DANCE SHOWS
(All directed by Sleep unless otherwise stated.)
A DASH of Christmas
Bits and Pieces
Dance
DASH

DASH (2)
DASH (The Wayne Sleep Dance Consort)
Hollywood and Broadway Parts 1, 2 and 3
   (singer, dancer, choreographer – other
   director/choreographers: Richard Samson,
   Chris Power and Alan Harding)
Hot Shoe Show
Sleep with Friends
Steps, Notes and Squeaks (dir. Gielgud)
Wayne's World of Dance (cabaret act)

PERSONAL APPEARANCES
   (TELEVISION)
Guest on *Parkinson, Harty, Hunniford,*
   Aspel, Wogan (also with Ben Elton),
   Andrews

OPERA (COVENT GARDEN)
Aida (The Golden Slave) with Placido
   Domingo
A Midsummer Night's Dream (Puck) with
   Geraint Evans

INDEX